Property of
FAMILY OF FAITH
LIBRARY

W9-BIR-252

clinical teaching

METHODS OF INSTRUCTION
FOR THE RETARDED

McGraw-Hill Series in Special Education

Robert M. Smith, Consulting Editor

Cartwright and Cartwright: DEVELOPING OBSERVATION SKILLS
Smith: CLINICAL TEACHING: Methods of Instruction for the Retarded
Smith: INTRODUCTION TO MENTAL RETARDATION
Worell and Nelson: MANAGING INSTRUCTIONAL PROBLEMS: A Case Study Workbook

clinical teaching

METHODS OF INSTRUCTION FOR THE RETARDED

SECOND EDITION

Robert M. Smith
The Pennsylvania State University

McGraw-Hill Book Company
New York   St. Louis   San Francisco   Düsseldorf   Johannesburg
Kuala Lumpur   London   Mexico   Montreal   New Delhi   Panama
Paris   São Paulo   Singapore   Sydney   Tokyo   Toronto

CLINICAL TEACHING
Methods of Instruction for the Retarded

Copyright © 1968, 1974 by McGraw-Hill, Inc. All rights reserved.
Printed in the United States of America. No part of this publication
may be reproduced, stored in a retrieval system, or transmitted, in any
form or by any means, electronic, mechanical, photocopying, recording, or
otherwise, without the prior written permission of the publisher.

234567890MAMM798765

This book was set in Helvetica by Black Dot, Inc. The editors were Robert C. Morgan
and Phyllis T. Dulan; the designer was Jo Jones; and the production supervisor was
Thomas J. LoPinto. The drawings were done by Vantage Art, Inc.
The Maple Press Company was printer and binder.

Library of Congress Cataloging in Publication Data

Smith, Robert McNeil.
    Clinical teaching.

    (McGraw-Hill series in special education)
    1.   Mentally handicapped children—Education.
I.   Title.   DNLM: 1.   Education of mentally
retarded.   LC4620   S658c   1974
LC4601.S67   1974   371.9'28   73–17097
ISBN 0–07–058906–2

contents

preface

This new edition of *Clinical Teaching* has been organized into two major sections. Following some brief introductory comments in Chapter 1, the next three chapters establish a general philosophy concerning educational programming for mentally retarded persons. The tenets of the philosophy reflect contemporary thought and evidence. The main theme throughout the book is that appropriate education for the mentally retarded must be based on (1) accurate evaluations of individual performance and a characterization of each child's environment, (2) clear and unambiguous statements about what you would like each child to be able to do, (3) the correct application of appropriate principles of educational methodology, (4) the selection of materials of instruction that are compatible with the instructional procedures that have been selected, and (5) the assignment of each child to a setting in which his individual program of educational management can best be fulfilled. All the issues surrounding these important fundamentals are discussed in this first section.

The second section of this new edition identifies and describes the prominent subject or content areas that pertain especially to the mentally retarded. The material in each chapter has been updated according to the new research that has been done since the original text was published.

Although the book continues to have as its primary target those teachers who have responsibility for providing instructional programs to the mentally retarded, the fundamental point of view has much wider applicability. The process and techniques of diagnosis and management have direct pertinence to children with various and multiple educational problems. Special efforts were made to use illustrations and suggest management guidelines that will have meaning to teachers, aides, parents, administrators, and psychologists.

As with the first edition, I hope that this book will be found useful by practitioners who often do not have time to become acquainted with the current concepts and techniques that pertain to a field such as mental retardation. I have tried to provide a book in which these newer approaches are discussed, justified, and illustrated. The ultimate goals, of course, are that mentally retarded individuals become both increasingly capable problem solvers and more thoroughly integrated into the open community. I believe that the approaches outlined in this book can lead to the realization of these goals.

I acknowledge with especial gratitude the effort Karen Lewis gave in helping to process the manuscript. It is also a pleasure to recognize the assistance and support Robert Morgan of the McGraw-Hill Book Company has given throughout this project. Finally, my wife, Bette, and six children have been very patient and encouraging during the preparation of this revision.

Robert M. Smith

clinical teaching

METHODS OF INSTRUCTION FOR THE RETARDED

1

ISSUES OF PROFESSIONAL CONCERN TO EDUCATING THE MENTALLY RETARDED

Recently our society has begun to show more concern for the problems of the mentally retarded than it has at any time since the middle 1800s. All the reasons for this increased interest are unclear; however, there is no question but that the following should be considered among the most prominent:

1 Heretofore, the diagnosis of mental retardation has been viewed as restricting—that is, the child who allegedly has this condition has been seen as having an irreversible, irremedial, and unmodifiable prognosis for developing skills at an acceptable level and rate. Research has shown this assumption to be untrue. It is now clear that changes can be made in the performance of children who have been identified as mentally retarded, whatever their level of retardation.

2 Much of society has begun to recognize that it is inappropriate to insist that the mentally retarded adapt to society in order to have opportunities for normal experiences. Indeed, the emphasis has become reoriented to a more realistic belief that the environment must adapt to the mentally retarded by providing appropriate training, employment, social experiences along a full and normal range, and as much a chance as others have to live in an open community. The evidence suggests that this is possible if the environment provides for individual needs.

3 It has become clear that there is no single way to look at the mentally retarded—they are as different as any other group of people. As such, then, they need individually tailored programs to facilitate the development of their skills. Moreover, our society is beginning to recognize that the mentally retarded deserve the best. For too long they have been viewed as subhuman, social noncontributors, and unworthy, and it has taken a long time to reverse the tide of dehumanization, indiscriminate warehousing of the retarded into institutions, and absolutely no educational programming.

4 There have been encouraging medical breakthroughs in mental retardation as well as in tangential areas. These new techniques and understandings provide alternatives, unavailable in the past, for preventing the condition in many instances, for more effectively managing the condition, and for reversing the consequences of the problems that attend mental retardation.

5 Behavioral scientists have recognized through theory, research, and practice that the basic principles of behavior that have "stood the tests of time" with normal individuals are no different for the mentally retarded. This realization has resulted in an enormous renaissance in thinking concerning the means by which retarded children can best be managed. Well-researched and/-documented guidelines are now available concerning the arrangement of the instructional environment to accelerate rate and level of performance of children who have not progressed in the past. No longer, then, does a teacher have to follow hunches about how best to design an educational program for retarded children.

6 Parent groups have also been extremely active in the 1960s and 1970s on behalf of the mentally retarded. They have insisted (through lobbying, use of the courts, and public pressure) on attention being focused on equal free public education for all children, including the severely and profoundly mentally retarded. Their efforts have resulted in court suits in which states have been ordered to provide appropriate programs for all children.

7 All levels of government have become more active in supporting research and training efforts on behalf of the mentally retarded. The President's Committee on Mental Retardation initiates and coordinates a host of activities throughout the country and the world with the main object being to provide leadership in developing and implementing new programs for the mentally retarded. President Kennedy was instrumental in stimulating the federal government to begin considering the role it should have in dealing with the problems of mental retardation in society. The Report of the President's Panel on Mental Retardation entitled "National Plan to Combat Mental Retardation" (1962) has been used as a broad mandate for stimulating program development for and directing public attention to this problem. More recently President Nixon has determined (1) to try to reduce the incidence of mental retardation by one-half by the year 2000, and (2) to return to the community as soon as possible one-third of all presently institutionalized retardates.

the focus of professional involvement

Many kinds of professionals are interested in mental retardation. Medical specialists, including pediatricians, obstetricians, physiologists, biochemists, teratologists, and geneticists are concerned with the causes, or etiological patterns, that are related to retardation. A major focus of their attention is on identifying and eventually controlling those mechanisms that result in the condition.

Psychologists have a history of working with the retarded. They are concerned, basically, with assessing behavior specific to the retarded and with comparing their behavior with that of the normal population. Even within the general area of psychology, specialists have concentrated on specific areas such as learning, motivation, personality characteristics, and social competencies of the retarded.

Educators have used the principles of behavior management to manipulate the environment of retarded persons in order to foster more effective learning. Primary attention has been focused on altering the physical environment, applying the most powerful and effective methodological procedures in a way appropriate to each situation, and in developing curricula. Although dimensions such as etiology and psychological techniques for assessing factors of strength or particular weakness of the mentally retarded may be of academic interest, these have not been nor should they be areas of primary concern to the teacher.

Sociologists, anthropologists, lawyers, and other professionals have also examined problems related to retardation. But the accelerated interest in the study of this condition and the resulting activity has been bought at a price. There is difficulty in the communication of ideas among interested disciplines and sometimes even within specialities. Because of the precise and restricted nature of each discipline, practitioners have been forced to use definitions and esoteric language peculiar to their own perspective, which has resulted in poor interdiscipline communication.

A major reason for this poor communication is the minimal effort exerted by investigators to translate their findings and interpret them for scientists from other fields. Some effort has been made by federal agencies and professional organizations to facilitate communication through support of interdisciplinary conferences and large research and development centers, wherein, for example, a medical school and a college of education look at mutual problems with a team approach. The President's Committee on Mental Retardation has been especially helpful in fostering interspecialty communication.

Finally, difficulty in communication among specialists is owing in large measure to the lack of a generally accepted, systematic, theoretical position concerning mental retardation, an appropriate definition, what it means to society, how best to deal with it, and so on. Such basic questions are the subject of great debate among disciplines.

Although communication difficulties exist among the specialties, it should be emphasized that their basic goals are quite compatible and their approaches to achieving these goals are similar. Three basic objectives characterize any scientific inquiry. The first objective is to *describe* phenomena and to relate to them other variables that may exert significant influence on their manifestation. The second objective is to *predict* the occurrence of the phenomena. To be sure, some overlap exists between these two stages of inquiry; however, accurate prediction depends on adequate description. The final goal is to *control.* To effectively control a condition, it must be describable and it must be predictable.

Each stage of inquiry can be viewed in either a global or a narrow perspective. For example, a teacher can be concerned with describing, predicting, and controlling the total environmental situation of retarded children in her class in order to effect adequate social, personal, and intellectual development. This would involve a global attack on areas of concern. Simultaneously, the teacher may be concerned with describing, predicting, and controlling one child's very specific type of atypical behavior that occurs under certain, rather specific, circumstances. This "ugly" behavior may be antagonistic to the general goals of the educational program and to the effective learning of the child.

To emphasize again, disciplines concerned with the study of mental retardation attack problems similarly, in the same relatively sequential fashion, and with the same goal in mind—control of the phenomenon. When characteristics of conditions such as retardation are stable and occur under the same circumstances, in the same fashion, and to the same degree on each occurrence, the goals of describing, predicting, and controlling the condition can be realized relatively quickly. Mental retardation is not a singular phenomenon; it is characterized by many variations and nuances. For example, certain behavior may be related to intellectual retardation with one group of subjects and not with another.

Substantial variation exists among the mentally retarded in the degree of disability, primary etiological factors, appropriate habilitation practices, and prognosis for social or occupational success as adults.

Because of the multifaceted and heterogeneous nature of the condition, it must be realized that no one population of mentally retarded individuals exists. In fact, retardation is represented by a number of unique populations each of which may differ in characteristics which in themselves are of different magnitudes of significance to each discipline. Because of this heterogeneity, scientists have had great difficulty proceeding beyond the level of description. A group of characteristics typical of a particular population of retarded persons may not be descriptive of other retarded populations, although the same degree of intellectual subnormality could be exhibited. There is great difficulty, therefore, in generalizing results of scientific observation. Moreover, scientific work in disciplines investigating mental retardation is proceeding at different speeds through the three levels of scientific inquiry.

Research related to mental retardation historically can be characterized as being more basic than applied. Studies dealing with biochemical correlates of the condition, specific psychological characteristics of the retarded, and the type and degree of anatomical deviations from the normal illustrate the prevailing focus of much of the research. Less interest has been shown in conducting *in situ* types of experimentations, most of which have direct and obvious applicability to management of the retarded.

Moreover, the traditional research emphasis in this field has been molecular rather than molar. Investigators have chosen to study small, well-defined problems and not large, general areas of concern. For example, substantial effort has been given to investigating discrimination learning or other specific factors of cognition. Fewer studies have considered more global concerns, such as the efficacy in placing certain groups of retarded persons in a specific kind of environment which theoretically should influence behavior and performance in specified areas of functioning. The laboratory approach characterizes the former technique; an *in situ* strategy describes the latter.

Aside from the fact that much of the research has come from medicine and allied fields such as physiology, biochemistry, and psychology, there are specific reasons why past research efforts are molecular and basic. Fundamentally, these are the result of certain research methodological considerations.

Scientists have been concerned about the heterogeneous nature of the retarded. To generalize findings from a specific sample of subjects to all groups of mentally retarded is, indeed, hazardous. Fortunately, in the early stages of research, investigators have exercised caution by identifying research problems which could be finely delineated and by using subjects whose characteristics are readily descriptive and who represented a large population of the retarded. The collection of a substantial number of studies on specific topics allows for their synthesis and the observation of common threads. This provides movement toward a more global or molar attack characteristic of *in situ* research.

A word should be said concerning sampling difficulties. Locating an adequate sample of subjects for study is a particularly difficult problem because of the relatively small incidence of mentally retarded subjects in the population and the variability in their characteristics. Sampling bias may occur frequently because of nonrepresentation. For example, in a study designed to assess a specific reading characteristic, such as comprehension, among environmentally deprived retarded children, it may be desirable to exclude children with minimal neurological involvement since comprehension could be related to the variable being studied for that group and not for non-organically involved children. To include subjects from both groups might obliterate significant findings that would have been evident if the groups had been studied independently. Researchers, therefore, must identify homogeneous groups for study and identify other variables which could actively influence factors being studied.

To further complicate the research effort, in addition to cognition, other dimensions influence the performance and behavior of the mentally retarded. For example, the social milieu in which individuals are reared influences patterns of behavior and styles of living. The retarded are no less influenced by the dynamic nature of social expectations and pressures. Indeed, one might speculate that they are more vulnerable to social pressures and at the same time less adept at effectively responding to such demands. The consequences of this inadequacy are likely to be felt in other areas of life, such as emotional development and mental health. Moreover, the range of characteristics of the various social situations among mentally retarded children makes it difficult to control these potentially important variables. The researcher, therefore, must give careful consideration to such dimensions.

Because research with the mentally retarded offers opportunities for exploring new aspects of the condition, there have been relatively few attempts at replicating other studies. This presents a problem for those interested in making use of research findings. A basic requirement of research is that findings be reliable. One would hesitate to alter an existing program on the basis of a single, circumscribed research report, irrespective of how dramatic the findings. The safe strategy is to adhere to the status quo. Because of this legitimate hesitation of educators to change programs without adequate documentation and because of the minimal effort exerted by researchers to interpret and translate findings into practical considerations, much of the research in mental retardation has not become part of the general habilitative program.

The history of research in mental retardation, moreover, has shown a hesitancy on the part of investigators to explore areas potentially unfruitful. If an investigator reports findings which are not significant, few would be inclined to replicate the experiment unless there were obvious gross errors committed. This is an unfortunate fact of life since chance alone could account for nonsignificant findings when, in fact, a significant difference may exist.

To illustrate, assume that a certain theory suggests that technique A will foster more rapid learning than technique B with mentally retarded children. When tested, this difference was not observed. Typically, this research is duly reported, filed, and most often lost in the archives. Even assuming an appropriate research method and design, chance alone could result in treatment A not being significantly superior to treatment B. Such studies are rarely replicated because investigators are hesitant to study areas which have been relatively unproductive in the past. Therefore, the possibility of a research breakthrough could be stymied. This situation is not peculiar to research efforts in mental retardation; indeed, it is characteristic of other large unexplored territories.

Studies in the behavioral sciences are often characterized by relating many variables to one another. Correlational analysis is the statistical technique most frequently used. This approach makes possible the study of the degree of relationship which exists between variables and is often employed in research with the mentally retarded. An investigator who wishes to correlate social class with mental retardation may observe a moderately high relationship between these two variables, perhaps on the order of .60 to .75. It is possible to relate any number of variables. For example, hair color, number of push-ups, size of the right foot, and intellectual ability could be correlated. We cannot assume that one variable causes the occurrence of another simply because a high relationship among variables was observed. Obviously, the color of one's hair or the size of a right foot does not cause intellectual subnormality. Factors characteristic of one's social class, however, may influence to some extent the intellectual ability of an individual. The fact that *correlation does not necessarily mean causation* is important and should be kept in mind in reviewing results of research.

It was stated earlier that research in mental retardation has been primarily basic. Increased financial support has not only escalated basic research in mental retardation, but it has caused a definite trend toward more applied research. Research and development centers are being established to study the educational problems of retarded children in a more global fashion. Dissemination of research results is another major objective of these centers. These trends will result in more attention being given to the interpretation and translation of research for those working directly with the mentally retarded. Findings from studies will be applied to classroom problems much more rapidly. This, then, will lead to an increase in applied *in situ* studies which test out habilitation procedures under existing conditions.

the attention of educators
to problems of mental retardation

HISTORICAL OVERVIEW
The first systematic attempts at training and educating the mentally retarded began during the late 1700s and were primarily the result of attention by physicians. The focus of their educational procedures dealt with techniques for training the senses. Training of the retarded began initially in France with the early attempts to provide systematic instruction located in institutions for the blind and in institutions for the deaf.

Itard is considered to have conducted the first systematic training program by attempting to educate Victor, the wild boy of Averyon.[1] Although Victor had been diagnosed as an "incurable idiot," Itard provided him with a program which was designed to:

1 Create an interest in the social life as opposed to the nomadic, vagabond existence to which he was accustomed
2 Produce refinement in understanding the significance of sensory experiences by exciting those organs concerned with sensation
3 Encourage speech development through imitation by making vocal communication necessary
4 Expand his world of social experiences and create a breadth of desires and wants
5 Encourage Victor to use simple mental operations to satisfy his physical needs

---

[1]For a description of Victor's characteristics and Itard's report of the educational program, see Itard, 1962, as translated.

For more than five years Itard worked with Victor, systematically and continually, attempting to lead the boy from the life of a savage to that of a civilized person. The program terminated when Victor left in a rage. Itard perceived his efforts as being in vain and reported his findings in general publications and in a report addressed to the Minister of Interior.

The French Academy of Science, however, acknowledged the effort Itard had made in training Victor by recognizing the substantial contributions he had made to education. Perhaps one of the most educationally significant points made by the Academy was to remind Itard that it was most appropriate that Victor be compared only with himself by measuring his degree of growth. This may have been the first instance in which the educational value of intra-individual assessment was emphasized.

Itard's influence in the education of retarded children, and the subsequent statement by the French Academy of Science, was quickly felt elsewhere. Itard was Séguin's teacher and influenced many others, including Madame Montessori, who developed self-instructional teaching devices.

Based primarily on the work of Itard, Séguin viewed the possibility of educating the mentally retarded in a more optimistic light than was characteristic of many during the middle 1800s. At the age of twenty-five, Séguin endeavored to train an idiot boy to use his senses more effectively. After eighteen months of training, the child had made substantial progress in cognitive and communication activities. The significance of the event was acknowledged by professional and lay people interested in the retarded, and Séguin began using his training procedures with a larger number of retarded children. His classic book, published in 1866, described his procedures. Doll has characterized these methods as involving ". . . orderly sequences from passive to active, from sensation to perception, from gross to the refined, from known to the unknown, from observation to comparison, from attention to imitation, and from patterned activity to spontaneity."[2]

Paralleling present-day thinking, Séguin emphasized the need to teach in context, utilizing actual life situations as the basis for instruction. These, it was hoped, would assist the retarded child to develop a conceptual understanding instead of rote. The need to vary the mode of presentation and to help the children associate perceptions from

---

[2]Eugene E. Doll, "A Historical Survey of Research and Management of Mental Retardation in the United States," in Trapp and Himelstein (eds.), *Readings on the Exceptional Child* (2d ed.), Appleton-Century-Crofts, Inc., New York, 1972, pp. 47–98.

various sense modalities was emphasized in his program. Although Séguin stressed sensation, he was conscious of the need to provide the retarded with opportunities to develop social skills through group play and for the teacher to exhibit concern for moral development of the child.

The similarity between the basic tenets of Séguin's method and contemporary thinking by educators is striking. Without empirical data to support his techniques. Séguin was aware of the need for the teacher to use fundamental principles of learning in the instructional program. For example, he suggested actively involving the child, assisting him in observing relationships and associating incoming stimuli with the existing repertoire, helping him to develop skills related to socialization, and teaching for a conceptual instead of rote understanding. All these suggestions, although consistent with contemporary thinking, originated with Séguin. There is no doubt that his work has had substantial impact on education generally, although his notoriety outside of special education circles has not been consistent with his contributions.

The training procedures developed by Séguin were elaborated upon by Maria Montessori, an Italian physician. Her techniques, emphasizing self-teaching on the part of the child through the manipulation of materials, were developed primarily for children in residential schools. European schools have employed her techniques and materials much more than have American schools. Basic to her procedures was the feeling that children should (1) proceed at their own rates, (2) be exposed to a flexible program which capitalized on the spontaneous interest inherent in young children, (3) be provided with a learning situation and environment which was fun and pleasurable, (4) be given opportunities for repetition to the extent desired by the individual child, and (5) make use of the environment for self-improvement. There has been a revival of interest in the Montessori procedures in America. Montessori schools have been established to train teachers and to provide preschool instruction, in most instances, to children who show potential as being intellectually bright.

Various points of view concerning the education and training of the mentally retarded were expressed during the early and middle 1900s. During this time there had been a gradual shifting from a physiological orientation to a more psychosocial emphasis. Descoeudres (1928) emphasized the Dewey concept of "learning by doing"; Duncan (1943) encouraged enhancing relative weaknesses in verbal areas by assisting children to relate nonverbal (manual) abilities to academic areas using a project technique; and Inskeep (1926) suggested modifying the regular school program by teaching retarded children fewer skills, presenting them with less complicated materials of instruction, and gauging instruction at a lower level.

CONTEMPORARY EDUCATIONAL TRENDS

Beyond the middle 1950s, educational practices employed with the retarded have been based primarily on evidence and theories from fields other than education. Psychology, for example, because of the basic nature of the research, has provided direction for educational practices. Application of the basic principles of behavior to the whole range of performance problems of children with retarded mental development has been very effectively implemented within various educational contexts. Psychologists have thoroughly documented the appropriate methodological procedures to use with retarded children who exhibit the whole range of anomalous behaviors. This is an excellent illustration of how theory and technology from one field (in this case psychology) can have complete relevance to the applied problems faced by another field (special education). These principles are discussed and illustrated in great depth in the remaining chapters in this book.

Research in special education problems, per se, unfortunately has not been as farsighted or productive as it has been in many of the other professions. A great deal of attention has been given to the pros and cons of special education placement in contrast to other forms of administrative management practices. While placement is of obvious importance, more basic questions related to evaluation of human performance, construction of a proper and flexible curriculum, and the essential characteristics of an excellent special education teacher still await the attention of researchers and academicians.

The course of study, indeed, is an extremely vital consideration; the need for sequencing of instruction and the identification of a reasonable program scope are basic to achieving the goals of education. The development of curricula has been based on two considerations: (1) the unique characteristics the children exhibit, and (2) their predicted level of accomplishment in social, personal, and occupational areas. Whether these are appropriate bases for curriculum development deserves a great deal of thought—especially in light of the recent revelations concerning the ease with which errors can be made in accurately characterizing a person's mental ability and the difficulties inherent in speculating about anyone's potential to do anything!

Although the curriculum and administrative plans are important concerns, most educators would agree that methods of instruction, or what the teacher does in the classroom, are basic to effective teaching and learning. The inherent difficulties in studying teaching and learning processes and the slowness in interpreting and translating basic research into clear and manageable educational constructs have hindered progress in this area. It is clear that a single "cookbook" approach for teaching the retarded will not work.

the preparation of teachers:
some crucial needs and issues

Because of the unique learning problems of the retarded and the substantial alteration required in the basic objectives of the school program, it is necessary for a teacher to receive special clinical and remedial preparation. Moreover, it is desirable that the special education teacher exhibit certain personal traits. In addition to those traits desired of a good teacher of intellectually normal children which result in a classroom environment conducive to effective learning, a teacher of the mentally retarded must be satisfied with demonstrations of minimal change by the children. The retarded will usually learn at a rate substantially slower than intellectually normal children. Not only will it take longer for them to learn a concept or fact, but a lesson will need to be repeated several times, in a variety of ways, and perhaps using many sense modalities. Children will forget quickly, and the teacher will need to review and repeat material. Many teachers find this situation difficult to tolerate, perhaps because of a personal need to see dramatic changes in behavior and intellectual growth on the part of the students. To press students for a performance beyond their present level because of a desire to see more dramatic change is inconsistent with good teaching for the retarded.

Flexibility is a second important characteristic for teachers of the retarded. Teachers must be able to switch quickly from one procedure to another when a child has difficulty with a concept. Frequently it is necessary to abandon a lesson plan entirely and return to an earlier level of development when it is obvious that more work is needed in a prerequisite foundation area. Not to adapt spontaneously can result in ineffective teaching and perhaps in the student's developing negative feelings toward the total school program.

Universities and colleges are constantly faced with the problem of deciding what constitutes adequate preparation for teaching mentally retarded children. Quite frankly, we really do not know. Just taking courses is clearly not satisfactory. But, in a general sense, it seems reasonable that any teacher will be more successful if the following types of competencies are stressed in teacher-training programs.

1 A stable and comprehensive philosophical point of view should be developed that considers, among other things, the fact of individual variation, the worth of the individual, the place of the mentally retarded in society, and reasonable goals and expectations in training and educating the mentally retarded.

2 The teacher should have a firm understanding of appropriate objectives and goals for all the populations of mentally retarded in general as well as for each child specifically. A sensitivity to and a concern for educationally significant individual differences should be focused upon in teacher-education programs.

3 Teachers of the mentally retarded should have a complete understanding of some basic theory that will serve as the basis for educational programming. The theory chosen should be sufficiently broad to include all areas relevant to normal functioning within society. It should provide direction concerning appropriate sequencing of activities and the foundation skills basic to effective learning.

4 Teachers of the mentally retarded should have some sensitivity to and minimal skill in elementary and informal educational diagnostic procedures appropriate to the classroom. The teacher must constantly assess a child's performance and alter the mode of instruction, materials, and curriculum according to each child's pattern of strengths and weaknesses.

5 Since the teacher of the mentally retarded is interested in appropriately manipulating a child's environment in order to provide the most propitious conditions for learning, there is needed, first, an awareness of what constitutes an ideal environment for learning and, second, an understanding of techniques available for effecting such environmental conditions. It is possible to view this manipulation of the child's environment from a general perspective (e.g., the total special-class environment) as well as in terms of a specific technique for organizing materials and the instructional strategy for teaching, for example, discrimination among shapes.

6 Teachers should be provided with an opportunity to develop basic skills in interpreting and translating research findings from various disciplines into practical classroom activities.

7 Teachers of the mentally retarded should feel comfortable serving as consultants to other teachers on issues related to possible ways for dealing with complex problems in learning and classroom management.

selected references

Descoeudres, A.: *The Education of Mentally Defective Children*, D. C. Heath and Company, Boston, 1928.

Doll, E. E.: "A Historical Survey of Research and Management of Mental Retardation in the United States," in Trapp and Himelstein (eds.), *Readings on the Exceptional Child* (2d ed.), Appleton-Century-Crofts, Inc., New York, 1972, pp. 47–98.

Duncan, J.: *Education of the Ordinary Child*, The Ronald Press Company, New York, 1943.

Inskeep, A. L.: *Teaching Dull and Retarded Children*, The Macmillan Company, New York, 1926.

Itard, Jean-Marc-Gaspard: *The Wild Boy of Aveyron*, translated by George and Muriel Humphrey, Appleton-Century-Crofts, Inc., New York, 1962.

President's Panel on Mental Retardation: *A Proposed Program for National Action to Combat Mental Retardation*, Government Printing Office, Washington, D.C., 1962.

Séguin, E.: *Idiocy: Its Treatment by the Physiological Method*, William Wood, New York, 1866.

2

THE NATURE AND IMPLICATIONS OF DISCREPANT FUNCTIONING

This chapter discusses a number of prominent issues pertaining to the foundation on which educational planning for the mentally retarded might be based. Some of the concepts presented will no doubt differ from anything you have ever read or heard. Debatable issues will be singled out and attention given to the points of view that surround each. By the time you have studied this chapter and the next you will have been exposed to the essence of the author's beliefs concerning how educational programming for the mentally retarded can best be done. It is not necessarily intended that you adopt the total philosophy expressed here, but hopefully the content in these chapters will stimulate you to acquire your own beliefs that will direct you in your teaching behavior and lead to an increase in the effectiveness of learning on the part of the children for whom you are responsible. Armed with systematic guidelines, then, your approach to dealing with the learning problems of the mentally retarded will become consistent, will provide the means for you to properly document the procedures you select, will be pertinent to all levels of intellectual and physical development, will allow you to translate the tenets of your philosophy into practice, and will facilitate the discussion of professional issues among you and your colleagues.

dimensions of intelligence

To understand mankind, his society, feelings, motives, and achievements, one concern must be with investigating the nature of man's intellect. It is relatively simple to describe, predict, and control phenomena that are manifestations of the physical world. More difficult for man is the study of himself, particularly one basic aspect of himself—his intellect. Only within the last sixty-five years has man even described the factors of intellect in any scientific way. The other two basic objectives, to predict and to control, have not been scientifically considered to the same degree because of the problems involved in identifying, measuring, and quantifying mental attributes.

EARLY SCHOOLS OF THOUGHT

Late in the 1890s investigations concerned with understanding the nature of intelligence moved from the philosophical to the empirical. The scientific developments precipitating this change included the improvement of research methods and tools for explaining and measuring behavior. Of equal significance was the movement toward emphasizing individual differences.

One early approach to explaining intelligence—since repudiated—was called *faculty theory*. Intelligence was conceived as a number of abilities located in specific areas of the brain. It was thought that bumps on one's head presented an external manifestation of intelligence and that mental abilities could be evaluated by a trained observer "reading" the bumps.

In 1905, Binet, a French psychologist, devised one of the first intelligence scales. He believed that intelligence is expressed as a combined mental operation in which processes operate as a unified whole. Binet's idea of mental age evolved from his adoption of the concept of developmental tasks and levels and the idea that children of certain ages are capable of specific types of tasks that increase in complexity with advancing years. Binet collected a number of simple tasks, found the average age at which a large group of children could accomplish each task, then sequenced the tasks in order of difficulty. The performance data collected on children of different ages allowed Binet to develop reference points for comparing responses. His scale emphasized verbal factors of intelligence.

The Binet Scale seemed appropriately useful with retarded children. Others have adapted this scale for specific purposes. In America, Terman revised the Binet Scale, and it was published in 1916 as the Stanford-Binet Intelligence Scale. Subsequent revisions were made in 1937 and 1960.

In the early 1900s Spearman (1923) devised a two-factor theory of intelligence. His belief was that intelligence is composed of one general ability and several specific abilities. Thurstone (1926) expanded this two-factor theory by suggesting that a group of factors, termed primary

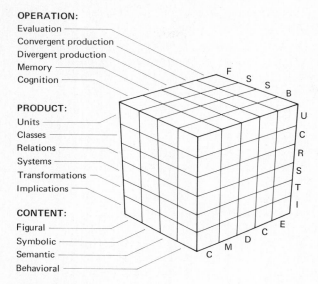

Figure 2-1
The Structure of Intellect Model. (From: *The Nature of Human Intelligence*, J.P. Guilford. Copyright © 1967 by McGraw-Hill Book Company. Reprinted by permission of McGraw-Hill Book Company.)

mental abilities, more accurately describe intelligence. The abilities he identified were number, spatial, memory, verbal, word fluency, and reasoning.

STRUCTURE OF INTELLECT MODEL
Continued advances in testing theory and statistics allowed for the further development of models to explain the nature of intelligence. Guilford and Hoepfner (1971) proposed a structure of intellect that is similar in concept to the periodic table of elements. They hypothesized 120 possible factors of intelligence, more than 80 of which have been identified with a specific test. Figure 2-1 represents Guilford's Structure of Intellect Model.

Much research has been devoted to the development of devices to measure the hypothesized factors within the model that are viewed as elements of intelligence. For example, the Unusual Uses Test is often used to measure spontaneous flexibility, i.e., the divergent production of semantic classes. The subject is asked to list as many ways as he can think of to use a common object, such as a brick. Each response is then

Table 2-1
RESPONSES OF TWO CHILDREN TO THE
BRICK QUESTION ON THE UNUSUAL USES TEST

MALCOLM'S RESPONSES	CATEGORY	SHIFT	OSCAR'S RESPONSES	CATEGORY	SHIFT
1. Build a house	Construction		1. Hold a door open	Support	
2. Build a barn	Construction	No	2. Line a walk	Decoration	Yes
3. Build a garage	Construction	No	3. Heat and use as a bed warmer	Who knows?	Yes
4. Line a walk	Decoration	Yes	4. Build a garage	Construction	Yes
5. Hit a nail	Tool	Yes	5. Use as a pillow	Support	Yes
6. Hit a schoolhouse	Weapon	Yes	6. Build a house	Construction	Yes
7. Pound a stake	Tool	Yes	7. Use as a hammer	Tool	Yes
8. Make a sidewalk	Paving	Yes	8. Support a car	Support	Yes
9. Make a road	Paving	No	9. Use as stepping stone for "follow the leader"	Recreation	Yes
10. Make a fence	Construction	Yes	10. Use for bookcases	Support	Yes
Flexibility Score		6	Flexibility Score		9

assigned a category. For the brick question, categories such as construction, paving, weapon, tool, recreation, and decoration could be used. A count is then made of the number of times the category changes from one response to the one immediately following it (as from weapon to tool, as opposed to remaining weapon twice in a row) and that count is the flexibility score. An illustration of the responses given by two subjects, Malcolm and Oscar, and the spontaneous flexibility scores of each is given in Table 2-1. The question each child was asked is, "How many ways can you think of to use a brick?"

This is only one of the many tests that Guilford, his associates, and other researchers have developed to measure the hypothesized factors of intelligence from his Structure of Intellect Model. The tests, their scoring systems, and the dimensions that each evaluates have been described elsewhere.[1]

After this historic presentation by Guilford, it soon became obvious that tests such as the Revised Stanford-Binet Intelligence Scale and the Wechsler Intelligence Scale for Children (WISC) sample only a small group of intellectual abilities, perhaps as little as 25 percent of the factors postulated by Guilford. For example, verbal fluency, flexibility, originality, and elaboration are not evaluated by the standard intelligence tests.

Although some psychologists have criticized the Structure of Intellect Model proposed by Guilford, it has acted as a stimulus for new research on the nature and development of cognition, and has resulted in scientists looking at intelligence as a multifaceted phenomenon.

the openness of human ability

Now let us turn to a brief discussion of some different positions about how intelligence is thought to develop. You must realize that these are still theoretical concepts and, as such, they require a great deal more research to validate. In fact, even now spirited debate is taking place among academicians concerning these positions.[2]

At the turn of the century a major controversy arose between those

---

[1]For a comprehensive review of Guilford's model and the tests that have been designed to assess the various factors of intellect, the reader is referred to Guilford (1967) and Guilford and Hoepfner (1971).

[2]A very interesting group of presentations on subjects pertaining to the development of cognitive skills resulting from one's hereditary background and/or environment appear in Zigler (1970) and in Reprint Series No. 2 of the *Harvard Educational Review* (1969).

who believed that intellect depended on heredity and those who believed that environment was more important. This controversy paralleled the development of theories that attempted to explain the nature of intelligence. The hereditarians and the environmentalists justified their respective positions with evidence that was often biased or inadequately analyzed. For example, the hereditarians recalled that men of distinction in Great Britain came from a small group of families. They overlooked the fact that these gifted people also lived in a peculiarly enriched environment.

The report of the Kallikaks by Goddard (1913) was cited by this group as evidence of the predominant influence of the genes on intelligence. This study compared the descendants of an illicit union of Martin Kallikak with those who were descendants of his lawful wife. More social degenerates and mentally deficient persons were found to be descended from the illicit union than from the lawful marriage. The conclusion reached was that the difference was due to heredity. Again, Goddard did not indicate the inferior environment in which the illegitimate family lived.

The environmentalists, too, had difficulty explaining their position. Studies that compared the performance of children who were given early practice on tasks as opposed to children who were given none indicated that the latter group caught up with the former after very little practice (Shirley, 1931). Observation suggested that behavioral development, like somatic development, seemed to follow a predetermined course (Coghill, 1929). The environmentalists attacked the dissonant evidence presented by the hereditarians by indicating the uncontrolled nature of the studies cited. They also countered with evidence that showed that deprivation of experience decreased the rate of behavioral development in *infant organisms.* Research by the environmentally oriented scientists emphasized that the age at which the organism was deprived was of significance.

GENETIC AND ENVIRONMENTAL INTERACTION
Even now the specific influences of the environment and the genes on intellectual development are unknown, although studies using both animals and human beings as subjects are leading gradually to clarification of this issue. It is apparent that intellectual ability is not the result of genetic inheritance alone nor of environment alone. The fact that some type of interaction occurs is no longer in dispute.

Dobzhansky (1955) has conceptualized the hypothesized relationship between an individual's inherited characteristics (genotype) and the degree of his environmental favorableness. Accordingly, a person's genetic endowment establishes a range within which behavior (in this

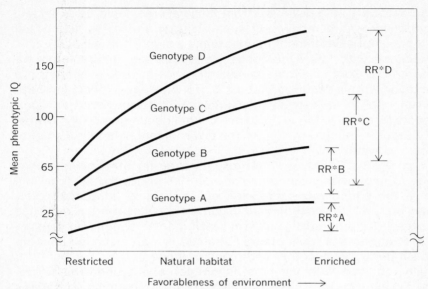

Figure 2-2
Concept of reaction range; four hypothesized genotypes. (From: *Handbook of Mental Deficiency*, edited by N. R. Ellis. Copyright © 1963 by McGraw-Hill Book Company. Reprinted by permission of McGraw-Hill Book Company.)

instance, intelligence) develops. The specific pattern of behavior an individual develops within this hypothesized range depends on the degree of restrictiveness of the environment. The observable results from the interaction between a certain genotype and a specific environment is called *phenotype.*

Gottesman (1963) has schematized these hypothesized relationships according to Dobzhansky's conceptualization. Figure 2-2 presents the components of this schema. From this diagram it is apparent that those individuals with poor genetic endowment (Genotype A) have less potential for responding to environmental stimuli (whether favorable or unfavorable) than those who have been blessed with more ideal genetic characteristics (Genotypes C and D).

The genotypes described in the figure are only four from an infinite number and an infinite range of possibilities. As such, they are only a hypothetical characterization of subgroups of individuals within this very broad range. For example, children who are represented by Genotype A have serious genetic weaknesses. Under normal environmental circumstances these youngsters would probably score around 25 or 30 on an intelligence test. In either a deprived or an enriched environment very little deviation from these scores could be expected. The genotypic characteristics of such children are so restricting that even a powerful environment cannot make a significant impact.

Continuing with this hypothetical construct, the children who are represented by Genotype B are genetically more favored than are those of Genotype A. This suggests that the B group can be expected to have more potential for change in their intellectual development and performance. Not only is the expression of intelligence greater for B than for A, but the range of reaction to the environment, whether dismal or favorable, is wider.

The curve for Genotype C represents a group of persons whose average IQ under typical circumstances is 100. Notice that the possible range in the phenotypic expression of intelligence is approximately between 65 and 125, depending on the environment. Empirical evidence from preschool programs and from placing some siblings in orphanages or foster homes while others remained in more deprived environments supports this hypothesized reaction range.

Finally, children with the most favorable genetic endowment (Genotype D) exhibit the widest possible range for reacting to various environmental situations.

The hypothesized cause-and-effect relationship that exists between heredity and type of environment is subtle and not completely understood. Genetic transmission is important and research is beginning to point to the possibility of eventually controlling some aspects of heredity, such as by manipulating DNA and RNA molecules. Moreover, some very significant breakthroughs in areas such as chromosomal analysis are rapidly increasing scientific precision in explaining, predicting, and controlling certain forms of mental retardation. These issues are as yet of academic interest, however. The teacher's main focus must be on manipulating the child's environment to maximize his hypothesized genotypic potential.

Fewer children are retarded because of inadequate inheritance than because of some type of environmental difficulty, whether it occurs prenatally, at birth, or postnatally. Behavioral scientists have focused their attention on the postnatal period. By attempting to control genetic components and to manipulate the environment in various ways, researchers have found evidence concerning the learning characteristics of organisms reared in different environments. For example, by using animals from similar genetic stock, it is possible to investigate the influence of various types of environments.

Hebb (1949) found that by blinding rats at infancy and then comparing their performance on an "intelligence test" with littermates who were blinded later that the latter group made fewer errors. This result suggested that the extra experience gained from being able to see even briefly facilitated "mental" development. In another experiment (Hebb, 1949), some rats were raised as pets while their littermates were raised in laboratory cages. On the Hebb-Williams Intelligence Test, the rats reared as pets performed in a significantly superior manner to the cage-reared rats. Moreover, they profited more from continued training, which was concomitantly received by the cage-reared animals, suggesting that the richer early experiences of the pet group facilitated later learning.

It is becoming clear from the results of such studies that intelligence is plastic; it is not totally fixed nor predetermined. Animals exposed to stimulating experiences at specific periods of life perform at a higher level on various intellectual and social dimensions than do their nonstimulated but genetically similar counterparts.

PHYSIOLOGICAL CORRELATES
OF ENVIRONMENTAL MANIPULATION

Not only does it appear that certain stimulation elevates the rate of mental development, but there is evidence that an alteration in brain chemistry of either stimulated or deprived animals occurs as a result of the environment. Rosenzweig and his colleagues (1961, 1962, 1964, 1971) have reported results of an interesting series of experiments in which they have explored relationships among learning, environment, brain biochemistry, and heredity. Figure 2-3 describes the general design of these experiments.

In studying the relationship between heredity and learning capacity (line *a* in the figure), the experimenters selected two strains of rats. One group was selectively bred for maze brightness and the other group for maze dullness. For a time both groups were reared in the same environment. Then they were engaged in a series of complex problem-solving tasks that experimental psychologists agree are indicants of learning capacity. On these activities the genetically smart rats performed significantly better than their genetically dull peers.

Another group of genetically smart and genetically dull rats was allowed to mature in an identical environment, was subsequently sacrificed, and the neural structures of both groups were studied under strict biochemical conditions (line *b* in the figure). The genetically bright rats showed a significantly greater amount of activity in certain important neural enzymes that are known to foster cortical transmission than did the genetically dull group. It is clear from these and other

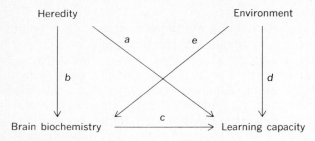

Figure 2-3
Schematic design of variables studied by Rosenzweig.
(From M. R. Rosenzweig, "Heredity, Environment, Brain
Biochemistry, and Learning," in *Current Trends in Psychological Theory*, The University of Pittsburgh Press, Pittsburgh, Pa., 1961. Reprinted by permission of The University of Pittsburgh Press.)

successive experiments on different species of animals that heredity not
only influences learning capacity to some degree but is also related to
neurological functioning.

These same scientists conducted experiments in which the genetic
strains of their rat subjects were controlled and the kind of environments varied (lines *d* and *e*). Littermates, whose genetic character is
known, were divided at birth. One group was placed in an enriched,
playground environment, while their siblings were raised in bare, bleak
cages with no opportunities for interesting stimulation. The playground
group later proved significantly superior in problem-solving tasks.
Moreover, when their brains were analyzed the stimulated rats proved to
have heavier and thicker cortex material, increased activity among
various important neural enzymes that facilitate neural transmission,
and other more favorable biochemical and anatomical characteristics.
These exciting findings suggest that an association with an enriched
environment not only increases problem-solving ability but also alters
the characteristics of the brain in several very important ways.

To be sure, there are differences among species, and you should be
cautious in directly applying these findings to humans. However, in the
behavioral sciences, especially in the field of psychology, the study of
animal behaviors has usually preceded and enriched the subsequent
study of human behaviors. This type of experimentation offers proto-
types, new insights, and provides a map for more-productive inquiries
into the study of man. There may not now be a direct translation that can
be made to man from the results of Rosenzweig's experiments with rats,
but there may be later as additional results are obtained.

EARLY INTERVENTION

It is obviously impossible to assess the impact of man's environment on physiological changes in the same fashion in which Rosenzweig evaluates the neurological condition of rats who have been reared in different environments. There does, however, appear to be a functional difference in the intellectual performance of children who experience enrichment at an early age in contrast to their counterparts who come from relatively uninteresting environments. Behavioral scientists are no longer in dispute over whether planned programs of intervention will facilitate higher levels of performance in young children. The debate has moved beyond determining the value of early programming to discussion about the age at which programming should best take place and the type that should be provided. For example, in the late 1960s and early 1970s much theoretical and empirical support was offered in texts, conferences, and professional journals for providing certain infants, beginning at age six months, with a program of educational stimulation. You may be interested in tracing the development of professional thought concerning the efficacy of early intervention by reviewing the writings of people such as Hess and Bear (1968), Skeels and Dye (1939), Wellman (1940), Skeels (1966), Denenberg (1970), and Ambrose (1969).

One of the landmark studies conducted on preschool children adjudged to be functionally retarded or of high-risk potential was conducted by Kirk (1958). Despite an enormous array of logistic difficulties, Kirk studied children who were removed from deprived environmental settings and given preschool experiences and/or placed in foster homes. Significant increases were observed in the rate of intellectual development when these children were compared with sibling controls who had remained in the home and/or did not receive the preschool experience. In fact, this research reports that children who were left in the deprived environment remained at their initially tested level and in some cases, even tended to decrease or lower their levels of intellectual functioning.

This research stimulated a sizable number of other investigators to begin looking at the whole range of issues about early education that might lead to a more careful and specific delineation of how best to prevent mental retardation from ever occurring in certain high-risk children and how to improve techniques for dealing with those children who already showed retardation. During the latter 1960s, a number of demonstration, evaluation, and research projects were conducted that resulted in various curriculum guides to be used with children who could especially benefit from a program of early intervention to possibly control or otherwise effectively deal with mental retardation. Some of the early education programs in this important area are those of

Spicker, Hodges, and McCandless (1966), Painter (1969), Bereiter and Engelmann (1966), Gray and Klaus (1965), Karnes, Studley, Wright, and Hodgens (1968), Kohlberg (1968), Weikart, Kamii, and Radin (1964), Weikart and Lambie (1968), Connor and Talbot (1964), and Parker et al., (1970).

inferences about mental development

Because there are so many unanswered questions about cognitive development—the manner in which it occurs and the necessary conditions for its occurrences—various theoretical explanations have been presented to try to describe its major dimensions. Neisworth and Smith (1973) have broadly grouped these explanations into four major categories. First, there are those interpretations of cognitive development that focus on hypothetical internal states of an individual. These phenomena cannot be seen and are illustrated by the Freudian approach to describing human behavior. Second, some theories explain behavior, such as intellectual development, by using hypothetical constructs that focus on dimensions external to an individual. These forces, also, cannot be seen and are illustrated in the work of those behavioral scientists who believe that the so-called social presses or one's phenomenological field largely dictate the direction and development of intelligence and personality. Third, some schools of thought explain mental development, or the lack thereof, according to conditions that are internal to an individual but that can be seen. Observable brain damage, metabolic imbalances, and genetic characteristics can be studied, and one can translate these data into valid explanations for a certain degree of mental development. This approach is restricted because scientists, in most instances, are not able to study a person's actual internal state until death. A fourth group of explanations focuses on observable conditions that are external to a person and that are known to influence behavior and development. Factors such as temperature, noise, light intensity, and rewards following certain behavior illustrate external conditions that affect the direction and extent of one's cognitive, personal, and social behavior and development.

It is important to note that each of these four categories is not independent and mutually exclusive. Certain internal conditions, for example, can be observed and others cannot. Certain theorists have developed explanations of mental development that contain some components that are readily observable and others that are inferences—some of which reflect on states that are internal to the individual with other factors that are in a person's external environment. Let me illustrate this point by describing one theory of mental development that overlaps these categories.

HEBB'S THEORY OF MENTAL DEVELOPMENT

In explaining his position concerning cognitive development, Hebb (1949) differentiates between innate potential in the development of intellectual functioning (Intelligence A) and the functional or measurable level (Intelligence B). Intelligence A cannot be measured since it is a manifestation of dimensions such as the quality and robustness of brain functioning, one's genetic contributions, and other components quite apart from the experiential determinants of intellect. On the other hand, Intelligence B is more measurable and, although perhaps a rough estimate of Intelligence A, basically dependent on the nature of an individual's environment and the degree of variety of experiences the organism has encountered.

Hebb has suggested that the ratio between the amount of neural tissue concerned with the function of association and the amount concerned with sensory input and output determines the potential of an organism for learning. Presumably, organisms with a higher association/sensory ratio can develop more complex networks of association at maturity. Organisms lower on the phylogenetic scale, with lower ratios between the association and sensory areas, have progressively less ability and skill for more complex learning. For example, although an elephant has more neural weight than a man, the elephant's A/S ratio is substantially smaller.

Although more complex relationships can be learned by species with high A/S ratios, simple relationships can be learned as rapidly by lower as by higher species. For the more phylogenetically advanced organism, first learning is slower than in lower species. Consider, for example, the speed of motor learning in the newborn calf in contrast to that of higher species.

Perception of Events   Basic to Hebb's theory is the notion that an organism experiences a variety of perceptions related to an event. As this myriad of perceptual experiences associated with an event is repeated, a network of neural cells fires as a unit. Eventually, as the organism experiences this event on repeated occasions, and the associated combination of perceptions related thereto, the stimulated neural cells begin to establish a closed system in which firing continues after the stimuli have ceased. Cell assemblies of single stimulated neurons become established in the course of repeated excitation.

As these perceptual acts are repeated, the intercellular bonds become strengthened and lead the assembly to function as a unit. The assumption is made that whenever an impulse crosses a synapse, subsequent transmission between these neurons is easier. If this synapse cross occurs frequently enough, a physiological alteration at the synapse is effected either as an anatomical growth (*synaptic knob* in Hebb's terms) or as a metabolic change.

Presumably a given cell assembly consists of numerous neurons widely dispersed over a large portion of the brain. This apparently accounts for the finding that lesions in adults, resulting from some type of trauma, often do not destroy abilities; whereas, in young children who have not developed these complex associational networks, cortical lesions are much more permanently damaging.

As experience proceeds in time and sequence, cell assemblies become associated with each other and form an exceedingly more complex associational pattern, which Hebb labels as *phase sequences*. Thus, a large and extensive associational network becomes established around several related events, each of which has idiosyncratic as well as similar and shared perceptions.

To illustrate, suppose you were involved in the event of cooking a steak over a charcoal fire in your backyard. Associated with this event are a variety of perceptions of an auditory, visual, tactual, and olfactory nature. In each of these areas a variety of rather discrete perceptual events can be experienced. For example, you would not only hear the fire, but also receive the auditory perceptions of steak sizzling, the metal of the burner expanding and contracting, and the admonishments of your guests to be sure that their steak is either rare or well done. Similarly, a variety of rather discrete perceptions in the other areas would be evidenced.

As these perceptual experiences occur over and over every time you charcoal steaks, they tend to become associated with one another. These perceptions are transmitted to various neurons resulting in an associational network eventually being established. Following the establishment of this cell assembly, the reception of one or more of the perceptual experiences, such as *smelling* a sizzling steak, immediately results in the total cell assembly firing. Simply smelling a steak, without having received other associated percepts, will result immediately in an image being established around the event of cooking a steak. Figure 2-4 diagrams the hypothetical interaction among such perceptions.

Cell assemblies become associated with one another and form phase sequences. For example, the event of cooking a steak could become associated with a birthday, anniversary, inviting the boss for dinner, receiving a raise, or some other type of event. Perceptions associated

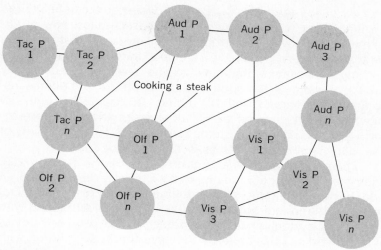

Figure 2-4
Interrelationship of perceptual experiences concerned with a specific event
(infinite number of possible associational bonds).

with each of the cell assemblies become related to perceptions from
other assemblies. When you smell a steak cooking, the appropriate cell
assemblies immediately become active and in turn, stimulate networks
related to other events. Close temporal and spatial contiguity must be
present for cell assemblies to become associated and form phase
sequences. These higher-level associational structures will develop
only after a certain amount of interassembly facilitation has been
established through repeated excitation.

According to Hebb, intelligence develops as the organism forms
these complex and diffuse associational patterns. The more complex
the patterns, in terms of the number and degree of perceptual associations, the more intelligent the organism. The intellectually superior,
therefore, is one who has experienced a variety of events, become
sensitive to the perceptual experiences associated with these events,
related perceptual experiences through the development of cell assemblies, and elaborated on the cell assemblies by making possible their
higher-level association into phase sequences. The development of
such associational systems assumes a potential of Intelligence A.

Intelligence Defined   In Hebb's terms intelligence may be defined as
the *"number of strategies for processing information that have been
differentiated and have achieved the mobility which permits them to be*

available in a variety of situations." "Number of strategies" refers to the extent to which associational networks (cell assemblies and phase sequences) have been developed. Mobility is an important feature of the definition in that emphasis is placed on the need for flexibility within the system. Not only is it essential that networks be developed; it is equally crucial that the system allow additional perceptions to become associated so that elaboration of cell assemblies can occur. This will lead to a system which, because of its high level of associational patterning, is able to arrive at a variety of solutions to problems since flexibility of the organism allows more complex associations to be formed.

Hebbian Explanation for Mental Retardation　Benoit (1957, 1959) has explained mental retardation using Hebb's theory. Certain children are retarded because of deficits in Intelligence A. For a variety of possible reasons, the innate potential of the organism is reduced with the result that the system is less amenable to the development of associational networks. This would be the case for those children with genetic aberrations or gross cortical damage resulting from intrauterine difficulties and for those children who have experienced some type of central-nervous-system damage at birth. In each case, the child's potential for using experiences and perceptions in the establishment of cell assemblies and phase sequences has been damaged or not developed.

The largest group of mentally retarded children exhibits mild intellectual deficits (i.e., IQ between 50 and 80), not because of an inadequate Intelligence A, but because it has not had the opportunity to experience many perceptions around a variety of events within the environment. These children typically come from low socioeconomic situations and are usually classified as culturally deprived. There is no reason to believe that these children do not have basic potential (Intelligence A) for taking advantage of their environment; however, in most instances the opportunity is not provided at an early enough age. These children, because of their paucity of experiences, develop weak and inadequate associational patterns which are extremely limited in scope. Little wonder that they are unable to solve problems effectively, do well in school, or operate as intellectually normal individuals. Indeed, if the lack of opportunity for experiencing a variety of events is severe enough, they will not develop an adequate repertoire of associations and will function as mentally retarded persons.

From research on human beings at various ages, it is well established that plasticity of the organism decreases with increasing age. That is, if an impact is to be made on an organism, it is much more efficient and effective to work with a young individual than with one who is older.

Some scientists believe that plasticity decreases substantially after age six. Relating this point to Hebb's theory, there is obvious wisdom in providing the young child with a variety of stimulating experiences in order to foster the early development of associational networks leading to higher levels of intellectual functioning. The difficulty in training and educating a relatively more rigid organism is substantial.

Implications of Hebb's theory for education of the retarded follow.

1 To provide the neonate with as robust an Intelligence A as possible, parents, particularly the mother, should receive instruction during the prenatal period. There are certain considerations about which an expectant mother should be aware as they can influence the infant's health. If expectant mothers are unaware of or unconcerned about personal health during pregnancy, a variety of difficulties could reduce the infant's potential. In a broad sense, this area is of educational concern.

2 One of the most obvious implications of Hebb's theory for the retarded is the need to enlarge these children's stimulus fields. They need to be engaged in a wide variety of experiences that provide distinctive perceptual experiences to facilitate association.

3 To control the development of inaccurate and incomplete associational networks and to take advantage of the greater plasticity of the young child, emphasis should be placed on early educational programs. There is a definite advantage in working with children when they are young and while new organizational structures are being formed.

4 The teacher must provide the child with consistent, clear stimulus patterns during the early phases of training. If the child is presented with different stimuli at different times, each of which is related to the same event, confusion will result, and the opportunity for developing a stable associational pattern will be substantially reduced. The stimulus value of the stable percepts should be increased, the irrelevant stimuli should be decreased, and associations between percepts explicitly called to the attention of the child. To leave such associations to chance is hazardous.

5 Effective learning occurs only after the child's attention has been focused. If the child is inattentive or receives only a segment of the perceptions of an event, inadequate or erroneous associations will take place. The teacher must gain and hold the attention of the child before proceeding with the activity.

6 The teacher must constantly repeat stimuli if associational chains are to develop. This repetition is desirable not only to develop associational patterns but also to maintain those cell assemblies and phase sequences that have previously been formed. Without repetition, obliteration will occur. This is particularly true with the retarded because they often have a short-term memory.

7 Early cortical stimulation is desirable for subsequent learning. The infant's natural tendency for sensory motor activity should be encouraged by providing him with opportunities for moving about and experiencing various events. There is reason to believe that early sensory motor activity will lead to the more rapid development of perceptual skills—a basic ingredient in Hebb's theory. To restrict a child's movement or to reduce stimuli during the early years will negatively influence subsequent cognitive development.

assessing intellectual development

The measurement of intellectual development, capacity, or potential is tricky and is fraught with controversy. People tend to take extreme positions on the subject. Many believe that it is impossible to evaluate intellectual capacity. Others feel that standardized intelligence tests are heavily biased against children from lower socioeconomic environments, and, as such, they provide invalid data. Believing that contemporary intelligence tests assess only a small segment of what is presently felt to constitute intelligence, some behavioral specialists suggest that the future use of such instruments can only lead to erroneous conclusions about an individual's cognitive development and state.

Let me emphasize that it is impossible to accurately measure a person's real capacity or potential to do anything. For example, how would you decide on a child's potential capacity to throw a ball a certain distance, your own potential capacity to run a mile, or your close friend's potential capacity for climbing a rope? Would you begin by measuring physical fitness? Experts in this area of study disagree about which dimensions you should focus upon. Moreover, they have not considered such important factors as a person's attitude toward participating in an activity that presumably measures potential capacity to throw a ball, run a mile, or climb a rope. Perhaps the most accurate way to measure these capacities would be to study such basic components as muscle cells and fibers, percent of oxygenation of the tissues, circulatory efficiency and effectiveness, oxygen–carbon dioxide exchange, and all the host of emotional-social components that directly influence how well a person really should be able to do something.

It is all the more difficult, then, to adequately assess intellectual capacity or potential. It involves an extraordinary conceptual leap to infer a person's basic intellectual capacity from results obtained on an intelligence test. They were not designed to assess innate cognitive potential. Intelligence tests historically have the functions of

1 Predicting how well a child should achieve in school on the basis of his present achievement on the intelligence test

2 Discovering those areas of intellectual development, within the limits imposed by the character of the test, in which a child is relatively weak and/or strong so that more precise and meaningful educational planning can be initiated for him

If, after collecting data on a child from an intelligence test, your conclusions about the child diverge from the two functions that intelligence tests were designed to fulfill, you will be engaging in extreme speculative behavior. Do not conclude that a child's "intellectual bucket" is really of a certain volume or capacity on the basis of an intelligence test score. It was not designed to allow anyone to make such a conclusion.

Even if intelligence tests were designed to assess one's intellectual capacity or potential (which they were not), consider these acknowledged weaknesses and decide for yourself how comfortable you would feel in declaring that a person had a certain intellectual upper limit.

1 Even the more sophisticated tests currently used to evaluate intellectual ability provide inadequate estimates of total mental abilities and are based on an incomplete sample of the presently known factors of intellect. Current standardized intelligence tests do not identify and assess talents such as originality, fluency of ideas, sensing problems, foresight, and evaluation abilities. It is possible, therefore, for a child to test low on a standardized test but to score higher on other factors of intelligence, such as those associated with creativity. Likewise, many specific learning disabilities are not identified by current tests because of the circumscribed constellation of factors that the tests sample.

2 Despite the fact that test designers work hard to reduce errors caused by invalid and unreliable items, unclear wording, inadequate directions, and subtests that do not measure factors they purport to measure, every test has certain errors of measurement that exert a biasing effect on the performance of certain children and that therefore lead to erroneous conclusions.

3 Incorrect test administration has a substantial limiting effect. To either administer or score a test without proper knowledge and training violates a major assumption underlying these instruments and can substantially alter a subject's score.

4 Most educators and psychologists realize that children quickly become "test wise." To examine a child many times using the same test often results in wide variations among scores because the subject remembers the dimensions measured and, in some cases, even remembers specific questions. For these and other reasons test-retest reliability is frequently lower than desired.

There is no question that each of us has certain real potential in all areas of development—cognitive, social, emotional, motor, and so on. However, a true determination of these basic capacities cannot be made. Perhaps even trying to estimate capacities is a waste of time for a teacher. Let me simply highlight some of the factors that have been presented concerning the issue of intellectual capacity.

1 At this time we cannot identify and agree upon all the components involved in intellectual development.

2 No satisfactory measurement device has been developed to allow us to conclude anything at all about a person's intellectual capacity or potential—even in those areas that have been clearly identified and agreed upon as being components of intellectual development.

3 Standardized intelligence tests do not measure real capacity and scores from these tests should not be used as indexes of intellectual potential.

4 The use of intelligence tests as a measure of a child's future success in school-related activities and as an indication of areas of strength and weakness should be tempered with the realization that there are errors inherent in each instrument and in various assumptions that must be made regarding the training and experience of the examiner.

5 Intelligence tests, to the extent that they are used as predictors, presume that an optimal learning environment has been provided and that no educational intervention can be used that has not been used.

By using such tests as the Revised Stanford-Binet Intelligence Scale, the Wechsler Intelligence Scale for Children, the Pictorial Test of Intelligence, and the Peabody Picture Vocabulary Test, a trained psychologist or psychometrician can assess how well a child is developing in the various intellectual areas. Of course, the examiner must have some notion about which factor he is interested in testing, some idea of when and at what level of performance each dimension is usually evidenced, and some general criteria that can be used to denote an abnormally slow rate of development. These data, then, can be analyzed to determine core areas of weakness and strength in basic factors involved in the development of cognitive skills. More will be said later about these and related issues.

interindividual differences

Although it is almost too obvious to mention, nonetheless the extreme importance for teachers to be aware of the ways and the extent to which children differ from each other must be emphasized. Even within a group of children generally considered homogeneous you will often notice some rather extreme interindividual variability. For example, in a class of children of approximately the same chronological age many physical differences will be evident. Some youngsters will be much taller than others—some may be extremely short. However, in spite of some very obvious differences in certain children, the group as a whole will probably be much more alike than unlike in many individual characteristics. When one describes the average characteristics of populations of subjects a measure of central tendency, such as the mean, mode, or median, is often used. For example, the mean intelligence quotient for children on the Revised Stanford-Binet Intelligence Scale and the Wechsler Intelligence Scale for Children is 100. Or, a group of third-grade children might average 48 inches in height. Such averages reflect the status of most of the children within a circumscribed and defined group. They do not indicate the extent to which the scores of the group spread out or vary from the mean.

To be sure, special educators are interested in group averages; however, *their main concern is usually those children whose performance in educational areas is significantly different from that of other members of the group of whom they are a representative.* These deviations, then, are extreme enough to require some form of special educational programming. Suppose we consider some of the dimensions that apply to this statement that broadly describe a main thrust of the special educator's concern for interindividual differences among children.

First, notice that emphasis is placed on the performance of a child in contrast to that of his contemporaries, and that deviations in performance should focus on areas that relate to educational factors. It is deceptively easy to focus on educationally inconsequential variables. Physical stature, shape of head, body odor, cleanliness of fingernails, and other obvious characteristics cry out for your attention when they are present in only a child or two in a group. It is the teacher's duty to determine if any of these factors really warrants special attention. Sometimes they may be relevant, but usually they only distract attention from behaviors that are more directly educational. Look at performance differences among children on specific facets of arithmetic achievement (e.g., counting, grouping, carrying and/or borrowing), reading achievement, spelling, language, and in any other areas you consider to be important. You can be fairly certain that children judged to be mentally retarded on the basis of their performance on an intelligence test will usually manifest other specific achievement difficulties.

Another factor that must be considered in deciding on the extent and type of special education programming desirable for a child is the degree to which his performance deviates from that of his peers. It is not possible to define the term "significantly different from" in an absolute sense. People disagree on what is an appropriate level for differences to be significant; the same level of performance discrepancy may be significant in one subject area but not in another—and the chronological age of the child is a compounding factor. For example, a relatively small performance discrepancy in a certain skill area usually warrants much more attention for a very young child than does a much larger performance deviation for a high school youngster. This is because the early readiness skills are essential for subsequent learning, whereas if an older child is a year or two behind his peers in reading the consequences are not nearly so severe.

Finally, in looking at interindividual differences it is important to know the reference group against which a child's performance is being compared. If a youngster with a serious hearing problem is administered a predominantly verbal test, such as the Stanford-Binet Intelligence Scale, one could expect an inordinately poor performance not only because of the difficulty hearing-impaired children typically have in dealing with verbal communication skills, but also because the test was standardized with children whose hearing was normal. Although such measuring devices were not developed to explain why a child might do poorly, it is nevertheless important for a teacher and/or school psychologist to select an instrument that will

1 Give a maximum amount of reliable information about a child's performance in specified target areas

2 Allow for a comparison of the child's achievement with a population from which the youngster is a member

3 Not penalize the child because of certain serious limitations in understanding the stimuli or in responding to them, as in the case of a blind or deaf child being administered the standard version of the Stanford-Binet Intelligence Scale

Some control, therefore, should be exercised over the various elements that could bias the results of an interindividual assessment. When experimenter or subject bias is introduced, the validity and generalizability of the findings are reduced, which leads to less precision in formulating an appropriate educational program. The teacher should know about these possible sources of bias as educational and psychological reports are interpreted.

intra-individual differences

Interindividual assessment uses the performance of other children as the reference for determining an individual's level of competence; intra-individual assessment uses the individual's own performance level as the reference. The child is compared with himself, and a profile of relative strengths and weaknesses is determined.

As suggested earlier, most individuals show areas of relative strength and others of comparative weakness. Even among intellectually normal or superior people uneven competencies are often observed. For example, many people are extremely unskilled in artistic or musical performance but are highly effective in other areas. Depending on the number of areas assessed, most of us would show an extremely uneven profile.

Awareness of a retarded child's level of success in academic areas is important; however, awareness of disabilities in more specific areas (e.g., memory, transfer, incidental learning, and vocal expression) provides a more practical basis for planning an educational program. It is true that teaching and learning would be greatly simplified if one could give teachers a cookbook of methods that would enable them to deal with all the problems they might encounter in the classroom. Obviously this is impossible because (1) you could not dream of all the problems that will occur in one classroom during the school year, and (2) even if you *were* able to specify the problems there are no specific, foolproof techniques for dealing with all their manifestations as you find them among heterogeneous populations of children such as the mentally retarded. This situation, then, demands that you look at each child's performance on an individual basis, comparing his competencies with those of other youngsters but, most important, looking at his own individual skills. The strengths and weaknesses that he exhibits, then, act as the pivot point for designing an individually appropriate educational plan.

To illustrate, two retarded children of the same age, with the same general intellectual skills, may demand entirely different programs. One child may be weak in areas related to visual-motor performance but relatively strong in use of the auditory channel. The other child may show the opposite profile. If the teacher has been trained to use phonics, based on auditory capabilities, the first child will be in a much better position to learn than the second youngster. If, on the other hand, the teacher has been trained to emphasize visualization, the first child will be penalized. Teachers of these children soon learn that "standard ways" for teaching reading, arithmetic, spelling, or talking do not work. The upshot is that everyone, the child as well as the teacher, becomes frustrated.

Let me emphasize again, then, that to base an educational program for the retarded solely on interindividual assessment is being insensitive to differences within children and implicitly supports a cookbook approach to teaching. Instead, moving beyond the interindividual procedure to a within-individual analysis transcends the use of traditional disability categories and focuses attention, properly, on educationally relevant factors. Special educators most often deal with children who show extremely diverse patterns of performance and have multi-disabilities. The onus is on the teacher to be aware of this pattern and to structure a program for each child on the basis of individual and relevant educational characteristics.

some prominent learning characteristics of the mentally retarded

The opinion expressed in the preceding sections emphasized the value of dealing with children who are unsuccessful in school, such as the mentally retarded, on an individualized basis. This approach should be used in all efforts involving the evaluation of a child's educational problems and the specification of an appropriate instructional plan. If you believe in this philosophy then you will not classify, plan for, or group youngsters according to factors that are anything other than educational. For special educators, such terms as *brain injury*, *mongolism*, *Strauss Syndrome*, and even *mentally retarded* lack specificity and do not lead to individual education plans. These are immaterial characteristics that are in no way germane to teaching and learning. There are two issues, then, on which an educator must focus special attention. First, he must decide whether the variables he has selected for investigation have pertinence to educational intervention. Second, he must collect relevant inter- and intra-individual performance data on each child for whom a plan is desired.

Although there are often pronounced individual differences among the mentally retarded, at any age level, at the same time there are also some common behavioral characteristics—that is, traits that occur with measured frequency among most such populations. It does not do violence to our previously expressed emphasis on the need to deal with each child individually to describe here some of the usual characteristics of the retarded. The following section, then, presents results from a sample of studies in several areas of learning in which retarded and normal children have been compared. The findings of much of the research do not agree, *except* on certain learning variables. Also, these studies show but a few of the numerous areas of learning in which the retarded show characteristic deficits. Gardner and his colleagues (1970) have developed a comprehensive bibliography of most of the significant literature in this area.

There are some other problems in conducting research on retarded individuals of which you should be aware, the most pronounced of which concern sampling, testing, and instrumentation. This is particularly true with public school retarded children. Therefore, investigators have conducted most of their research using more moderately or more severely retarded subjects.

SHORT- AND LONG-TERM RETENTION
The research literature strongly suggests that retarded youngsters often exhibit weakness in short-term memory (Scott and Scott, 1968). Their ability to store auditory or visual material for more than a few seconds or minutes is decidedly poor. Hermelin and O'Connor (1964) found that, two to six seconds after presentation, intellectually normal children remembered an auditory sequence better than retarded children. No differences were observed between the groups when a longer time interval ensued after the stimulus was presented. Similar findings have been reported by others using visual stimuli and requiring some type of motor response (Headrick and Ellis, 1964; Baumeister, Smith, and Rose, 1965).

With respect to the short-term memory of mentally retarded children, several common threads seem to be evidenced throughout the empirical literature. First, in addition to retarded children being poorer in immediate recall than normal youngsters, they appear to be overly influenced by irrelevant stimuli and have more difficulty focusing on a task (House and Zeaman, 1961). Both normal and subnormal children tend to be hindered in short-term memory by items which intervene between the stimulus presentation and the test for recall. When verbal labels are used in association with the stimuli, significant improvement in the short-term memory of retarded persons has been observed (Barnett, Ellis, and Pryer, 1959; Jensen and Rohwer, 1963). Children, irrespective of intellectual level, do less well in short-term memory when

1 The complexity of the stimulus is increased
2 The delay between presentation and recall becomes excessive
3 Some type of psychological threat is perceived by the child
4 Anticipation of reward is too great
5 Some type of interfering material is presented

Long-term memory deficits in retarded individuals have not been observed when comparisons were made with intellectually normal subjects (Jensen and Rohwer, 1963; Johnson and Blake, 1960). Generally, retarded youngsters are able to remember material as well as normal subjects if (1) they have overlearned the fact or concept beyond a minimal criterion level and (2) they have had an opportunity to reinforce this learning through constant use. If a retarded child does not have a chance to employ the material which has been learned there is greater likelihood of obliteration occurring.

Hebb's theory supports the empirical findings concerning the retention characteristics of retarded children. If, for some reason, a child has impaired cortical tissue, it is reasonable to expect that the development of associational networks (cell assemblies and phase sequences) will occur to a very limited degree. Retarded children without obvious organicity may be faulty in short-term memory and in the concomitant development of associational patterns because of the ambiguous nature of the stimuli, the vague or reduced stimulus value of the perceptual events, the short duration period of the stimuli, the lack of clarity in relationship among various types of stimuli concerning an event, the lack of attention on the part of the child, the introduction of irrelevant perceptions at a time when relevant stimuli are presented, or because of faulty peripheral systems such as the auditory or visual. Any or all of these difficulties would result in either a reduction in or a confusion among the various perceptual experiences of an event and lead to the less precise development of cell assemblies and phase sequences. This, then, would result in the child experiencing difficulties in short-term memory.

If the child has developed a stable repertoire of associational patterns, the theory suggests that obliteration or decay will occur only with disuse. There is no reason to suggest that this position would not be true of retarded individuals. The empirical documentation for validating this postulation shows that once the retarded learn a fact or concept they are likely to remember it as well as the intellectually normal, provided they are given opportunities to use the material. By using information available from existing cell assemblies and phase sequences, the individual establishes a firmer entrenchment of the network in the cognitive structure, and an opportunity is provided for elaboration with other old and new assemblies. In using existing networks, the individual will infrequently experience precisely the same stimuli which were initially instrumental in the formation of networks. Because of this, elaboration is extended to other perceptions related to the same event which, in turn, leads to opportunities for greater flexibility and generalization on the part of the individual. The use of existing information in the repertoire, therefore, is important for long-term retention, application, and generalization.

DISCRIMINATION LEARNING

Discrimination among auditory or visual stimuli is a skill which is basic for effective and efficient learning. Children must develop skill in discriminating among shapes, configurations, symbols, and sounds in order to learn how to deal with complex stimuli that are contained in the various symbol systems or academic and nonacademic subject areas. Even in social situations discrimination is required of adults. For example, it is often necessary to discern the intentions of people in social interaction.

Studies in discrimination learning have typically offered to subjects several stimuli which are closely related in their characteristics. The subjects are asked to choose one of the objects, and their response is either acknowledged as being correct or wrong according to an a priori decision by the experimenter. For example, in a series of these experiments the correct choice, as determined by the researcher although not explicitly told to the subjects, might be the one object shown each time with two or more rounded corners. From the experiments the investigator can choose any number of variables for study. For example, the speed of learning, various types of punishment or reward schedules, types of rewards (candy versus toys), face-to-face versus machine presentation, influence of labeling objects prior to selection by the subjects, and other variables have been used as dependent variables in discrimination-learning experiments. A number of studies in this area have been done using mentally retarded persons as subjects, and their performance has been compared with intellectually normal children of either the same MA or CA.

The studies which have contrasted retarded and normal children in discrimination learning are inconsistent in the direction of their findings.[3] Several studies indicate that retarded children learn more slowly than normal subjects (Stevenson and Iscoe, 1955; House and Zeaman, 1959; Rudel, 1959); whereas other researchers have found no difference between these two groups in their rate of discrimination learning (Ellis and Sloan, 1959; Stevenson, 1960). The differences in the results of these studies are probably due to methodological variation in the procedures of experimentation more than to differences among subjects. In fact, most of the research in discrimination learning has employed subjects from institutions, comparing these individuals with noninstitutionalized normals. It is difficult to precisely specify their discrimination-learning characteristics apart from considering the possible influence of institutionalization.

Although difficulties in research design have tended to confuse the findings of studies in discrimination learning, the research does suggest that retarded children will learn patterns of discrimination more rapidly if they are encouraged to name or label the stimuli (Zeaman, House, and Orlando, 1958; Dickerson, Girardeau, and Spradlin, 1964), provided with stimuli which are novel (Zeaman, House, and Orlando, 1958), and given a reward for a correct response (Cantor and Hottel, 1955). Caution should be exercised in generalizing these findings to all populations of retarded youngsters since, in many cases, trainable-level children were used as subjects in these studies. The applicability of these findings to the noneducable child remains somewhat speculative.

LEARNING SET
The term *learning set* refers to the ability of a person to learn how to solve additional problems because of previous experience with similar situations. For example, it takes fewer trials to solve discrimination problems after a person has earlier been required to respond to the same type of problem. The decrease in the number of trials required to learn the techniques for solving subsequent problems indicates that the individual learns how to solve such problems. This phenomenon has been called "learning how to learn."

---

[3]For a review of a representation of the studies conducted in the area of discrimination learning see Stevenson (1963) and Baumeister (1967).

Studies of learning set show that retarded children generally are capable of learning how to learn. The ability to establish a learning set seems to be directly related to MA, the phenomenon occurring more rapidly for subjects with a high MA (Ellis, 1958; Stevenson and Swartz, 1958). In studies in which retarded and normal children of the same MA were compared, the retarded children tended to be somewhat slower in establishing a learning set, perhaps because of a tendency toward increased perseveration.

One additional generalization seems warranted from the literature. When retarded youngsters are given an opportunity to solve and master easy problems prior to their being exposed to more difficult problems, the establishment of a learning set is effected more rapidly. The most obvious educational implication of these studies is that the retarded need to be exposed to a sequential presentation of facts and concepts.

INCIDENTAL LEARNING

Relatively few studies have endeavored to ascertain to what degree retarded children are able to acquire knowledge from stimuli which are peripheral to those perceptions involved in a directed learning task. The ability to be sensitive to incidental clues from the environment is a competency which will lead directly to the establishment of a more elaborate response repertoire.

Goldstein and Kass (1961) compared educable retarded with gifted subjects of the same MA and found that the retarded children were capable of incidental learning in terms of the number of responses given. The retarded, however, gave significantly more incorrect responses than did the gifted. Hetherington and Banta (1962) indicate that familial retarded and normal children score higher on incidental learning tasks than retarded children with organic involvement.

Several investigators have tried to teach for incidental learning. Williams (1970) investigated the effects of readiness training on the enhancement of incidental learning and concluded that such preparation definitely has value for the educable mentally retarded. Ross (1970) found that a nine-month game program designed to teach game skills resulted in educable retarded children acquiring skills, on an incidental basis, in basic number concepts, and at a level that was significantly greater than for control subjects.

Although the retarded appear to have the potential for making use of stimuli which are incidental to a direct task, the empirical evidence describing any specific deficit in this area is fragmentary. The retarded are less perceptive and selective of stimuli within their environment and much less able to make use of such peripheral stimuli. If maximum benefit of the potential value inherent in incidental stimuli is to accrue to the retarded, their attention must be directed to perceptual events. The association of these perceptions with stimuli from intentional learning should be encouraged. By intentionally following this procedure, maximum advantage is made of the environment, and the associational patterns developed in the cognitive structure become much more elaborate.

REACTION TIME
There is almost complete consensus in the literature that the retarded are significantly weak in reaction time. A significant negative correlation between MA and reaction time has been consistently found with various samples of retarded children (Ellis and Sloan, 1957; Bensberg and Cantor, 1957). Studies dealing with reaction time show that retarded children with organicity do less well than familial retarded children. Further, children with perceptual difficulties and attention difficulties appear to be slower in their reaction to stimuli than children without these behavioral traits. Some evidence suggests that greater stimulus intensity will result in more favorable reaction time among the retarded (Baumeister, Vrquhart, Beedle, and Smith, 1964).

TRANSFER
A certain amount of conceptual overlap exists between the notions of transfer and learning sets. In the following discussion, transfer should be viewed in a more general way. Transfer, therefore, is to be considered as skill in using and applying response patterns and experiences formerly learned to another problem which has components similar to the previous situation. In order to be skilled in transfer, an individual must have concepts and facts stored in the cognitive structure, be able to choose and select those concepts relevant to the problem, and appropriately apply them to another situation.

The research designed to investigate the retardeds' ability to transfer indicates that they show a definite tendency to transfer negative rather than positive learnings. The retarded remember with much greater facility what they are *not* supposed to do instead of what they are supposed to do (Bryant, 1965). The reverse tends to be true for intellectually normal children. This finding is of great instructional significance.

Orton, McKay, and Rainy (1964) suggest that educable mentally retarded children perform better in transferring when the instructional presentation is concrete, the materials used can be manipulated, and the tasks involve a minimal need for abstraction. In contrast, bright students transfer best when the method of instruction involves the use of rules, principles, and generalizations.

In teaching retarded children to transfer, the teacher should

1 Logically sequence instruction and make liberal use of materials and concrete examples before a principle or rule is considered
2 Place the retarded youngster in a situation which will be successful for the child, thereby encouraging positive transfer
3 Provide a variety of rewards for correct responses
4 Stress relationships between situations and problems by explicitly showing the children commonalities which exist

PRODUCTIVE THINKING

The terms *creative* and *divergent* are frequently used as synonyms for *productive thinking*. The research in productive thinking has been based primarily on the work of Guilford (1967) by employing instruments which assess fluency, flexibility, and originality in thinking.

Since low, nonsignificant relationships are known to exist between scores on intelligence tests and factors of productive thinking, researchers have endeavored to evaluate the extent to which retarded children are able to perform in the areas of creativity. Some effort has been directed toward determining the influence of training programs for the retarded which have been especially designed to foster skill in productive thinking.

Tisdall (1962) compared the productive-thinking abilities of educable mentally retarded children in special classes with those of educable-level children in the regular grades. On the verbal tests of productive thinking, the special-class children performed better than the children in the regular classes. Differences did not exist between the groups on the nonverbal measures. Low relationships existed between intelligence-test scores and all productive-thinking scores.

Rouse (1965) gave a group of educable-level children a special training program designed to enhance productive thinking. Their performance was compared with that of a group of educable children who had not received the special training program. As might be anticipated, the trained children were significantly superior in all areas of productive thinking.

These studies indicate that retarded children are poorer in spontaneous productive thinking than are intellectually normal children. They also show that educable retarded children possess the potential for being trained in productive thinking. A planned program in productive thinking would probably enhance the *total* verbal performance of educable children, which is their greatest area of difficulty. Other, somewhat tangential, benefits could accrue in areas of cognition such as in transfer, retention, and establishment of learning sets.

A productive-thinking program for the retarded should not have as an objective the training of these people to be unusually creative. A more appropriate emphasis should be on developing a more extensive repertoire of general information and associations which will allow for flexibility in retrieval at the most appropriate time.

selected references

Ambrose, J. A. (ed.): *Stimulation in Early Infancy*, Academic Press, New York, 1969.

Barnett, C., N. Ellis, and M. Pryer: "Stimulus Pretraining and the Delayed Reaction in Defectives," *American Journal of Mental Deficiency*, vol. 64, 1959, pp. 104–111.

Baumeister, A. A.: "Learning Abilities of the Mentally Retarded," in A. A. Baumeister (ed.), *Mental Retardation: Appraisal, Education, and Rehabilitation*, Aldine Publishing Company, Chicago, 1967, pp. 181–211.

————, T. Smith, and J. Rose: "The Effects of Stimulus Complexity and Retention Interval upon Short-Term Memory," *American Journal of Mental Deficiency*, vol. 70, 1965, pp. 129–134.

————, D. Vrquhart, R. Beedle, and T. Smith: "Reaction Time of Normals and Retardates under Different Stimulus Intensity Changes," *American Journal of Mental Deficiency*, vol. 69, 1964, pp. 126–130.

Benoit, E. P.: "Relevance of Hebb's Theory of the Organization of Behavior to Educational Research on the Mentally Retarded," *American Journal of Mental Deficiency*, vol. 61, 1957, pp. 497–507.

————: "Toward a New Definition of Mental Retardation," *American Journal of Mental Deficiency*, vol. 63, 1959, pp. 559–564.

Bensberg, G. J. and G. N. Cantor: "Reaction Time in Mental Defectives with Organic and Familial Etiology," *American Journal of Mental Deficiency*, vol. 62, 1957, pp. 534–537.

Bereiter, C. and S. Engelmann: *Teaching Disadvantaged Preschool Children*, Prentice-Hall, Inc., Englewood Cliffs, N.J., 1966.

Bryant, P. E.: "The Transfer of Positive and Negative Learning by Normal and Severely Subnormal Children," *British Journal of Psychology*, vol. 56, 1965, pp. 81–86.

Cantor, G. N. and J. V. Hottel: "Discrimination Learning in Mental Defectives as a Function of Magnitude of Food Reward and Intelligence Level," *American Journal of Mental Deficiency*, vol. 60, 1955, pp. 380–384.

Coghill, G. E.: *Anatomy and the Problem of Behavior*, Cambridge University Press, London, 1929.

Connor, F. P. and M. E. Talbot: *An Experimental Curriculum for Young Mentally Retarded Children*, Teachers College Press, New York, 1964.

Denenberg, V. H. (ed.): *Education of the Infant and Young Child*, Academic Press, 1970.

Dickerson, D. J., F. L. Girardeau, and J. E. Spradlin: "Verbal Pre-training and Discrimination Learning by Retardates," *American Journal of Mental Deficiency*, vol. 68, 1964, pp. 476–484.

Dobzhansky, T.: *Evolution, Genetics, and Man*, John Wiley and Sons, Inc., New York, 1955.

Ellis, N. R.: "Object-Quality Discrimination Learning Sets by Mental Defectives," *Journal of Comparative and Physiological Psychology*, vol. 51, 1958, pp. 79–81.

——— and W. Sloan: "Oddity Learning as a Function of Mental Age," *Journal of Comparative and Physiological Psychology*, vol. 52, 1959, pp. 228–230.

——— and ———: "Relationship Between Intelligence and Simple Reaction Time in Mental Defectives," *Perceptual and Motor Skills*, vol. 7, 1957, pp. 65–67.

Gallagher, J. J. and L. Lucito: "Intellectual Patterns of Gifted Children Compared with Average and Retarded," *Exceptional Children*, vol. 27, 1961, pp. 479–482.

Gardner, J. M., S. Selinger, L. S. Watson, D. T. Saposnek, and G. M. Gardner: "Research on Learning with the Mentally Retarded: A Comprehensive Bibliography," *Mental Retardation Abstracts*, vol. 7, no. 3, July–September, 1970, U.S. Government Printing Office, Washington, D.C., pp. 417–453.

Goddard, H. H.: *The Kallikak Family*, The Macmillan Company, New York, 1913.

Goldstein, H. and C. Kass: "Incidental Learning of Educable Mentally Retarded and Gifted Children," *American Journal of Mental Deficiency*, vol. 66, 1961, pp. 245–249.

Gottesman, I.: "Genetic Aspects of Intelligent Behavior," in Norman R. Ellis (ed.), *Handbook of Mental Deficiency*, McGraw-Hill Book Company, New York, 1963, p. 255.

Gray, S. W. and R. A. Klaus: "An Experimental Preschool Program for Culturally Deprived Children," *Child Development*, vol. 36, 1965, pp. 887–898.

Guilford, J. P.: *The Nature of Human Intelligence*, McGraw-Hill Book Company, New York, 1967.

———: "The Structure of Intellect," *Psychological Bulletin*, vol. 53, 1956, pp. 267–293.

———: "Three Faces of Intellect," *American Psychologist*, vol. 14, 1959, pp. 469–479.

——— and R. Hoepfner: *The Analysis of Intelligence*, McGraw-Hill Book Company, New York, 1971.

Harvard Educational Review (Reprint Series No. 2): *Environment, Heredity, and Intelligence*, Harvard College, Cambridge, Mass., 1969.

Headrick, M. and N. Ellis: "Short-Term Visual Memory in Normals and Retardates," *Journal of Experimental Child Psychology*, vol. 1, 1964, pp. 339–347.

Hebb, D. O.: *The Organization of Behavior*, John Wiley and Sons, Inc., New York, 1949.

Hermelin, B. and N. O'Connor: "Short-Term Memory in Normal and Sub-normal Children," *American Journal of Mental Deficiency*, vol. 69, 1964, pp. 121–125.

Hess, R. D. and R. M. Bear (eds.): *Early Education*, Aldine Publishing Company, Chicago, Ill., 1968.

Hetherington, E. M. and T. J. Banta: "Incidental and Intentional Learning in Normal and Mentally Retarded Children," *Journal of Comparative and Physiological Psychology*, vol. 55, 1962, pp. 402–404.

House, B. and D. Zeaman: "A Comparison of Discrimination Learning in Normal and Mentally Defective Children," *Child Development*, vol. 29, 1959, pp. 411–416.

——— and ———: "Effects of Practice on the Delayed Response of Retardates," *Journal of Comparative and Physiological Psychology*, vol. 54, 1961, pp. 225–260.

Jensen, A. and W. Rohwer: "The Effect of Verbal Mediation on the Learning and Retention of Paired Associates by Retarded Adults," *American Journal of Mental Deficiency*, vol. 68, 1963, pp. 80–84.

Johnson, G. and K. Blake: *Learning Performance of Retarded and Normal Children*, Syracuse University, Monograph 5, 1960.

Karnes, M. B., W. M. Studley, W. R. Wright, and A. S. Hodgens: "An Approach for Working with Mothers of Disadvantaged Pre-school Children," *Merrill-Palmer Quarterly*, vol. 14, no. 2, 1968, pp. 174–184.

Kirk, S. A.: *Early Education of the Mentally Retarded*, The University of Illinois Press, Urbana, Ill., 1958.

Kohlberg, L.: "Montessori with the Culturally Disadvantaged: A Cognitive-Developmental Interpretation and Some Research Findings," in

R. D. Hess and R. M. Bear (eds.), *Early Education*, Aldine Publishing Company, Chicago, Ill., 1968, pp. 105–118.

Neisworth, J. T. and R. M. Smith: *Managing Retarded Behavior*, Houghton Mifflin, Boston, Mass., 1973.

Newland, T. E.: "Psychological Assessment of Exceptional Children and Youth," in W. M. Cruickshank (ed.), *Psychology of Exceptional Children and Youth*, 2d ed., Prentice-Hall, Inc., Englewood Cliffs, N.J., 1963.

Orton, K. D., E. McKay, and D. Rainy: "The Effect of Method of Instruction on Retention and Transfer for Different Levels of Ability," *The School Review*, vol. 72, 1964, pp. 451–461.

Painter, G.: "The Effect of a Structured Tutorial Program on the Cognitive and Language Development of Culturally Disadvantaged Infants," *Merrill-Palmer Quarterly*, vol. 15, no. 3, 1969, pp. 279–294.

Parker, R. K., S. Ambron, G. I. Danielson, M. C. Halbrook, and J. A. Levine: *An Overview of Cognitive and Language Programs for 3, 4, and 5 Year Old Children*, Monograph 4, Southeastern Education Laboratory, Atlanta, Georgia, April, 1970.

Rosenzweig, M. R.: "Effects of Environment on Development of Brain and of Behavior," in E. Toback (ed.), *Biopsychology of Development*, Academic Press, New York, 1971.

————, E. L. Bennett, and D. Krech: "Cerebral Effects of Environmental Complexity and Training Among Adult Rats," *Journal of Comparative and Physiological Psychology*, vol. 57, 1964, pp. 438–439.

————, D. Krech, and E. L. Bennett: "Heredity, Environment, Brain Biochemistry, and Learning," *Current Trends in Psychological Theory*, The University of Pittsburgh Press, Pittsburgh, Pa., 1961.

————, ————, ————, and M. C. Diamond: "Effects of Environmental Complexity and Training on Brain Chemistry and Anatomy: A Replication and Extension," *Journal of Comparative and Physiological Psychology*, vol. 55, 1962, pp. 429–437.

Ross, D.: "Incidental Learning of Number Concepts in Small Group Games," *American Journal of Mental Deficiency*, vol. 75, no. 6, May, 1970, pp. 718–725.

Rouse, S. T.: "Effects of a Training Program on the Productive Thinking of Educable Mental Retardates," *American Journal of Mental Deficiency*, vol. 69, 1965, pp. 666–673.

Rudel, R. G.: "The Absolute Response in Tests of Generalization in Normal and Retarded Children," *American Journal of Psychology*, vol. 72, 1959, pp. 401–408.

Scott, K. G. and M. S. Scott: "Research and Theory in Short-Term Memory," in N. R. Ellis (ed.), *International Review of Research in*

Mental Retardation, vol. 3, Academic Press, New York, 1968, pp. 135–162.

Shirley, M. M.: "A Motor Sequence Favors the Maturation Theory," *Psychological Bulletin*, vol. 28, 1931, pp. 204–205.

Skeels, H. M.: "Adult Status of Children with Contrasting Early Life Experiences," *Monographs of the Society for Research in Child Development*, no. 3, 1966.

———— and H. B. Dye: "A Study of the Effects of Differential Stimulation on Mentally Retarded Children," *Proceedings of American Association of Mental Deficiency*, vol. 44, 1939, pp. 114–136.

Spearman, C.: *The Nature of Intelligence and the Principles of Cognition*, Macmillan and Company, Ltd., London, 1923.

Spicker, H. H., W. L. Hodges, and B. R. McCandless: "A Diagnostically Based Curriculum for Psycho-Socially Deprived Preschool Mentally Retarded Children," *Exceptional Children*, vol. 33, 1966, pp. 215–220.

Stevenson, H. W.: "Discrimination Learning," in Norman R. Ellis (ed.), *Handbook of Mental Deficiency*, McGraw-Hill Book Company, New York, 1963, pp. 424–438.

————: "Learning of Complex Problems by Normal and Retarded Subjects," *American Journal of Mental Deficiency*, vol. 64, 1960, pp. 1021–1026.

————, and I. Iscoe: "Transposition in the Feebleminded," *Journal of Experimental Psychology*, vol. 49, 1955, pp. 11–15.

————, and J. D. Swartz: "Learning Set in Children as a Function of Intellectual Level," *Journal of Comparative and Physiological Psychology*, vol. 51, 1958, pp. 755–757.

Thurstone, L. L.: *The Nature of Intelligence*, Harcourt, Brace & World, Inc., New York, 1926.

Tisdall, W. J.: "Productive Thinking in Retarded Children," *Exceptional Children*, vol. 29, 1962, pp. 36–41.

Weikart, D. P., C. K. Kamii, and N. L. Radin: *Perry Preschool Project Progress Report*, Ypsilanti Public Schools, Ypsilanti, Michigan, 1964.

Weikart, D. and D. Z. Lambie: "Preschool Intervention through a Home Teaching Program," in V. Hellmuth (ed.), *The Disadvantaged Child*, vol. 2, Special Child Publications, Seattle, Washington, 1968.

Wellman, B. L.: "Iowa Studies on the Effects of Schooling," 39th Yearbook, *National Society for the Study of Education*, 1940, pp. 377–399.

Williams, E. H.: "Effects of Readiness on Incidental Learning in EMR, Normal, and Gifted Children," *American Journal of Mental Deficiency*, vol. 75, no. 2, September, 1970, pp. 117–119.

Zeaman, D., B. J. House, and R. Orlando: "Use of Special Training Conditions in Visual Discrimination Learning with Imbeciles," *American Journal of Mental Deficiency*, vol. 63, 1958, pp. 453–459.

Zigler, E.: "The Nature-Nurture Issue Reconsidered," in H. C. Haywood (ed.), *Social-Cultural Aspects of Mental Retardation*, Appleton-Century-Crofts, New York, 1970, pp. 81–106.

3

DESIGNING AN INSTRUCTIONAL
ENVIRONMENT: DIAGNOSIS

It is imperative that teachers of the mentally retarded be highly efficient in planning their educational programs. The primary reason for emphasizing this need is that, even under optimum circumstances, these teachers have less time available for the formal aspects of instruction than do the teachers of intellectually normal children. Because of their subaverage intellectual performance, mentally retarded children do not reach the stage at which specific skills in the tool subjects can be taught effectively until they are approximately eight years of age. Therefore, these children often spend their first few years in school working on prereadiness and readiness activities, while their intellectually normal peers are moving along to reading at the second- or perhaps third-grade level. Thus, retarded children can be considered as less efficient information processors than their normal peers, children for whom instruction in the tool subjects begins late, but from whom as adults society expects a reasonably normal performance. Indeed, it is paradoxical that the teacher has less than the usual time in which to produce self-sufficient individuals from the less able, but society's demands are in many ways similar to those it makes of the intellectually normal. This contradictory situation imposes critical demands on the teacher and necessitates the construction of very efficient educational experiences for the mentally retarded.

educational objectives for the retarded

The general objectives of education for the intellectually normal as listed by the Educational Policies Commission (1946) are also appropriate for the mentally retarded. Civic responsibility, human relationship, self-realization, and economic efficiency are suitable broad objectives for all school children. They express the fundamental tenets of education in a democracy. The specifics of a program that evolves from these broad goals, however, are less precise and are subject to personal interpretation.

Kirk (1951) has enumerated eight aims of education for the mentally handicapped, each of which emphasizes occupational adequacy, social competence, and personal adequacy. The point of view taken in this book is not inconsistent with the objectives suggested by others. The emphasis here, however, is that teachers must accept the primary responsibility for helping the retarded to develop basic skills, which, in turn, they can use to effectively deal with problems in all these broad areas. We want the child to develop a style of behavior that will lead to the generation of adequate responses to social, personal, and occupational situations. All this has the basic aim of developing as much self-sufficiency in the child as possible.

In this context, the following educational objectives are viewed here as fundamental for all mentally retarded children.

1 The educational program should be designed to help the child to develop a progressively larger repertoire of general information that he can retrieve quickly and at the appropriate times.
2 The educational program should help the child to develop skills necessary to become socially, personally, and occupationally self-sufficient through the effective use of a consistent method of problem solving. The following sub objectives are directly related to this primary aim:
a. The educational program should assist the child to develop competence in predicting the consequences of his behavior in areas concerned with effective social, personal, and occupational interaction with his environment
b. Emphasis should be placed on the child's developing a conceptual understanding of issues and proper responses rather than a rote association between a problem and a single acceptable reaction

Each of these objectives will be achieved in direct relationship to how well each child's instructional environment is arranged. Proper manipulation of the environment will help a child acquire a repertoire of facts, concepts, and associations. The youngster must be able to retrieve appropriate information bits (facts) quickly and to use them in solving problems across concepts if he is to become self-sufficient.

If the child has developed an adequate repertoire of general information and is able to accurately and quickly associate segments of this knowledge with a problem, he is immediately faced with the need to assess the consequences of acting or reacting in a certain fashion. With the second objective, emphasis is on helping him to think of a number of possible alternatives to a problem and to predict the consequences of using each of these possibilities. His accurate evaluation of cause and effect and a reasonably clear notion of the consequences of using each of the alternatives will result in less impulsive behavior.

The use of a consistent method of problem solving is important for each retarded child to learn. The ability to associate a particular problem with a particular response is not a broad enough target; the retarded must be helped to develop conceptual understandings instead of rote responses to problems. They must learn to see relationships among problems, responses, concepts, and issues; and emphasis must be placed on the applicability of various solutions to an entire spectrum of problems. They need to know when and under what conditions a certain response is most appropriate and not which single response is always to be used in a particular circumstance. Their usual weaknesses in retention mean that they will have difficulty in learning from past experiences. This is all complicated by the obvious fact that the school calendar simply does not allow enough time for a teacher to cover the full range of possible problems the child might be expected to en-counter in adult life. However, the child can be successful in dealing with daily problems if he learns to make his own deductions from standards he understands well. Standards, in this case, means guide-lines, such as always choosing the safest, most careful procedure over the unsafe, the kind response over the rude, or the technique in which he has had some experience over the unknown and untried.

It is of utmost importance to recognize that if a youngster fails to a-chieve any of these broad objectives, or any of the smaller sub-objec-tives subsumed under the more general ones, it is misplaced to blame the failure on the child or on any of the internal conditions (such as "brain injury," "bad genes," etc.) that you may believe he has. Notice that each broad objective specifically emphasizes that the educational environment must be properly arranged so that certain types of behav-ior will be evoked. From this perspective, then, if a child fails to accomplish a certain skill or to perform as you would like in a specific area, you can only assume that his instructional environment has not been suitably arranged to allow him to develop competence in the skill in question. To attribute his failure to "brain injury," "sluggish associa-tional networks," poor family background, or to any similar type of ex-planation serves to accuse the child for his failure; it assumes that we can tell more about his "insides" than is readily obvious; and it does not lead to the identification of an alternative instructional approach. You see, then, the proper emphasis must be on answering the question "Given certain relevant educational characteristics that pertain to this specific child and to his environment, how can I arrange his instructional environment to help him efficiently and effectively acquire a certain level of competence in a prespecified skill area(s)?"

The remainder of this chapter will be directed toward suggesting a method by which teachers of the mentally retarded, as well as teachers of other children, can effectively answer this question. To this end, the broad dimensions of a model will be presented followed by a detailed discussion of each of its components. A separate chapter (Chapter 4) will be given to the last dimension of the model, i.e., the issue of assignment.

a model to direct teacher action

Figure 3-1 describes a general plan for the development and provision of appropriate instructional services to children who have problems in school, as do many of the mentally retarded. This simple, basic model, if followed properly, should lead to clearly demonstrated performance differences among children. The following discussion will explain the most important elements of each of the stages within the segments of this hierarchical model. As you proceed through these stages notice that the extent to which any one stage can be fully implemented and realized is inextricably dependent on how well each earlier stage has been fully realized. An appropriate placement decision, for example, cannot be properly decided upon without a clear statement about a preferred educational plan. Neither of these issues—placement and educational programming—can be confronted until pertinent diagnostic data are correctly analyzed, and this information cannot be gathered until the child has been referred into the system.

REFERRAL—(LEVEL I)
It is of utmost importance that children who have trouble in school or who, it can be reasonably forecast, are destined to have school-related disorders be identified at the earliest possible moment. It is of obvious advantage to the child and to his parents, since early identification leading to proper management of educational problems can save untold moments of anguish and can prevent a multitude of possible secondary disorders. Moreover, the earlier in a child's life a proper educational program can be implemented the greater is the possibility

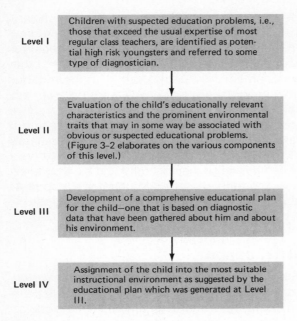

Level I — Children with suspected education problems, i.e., those that exceed the usual expertise of most regular class teachers, are identified as potential high risk youngsters and referred to some type of diagnostician.

Level II — Evaluation of the child's educationally relevant characteristics and the prominent environmental traits that may in some way be associated with obvious or suspected educational problems. (Figure 3-2 elaborates on the various components of this level.)

Level III — Development of a comprehensive educational plan for the child—one that is based on diagnostic data that have been gathered about him and about his environment.

Level IV — Assignment of the child into the most suitable instructional environment as suggested by the educational plan which was generated at Level III.

Figure 3-1
A diagnostic teaching flowchart (arranged in a postulated hierarchy).

that a wide range of lasting changes can be anticipated. This expectation is true for every child. In addition to the host of personal advantages that result from early identification of problems, society too can benefit, both in terms of having available more productive manpower and in terms of having a healthier environment.

Some mentally retarded children can be readily identified in kindergarten or first grade. These are youngsters who are more severely involved and whose motor behavior, social development, intellectual skills, and/or personal characteristics stand out as being greatly inferior to those of their peers. These children are usually impaired in almost all the behavior dimensions; i.e., they usually exhibit gross general disability in functioning as distinct from children who are weaker than their contemporaries in only one or two areas. The teacher can usually tell which children, if any, are so impaired in their general functioning as to warrant more careful scrutiny by a well-trained educational examiner. Such youngsters should be referred immediately to a professional diagnostician for a comprehensive evaluation.

It is not so hard to notice a young child with relatively serious or pronounced disorders in functioning as it is to identify a child with milder disorders, such as the mildly retarded youngster. For the most part, regular teachers are not trained to observe the subtle qualities of what may later develop into a serious educational problem. It is in this very area that special education teachers and supervisors can be of enormous help. More so than perhaps any other group of school professionals, special education teachers are usually trained in techniques of behavior observation, and they are sensitive to the general range of normal behaviors in the various areas pertaining to educational performance. Their training, which often includes opportunities to work with average children, typically focuses on the importance of noticing and screening for atypical patterns of performance. With such training, then, and with the greater awareness special education personnel usually have about proper referral channels and pertinent agencies, it is vital that they view themselves and be considered by others as "front-line consultants" to other school personnel. To that end, it is obligatory that special education teachers take definite steps during their initial training and consistently throughout their teaching experience to

1 Develop a library of activities (such as behavior checklists or rating scales) that they can use, or suggest for use by other teachers, to screen for suspected performance defects in various areas that have educational relevance

2 Develop, along with the library of activities for screening for gross disorders, specific behaviors that a child can usually be expected to demonstrate in connection with each activity

3 Specify the various performance components involved in each activity within which, individually and collectively, a child might have difficulty

4 Suggest comprehensive diagnostic techniques that might be used by a regular teacher alone or in collaboration with a special education professional either to follow up on tentative hypotheses concerning the character of a youngster's problem, or to test the child's performance if it is disparate enough to warrant further study

5 Be prepared to suggest steps that regular teachers might take to determine if a change in a specific child's behavior could be affected by an early and rapid change in instructional procedures or educational targets

Regular teachers are usually fearful of referring a young child to special education. This concern is natural because history suggests that once a child is identified as being mentally retarded and is placed in a special class, special school, or institution, there is little promise of the youngster's situation being reconsidered on a continuing basis. In addition, many teachers are concerned over using scores from psychological tests as the sole determinants for classification and placement; they are determined not to be the culprits in any erroneous conclusion being drawn about a child. Special education teachers face a situation in which they can offer a great deal of help by responding in a cool and informed way to questions from regular school personnel about general issues, such as those mentioned above, as well as about specific ones, such as the possible need for an individual child to receive a more intensive evaluation and/or some form of change in the instructional program.

Beyond these more obvious factors in the accurate identification of possible problems in children, and the proper referral of youngsters for intensive care, lie the attitudes that the special education person brings to the consulting role. So many well-trained special educators hesitate to act as consultants because they refuse to believe that they have anything of importance to offer. This is usually not true and the problem is not one of being undertrained but rather one of having a poor concept of self in such a role. The situation is much like that of a baseball player who has all the skills to be a bona fide star but ends up in a batting slump because for some reason he has come to believe that he is going to have difficulty hitting the ball—and so he does. It is vital that the special educator value his skills and that he recognize that these skills should be shared with the regular school people, especially during the initial screening and referral stages of the diagnostic-referral process.

Perhaps one of the most important concepts the special educator can impress upon regular teachers is that they should consistently collect data and keep records on children who seem to be having difficulties. The data should have no vague statements about a child's presumed psychological or neurological state but should focus completely on his performance. What the child does within a certain environment is important. It will be helpful for the special educator to help construct scales and checksheets that deal with very specific areas of achievement (including intellectual, social, personal, communication, and motor dimensions) so that the regular teacher can direct her information-collection energies in the most potentially profitable direction.

Some of the reasons for teachers hesitating to refer a child who is suspected of being mildly retarded have been alluded to throughout this section. Also, it is not pleasant to inform parents that their youngster may be having such difficulty in school that some form of special education is needed, whether on a temporary or continuing basis. Teachers and administrators should realize, however, that early identification of problems and proper referral of a youngster are educationally sounder and more humane than is simply ignoring what may be significant diagnostic signs in the hope that the child will outgrow the problems. It presents less of a problem in every way to err on the side of over-referral during the first two or three grades of school, fully realizing that some children may be identified as potential problem cases when further evaluation will reveal that they are not, than not to refer or to wait until the child experiences serious educational crises later on.

Finally, following the tentative identification of children with obvious or potential educational problems, it is most important that proper referral alternatives be made clear and available to the regular school personnel. Here again, the special education teacher and supervisor can help by suggesting school and community agents to whom each youngster might be referred. As the child's case is turned over to a school psychologist, or to someone else inside or outside the schools, clear lines of responsibility and authority should be specified so that the parents and school personnel are fully aware of the anticipated flow and organization of subsequent diagnostic and management information and activities to which the child will be exposed, along with the name of a person to whom they can relate at each point in the process.

DIAGNOSIS (LEVEL II)

After a child has been identified as having difficulty in dealing with the usual school environment, and after a referral has been made requesting that some other school professional (such as a special educator, resource teacher, school psychologist, or educational diagnostician) further analyze how best to deal with the situation, the information collecting and diagnostic phase begins. It is almost excessive to dwell again on the fact that mentally retarded children are not sufficiently alike to require the same type of instructional program. Although retardation is still used as a single criterion in many schools, it is an irrefutable fact that mental level alone, even if it were possible to determine in a consistent and valid way, is an inaccurate and inadequate indicant of the types of programs required by various populations of mentally retarded people. One cannot structure anything other than the most amorphous and imprecise instructional program on the basis of an IQ score or MA equivalent. These scores lack specificity, and they do not lead to precise programs of management that a teacher can implement immediately. The one responsible for conducting the diagnosis (and this is most often the special-education teacher) must systematically gather information that is germane to program development.

There are several levels of diagnosis involved in assessing a child's pattern of educational problems. The process is one of moving from a gross estimate of general performance to a more specific characterization of individual areas of weaknesses, including the processes used in dealing with stimuli, in relating new information to the existing repertoire, and in expressing ideas. All these stages in the evaluation process will be presented generally here, and then in detail in subsequent chapters. First, however, let me mention four points that apply to all levels of diagnosis and that have clear implications for the proper characterization of a child's performance in all subject areas.

1 One must not lose sight of the assumptions, and their possible violations, that must be made about diagnoses. For example, we assume that the observer or examiner is trained to know both what to look for and the preferred procedures for collecting data related to that goal. We hope the data are reliable and valid and give as true a characterization of the child as possible. We trust that the examiner has the necessary competencies to evaluate the child and that his skills are equally keen in the analysis of the information that has been collected. Parenthetically, it is worth mentioning that the child's teachers have an important role to play in continuously gathering data about a youngster in an informal fashion and in matching their observations with those of a diagnostic specialist. This type of confirmation has obvious value.

2 It is most important that each child in question be fully described in terms of his performance in those areas about which the teacher and/or the diagnostician are concerned. In addition, and of equal importance, the means each child uses to deal with the presented stimuli must become a standard component of every diagnosis. Let me highlight the importance of considering both these dimensions by using an example of two high jumpers, both of whom share similar physical and, presumably, mental characteristics. To simplify the argument, suppose we assume that they are identical twins. We ask each young man to high jump and find that their performance or achievement level is identical—3 feet 6 inches. Both lads have a deep interest in becoming competitive high jumpers; however, they realize that their present level of achievement, which is so personally important, is far below competitive standards. The results of their performance, or the product of this form of motor behavior, is too vague to be of any precise remedial value. That is, there is no way of determining which of a multitude of possible remedial programs would be most appropriate for each youngster. One answer to this problem is to study, on a reasonably intensive basis, how each lad goes about his jumping. Let us assume that our observation of Charles revealed that he approached the high jump bar properly, but he consistently took off from the wrong leg. James, his brother, approached the bar correctly, took off from the correct leg, but lowered his head and thrust his arms behind his back in his attempt to get over the bar. Each youngster presents an entirely different remedial problem because the approaches are inadequate in different ways.

The nature of the preferred remedial strategy for Charles and James could never have been discovered if the diagnostician had been satisfied with achievement-level data alone. This argument for observing and analyzing the process, style, or technique a child uses in dealing with stimuli or situations has equal validity in all areas, including reading, arithmetic, social interaction, and so on. It is important, for example, for the diagnostician to try to ascertain the method a youngster uses in attacking words, counting, working in groups as a leader, and in the whole range of behavioral areas.

3 In addition to collecting information about the child, it is vital to characterize the environment in which he is performing. Our behavior, whether it be in reading, speaking, social, or personal areas, is determined by various internal peculiarities as they interact with the components of the environment. A child may have inarticulate speech because of a "lazy tongue" in combination with a poor model for speech at home or a lack of understanding on the part of the teacher on how best to facilitate proper speech in a youngster. Behavior, then, springs from this person-environment interaction; hence, every diagnostic effort should include an assessment of both these factors in as complete a form as necessary to construct a workable remedial program.

4 Diagnosis of educational problems of children, including the mentally retarded, should be continuous at all levels and should include the observations of various people who have any dealings at all with the youngsters. The process begins when a teacher or parent observes that a certain child is failing to develop or to perform as might be reasonably expected. This observation may be informal and may eventually lead to the use of more structured and formal evaluative techniques by a school psychologist or counselor. It is important for the child's teachers to be viewed by others—and to consider themselves—as active participants in the data-collection and analysis phases of the whole process. In addition to using formal data collected by competent examiners, teachers must consistently employ informal educational evaluations by unobtrusively, and within the natural school environment, engaging a child or group of children in specified activities to determine whether certain skills have been achieved. As Smith (1969) has pointed out, in this way teachers can provide vital diagnostic information which is of central importance in the formulation of an appropriate instructional program.

The fact that teachers are affiliated with youngsters in a natural environment is of inestimable value from a diagnostic viewpoint. This natural setting affords a unique opportunity to observe the level at which and the style by which each child functions under uncontrived circumstances. There is no question that the teacher is the key person in establishing a realistic picture of a child's strengths and weaknesses within the context of the school environment.

These four generalizations should be given careful thought by all who are involved in evaluating human behavior and in making diagnostic judgments about the character and meaning of such behaviors. No matter what the level or depth of your involvement, these generalizations pertain throughout and for all.

Mention was made at the beginning of this section that the diagnosis of educational problems in children who show retarded development is of several levels of involvement and complexity. Figure 3-2 describes four stages in the diagnosis. The assumption is made here that each stage depends on some measure of effort having been completed at the preceding stage. Let me spend some time discussing the diagnostic flowchart that appears as Figure 3-2. I do not want you to become confused or to lose your place in this discussion, and so let me point out that all the stages in Figure 3-2 are nothing more than an elaboration of the major factors contained in Level II of Figure 3-1. You will encounter the same type of elaboration when we consider Level III in Figure 3-1, namely, components of an educational plan or program. And now, let us return to the factors involved in an educational diagnostic effort.

Stage A   There are many obvious conditions that a youngster might have that could restrict his performance and delay the development of educational skills. Even though such problems are often very obvious, teachers and parents frequently either ignore them or fail to recognize that they exist to a sufficiently significant degree to warrant special attention. For example, the lazy eye syndrome, perpetual hearing disorders, runny eyes, speech that cannot be understood, motor problems, self-destructive behavior, unusually small stature, or constant

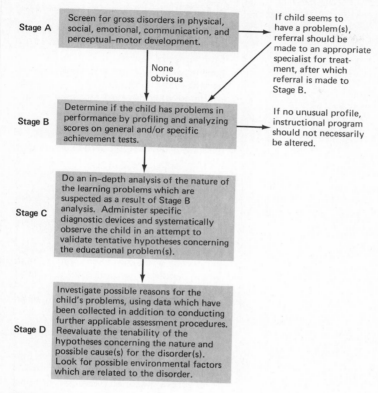

Stage A Screen for gross disorders in physical, social, emotional, communication, and perceptual–motor development.

If child seems to have a problem(s), referral should be made to an appropriate specialist for treatment, after which referral is made to Stage B.

None obvious

Stage B Determine if the child has problems in performance by profiling and analyzing scores on general and/or specific achievement tests.

If no unusual profile, instructional program should not necessarily be altered.

Stage C Do an in–depth analysis of the nature of the learning problems which are suspected as a result of Stage B analysis. Administer specific diagnostic devices and systematically observe the child in an attempt to validate tentative hypotheses concerning the educational problem(s).

Stage D Investigate possible reasons for the child's problems, using data which have been collected in addition to conducting further applicable assessment procedures. Reevaluate the tenability of the hypotheses concerning the nature and possible cause(s) for the disorder(s). Look for possible environmental factors which are related to the disorder.

Figure 3-2
Flowchart describing various levels of diagnosis. (Adapted from R. M. Smith, *An Introduction to Mental Retardation.* Copyright © 1971 by McGraw-Hill Book Company, New York, 1971. Reprinted by permission of McGraw-Hill Book Co.)

withdrawal from other children, if overlooked, will probably result in a whole range of subsequent classroom problems. Unfortunately, teachers and others often elect not to call attention to a possible borderline situation because they do not want to alarm the child or his parents, or they may fully expect that the youngster will eventually outgrow the problems.

Teachers, and especially those who are involved in early education programs, *must* screen for possible gross disorders by observing the behavior of children that might be viewed as unusual in comparison to that of most youngsters of the same age or in the same classroom. No time should be wasted in referring such a child to an appropriate

Table 3-1

EXAMPLES OF GROSS DISORDERS THAT SUGGEST NEED FOR
IMMEDIATE PROFESSIONAL ATTENTION

Area	Behavior or Symptom
1. Seeing	a. red eyes, crusty eyelids, or discharges from the eyes
	b. turning in or out of an eye or eyes (either permanent or temporary)
	c. squinting while looking at a near or far-point stimulus
	d. unusual sensitivity to light
	e. excessive rubbing of eyes
	f. difficulty in seeing the board or working at close range
	g. bumping into objects or general problems with orientation and mobility
	h. lack of spontaneous response of the pupil of the eye to brightness or darkness
	i. leaning either to the right or left while working on an activity
	j. pushing a finger, hand, or object against the corner of an eye when trying to read
	k. lack of apparent response to peripheral stimuli
	l. excessive blinking, tearing, or pain when opening and closing eyelids
2. Hearing	a. low tolerance for noise or changes in usual patterns of sound
	b. requesting that an order be repeated, that the radio or television volume be turned up beyond a reasonable level, or ignoring a direction presented verbally
	c. showing no startle in situations that would normally result in some such response pattern
	d. discharges from the ears
	e. complaining of a buzzing or ringing in an ear
	f. turning head in one direction as if attempting to locate or tune in on a sound
	g. rubbing ears
3. Motor	a. limping or showing difficulty in extending extremities
	b. exhibiting swollen joints
	c. getting fatigued while walking, running, or engaging in a normal amount of exercise for children of the same age
	d. seeming to bend or veer to one side while walking
	e. "favoring" one side of his body to a relatively extreme degree

Table 3-1 *(continued)*

Area	Behavior or Symptom
	f. having unusual trouble grasping and/or holding objects
	g. having pain in an extremity or in the back while walking or bending
4. Personal/Social	a. seeming to have a low threshold or tolerance for frustration
	b. having excessive trouble in socializing with people
	c. throwing toys or other objects whenever things do not go his way
	d. yelling, shouting, or cursing to excess at other people
	e. seeming to enjoy being alone most of the time; not apparently interested in being with children his age
	f. exhibiting unusual behavior patterns such as whirling hands, butting his head against objects, rocking his body back and forth, eating unusual things, or picking at certain areas of his body
	g. giving verbal responses that appear excessively disconnected from his surrounding or from reality
	h. crying at inappropriate times or in unstressful situations
5. Speech and Language	a. making sounds that are so unclear, in contrast to those of other children his age, that the listener cannot understand what is being said
	b. exhibiting excessive nasality, stuttering, being hoarse, speaking too high or low, or hesitating in his speech
	c. pointing at an object when making a request instead of speaking
	d. seeming to have problems in understanding what is being said or in following directions
	e. choosing not to respond to a question or to speak spontaneously at a level usually characteristic of peers of the same age
6. General Areas of Functioning	a. being active or inactive at inappropriate times or to an excessive degree
	b. coughing, wheezing, or exhibiting other similar types of characteristics that suggest possible health problems
	c. being absent from school on a continuing basis
	d. having constant problems keeping up with classmates in physical activities

specialist. Table 3-1 illustrates a few instances of behaviors or characteristics that should probably be brought to the immediate attention of a specialist.

The kinds of behavioral symptoms and their associated characteristics that it is important to identify at this first stage are usually obvious even to an observer who has not been with the child for an extended time. Parents and teachers who literally grow up with a child might not notice the presence of a significant problem if it is of the type that grows over a lengthy period. In such situations, it takes a keen observer to be alert to the subtle development of possible problems that could eventually jeopardize the child's level and quality of functioning in school. Even at this screening level of observation and diagnosis it may be worth your asking another teacher to observe and advance an opinion about the functioning of a child whose performance and/or symptoms you feel are suspicious but about whom you may question your own ability to give an objective opinion. Take care not to bias the observations of your colleague who is aiding in this venture.

This is a very important, but often overlooked, stage in the total planning of an educational program for mentally retarded children. It is of utmost desirability to identify which children, among those who enter school each year, have possible problems that require special attention. One can no longer dispute the immeasurable advantage of early identification if it leads to prompt treatment. If the problems are identified early, and if appropriate remediation takes place, the prevention of subsequent, complex educational problems is increased proportionately. If these major developmental disorders are not identified, and the youngster is allowed to move through the school program without intervention to reduce the impact of his disorders, his educational future will be seriously impaired.

The kinds of problems being discussed at this level do not require the use of formal rating scales, checksheets, or other types of measuring instruments. They usually stand out to a person who does not know the child well. Every effort should be taken to refer such a child to an appropriate specialist. Do not wait in the hope that the child will outgrow the difficulty or that you will feel embarrassed because of possibly making a mistake in judgment. It is better to err at this level by over-referring children than not to refer when a child needs prompt attention. Missing children at this stage can have serious, long-term consequences. And, also, let me emphasize that it will often be necessary for you, the teacher, to check on how much attention is being given to your referral. You probably know better than your principal to which specialist a child should be referred and whether he has been seen by a reasonably competent professional. The safest posture to take is to

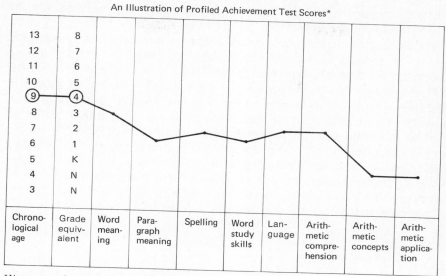

An Illustration of Profiled Achievement Test Scores*

Chrono-logical age	Grade equiv-alent	Word mean-ing	Para-graph meaning	Spelling	Word study skills	Lan-guage	Arith-metic compre-hension	Arith-metic concepts	Arith-metic applica-tion
13	8								
12	7								
11	6								
10	5								
⑨	④								
8	3								
7	2								
6	1								
5	K								
4	N								
3	N								

*Not necessarily considered an example of a child with retarded mental development.

Figure 3-3

assume that no one else will be lobbying in the best interests of your student, and that it is important that his possible problem receive prompt attention. Document why you believe the child needs help, and then gingerly apply pressure until you are satisfied that all possible avenues have been considered. Children get lost in the mountains of paperwork in a school system. The individual teacher must be willing to serve as the child's advocate in a situation such as this, i.e., where a possible developmental disability is present that could subsequently hinder the youngster's progress in school, and where the likelihood exists that the child's disorder will not receive the attention it deserves.

Stage B Among children with mild to moderate degrees of retardation, one will often see marked differences in the levels of achievement among various performance areas. At this second stage of diagnosis, focus is on obtaining achievement data in those areas that the special educator views as important for each child. These data can be obtained from any broad-spectrum group or individual achievement test, such as the Stanford Achievement Test, Metropolitan Achievement Test, or the Peabody Individual Achievement Test. The use of standardized instruments provides the most accurate indicator of achievement, although school grades can be used for informal assessment. After a child's performance has been assessed in the various subject areas, simply place the scores on a grid and construct an achievement profile, as illustrated in Figure 3-3.

Although the profiling technique helps to summarize the presumed status of a child in the various areas, you must be careful not to overinterpret or misinterpret such profiles. Placed on a graph, scores that are really not very disparate can be made to look "miles apart." In addition, you must remember that there is always some degree of unreliability in each subtest area. This clearly suggests that one must look at the child's performance in terms of a range of possible scores and not as a definite point. For example, let us suppose that you tested a child and arrived at general reading and arithmetic scores. Upon profiling these two scores, you may decide that the child is quite low in reading—to a point where something needs to be done. This judgment is made on the basis of a specific point estimate of performance.

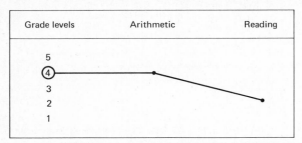

Let us suppose, though, that the test, the administrator, and/or the child's performance contributed to an unreliable measure of reading and/or arithmetic achievement. In fact it may be more accurate to view the child's achievement level, in this case, as a range of possible scores between a grade above and a grade below the actual score he received in both reading and arithmetic. By viewing the child's performance in terms of a band of possible scores, one is able to account for possible errors of measurement that characterize every evaluative attempt. The profile that we would construct, then, should more accurately be characterized thusly:

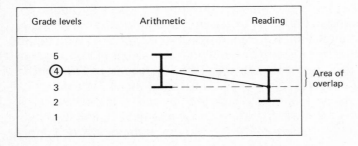

Using the concept of a band of possible scores instead of a specific point score as an indicator, one can conclude that the child is not necessarily weak in either area. In fact, the opposite conclusion might well be reached if a single score is used as the basis for deciding whether a disability exists. The previous example highlights just such a situation. For example, using absolute scores (the first profile), one might conclude that a one-year difference exists between the child's reading and arithmetic performance. In contrast, using the band notion (the second profile), one might conclude that some degree of overlap exists between the lower end in arithmetic and the upper end of reading (assuming that plus or minus one grade-level equivalent is legitimate in this case). It is possible that the child's true performance in these subject areas might well be within this overlapping area, and thus no significant difference would exist between the child's performance in these two areas.

I hope that you see the importance of not automatically assuming that a child is weak in certain areas. It is of utmost importance for you to consider the standard error of measurement (which is usually published in the examiner's manual for their respective subtests) before you decide whether or not a child's performance is subpar. Remember, also, that for any test, average scores for groups are more reliable than are scores for individuals. Thus, a test may be very reliable in describing score differences between subtests for a group of children, but the same test may not be reliable when comparisons are made for an individual child on the same subtests.

Stage C If a child consistently scores significantly below his own general achievement level in one or more subject areas, or if his general performance level is greatly depressed across all subject areas in contrast to his peers' performances, a more thorough investigation of his learning characteristics should be initiated. What this really involves is analyzing the characteristics of the child's performance in those sub-areas in which weaknesses have been demonstrated. This more detailed analysis of performance could involve testing the child with formal diagnostic instruments that are designed to probe into very specific skill areas. For example, tests such as the following are narrow in subject focus, intensively sample specific areas of competence, and usually require that the examiner have been trained in their administration and interpretation: Illinois Test of Psycholinguistic Abilities, Gates-MacGinitie Reading Tests, Templin-Darley Tests of Articulation, and Oseretsky Motor Proficiency Tests. Although the use of such tests is often highly desirable, and there is a clear need for them to be administered and the data from them interpreted by a trained and competent examiner, there are many other ways that a teacher can conduct an in-depth analysis of a child's performance without using formal diagnostic devices. Let me pursue this thought.

Let us assume that you conclude that a certain child, Andy, has trouble in arithmetic. Knowing that fact alone, that his general arithmetic performance is substantially lower than his reading, spelling, and language scores, does not provide precise enough information about Andy's arithmetic performance to lead to the development of an arithmetic program that will predictively work for the youngster. The need, of course, is to identify (or task-analyze) the principal skills embodied in the arithmetic activities in which Andy was engaged and then determine where within the group of skills he seems to have difficulty. The process is much like the technique of profiling that was suggested in Stage B, but this time the variables that are analyzed are contained within the broad subject of arithmetic.

After we have decided that Andy's arithmetic performance needs attention, the next step is to identify the components of arithmetic performance. This information is often available from the achievement test that was used in the original evaluation. Let us say that the Stanford Achievement Test was used, in which case arithmetic concepts, arithmetic computation, and arithmetic applications constitute the major dimensions evaluated. For the sake of this illustration, suppose we say that Andy's performance in each of these areas looks like this:

Arithmetic computation—stanine of 7[1]
Arithmetic concepts   —stanine of 8
Arithmetic applications —stanine of 3

From these data, then, we can validly conclude that Andy does well on all of those skills that are involved in arithmetic *computation* and *concepts.* In contrast, we can see that his overall arithmetic performance was depressed because of an inordinately poor performance in arithmetic *applications*—that is, he had trouble using his conceptual and computational skills to solve problems.

---

[1]A stanine is a value along an equally spaced nine-point scale (expressed from 1 [low] to 9 [high]) with the value of 5 always representing average performance for students in the norm group. A child's scores are converted to stanines. Using these scores one is able to compare a child's performance with the norm group and also against his own performance in other areas of the test. Stanine scores of 1, 2, or 3 are considered below average; scores of 7, 8, or 9 are viewed as above average. Since stanines have the same standard deviation from one subtest to another, comparisons of performance across achievement areas can easily be done.

The next step within Stage C is to analyze the skills involved in arithmetic applications to see where within this area Andy has trouble. He may have had difficulty in any one or more of the following areas of application:

1 Recognizing that a problem has been posed and defining its dimensions, including what is being requested
2 Analyzing the components of the problem and determining the sequence of steps that must be taken to arrive at a solution
3 Translating the narrative components of the problem into a proper symbolic form that will lead to a solution
4 Recalling facts, concepts, and notations that have possible pertinence to the solution of the problem
5 Recalling whether the problem could be solved in more than one way and, if so, which strategy is the most efficient
6 Performing the required mathematical steps in proper sequence and with accuracy and efficiency
7 Arriving at a conclusion that is based on the solution achieved from working the required mathematical steps

Some of these sub-skills can be evaluated by administering parts of various analytic achievement tests, such as the (1) Cooperative Sequential Tests of Educational Progress (higher elementary-grade levels), (2) SRA Achievement Series (lower and middle elementary-grade levels), (3) Comprehensive Tests of Basic Skills (lower and middle elementary-grade levels). None of these tests will extract and then individually assess all the segments of arithmetic applications; however, they will provide a general measure of a child's performance in this broad dimension. Moreover, tests that are highly specific and analytic (such as the Illinois Test of Psycholinguistic Abilities, Durrell Analyses of Reading Difficulty, and Gates-McKillop Diagnostic Reading Tests) require that a trained examiner administer and interpret them.

Although these tests are frequently helpful in characterizing a child's performance on progressively smaller dimensions, for many reasons they are often not available to teachers. If a teacher elects to follow the procedures of diagnosis that are recommended here it will be necessary for her to observe the performance of a child, like Andy, and make some tentative judgment about where within the process of arithmetic applications he seems to be having difficulty. This precise bit of information is vital because each of the above seven steps, all of which are considered necessary skills in performing arithmetic application problems, requires a different remedial focus. If Andy's problem is that he is unable to translate the narrative components of a problem into proper symbolic form, he does not need an educational program that helps him to recognize the problem, to recall facts, or to study which processes of arithmetic need to be used.

In the absence of formal instrumentation, but at the same time realizing that a proper educational program can only emerge from a detailed analysis of individual performance characteristics, the teacher will need to study each child's performance in the subtasks that are involved in an activity. All of this means that the teacher must carefully observe and question a child like Andy as he attempts to solve an arithmetic problem. Given a certain problem, and given the various steps contained in it, a teacher can begin by observing the steps that Andy takes. First, be sure that he can read the problem. And which, if any, of the words does he not understand? Next, ask him to cite what is being requested and to identify the major components of the problem. Then, follow the same procedure throughout all the tasks that have been identified as necessary components of solving problems of arithmetic application.

Indeed, this process takes time, and one can legitimately ask who is going to take care of the rest of the troops while the teacher deals with this type of individual problem. There is no easy answer to this question, for every special education teacher does not have the luxury of having an aide, resource room, or itinerant teacher available to deal with the regular program while the special teacher tracks down the character of a child's educational problem. In the absence of such important auxiliary personnel, and assuming that there is little if any free time before, during, or after the school day for short periods of individual diagnostic attention, the only recourse left to the teacher is to informally observe the child during those periods when he is working on a pertinent activity either alone or with a small group. In these situations, however, you must set up very specific activities that are aimed at obtaining one certain bit of information. If, for example, you believe that the child cannot satisfactorily do his word problems in arithmetic because he is using a wrong process, such as subtraction instead of addition, then set up a problem where all the prerequisite steps have been done for him so that his focus is on the decision of which arithmetic process to use. If he accomplishes this task at a satisfactory level, you can then continue studying his performance at subsequent levels. Let me emphasize a subtle point here. If you have an objective in mind about the specific kind of behavior you want to observe, it is relatively easy to select an activity in which you can engage the child in order to observe that specific behavior. If you do not specify the "little behavior bit" you wish to study, or if you fail to arrange the child's activities so that his performance can be readily observed, much too much "fishing" will go on, you will get lost in irrelevant side behaviors, and time will be wasted. The secrets to success in analyzing the child's performance at Stage C are

1 List the specific tasks or behaviors that the child must accomplish to satisfactorily perform the activity
2 Order the tasks in a presumed hierarchy so that the most basic are listed first
3 Select a simple problem from those in the area in which you are studying the child's performance
4 Before you engage the child in the problem you have selected, decide what you are looking for, how you will know when the child has been successful, and how you will record the behavior
5 Have the child begin the activity after you have arranged it so that the behavior you are interested in is separated as much as possible from other confusing aspects so that the behavior in question stands out. The situation is analogous to the surgeon who, when evaluating your appendix for possible removal, pushes all other viscera out of the field of vision so that he can get a thorough look at the organ in question. Obviously, school problems cannot be observed as clearly as an infected appendix; however, the principles underlying the idea are the same.

Observation of a child's achievement level, along with the technique(s) by which he deals with specific stimuli of Stage C, should lead to the gathering of very precise information about such behaviors as left-to-right progression in reading, carrying difficulties in addition, problems in translating a spatial phenomenon into a temporal dimension (such as in hitting a ball that has been tossed into the air), errors of substitution or omission in speech, difficulty in discriminating among consonant-vowel blends, inattentiveness, seeing prefixes or suffixes as units, writing specific letters in script, or discriminating between one-quarter- and one-eighth-inch units of measurement. At this level of diagnosis, then, the behaviors that are troublesome and that are major contributors to the youngster's problems of achievement are identified with as much precision and reliability as possible. It is emphatically suggested here that you not judge a child to be defective in any of these behaviors from only one evaluative session. It is of utmost importance that such observations and conclusions be based on evidence that has been gathered in diverse formal and informal encounters with the youngster; data must be conscientiously collected over a period of time.

Stage D In several sections of this chapter the notion was presented that a youngster's behavior or performance is in large measure dictated by the characteristics of his environment. Through the previous four stages of the diagnosis attention has been directed toward establishing a reliable and valid portrait of the child's achievement strengths and weaknesses. At this last stage the observation switches to depicting those aspects of the youngster's surroundings that are either related to or allegedly directly the cause of the educational difficulty. However, do not lose sight of the fact that a child's poor performance may be the result of previous environmental problems that no longer exist. For example, poor teaching in earlier grades, exposure to an inconsistent or ambiguous curriculum, teacher attention given to inappropriate behaviors, and emphasis placed on areas of instruction that are of secondary importance for the child are all illustrations of environmental events that could well cause a child to do poorly in school. You really cannot do much about such problems other than make sure that the situation does not continue, either for that child or for others.

As a teacher, there are a number of questions you can ask yourself as a check on how good an instructional environment you are providing. The answers you give are self-diagnostic in that they deliberately focus your attention on your own behavior which, in turn, constitutes the major part of the youngsters' environment. I hope I have made this point clear—at this final stage of diagnosis you, the teacher, are actually looking at your behavior (the child's environment) with the aim of trying to discover which, if any, aspects of your own performance are causing a child, or group of children, to perform poorly in school. This is of inestimable importance for teachers of retarded children, since these youngsters, more than possibly any other single group, need an environment that has all the components necessary for maximizing their school performance. Here are four examples of questions you might ask yourself:

1 To what extent has the child's previous instructional environment been conducive to the development of such skills as being a good listener, sticking to a task until it is completed, systematically figuring out solutions to problems, being interested in trying to solve problems, and being spontaneous in expressing ideas?

2 Do the areas in which the child appears weak suggest that one aspect of his previous environment may have been inadequate? For example, when he attempts to read does the youngster try to figure out words by using several different approaches and have little or no success with any of them? If so, one might hypothesize that his past instructional environment in reading has confused him in the word-attack area, perhaps because different teachers at various levels exposed him to several forms of word attack. This could have resulted in the youngster not developing a consistent approach on which he can depend. Parenthetically, it is worth mentioning that the child's learning problems, in this example, are not of his own making; the situation can be more appropriately described as a teaching or environmental disability.

3 Has or is the physical environment of the classroom possibly confusing to the child(ren)? For example, are sections of the classroom set aside for certain activities or can the children do anything they wish in every area of the classroom? Later in this chapter the proposal will be advanced that establishing centers within the classroom in which only certain types of activities are allowed is a promising technique for enhancing the discrimination skills of children and will not only control their deportment but will facilitate their achievement in other content areas. An environment in which guiding rules have not been specified will usually confuse children with retarded intellectual development and will restrict their general performance. The physical environment, then, must be controlled and arranged to encourage learning.

4 How much is known about the reinforcement preferences of each child in the class? Have the appropriate reinforcing stimuli been provided in a consistent and proper fashion?

For the most part, all the steps in this suggested plan for evaluating a child's performance and attempting to identify the specific areas in which he is deficient, along with identifying the possible reasons for such problems existing, can be accomplished by the teacher. It is certainly true that one must consult with and obtain the services of specialists (such as school psychologists, educational diagnosticians, speech therapists, audiologists, and counselors) in those instances in which especially difficult educational problems persist—that is, the kind that require professional skills which exceed those of the teacher. Make certain though that you do not betray your own repertoire of skills by automatically assuming that a problem is beyond your comprehension or ability. There is nothing particularly sacrosanct about consistently observing a child's performance in a given number of performance areas over a period of time and making some educated guesses (hypotheses) concerning the nature of his problem and how one might best construct his environment to help alter the manner in which he deals with his problem, thus affecting his performance level. In short, do not automatically call in specialists until you have done some observing of the child and reached some tentative conclusions about him and his environment. To repeat a statement that was expressed earlier, the teacher is in the best position to reliably observe a child. The secret of success is to prespecify the precise behavior you intend to observe (e.g., simple counting, borrowing, or hitting other children on the playground), construct a simple checksheet or frequency table on which you can note how often or how much each behavior occurs and, if applicable, the circumstances surrounding the incident, consistently record data that pertain to the behavior in question, and begin to construct hypotheses about how to change the child's behavior (or performance) according to the goals of your program for him and the class.

4

DESIGNING AN INSTRUCTIONAL ENVIRONMENT: STRATEGIES FOR TEACHING

developing an education plan (level III)

We have finally reached Level III on the Diagnostic-Teaching Flowchart that appears in Figure 3-1. At this level we are concerned about generating an educational program for a child or group of children who are alleged to be retarded in intellectual development. At this point I hope that you recognize that it is virtually impossible to know what type of emphasis to place on any kind of instructional program without having some notion about what a child needs, i.e., where the educational program should be focused for each youngster in order to accurately reflect on those specific skill areas most in need of attention. For certain children this focus might be on a whole range of auditory skills, for another group the visual area might need attention, and still others might need a program structured to enhance and stabilize social control. It is impossible to decide on the character an instructional program should *best* take without having first described the child and his environment—all of which should have been done during the diagnostic portion of this broad education model. To leap into suggesting an educational program before conducting as adequate a diagnosis *as is needed* will cause the teacher to fish around for what she supposes to be the kind of program each youngster needs, but without having proper documentation. A competent physician does not operate or plan a program to manage an illness until he has collected data about you, your condition, its history, and the environmental circumstances that may have contributed to the illness. This analogy is a direct one in the case of designing an educational plan for retarded children. Their problems are not the same across groups, and this heterogeneity frequently demands unique program emphases that can only be determined by diagnostic efforts, such as those that have just been described. In like manner, the assignment decision, which is discussed in the following chapter, depends on information about the type of educational program the child needs. Only then can one determine where within the existing school system the plan can best be filled.

A plan designed to deal effectively with the educational problem of children with retarded intellectual development can be thought of as containing three principal components: the course of study—or goals and objectives—that one desires the children to cover—or achieve—in a specified time; the instructional methodology or strategy of intervention that has particular appropriateness for individual children; and the materials or media that can best facilitate the acquiring of those skills that the teacher has identified as of high priority. Each of these three broad areas contains numerous subareas, some of which will be emphasized in this section. Let us take each of the three components of an educational plan in sequence and consider their meaning as one begins to generate an educational plan.

Curricular Considerations How does one decide what to teach children with retarded mental development? Most teachers and special education personnel approach this problem by adopting an existing curriculum guide or by modifying various curricula according to what they believe reflects an appropriate focus and orientation for their particular group of children. But recognize that, when this approach is used by individual teachers without agreement or clearly stated singularity of purpose, the total special education program will lose continuity, become filled with gaps in important areas, and result in unnecessary repetition. Special education administrators and supervisors usually assign members of their special education program to the enormous task of designing a broad curriculum that is especially appropriate for their school system. Hour upon hour of valuable teacher time is devoted to this type of project. The final product is typically greeted with mixed emotions and unsure acceptance because, as is so often the case, by the time such a project is completed new personnel with different ideas have joined the staff. The upshot of this situation is that teachers who either do not understand the curriculum or are unenthusiastic about it begin to improvise and stray away from the specifics for which they are individually responsible.

It is also true that special education teachers who are without a general curriculum plan, or who have become especially enamored of some earlier program with which they have been associated, often determine what to teach their children on the basis of intuition, hunch, or some immediate personal crisis that the children are experiencing. For example, to a teacher of retarded adolescents it may seem only natural that the program focus primarily on social and occupational issues and much less on such subjects as language, reading, and arithmetic. However, this type of improvisation can seriously undermine a total program because the exact objectives and components of instruction are left so imprecise that the necessary replication of the program by someone else is virtually impossible.

These improvisational approaches to developing curricula for retarded children are both traditional and somewhat inadequate because (1) they are so imprecise as to defy delineation of specific types of behaviors one desires of the students, (2) they do not clearly describe the kind of environment the teacher must provide in order to facilitate learning and skill development by the children, (3) they are antithetical to the establishment of clear lines of responsibility among various segments of the special education program, (4) they allow for much latitude for unproductive time on the part of teachers and students, and (5) they provide a flimsy basis for the establishment of individualized programs of management and the means by which the influence of each student's curriculum can be evaluated on a continuous basis.

Perhaps a more potentially productive approach to deciding what to teach retarded children is to switch from an emphasis on content, per se, to a focus on the specific skills or competencies professionals in special education believe to be pertinent for each child. Heretofore, special educators have designed curricula according to major subject areas, e.g., reading, arithmetic, language, perceptual-motor, and social. The components involved in each of these areas are usually identified and the goals stated in terms of what is to be taught at a specific level. For example, in the beginning intermediate grades one might focus on teaching carrying and borrowing in arithmetic, or, in social areas, on presenting materials about various governing bodies in the city or community in which the students live. This orientation has strong traditional roots.

The reorientation I am suggesting here is that curriculum for the mentally retarded concentrate on the kind of output, skills, or competencies that are considered to be appropriate for each youngster. This task leads to emphasis on *what is to be learned* by a child as opposed to *what is to be taught* by the teacher. There is a difference between these two foci, although it is obvious that learning cannot take place in reading, arithmetic, or other such areas without some form of content. Emphasis on the teaching dimension, though, forces one to assume that learning has or will automatically take place. Primary attention to the learning component provides direct evidence and does not force one to assume anything or to make any conceptual leaps. The child is either able to demonstrate proficiency in a prespecified skill at a certain level or he is not. If he can, then one might reasonably assume that the teaching has been effective; if he cannot, then the teaching strategy might well be reconsidered and reorganized.

This orientation provides a much easier means by which program and student goals can be evaluated, and it does away with the vague platitudes that are often used to justify courses of study that are mostly content-based and not "behaviorally" stated. After all, one can have the most widely accepted and glorious curriculum ever designed for retarded children, but if it does not effect changes in student behavior, skills, or understandings, it is virtually worthless. Any course of study, then, is only as good as the degree to which it helps to influence and alter student behaviors according to prestated goals.

To implement the concept of using student competencies as a basis for making curricular decisions, one might first identify a range of developmental areas that some theory, body of research, or extensive personal experience suggests is especially pertinent to the group of youngsters toward whom your program is directed. Taking each of the broad developmental areas individually, you might begin doing a task analysis by listing major skills that are subsumed by a larger developmental area, and then continue with your analysis by fractioning-down each segment into progressively smaller component parts. As the small skill areas are identified, it is helpful to restate each as a behavioral objective. Lindvall (1967) suggests that behavioral objectives be stated (1) in terms of the pupil, (2) in a fashion that allows the behavior to be directly observed without requiring conceptual extrapolations on the part of the observer, and (3) in reference to specific content to which the behavior applies.

Let us take an example and work through the process I am suggesting. In language arts, as well as in any other subject area, the first issue that needs to be considered is that of the skills that need to have been developed in order to perform at certain levels. What does it take to be able to read most newspapers? What skills are required to maintain a checking account? What specific competencies must one have to lay concrete blocks in a prescribed way? Each of these questions is about curriculum, but it is translated in terms of student performance required to accomplish a complex task. Moreover, each question demands that a precise task analysis be done in each of the major areas so that the instructor will know the focus of the program at each moment and will know exactly what to look for in terms of student behavior. In addition, one would also expect that a level of performance would be specified for each subtask that is an integral part of the broad skill. This is necessary so that the instructor can know when the sub-skill has been accomplished at an acceptable level.

The field of education is indeed fortunate that several excellent task analyses have been done in a number of complex subject areas. Although these analyses are still new and to be viewed as experimental, they are, nevertheless, very helpful starts toward the development of more complete and valid networks of skills. Even now, it is no longer really necessary for local curriculum committees to spend hours, days, and months re-creating skill sequences. I strongly recommend that the material developed by the Westinghouse Learning Corporation, the Instructional Objectives Exchange, and the Center for the Study of Evaluation be used as the basis for the curriculum in special- and regular-education programs. If a teacher, a department, or an entire school system wishes to elaborate on or to reorder the skill sequences suggested by any of these groups, that is fine, but there is really no rational justification for ignoring this important material by trying to do your own task analysis of large content areas.

Table 4-1 gives an abbreviated version of a task analysis of language arts as performed by the instructional Objectives Exchange. The example is incomplete since, for purposes of illustration, only one strand or trunk at each level of the task analysis has been given. At Level I you will notice that language arts has been fractioned into nine broad categories of which *decoding* is one. At Level II, decoding has been broken down into five major components of skills, including those involved in *discrimination.* At Level III, discrimination has been analyzed into two chunks of skills, *auditory* and *visual.* And finally, at Level III the auditory category has been split into three forms, *sounds*, *rhymes*, and *initial sounds.*

This same kind of task analysis can be done for the content areas of the remaining eight language arts categories, and, indeed, the personnel at the Instructional Objectives Exchange have done just that. Obviously, some of the areas are amenable to more detailed analyses than are others. This, then, allows the network of skills to become quite elaborate.

As soon as the content areas have been identified, one can begin to designate a behavior that will indicate whether the content area in question has been mastered at a suitable level of competence. Table 4-2 illustrates the transition one must make from a specific content area (discrimination—auditory—initial sounds) to a statement of expected behavior by the child. Notice the precision that characterizes the

Table 4-1
EXAMPLE OF A TASK ANALYSIS OF LANGUAGE ARTS BY THE IN-
STRUCTIONAL OBJECTIVES EXCHANGE

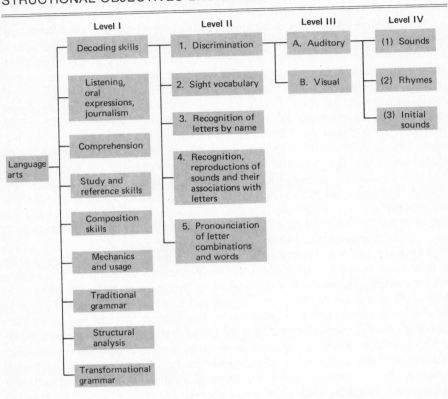

SOURCE: *Language Arts Series,* The Instructional Objectives Exchange, Box 24095, Los Angeles,
California 90024.

behavior statement. First, there is no ambiguity at all in the character of
the presenting stimuli—it is given orally, the words involved in each
activity are given, and the characteristics of the words are spelled out,
i.e., they begin with the same consonant sound. Second, the type of
response expected from the student is indicated, viz., that the child
respond orally. Finally, although in this illustration it is obvious, the
preferred response is specified. All these aspects of the behavior
statement, that were developed from a content analysis, fulfill the
criteria of Lindvall that were mentioned in this chapter.

Table 4-2

AN EXAMPLE OF A BEHAVIORAL OBJECTIVE IN THE CONTENT AREA "DISCRIMINATION—AUDITORY—INITIAL SOUNDS"

OBJECTIVE:	Given orally a group of commonly used words, a majority of which begin with the same consonant sound, the student will state orally the word(s) having an initial sound different from the majority in the group.
DIRECTIONS:	"I will speak four words. One will begin with a different sound from the others. You say which word it is."
SAMPLE ITEMS:	1 "house . . . hair . . . mother . . . happy" 2 "light . . . look . . . met . . . luck" 3 "very . . . terry . . . view . . . vex" 4 "doll . . . ball . . . bell . . . bill" 5 "mix . . . map . . . met . . . nap"
ANSWERS:	1 mother, 2 met, 3 terry, 4 doll, 5 nap

SOURCE: *Language Arts Series: Decoding Skills K-12,* Revised Edition, The Instructional Objectives Exchange, Box 24095, Los Angeles, California, 1972, pp. 15–16.

If you have followed the discussion regarding curriculum up to this point, you may wonder what is different between the curriculum for children with retarded development and that for those youngsters who are reasonably normal intellectually. So far as content is concerned, in the early elementary grades there is really very little difference in the kinds of skills that we would like to see all children achieve. To develop rudimentary skills in important content areas such as reading, speaking, and arithmetic, the mentally retarded, as well as the intellectually normal, must achieve some success in readiness and other basic competencies early in their training. Thus, the goals to be achieved by both groups are quite similar during the early stages. To be sure, though, it may be essential that the special education teacher be quite exacting in "fractioning-down" each skill area into very small skill components so that the retarded youngsters are not placed in a pedagogical situation in which they are expected to make inordinately large leaps from one set of skills to another without having first demonstrated competence in those smaller areas that lie between. For intellectually normal children one does not have to be as careful to delineate all the precise intervening skills (as well as teach for each) since these youngsters seem to have greater facility for filling in gaps and making larger conceptual leaps.

As the retarded children progress through the educational program and move toward adolescence, the curriculum focus diverges from that of the usual school program for the intellectually normal. The orientation for most retarded children approaching the teenage years becomes quite practical, occupationally, socially, and personally. The thrust is on engaging the youngsters in a wide range of activities in which they can practice using the tool subject skills they have acquired in their earlier school years to deal more effectively with problems associated with becoming as self-sufficient as possible. Obviously, there is a wide range of self-sufficiency among mentally retarded adolescents, and the instructional focus will most certainly differ among children of the same chronological age according to each child's repertoire of demonstrated skills in the various developmental areas.

The decision as to where one should concentrate the educational program for each retarded child is of great gravity, for it will in large measure cast the direction of all subsequent instruction. One must consider such factors as (1) how well each child has acquired important prerequisite skills in reading and in other tool subject areas, (2) the general prognosis for the child to become independent and self-sufficient in various areas of life, (3) the extent to which the youngster and his parents are willing to continue on in the school's programs, (4) how well the schools (and other community agencies) are equipped to provide for his instructional needs, and (5) the extent to which the climate of the community will be helpful to the child as he approaches adulthood.

To summarize this section, the proposition has been advanced that the schools must concentrate on describing terminal and intermediate skill goals for the mentally retarded in important areas of functioning. During those stages of instruction in which focus is on fundamental tool subject competencies, the major curricular difference between the special education program and the regular school program is in the degree of specificity with which objectives are described and emphasized. More precision is needed in describing objectives and in the necessary intensiveness of instruction in the early program for retarded children than for intellectually normal youngsters. As the retarded progress toward their adolescent years, the curricular goals diverge more sharply from the normal school program and veer toward a greater emphasis on using previously acquired skills to solve the numerous practical problems the youngsters will face as adults.

Methodological Issues The second issue in the chronology of developing an educational plan for the mentally retarded is the need to decide on an appropriate methodology (or methodologies). I emphasize that this is a second-order question to be considered only after careful thought has been given to the specific skills that the child should acquire. The individual goals must be established first, before one can determine the best route to take or tactic to employ in aiding the youngster to achieve a goal or become competent in a skill area.

It is clearly impossible to list all the instructional situations and problems that could arise for a teacher of retarded children. Even more remote is the possibility of describing how one might best deal with each of the problems. For these reasons and others, a teacher of the mentally retarded needs an understanding of a set of principles that can be used to deal with the full range of instructional situations for all children irrespective of their individual levels of achievement and rate of learning, the type of subject matter on which attention is focused, and the complexity of the problems. These principles should have wide applicability and an acceptable level of support from the research and theoretical literature from those fields of science that have been concerned with the learning problems of the mentally retarded.

The following section will list, discuss, and provide examples for two categories of instructional procedures that are especially appropriate for use with children who are intellectually retarded. In the first category, attention will be given to very broad principles of behavior management (again, behavior is used in the broadest possible sense). In the second category we will consider some of the prominent learning weaknesses of the retarded and suggest some practical ways for arranging the environment so as to reduce the possible harmful effects of these weaknesses and help the retarded to acquire the levels of skill that the teacher has, by this time, explicitly stated. Notice that the entire discussion of methodology is essentially dealing with teacher behavior, i.e., how best to arrange the educational environment, including the actions and reactions of the teacher toward the child.

I Fundamental Methodological Guidelines

  A Readiness for Learning—Among the factors inherent in the concept of readiness is the general belief that *a child must be mature enough to respond in a consistent and accurate fashion.* The validation of this finding in nonverbal areas has been well established. A child needs to acquire certain basic skills before adequate performance can be expected in areas such as walking, drawing, gross and fine motor movements, and other types of visual-motor activities. The influence of maturation on verbal skills, and more generally on cognition, is less well validated, since there is larger interindividual variation in these areas than in nonverbal skills. Some degree of extrapolation from observations in nonverbal areas to those involving more cognitive competencies has occurred, particularly as they relate to maturation.

Although it is without sound empirical documentation, this extrapolation seems to be valid clinically.

In order to receive incoming stimuli, engage in associational activities, and respond properly, *the child must be in a state of attentiveness.* Many believe that general lack of attention, the etiology of which may be multitudinous, is the primary reason that retarded children often do poorly in school. No doubt the problem is more complex than simple inattentiveness, and other difficulties contribute their share to readiness problems.

In addition to maturation, *readiness to learn a skill is based on the degree of competence the child has developed in precursive skills.* If the necessary basic skills upon which subsequent learning is dependent have not developed, any new skills will at best develop in an inefficient and disorganized manner, often totally out of context. Since deficits are cumulative, the area of readiness is particularly important. For example, if a child has trouble discriminating between the shapes of two objects, such as a square and a circle, he is not ready to choose the largest square among several sizes of circles and squares, because the skill of discriminating among shapes precedes the two-dimensional discrimination of shape and size.

The methods or processes the child uses for learning are related to readiness. If he has received primary instruction in using an auditory approach to solve problems but is subsequently given a task that demands a visual approach, the child may have difficulty in performing adequately. Methods of instruction to which the child has previously been exposed are related to readiness.

Finally, *the child's emotional adjustment and attitude toward school generally and learning specifically are related to readiness.* Those children who are antagonistic toward school activities or toward the teacher will gain little by being forced to participate. Time would be better spent attempting to alter attitudes.

The notion of readiness is also related to concept development. Although it is true that retarded children can be taught to memorize without having developed the basic readiness skills described earlier in this section, this strategy is inconsistent with the objectives of the special education program. Emphasis should be on the systematic and sequential development of skills leading to conceptual understanding and not rote memorization.

B Motivation to Learn—The term *motivation* is used frequently, but often erroneously, in educational circles. The most common misuse of the word is in connection with the wornout phrase "We must motivate the child." Children cannot be motivated. They can be stimulated, and appropriately rewarded, which can lead to their becoming eager or motivated to engage in an activity and to acquire certain associated skills.

There are several factors contained in the concept of motivation. If learning is to proceed in a stable fashion at an optimum level, children must perceive a need to participate in an instructional sequence of activities. For example, many primary- and intermediate-level retarded children are disinterested in activities related to acquiring basic skills in reading. Among the reasons for this attitude is the failure to perceive why they should learn to read. In the early school years, one can "get by" without being highly skilled in reading; this is particularly true if the child is with other retarded children in a homogeneous class in which peer pressures to learn are usually minimal. At the secondary level, however, retarded children begin to show a rather intense interest in learning how to read, for it is at this age that obtaining a driver's license becomes important. On several occasions I have seen dramatic increases in reading performance based primarily on this very clearly expressed need of the child. All reading problems cannot be interpreted using a motivational hypothesis, however. Obviously, many children have more complicated disabilities. But the degree of interest in and the amount of need for acquiring a skill are undoubtedly important to learning. Blindly launching into a lesson without preparing the class will generally result in the class becoming disinterested. To foster a desire to learn, the following points should be considered:

1 The children must see a reason for participating in an activity. This can be accomplished by judicious use of peer and social pressures or by the teacher relating a child's goal to the subject area in which his interest is not apparent.

2 For children to develop an interest in participating, they must have a history of success in related areas. Nothing inhibits interest more than continuous failure. To extend this notion, retarded children should be placed in situations in which they can be assured that their performance will be successful. Not only a history of success, but subsequent successful experiences will stimulate a level of motivation to participate even more.

3 Long- and short-term goals, established by both the teacher and by the child, should be realistic and sensitive to the child's individual strengths, weaknesses, and interests. If a child is

placed in a situation in which he is pressed to achieve beyond reasonable expectations, failure will result and he will quickly lose interest in participating. When this occurs frequently, the child may well generalize the negative feelings about that one activity to all school activities.

C Reinforcement of Desired Behavior—Perhaps the most influential technique that a teacher can use with intellectually retarded children is to provide appropriate reinforcement following a behavior that the teacher wants to see increased or strengthened. If the consequence of a child's behavior is personally rewarding to him, the chances of his engaging in that same kind of behavior on successive occasions is dramatically increased. If you are able to select an appropriate reinforcer for a child, and if you continuously provide this reinforcer *immediately* following the target behavior or skill, you should see significant changes in the child's performance. You must remember, though, that the goal or behavior target needs to be prespecified, that the reinforcer needs to be appropriate for each child (perhaps the best way to determine a child's interests regarding what is reinforcing is simply to ask him what he most enjoys among a variety of possibilities), and that the reinforcement must be provided immediately after the behavior and initially on a continuous schedule. Several other points regarding reinforcement should be mentioned.

1 Because it is virtually impossible for a teacher to immediately provide all the primary reinforcers that a classroom of children desire, there is real merit in establishing a credit system of "back-up" reinforcers that children can "cash in" at appropriate times. A token system, a punch card, or a green-stamp program can be implemented without distress. The children are simply given credit, by way of a token or a mark, toward some form of personal privilege after they have performed or behaved according to the prespecified target that the teacher has established.

2 When you are teaching for the acquisition of new behaviors, be sure to reinforce the child on every occasion during the beginning stages. Shift to a random, intermittent schedule of reinforcement—i.e., every once in a while without following a predictable pattern—only after the behavior has been stabilized. Usually you will have to begin by using tangible reinforcers, sometimes even food or candy, and always pair these reinforcers with a social stimulus. Gradually you can shift the child to more natural, social reinforcers.

3 Do not wait around for the student to achieve the target behavior if his entry behavior is miles away from what you wish for his terminal behavior. One important factor in changing behavior is to immediately reinforce *progressive movement toward* the final goal. The idea is to perform a task analysis of a behavior and to reinforce successive approximations—but never even the slightest hint of regression—toward the behavior.

4 If you want to stamp out certain behaviors of a child, try first to find behaviors that either oppose or are incompatible with the undesired behavior. As these contending behaviors occur, quickly provide the youngster with a heavy dose of appropriate reinforcing stimuli. In some cases you can also appropriately reinforce a neighboring child whose behavior is incongruent with that of the youngster in question. At the same time, you will find it effective to quickly remove any reinforcing stimuli from the child when the undesired behavior takes place. For example, if adult attention is reinforcing for a youngster, do not pay attention to him when his behavior is not consistent with a target(s) you have specified.

5 You will find that behavior of children can be changed by removing stimuli that are aversive. You may observe that some children are virtual non-talkers in certain situations that involve grouping with other specific children in the class. When they are not in the group, they talk. If verbal fluency is a target behavior, then you would most certainly want to remove the possible aversive stimuli from the child's environment. One sure way of determining if a certain factor in the environment is aversive is to observe the frequency of certain behaviors before removal of the stimuli and then observe them after. I hope that you can see how negative reinforcement, or the removal of aversive stimuli, can be combined with positive reinforcement, or the application of a desired reinforcer, to effectively change behavior.

6 After a behavior has become established, you can assure its stability by changing the reinforcement from a continuous to a variable-ratio schedule. This means that the youngster will be reinforced intermittently following the desired behavior. The influence is similar to that of a gambler who hopes that the next time will result in payoff.

D Exercise—Retarded children are generally less responsive to stimuli than are the intellectually normal. Moreover, the retarded are relatively inefficient in learning, usually acquiring skills much more slowly and laboriously than other children do. Fundamental to teaching these children is the advantage in offering them opportunities to repeat and practice experiences in a variety of ways.

The chance to exercise, practice, or repeat is necessary for two reasons. First, since stimuli will rarely occur again in the same form, children should be exposed to a range of stimuli around an event in order to become aware of the dimensions of a problem and to allow for a full opportunity to interrelate relevant stimuli. Second, wide experience on a number of occasions, and in different contexts, will direct the child's attention toward and help in the development of "associational bonds." Exercise and varied repetition will assist the retarded to practice correct responses. The true test of whether a concept has been established is if the child can scan his cognitive structure and respond in an appropriate fashion. This aim will be met more effectively if opportunities are provided to repeat responses in a variety of settings.

E Distributed Practice—Even under optimum circumstances, in which the material is interesting and the student is motivated, learning will become inefficient if the time for study or practice is massed instead of spread out. Distribution of practice should vary according to the characteristics of each student as well as of the type of materials used. With certain types of activities, for example, retarded children might profit most with four 10-minute periods of practice, whereas with other kinds of exercises, fewer and longer periods might be more efficient. When the interpretation of symbols is required to obtain meaning, more frequent shorter sessions will be more profitable than fewer longer periods. The reverse is probably true when computational and social-occupational lessons are being considered.

In distributing practice, moving to a different but somewhat related topic is often as effective as a rest period. Similarly, switching the materials used (such as from a piece of paper to the blackboard) will serve the same purpose as moving to another topic or providing a time for relaxation.

Although the evidence supports the value of distributing practice, it should be noted that a possible error can be made in the opposite direction. Practice periods should not be too short. The most desirable length of time has not yet been empirically determined, but the teacher should be aware of the students' restlessness and reduced efficiency so that activity on one task can be stopped and a switch made whenever necessary.

F Active Participation—Most educational psychologists agree that active involvement by the learner facilitates learning. Such participation has several advantages: (1) It helps to focus the child's attention on the task at hand, (2) it alerts the child to his importance in the teaching-learning process, (3) it fosters greater efficiency in learning, (4) it provides a more dramatic source of feedback, (5) it serves as a more accurate means of diagnosing the extent of learning which has taken place as well as any unusual weaknesses, and (6) it gives more opportunities for meaningful reinforcements for desired behavior.

If children are not provided with opportunities to actively participate, boredom results and the tendency for desired responses to be extinguished increases. If learning is to be profitable, a certain degree of alertness and anticipation is needed and, thus, an optimal level of stimulation must be provided. Too much stimulation should not be provided, however, since this is just as detrimental to learning as too little stimulation.

G Overlearning—This concept is defined as the practice of a task beyond the point of initial mastery. Retarded children do not have a complete understanding of a concept after having accurately responses on only the first few occasions. Since these children often have difficulty with attention, short-term memory, and association, there is a need for overlearning to be an integral part of the special program.

Improvement in learning, retention, transfer, and relearning will be facilitated if overlearning has taken place (Gilbert, 1957; Postman, 1962; Mander and Heinemann, 1956). According to Hebb's theory, overlearning provides the organism with opportunities to strengthen and elaborate on the "associational networks" that have developed around an event. The same types of stimulus conditions that were present when initial learning occurred should prevail on subsequent presentations. Gradually, additional perceptions, stimulus variations, and experiences can be introduced so that the generalization and elaboration of skills already established is possible.

When overlearning is allowed to occur, the teacher reduces the possibility of eliciting random responses from the child, enhances retention and transfer, and provides a means for increasing the child's general response repertoire. By presenting previously learned material in a variety of ways on numerous occasions, a more flexible and less rigid organism will develop.

As a general rule of thumb, you can be fairly sure that the child has overlearned a concept, skill, or task when, after switching from a continuous to an intermitten schedule of reinforcement, no discernible change occurs in the level of the child's achievement. If there is no deceleration in the rate or level of performance following the shift of schedule in reinforcement, overlearning has probably taken place at an acceptable level. Take care, however, to continue to give the youngster opportunities to use the concept or skill in ways that are meaningful, i.e., of practical value to him.

H Stressing Accuracy—To control the chance of children practicing errors, accuracy instead of speed should be stressed. This is especially necessary in the early stages of learning when new and basic concepts are formulated, which will later form the basis for subsequent learning. Competition between and within individuals often helps to stimulate interest in the child, and thus, as he learns, accuracy can be stressed by the teacher, who can also instill in the child the appropriate dimensions upon which such a competitive situation is to be founded. If children compete in terms of the time it takes to complete a task, accuracy will inevitably be sacrificed.

The teacher must see that the children develop stable response patterns that are characterized by lack of ambiguity. An early emphasis on speed will result in errors, which in turn will lead to a less clear and less firmly established network of interrelated and pertinent skills. To reduce the possibility of confusion on subsequent tasks, corrections must be stressed—not speed of response. Obviously, this can best be done by reinforcing accuracy and withholding all reinforcement for speed during periods of initial learning.

I Minimal Change—Retarded children learn most effectively if materials are programmed so that abrupt shifting between concepts and activities is minimized. Hegge, Kirk, and Kirk (1955) have developed remedial reading drills that follow this principle. For example, instead of a series of drill words that quickly shifts to a totally new series, only the last letter in the new series changes: "sat," "mat," "rat," followed by "sap," "map," "rap."

All activities cannot be developed to precisely follow the minimal-change principle illustrated above. Some consideration, however, must be given to a step-by-step progression of activities that does not require the child to make conceptual leaps. The previous discussions about the need to task-analyze activities and the notions of reinforcing successive approximations of behavior as a child approaches a terminal behavior target or goal both have a relationship to this minimal-change concept.

J Using the Child's Strengths—All of us are stronger in certain areas than in others. Retarded children typically show their greatest capabilities in nonverbal activities and their lesser ones in verbal activities. In teaching retarded children with uneven profiles of abilities and disabilities, it is wise to use areas of relative strength to enhance development of the weaker areas. For example, a child with this type of uneven profile should be encouraged to verbalize about nonverbal tasks. Telling the class what is being done as the child proceeds through an activity, answering questions posed by the teacher and other classmates, talking about an event, and being certain that you identify and properly apply appropriate reinforcers for individual children illustrate the principle to be followed.

The children should be encouraged to participate in activities that will strengthen areas of weakness and should be reinforced for it. At first, some children may hesitate to participate because of a history of failure in the weak areas or because the consequence of participating is not satisfactorily rewarding. The focus of the activities, thus, should not be on situations wherein the threat of evaluation is minimal. In fact, initially the children should be placed in situations in which there are no wrong responses. Gradually, evaluation and some degree of difficulty can be judiciously introduced without penalty.

II Prominent Learning Weakness of Retarded Children and Techniques for Reducing Their Potential Harmful Effects

  A Attention—Many feel that if the retarded were able to inhibit the effects of extraneous stimuli, learning could proceed in a much more orderly and effective manner. These children often have very short attention spans, which directly affect their ability to grasp material and acquire skills quickly. It should be pointed out here that attention span for the retarded, as for the nonretarded, is a variable that is often a function of the type of task as well as the extent to which the consequences of attending are valued by the child. The average child, however, typically attends to a lesson long enough to understand the major concepts involved; the mentally retarded child frequently loses interest and drifts away from the grasp of both teacher and material. Helping the retarded learn to attend to relevant stimuli is important for instructional effectiveness. Factors that affect the attention of the retarded include:

    1 Reducing extraneous stimuli by sectioning the room with partitions when small groups are at work, seating the children away from doors and windows, controlling interruptions, and establishing patterns of work and conduct that the children gradually perceive as being appropriate. For example, using the same classroom and seating positions helps to create a more stable atmosphere and eliminate irrelevant stimuli that occur when physical changes are made.

2 Emphasizing relevant stimuli and varying the mode of presentation by employing illustrations, examples, demonstrations, or audiovisual aids. The materials should be handled by the children and a definite attempt made to stimulate as many channels of communication as possible during the lesson. For example, when doing rational counting, have the child place a peg in a hole or drop a ping-pong ball into a jar. When saying a word, have the youngster trace the letters.

3 Spending very short periods of time on new, more difficult activities. The teacher should be alert to (a) situations in which children are reaching their tolerance for frustration because of lack of success, and (b) the point at which they are becoming restless or inattentive because the material is too difficult, boring, or unstimulating. Activities should be varied to offset these difficulties.

4 Encouraging questions during the activity and group interaction. Questions keep interest high and provide for a more complete understanding of the material. Introducing mildly competitive situations is desirable when all the children are performing at approximately the same level. Attention-maintaining devices such as saying, "Follow my finger with your eyes and don't let it get out of sight," will help mask irrelevant stimuli.

5 Rewarding attending behavior and ignoring other behavior. Again, this is one of the most powerful procedures for increasing attending behavior.

B Discrimination Learning—Learning to discriminate among objects and sounds assumes that the child can see and hear at an acceptable level. If he can, then his attention must be focused on the relevant stimuli in order to observe differences and similarities. Discrimination is important if the significance of information is to be correctly perceived, appropriately recorded and associated, and properly used in subsequent situations. For discrimination to occur, the following points should be considered:

1 Background interference and interruptions should be reduced to a minimum and task stimuli should be increased in value. It is often necessary to deliberately mask irrelevant stimuli.

2 Labels should be attached to each stimulus with emphasis on

making use of all sense modalities. For example, in discriminating among three objects, the child could be asked to choose the appropriate object and also to tell its name and hand it to the teacher. The unique characteristics of the object and how it is similar to and different from the other objects might also be discussed.

3 Stimuli should initially be distinct and novel with gross discriminations used first. The dimensions on which the children are to discriminate should be clear. If the teacher wants discrimination by size, the colors and shapes of the alternatives should all be the same. As the child gains skill in differentiating among various dimensions and begins to understand and correctly use the related language (e.g., larger, smaller, round corners, green, etc.), more complicated and finer discriminations can be required. In the beginning stages of instruction, either large or small objects are preferred to those of intermediate size.

4 Material should be sequentially presented according to the difficulty of the discrimination task. Difficulty can be increased either by requiring finer discriminations, with the alternative choices being more closely alike, or by asking for discriminations on more than one criterion. For example, the task might be to select the object that is green, largest, and longer than it is wide. Some of the options could be green but smaller than the correct choice, and other choices could be large but yellow.

5 Discrimination should logically lead into an understanding of classes and categories of things or the grouping of things that share a common characteristic. To assist in the development of this skill, verbal and visual stimuli should constantly be related.

6 All the learning phenomena discussed earlier, such as immediate reinforcement, success, active involvement, and spaced learning, are important for the development of skill in discrimination.

C Association—The ability to associate concepts or facts is part of intelligence. It permits us to react to stimuli in a rapid and proper manner. For example, when we are driving and see a red light, we stop. We react to this stimulus because in the past we have developed a network of perceptual associations that result in our stopping the car. It is apparent that for associational ties to become established, the individual must have clearly received the various stimuli common to an event. Many of the teaching considerations mentioned earlier apply to the development of association skills. In addition to these, the following should be considered:

1 The first association activity should require students to group together things which are alike. At first the criterion for "likeness" should be very general. For example, have them name all the animals they have seen. Cutting out pictures from magazines of things they can ride in, eat for dinner, or wear to school will help. The children should always be encouraged to verbalize about the various aspects of their activity. The teacher can ask a child why various pictures were put together just to have him verbalize and see the relationships that exist.

2 Children should learn that some events naturally precede others. The idea of sequence can be developed by showing a story illustrated on cards. Mixing the cards and asking a child to reconstruct and simultaneously tell about the story will help in the development of sequencing skills.

3 At a higher level, the retarded need to relate cause to effect. This task demands more conceptual skill than simply seeing likeness. For instance, the child might be told not to cross the street unless the light facing him is green or the crossing guard is there to help. He might also be taught that he should look both ways for cars on those streets that do not have traffic lights or crossing guards. A clear explanation of the reason for this behavior must be presented. The child should realize that if he does not understand this relationship, an accident might result. Always tell the children why one certain act will cause another. Frequent use of the question "Why?" will guide them to see the important components in cause-and-effect situations.

4 The school program should not be structured so that the retarded are led to believe that knowledge in reading does not have applicability in other areas, such as in arithmetic or occupational information. Associations will become strongly established if commonalities among activities are explicitly pointed out.

D Short-Term Memory—Mentally retarded children frequently have weak short-term memories. For the child to correctly perceive and record stimuli, and to form comprehensive patterns of skills that he can remember to use properly in appropriate situations, the teacher should plan her presentations with the following in mind:

1 She should see that the child's attention is focused on the task by reducing the environmental stimuli to a minimum and increasing the stimulus value of the task. The working stimuli must

be clear, unique, pertinent, and interesting. The class should be located in a quiet section of the building and the students faced away from any external distractions. All irrelevant visual and auditory stimuli should be masked. Auditory and/or visual stimuli directly associated with the activity should not only be increased in value and emphasized, but proper reinforcement should be offered whenever responses approximate the desired target.

2 Every component of the auditory or visual stimuli should be presented clearly with each aspect initially of equivalent stimulus value. If the children are asked to recall a sentence or a short song, every word of the auditory chain should be loud enough to be heard and articulated clearly. If they are asked to recall visual stimuli, whether in a certain sequence or not, the stimuli should be bold enough to allow for a clear view. Gradually, variations from this rule can be allowed as the children gain competence. However, at first the same perceptions should appear each time with variations occurring only after overlearning has been assured.

3 All tasks should move from the simple to the more complex. The children should be initially exposed to and required to remember small groups of stimulus chains. The objects or sounds should be different so that each maintains its unique identity. Objects grossly different from each other are remembered more easily than objects closely alike. For example, in short-term visual memory the teacher might place a spoon, a toy automobile, and a rubber ball in front of a child, in no specific sequence. The child would then be asked to close his eyes and, upon reopening them, to recall which object had been removed. If a pencil, a pen, and a crayon were placed before him, the task would be more difficult because of the similarity of shape, size, function, and perhaps color. To further complicate the task, the objects can be presented and the children asked to reproduce the sequence as it previously appeared. A similar gradation in levels of difficulty can be used with auditory stimuli. The ability to maintain attention and the degree of success should constitute the principal criteria for deciding if the task is too difficult.

4 Interfering material should not intervene between the components to be remembered, between the learning situation and the recall tests, or between the child's response and the reinforcement; if it does, memory will be inefficient and will decay.

5 To improve short-term memory, stimuli should be labeled. In the

earlier illustration, one-word labels for each object (spoon, car, and ball) would help the child to recall what he had seen. Encouraging the child to use verbal labels in connection with a visual stimulus, and vice versa, will help him to recall and will assist him in the formation of strong "intrasensory associations," such as auditory-visual, auditory-tactile, and visual-tactile.

6 Reward or reinforcement should be carefully controlled and monitored so that the child does not develop too high an anticipation, which has been found to have a detrimental affect on short-term memory. When a child succeeds, simply saying "fine" or "good" is often adequate reinforcement. When he fails, moving to another task or activity without comment, or saying, "Let's try this one now," is wise strategy. Undue attention should not be called to errors since retarded children tend to remember best what not or how not to do something rather than what to or how to do it.

7 Ample time should be provided for short-term memory activities. A tachistoscope, flash cards, games, records with sounds or songs, and various types of material recorded on tape can provide a medium for individual and small-group practice. It is important in such activities that accurate feedback be provided immediately after a response is given. To disregard this principle will result in inefficient learning.

8 Material used in practice should be integrated with other subject fields as often as possible, especially when it can make use of the child's successful experiences. If a retarded youngster is particularly interested in arithmetic, it would be advantageous to use numbers auditorally or visually in short-term memory tasks. If, on the other hand, the child particularly dislikes arithmetic, it would probably be more desirable to use material from some other area.

9 A great deal of dramatization and other forms of active participation of tasks that involve short-term memory should become a central part of the program. Remembering and executing commands of an auditory or visual nature and using sociodrama are illustrations of this technique.

E Long-Term Memory—Mentally retarded children seem to have less trouble with long-term than with short-term memory so long as frequent review of skills and concepts is made available on a continuous basis. This finding supports those Hebbian postulations that suggest that once networks of association are established, their maintenance becomes vital and can be accomplished through the constant use of the information within the networks. Although the long-term-memory performance of the retarded is relatively good, it is still necessary to constantly review, use, and elaborate upon previously learned facts and concepts so that forgetting will not occur easily. To this end, the following general teaching suggestions apply to various subjects areas:

1 Primary emphasis should be put on overlearning, during which time the concept being learned must be put to use in a practical and meaningful way. Repetition of the material being learned is easier when a variety of sensory modalities are employed. Telling about and dramatizing an event makes maximum use of response patterns, using more than a single modality of expression, and helps to develop transfer abilities. Acceptable criteria for overlearning, of course, demand more than one appropriate response by the child.

2 Since context, such as remembering what to do in a special situation, remembering a story sense, or remembering an arithmetic process, is of much greater importance in long-term than in short-term memory, the teacher should reduce each task to its simplest components and present material in a logical sequence. For example, she should not teach addition before teaching grouping, since the latter is basic to an adequate understanding of the former.

3 For maximum long-term retention, meaningful materials should be used. Pleasantly toned materials are also preferable to neutral or unpleasant; and recitation during learning activities should be incorporated into the general teaching strategy.

4 The teacher should be consistent in the presentation of materials, activities, and tasks. Retarded children who have learned a concept after having been exposed to one set of stimuli and who are later exposed to a different set of stimuli may have great difficulty arriving at the correct answer because no explicit association was made between the two sets. For example, if a child is taught to read a word using a "look-and-say" approach, but is later transferred to a room where the teacher emphasizes phonics, a severe reading problem could result.

5 The material committed to memory should be used in practical situations. In such situations, if information is remembered and applied appropriately, the major reason for learning is realized through opportunities for the child to repeat and reinforce the material in lifelike circumstances.

F Expression of Ideas—Ideas can be expressed by either word or gesture. Mentally retarded children tend to be poor in both areas, probably largely because of lack of exposure to stimulating contacts in the early years, and because of inadequate models in the home that are necessary for developing skills in expression. To overcome this difficulty, the teacher should consider the following:

1 The classroom atmosphere should be conducive to stimulating vocal and gestural expression. The children should feel that their productions will not be evaluated and criticized.

2 The teacher must take time to listen and must provide a good example of language by speaking clearly and talking about subjects that are enjoyable and pleasant to the children. Many of the retarded do not have an opportunity to listen to an adult speak unless the adult is reprimanding or punishing them. Sometimes, too, the children are not given a chance to express themselves because their parents, knowing they are retarded, do not ask enough of them.

3 Expression should be stimulated by using a variety of materials, such as hand puppets, flannel boards, costumes. Dramatization can also aid expression and help the children to increase their general information repertoire. For example, the children could stage a make-believe visit to the doctor, supermarket, dentist, or to another city to visit a friend. Or pantomime can be used, with most of the students trying to guess what one child is depicting.

4 Questions should be framed to enhance, not stifle responses. To increase expressive performance, questions should be open-ended and allow for a variety of responses. The children will not be encouraged to express themselves when asked a question for which a "yes" or "no" response is sufficient. Questions designed to enhance expression can be formulated so that there is no wrong answer and any response is acceptable. This approach should be used until the child becomes secure enough to tolerate corrections and suggestions concerning the content and technique of his answer.

G Initial Learning—When retarded children face a new learning situation, they have less of a chance than do normal children of initially learning the concepts inherent in the tasks. This is because of their limited intellectual ability, their history of failure, and their resulting traditionally low expectancy for success. Also, they often fail to see the rewards of learning that normal children usually perceive.

Research indicates that mentally retarded children, when

matched with normal children on chronological age (CA), do poorly at the outset but show rapid improvement with continued practice. Although some authorities believe that a child's mental age (MA) seems to determine the upper limit of task competency in areas related to cognition (assuming that the task is within the individual's range at all), sufficient practice could overcome certain initial performance disadvantages. It is within reason, therefore, to suggest that although retarded children learn slowly at the beginning, they have some potential for overcoming this slow start if they are provided with opportunities for success and practice. Studies have shown that after failing on some problems, the retarded have difficulty in solving easier problems with which they were earlier successful. If a child has success with easy problems, he stands a better chance of successfully and more quickly performing harder ones.

Practice, too, has its part in even the simplest initial learning task. These periods of practice must be varied and interesting, allowing the child to give full attention to the task. To form comprehensive associational networks in learning, the retarded profit from repetition, from exposure to many contexts, and from using all the senses together. More specific suggestions for helping the children in initial learning are:

1 New learning should be presented early in the day when the children are more alert. Early presentation of such material in each work period is also desirable. In addition, the entire day's activities should be scheduled so that low-preference tasks are always followed by especially enjoyed ones. A certain level of performance by each child in the low-preference activities should be required before the youngster has the privilege of participating in the more desirable experiences. Do not start the day with all pleasant activities and end it with the ones the children consider to be "icky."

2 The children must be impressed with the personal significance of their learning the material. This preparation is important and may take more time than teaching the new material.

3 New learning should be related to past learning and experiences. It is wise to provide a reference or anchor point to which the new material can be directly related.

4 The children should have chances to react to and explain in their own words the major concepts inherent in the new material. Illustrations of the practical application of the new learning should be solicited from the students.

5 New learning should be repeated in a variety of ways and applied to a variety of situations in order to stress the applicability, generalizability, and usefulness of the information.

H Incidental Learning—Incidental learning with the mentally retarded does not typically occur without concentrated effort. All of us are aware of certain peripheral stimuli within our environment; those who are intellectually normal tend to absorb this information with greater ease than do retarded children. Unfortunately for the retarded child, much of this peripheral information is basic and often establishes a foundation upon which subsequent learning is based. Consequently, some effort must be devoted to this important area. Although it is true that the retarded do not seem to be as weak in incidental learning as in other areas of cognition, the following teaching considerations will allow them to exercise their maximum capabilities in this area:

1 Retarded children must be given opportunities to experience a great number of events and stimuli, and this diversity must be explicitly called to their attention and clearly related to other events and stimuli. In short, those aspects of the environment that are learned incidentally by the normal must become areas of intentional learning with the retarded. The special education teacher, therefore, should frequently, but judiciously and with specific objectives in mind, take the children on meaningful field trips. Preparation and follow-up should be important parts of the experience.

2 Questioning and group discussions help to make the students more aware of their surroundings. Questions asked must initially be open-ended with every answer correct. For example, there is a difference between asking, "What else did you see this morning on your way to school?" and, "What color is the flower in the front of the school?" Gradually, more specific questions can be asked as the children become more alert to their surroundings.

3 Games and other types of competitive situations can be used as the students develop incidental learning skill. Studies seem to suggest that incidental learning is enhanced when reward or incentives are used.

The guidelines and principles presented in these two lists can be applied to various educational situations and to children of different degrees of retardation. It is important to think about the meaning of each guideline and about how each can be implemented to effectively react to the various situations. In fact, you should do much more than think about them. I suggest that you practice using each one, first by itself and then in different combinations. The final goal, of course, is to develop a pattern of instructional behavior toward each youngster that is consistent and that makes use of these principles in all areas of involvement.

To help you practice using these guidelines, take a situation such as helping children group objects according to a preestablished classification system. Next, take each of the first group of fundamental methodological guidelines and outline how you will arrange the specific stimulus and the child's general instructional environment so that the guideline is properly implemented. Continue with this procedure for each principle until you have identified in detail how your behavior will appear within the instructional environment. Next, choose another instructional situation and go through the same process. When you feel comfortable with your ability to analyze several types of instructional problems on paper, and to apply principles in a way that will allow a child to acquire a target behavior, begin working with a child on a real problem, using the same procedures that you used on paper. I suggest that you begin using the principles that deal with reinforcement concepts and then gradually include the others.

There is another group of instructional methodologies that is quite different from those that have just been discussed. They are equally important, however. Usually they are specific to a subject area and do not have broad applicability for children even within the same classroom, but in most instances you can decide which of several possible methodologies to use from data previously collected on individual children.

Perhaps one of the most obvious illustrations of a subject-specific instructional procedure is in the area of reading. Certain children seem to acquire basic reading skills better when an auditory or phonics approach is used and a strict visualization approach is deemphasized. Other children seem to deal best with the visual approach. It is an idiosyncratic matter which is often difficult to identify from a test performance alone. Fortunately, most youngsters do equally well with almost any approach so long as the teacher(s) is consistent in using it. It seems to be true, however, that children with difficult and complex educational problems have a relative preference in the manner in which certain stimuli of a specific subject should be presented. Some children seem to respond best when a tactile approach is used and the auditory and visual emphases are minimized. Other children do especially well when combinations of various types are employed.

Some other illustrations of subject-specific instructional procedures are

1 Use of the i.t.a. (initial teaching alphabet) approach versus the regular orthography in teaching reading
2 Use of three-dimensional objects—such as the Cuisenaire Rods or Sterns Blocks—in teaching arithmetic skills as opposed to two-dimensional ones
3 Use of role playing to elicit proper social responses by children in a social setting instead of small-group discussion or individual counseling
4 Sound-symbol approach in the teaching of spelling in contrast to a strictly written approach
5 Fernald approach as opposed to the Distar or Sullivan procedures in establishing word-attack skills

Instructional Materials The third major component in establishing an education plan for retarded children is the selection of appropriate instructional devices, materials, and media. However, this selection should not be considered until after the teacher has decided what precise skills the youngster is to acquire and what teaching methods are to be used in helping him to acquire them. After those determinations have been made, the search begins for media that are compatible with the instructional procedures. There must be a match, then, between the methodology and the instructional devices so that the influence of each is not counteracted, found to be contradictory, or generally incompatible. For example, the Hegge, Kirk, and Kirk reading drills are phonics oriented and are most effectively used with an auditory type of reading program, especially in the beginning stages of learning. One would not want to use a visualization format in teaching word attack in combination with the Hegge, Kirk, and Kirk phonics materials during initial periods of instruction.

As you evaluate an instructional material or educational device, keep in mind the broad principles of methodology that were previously discussed and that can be used as criteria in your evaluation. You should ask the following questions about each piece of material or device:

1 Is the material potentially interesting to the child or children for whom it is intended? Will it help to hold their attention? Are the skills it will help to develop necessary for a child to succeed beyond his present level of performance? Have the children had a previously dismal experience with the same material?

2 Does the material have explicitly stated goals or targets so that the children (and their teachers) will know whether they have been successful at all the stages of its use? Does the device lend itself to a task-analysis format so that a student can make successive approximations toward a goal? Also, is there opportunity for success to be guaranteed at each of the steps? To what extent is the sequence of steps properly ordered?

3 Does the material provide control so that a youngster is reinforced if and only if he performs in a fashion that is consistent with an appropriate target? Is it obvious to the student when he has correctly and incorrectly responded? Are criteria given for correct responses?

4 Can students actively participate with the instructional materials or are they structured so that the youngsters must play a more passive role? Are there ample opportunities for youngsters to independently practice making responses to situations that differ in content and yet have interest to children from diverse backgrounds and who vary in aptitude, level of performance, and previous experiences?

5 Are the materials restricted in scope or do they cover a broad range of performance areas? To what extent are multiple experiences by the child possible within each area of performance contained in the materials?

6 Are the materials useful with both individuals and groups? What adjustments in the classroom environment are necessary when the teacher switches from individual to group instruction but continues to use the same materials? How easy is it for children to cheat, misunderstand what has to be done, or lose their place when using the materials?

7 Are the materials so complex that teachers cannot determine how best to use them, or are directions so detailed that teachers lose interest in learning how to incorporate the materials into the instructional program, or does using the devices depend on extensive training before a teacher can employ them in a classroom setting?

8 Are the materials flexible enough to allow for additions, alterations, or deletions of content within the software program sequences? For example, could a teacher develop and add a small sequence of activities to an existing package of arithmetic materials without jeopardizing the integrity of the existing sequence?

9 How expensive are the materials? Could the teacher construct similar materials or have them constructed at a more modest cost? What other materials are available that focus on the same targets? Are the materials under consideration durable, consumable, of high quality, or so subject specific or time related as to be potentially worthless on subsequent occasions?

10 Do the materials contain the means by which a teacher can evaluate a child's level of performance or repertoire of skills to determine where within a given set of materials the child should begin? Are evaluative checkpoints included at critical positions within the package to allow a teacher to assess the instructional value of the device?

11 Are the materials under consideration portable, readily available from the distributor or manufacturer, and easily maintained? Are repair services obtainable when needed?

12 Has the manufacturer done a reasonable job on pretesting, field-testing, and generally evaluating the materials on various populations of children? Does the research based on the materials provide any clues to possible indications and/or contraindications for its use?

These are some of the questions you should ask about each of the instructional materials that you select for use in your classroom. Do not by any means succumb to a tendency to accept a device on the basis of a publisher's name, the clinical observations of your colleagues, the attractiveness of packaging, or a "hard sell" by a local representative. It is most important that you conduct your evaluation with prudence and in a coolheaded manner.

The United States Office of Education has established a number of Special Education Instructional Materials Centers (IMCs) throughout the country. These centers, in turn, support smaller, regional IMCs. Their major mission is to provide general information, advice, samples of materials, materials evaluations, and occasional seminars and institutes to teachers and administrators. This is an excellent resource for both a teacher and a school system. In many instances the local or regional IMC will be able to provide you with answers to the questions listed above. Moreover, each center has close contact with other IMCs throughout the country—all of which are willing to share information on various professional issues.

Integration of Factors at Level III   This section, which began on page 77, has discussed in some detail the major components involved in developing an educational plan for children with retarded intellectual development. As has been emphasized, these children usually exhibit such extraordinary instructional problems that most often it is necessary to plan their educational programs on individual bases. The foci of curricular goals, instructional methods, and teaching materials will differ, often in very dramatic ways, for each child.

Although the foregoing discussion has tended to separate the components of an educational plan—i.e., curricular targets, methods, and materials—into somewhat distinct categories, in actual practice this is impossible. The instructional environment must include all three components. The important factors to be sensitive to are that these components be (1) explicitly identified before instruction begins, (2) compatible among themselves, (3) consistently applied, and (4) continuously evaluated in terms of the impact that they have on each child's performance. An educational plan, then, should be based on actual data collected on the child and from his environment, and it should contain clear statements about the content of an emphasis to be placed upon each of the three dimensions.

Let me illustrate this point by providing a sample of statements that pertain to the kind of instructional environment considered appropriate for a hypothetical child. Let us assume that the youngster's performance has been observed and that he has difficulty in reading. Closer observation reveals that he is inconsistent in his differentiation among consonant sounds. He is able to make the sounds, but his primary problem appears to be a weakness in making the correct sound in association with the appropriate consonant. He switches among consonant sounds in response to the request "Tell me what a 'b' says." The same holds true for the letters "g," "p," "t," and "d."

The immediate educational plan for this child might well include specific suggestions such as the following:

I Curricular Targets[1]

There are a number of objectives or goals that are related to how well a child is able to associate the sound a consonant makes with the graphic form of the letter. To determine where to focus the instructional program for our hypothetical youngster, the teacher should try to determine the extent to which he has developed a reasonable level of competence in these percursive areas. For purposes of illustration, one might want to engage the youngster in activities that are aimed at determining that the following broad skills have been achieved:

A The student can identify like and different initial sounds and discriminate among initial sounds.
B The child can discriminate among different letters, figures, letter sequences (words or nonwords), and colors.
C The youngster can recognize uppercase letters by naming and printing them.
D The child can recognize lowercase letters by naming and printing them.

---

[1]Each of the curricular targets in this section comes from the *Language Arts Series* developed by The Instructional Objectives Exchange.

E The student can identify any lower- or uppercase script letter by naming and printing it.

The preceding five goals are illustrative of groups of possible prerequisite skills that a child might find helpful in associating a consonant sound with the appropriate graphic form. Assuming that this youngster can perform satisfactorily in each of these areas, the teacher should then focus total attention on single and initial consonants. The following general and specific objectives are examples of this curricular focus.

A The student will be able to recognize identical initial consonant sounds, and to associate single consonant sounds with their letters.

  1 Given orally a word that begins with a consonant, the student will be able to reproduce orally the initial consonant sound (with a vowel, if necessary).

  2 Given a set of pictures, the one on the left being set apart from the others, the student will be able to put an "X" through each object that begins with the same sound as the object in the picture on the left.

  3 Given a word orally or a picture depicting the name of an object that begins with a certain consonant sound, the student will be able to supply another word or picture that begins with the same consonant sound.

  4 Given an initial consonant sound orally, both in isolation and in a word, the student will be able to state or write the letter of the alphabet that corresponds to the consonant he hears.

  5 Given a word orally or a word picture, with or without a list of consonants, the student will form new words by substituting orally or in writing other initial consonants. The newly formed word must be an actual word.

  6 Given a picture of an object and its written name partially spelled out (initial consonant omitted), the student will say or write the initial consonant that completes the word.

  7 Given an orally presented consonant-vowel-consonant (CVC) word, the student will be able to identify it within a group of words or pronounce a written word having the same vowel sound and final consonant with different initial consonant(s).

Following the satisfactory accomplishment of these objectives, the teacher might proceed to a higher level of skills, including those that are subsumed under this general objective.

B The student will be able to recognize identical consonant sounds, identify or reproduce their location in a word (initial, medial, or final) and associate single consonant sounds with their letters.

II Instructional Procedures

The following brief statements show how one might specify or highlight certain instructional procedures that seem to be *especially pertinent to the child pursuing the objectives set forth under I.* Remember, however, that the instructional methods discussed earlier in this chapter should be implemented by the teacher whenever desirable.

A Be certain that the child's attention is on the stimulus before you ask him to respond. This situation can be enhanced by providing a reward following each correct response at the beginning stage of instruction.

B This youngster is greatly affected by verbal approval from adults. Make sure that you use this type of reward only in those circumstances in which the child is performing in a fashion that is compatible with your curricular targets.

C Before you engage this youngster in an activity designed to increase his skill in a certain target area, make sure that he knows what is expected of him (short-term goal) and the level of performance that you consider acceptable. Be certain that only a proper response is rewarded, and do not reward any behavior that is less than that already achieved.

D Ignore any response that is not compatible with movement toward the objective on which you are focusing.

E Establish the same stimulus situation each time you engage the child in activities that pertain to the above curricular goals—e.g., a certain location in the classroom, the same time of day, and so on.

F Do not move the youngster to a higher-level skill in this general area too fast. As a rule of thumb, practice a skill until 95 percent accuracy is demonstrated for three consecutive days.

III Instructional Materials

The instructional devices that one might use in combination with the methods suggested above might include:

A Single-colored flash cards with individual consonant sounds printed on each could be used as the primary stimulus during early stages of consonant recognition.

B Single-colored flash cards with CVC words could be used during the latter stages of instruction. Follow the minimal-change principle by having the initial consonant on each card be the only stimulus that changes. For example, "pat," "bat," "rat," "sat," "mat," and so on.

C Make wide use of the language master or a tape recorder throughout all the instructional sequences. Be sure that during the initial stages the youngster first hears the consonant and consonant-vowel blends uttered properly before he is asked to reproduce each orally. Audio recording devices facilitate this type of modeling and give the child an obvious means for self-evaluation of his productions.

This illustration highlights the type of integration that should exist among curriculum, methods, and materials in the design of an instructional program for children with retarded intellectual development. Notice that there is compatibility among the three dimensions in the example. Also, you will find that the more specific you can be in describing the components of the educational plan the more easily they can be implemented and evaluated.

In concluding this section, it might be helpful to simply list some general guidelines that pertain to the construction of educational plans.

1 Each plan should include precise statements about content objectives, preferred instructional procedures, and materials/media to be used.
2 Do not develop so complex a program of activities that it is either too difficult for others to understand, too time consuming, or impossible to implement within the limitations imposed by the usual classroom environment.
3 Make certain that the recommended activities can be carried out within the confines of the school and/or class.
4 Clearly identify priority goals and activities. The plan should tell what should be done, how, when, in combination with what else, and the criteria the teacher can use for determining when the child has performed in a satisfactory way.
5 By all means, guard against editorializing beyond the observed data that have been collected on each child. Do not engage in mystic psychologizing or neurologizing; such behavior can introduce unwarranted and perhaps dangerous teacher expectations and biases against a child before and during periods of educational intervention. Focus on the child's environment and less on his presumed internal weaknesses or characteristics.
6 In a child's educational plan, stay away from using terms and suggesting activities that are vague, ill-defined, controversial, or without reasonable documentation.
7 Begin by emphasizing procedures for dealing with the child's fundamental *educational* problem and then suggest ways in which the teacher can begin to work on problems that are less all-embracing.

8 Be sure to describe the broad sequence of activities to be followed. Also, try to suggest alternate methods that might be tried to accomplish the same goal.

9 Suggest specific ways in which other people with whom the child associates might get involved in the remediation or habilitation process. For example, parents, aides, speech personnel, or child-guidance workers all might have important roles to perform in designing and executing an educational plan.

summary

This lengthy chapter has outlined a broad model that teachers of retarded children might use to effectively deal with each child's educational disorders. The procedures recommended can be easily applied to older as well as younger children, and they have clear implications for implementation across all subject or content areas. The emphasis here has been on studying each child's characteristics and unique environment through consistent observation, and, on the basis of data collected, designing a preferred educational plan that specifies curricular objectives, methods, and materials.

After the educational program has been designed, the schools have a basic responsibility to provide an environment in which the program can be implemented. This is the final stage in the model that was proposed in Figure 3-1. The next chapter will deal with issues that pertain to organizing the resources in a school building and a school system to facilitate the accomplishment of each educational program.

5

ORGANIZATION AND ADMINISTRATION
OF SPECIAL EDUCATION SERVICES

After generating a preferred educational plan for a retarded youngster, one is next faced with the decision of where within the existing school system the child's educational needs can best be satisfied. This assignment decision (level 4 of Figure 3-1) can be made only after you have decided what he needs, and that decision is based on the data that have been collected on the child's performance and environment. This chapter will deal with various ramifications of the assignment of children to appropriate settings and the manner in which the range of special education services can be organized and administered.

placement possibilities

Before we consider how one might determine the best possible placement for a youngster in a given school system, let us consider the variety of options that usually exist and the alleged uniqueness of each. Quite obviously, only a few of the largest systems can provide the full range of placement resources on which this discussion will center. Aside from the fact that a majority of school systems cannot physically and fiscally provide a total of all possible assignment configurations, it is probably true that they need not be concerned about this inability if they can develop and maintain a reasonably flexible system at all levels throughout the district. As you read about the different assignment options, consider which types could be adapted to the school system in which you work so that the educational requirements of retarded children could best be satisfied. One additional important point— although the discussion will attempt to provide a general picture of the characteristics of each type of instructional environment, you must realize that a great deal of variation exists in the nature of each type of setting. These differences are to be encouraged so that unique local needs can be effectively served.

Historically, the problems of educational placement of children with retarded mental development centered on the advantages and disadvantages of putting these youngsters in special schools, special classes within regular schools, or in regular classes. The pros and cons of each type of assignment have been widely debated in the professional literature and most vociferously from the middle 1960s until the present. For example, advocates of regular class assignment have suggested that special classes unnecessarily isolate the retarded, stigmatize the child, encourage misplacement and dumping of children who need programs different from those the special class can deliver, and that these youngsters can make as much progress in regular classes as they can in special settings. Advocates of special class assignment cite research to document their arguments that the retarded in regular classes are rejected by their classmates, need a specially tailored program that reflects their unique educational characteristics, and that the provision of such special placement opportunities is completely congruent with a democratic philosophy of equal opportunity for all to learn. Advocates of special school placement emphasize that the efficiency with which special services can be delivered to children within such a comprehensive setting justifies this type of assignment on the basis of economics and cost-benefit criteria. They also argue that diagnostic-remedial efforts can best be organized and provided within a centralized school facility.

As you no doubt have gathered by this time, a basic belief of the philosophy expressed in this text is that the argument of regular or special class assignment alone is a waste of time. Not only is there tremendous diversity within each category of class (special or regular) that completely obviates the possibility of giving a responsible and informed answer to the question of which is the better placement setting, but the question misses the mark completely. The issue of central importance on the whole subject of placement is this: *Where within the existing resources of my school district can the individual educational plan required by each retarded child (based on valid and reliable data) best be provided at the present time?* An adequate answer to this question demands not only the documentation about the child and his environment that must be used as the basis for designing an appropriate educational program, but it mandates the clear specification of what can best be delivered in the various possible placement settings within a school or school district. The whole purpose behind appropriate placement is to match the child's educational needs and characteristics with the best available delivery system within the school.

To that end, the cascade system of special education services that Deno (1968, 1970) has conceptualized is basically compatible with the philosophy expressed in this book. Figure 5-1 presents the basic model of her system. Let us, then, briefly discuss some of the broad characteristics that pertain to each of the seven levels of this system.

Level I—Regular Class   Children with mildly retarded mental development have been and will continue to be assigned to regular class programs. There are several possible reasons for this. In certain instances a child may be able to perform the fundamental content competencies during the early school years in a minimally satisfactory way. The youngster could require and receive additional assistance on a periodic basis, such as medical, psychological, speech, or other forms of remedial attention. Another child may be assigned to a regular class program because nothing else exists for him within a reasonable distance in the school district. Still another youngster, who is usually unobtrusive in his behavior, is socially promoted through the grades until placement in any other setting in the latter school years would be unacceptable.

The regular class setting for mildly retarded children is typically no different than for other youngsters. Some minor adjustments may need to be made in instances where a physical disability accompanies intellectual problems—for example, a certain type of desk may be required, or extra space for a wheelchair. Any adjustments that occur in the course of study, instructional sequence, or methods of instruction within the regular class program are usually informal and individual insofar as a specific teacher is willing to diverge from the usual program so as to respond to the needs of a few children, such as the mentally retarded, who may be in her class.

In a number of school systems the problems engendered by having retarded children within the regular school program have become issues of substantial import during contract negotiations between teacher organizations and school systems. Many regular class teachers feel that they are not professionally and/or dispositionally prepared to deal effectively both with children who are adjudged to be mentally retarded as well as with large groups of "normal youngsters" within the same class, and insist that such children be placed in special education programs.

There is no question but that many retarded children can profit from experiences in regular classes. Two factors are unmistakable as indi-

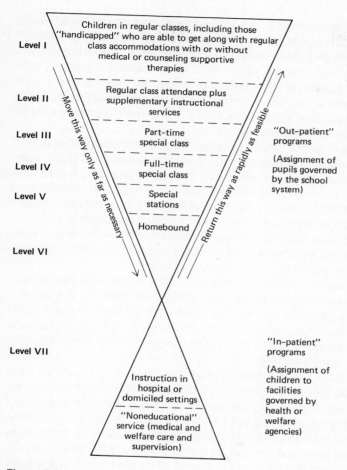

Figure 5-1
Deno's cascade of special education services. (From E. Deno,
"Special Education as Developmental Capital," *Exceptional
Children*, 37:229–237, 1972.) (Used with permission of author
and publisher.)

cators of the extent to which a regular class assignment can be
appropriate and facilitating. First, and of greatest importance, is the
attitude of the teacher. If the teacher views the mentally retarded as
being beyond help, feels that she is so untrained that her efforts will be

ineffective, or does not view her responsibilities as encompassing mentally retarded youngsters, one can guarantee that neither retarded nor normal children will profit from the experience of being together in the same class. In fact, her attitude will in large measure establish the direction and character of the social environment within the class-room—the degree of acceptance of the retarded, and the attitude of the retarded toward their normal brethren, are undeniably associated with the teacher's classroom demeanor.

The second factor is the extent to which the previous experiences of the children who are being integrated into the regular class have been successful. To be sure, this is related to the attitudes of previous teachers and the degree of retardation of each child. If a child has developed a distaste for the regular school program because of con-stant failure, further attempts at integration without concomitant adjust-ments in the curricular targets, methods, and materials will exacerbate the problems for all concerned—the child, his peers, the teachers, administrators, and parents.

The regular class for mentally retarded children should be recom-mended judiciously according to the child, his history within the school enterprise, the local setting, and the potential that such placement will have for helping him to develop the competencies specified by the educational plan without jeopardizing other equally crucial factors in his development.

It is important to realize that placement at any level in Deno's proposed cascade does not imply that the child will be there for an interminable period. Indeed, if the model is to operate with maximum effectiveness there must be complete latitude within the system for a child to be moved from one level to any other according to where his educational needs can best be met. In only very rare instances can you expect that every need will be met for the child by simply placing him in one or another setting. One must try to identify both where, within one type of setting, the goals of highest priority can be facilitated, and the type and extent of deleterious consequences that will inevitably occur in some form and degree as a result of such placement. The whole process involves negotiation, concession, and weighing the advantages against the disadvantages. Irrespective of the placement setting or the child in question, there will always be good and bad effects to be compared on a continuous basis.

Level II—Resource Room Program   With increasing frequency chil-dren who are mildly retarded are being maintained in a regular class setting but given regularly scheduled special-instructional programs for a portion of their school day. As is true of every other type of placement plan, the concept of the resource room varies widely. The usual model involves locating, within a regular school, an experienced and well-trained specialist in remedial instruction to whom individual children or small groups of youngsters can be referred. This specialist does not necessarily have to be a certified special education teacher. The important dimension is that the resource room teacher be able to evaluate the character of each youngster's educational problem and plan and deliver a proper program of management. For example, some schools use reading specialists as resource room teachers because of the preponderance of reading problems so often experienced among mildly retarded children during their early school years.

The resource room teacher, then, works with the children for at least one period each day on a consistent basis. The amount of time devoted to each youngster will vary according to the area being managed, its degree of severity, and the problems of the other children. All these factors influence the character of the resource room program in a given year—all of which may well change in subsequent years.

There is no debate regarding whether the resource room teacher should keep each child's regular teacher informed as to the individual program targets, methods, materials of management currently being used, and the progress of the student. Such open communication is of benefit to everyone. There is some difference of opinion among educators concerning how much broader a consulting role the resource room teacher should play within the school. As the resident specialist on how to deal with educational disorders, there is no question but that her advice would be widely sought. At the same time, however, it is readily acknowledged that her major responsibility is to those children with nagging, hard-core problems that defy change as a result of the program provided within the regular classroom. In an attempt to have the best of several possibilities, some school systems have employed more than one resource room specialist per school. This second person serves as a consultant in addition to being responsible for conducting detailed educational assessments of children who are experiencing problems.

The resource room placement option epitomizes individualization of instruction for children, including the mentally retarded. The basis for placement of a child and the character of the management procedures are both based solely on performance discrepancies and the needs of each youngster. Since the IQ score has little, if any, relevance in implementing the resource room concept, one might expect to find children from several "traditional categories of exceptionality" who are receiving similar modes of instruction aimed at identical targets. When a child achieves a satisfactory level, he simply moves out of the resource room to a different placement scene—or, if he stays within the resource room, the goals are altered with the expectation of higher performance levels.

Level III—Part-Time Special Class Certain retarded children have educational problems of such magnitude in terms of number, types, level of difficulty for remediating, and complexity, that placement in a special class is suggested. A number of these youngsters may function very effectively in a part-time special class program with the remaining portion of their day spent in a regular classroom and/or in some type of resource room setting.

There are several ways a part-time special education class can function. In large school systems there are often teachers who are specialists in one or several subject areas who can assume the major responsibility for working with children who require intensive programming in these areas—such as, for example, reading, writing, and speaking. Another teacher, perhaps in the same school, may have a part-time special class for children with prominent problems in certain nonverbal areas. The idea, then, is to provide a group of special classes on a part-time basis to children who have pronounced problems but who can otherwise function adequately elsewhere during the remainder of the school day. Moreover, these classes can be staffed so that each teacher is given responsibility in subject areas of greatest interest and strength.

Many school systems are not able to provide several part-time special classes within close enough proximity to each other to allow teachers to specialize in teaching responsibilities. This requires that one teacher provide special class instruction in all subject areas to children throughout the school day according to their individual instructional needs. Youngsters who are assigned to this type of placement move in and out of the special class during specified periods. A child may be assigned to the class for all aspects of language arts, which might consume half the school day. Another youngster may be assigned to the class for those periods during which the instruction is devoted to social and occupational issues, including, for example, an entire work-study sequence.

The part-time special class differs from a resource room in a number of ways. First, children who are candidates for the former usually have more severe, longer lasting, and more fundamental educational, and thus instructional, problems than do youngsters who receive resource room management. The special class, even a part-time one, typically emphasizes both developmental and remedial aspects of educational programming, whereas—usually—more attention is given to the latter in the resource room program. In addition, the part-time special class program must include continuity of content within that situation since many retarded youngsters will spend large chunks of their school lives within some form of special class setting.

As with the resource rooms within a given school area or district, the character of the part-time special classes will change from one year to the next according to (1) the types of educational problems exhibited by youngsters who can best be served by the part time special class program; (2) the total number of children who need special attention; (3) the experiences, characteristics, and interests of the teachers who are assigned to the program; and (4) the other types of placement possibilities available or feasible within a school district or area.

Level IV—Full-Time Special Class   Placement of a child in a special education class within a regular school building on a full-time basis may be desired under certain circumstances. When the youngster's performance is consistently poor across school areas, when his social and personal behaviors are sufficiently abnormal to detract from his own development in other areas or to hinder the progress of other youngsters, or when the community cannot provide other types of services, a full-time special class may be the best placement.

For obvious reasons, school personnel are hesitant to place any child, including those who are adjudged to be mentally retarded, in a special class on a full-time basis. There are serious possible consequences in such placement if it is done on an indiscriminant basis, if the reasons in no way relate to providing the optimum instructional environment for a child's educational needs, or if the child's regular teacher is confused about the proper course of action and forces the administration to relocate the youngster in a special education class. It is probably true that special classes do not usually provide as many opportunities for retarded students to interact with their non retarded peers as they would have if they were located elsewhere. This often results in the retarded special class child becoming less facile in the nuances of normal social and personal development. It also fosters a parochial character in an academic sense, thus making it more difficult for the child to learn how best to apply the solutions he has learned in class to the full range of practical problems he encounters within the open community. It is difficult enough for youngsters to face new, interesting experiences, but the problems become more pronounced when training is given in an environment that is totally different from the one in which the results of the training program are to be expressed.

While there are tremendous problems involved in cloistering children away from the main flow of the usual school program, a number of retarded children in every community are so handicapped educationally that they require a concentrated day-long special program. Whether a child is placed in a special class for the entire day will differ from community to community according to the available resources. The teacher in a special class of this variety must be a very well-trained professional, for she will be responsible for at least fifteen students, each of whom will exhibit significant developmental lags and difficult-to-remediate learning disorders. Moreover, the special education teacher must be a subject-matter specialist in all the prominent school areas that pertain to the education of these youngsters. In a part-time classroom there is more opportunity for the teacher to specialize, especially if there are several such classes within reasonable proximity of each other.

Let me emphasize one last point on the issue of special class placement. One must guard against becoming polarized against special class programming of all children in spite of the acknowledged potential negative consequences that frequently occur. With a teacher who is aware of these possible problems, but who is at the same time competent in delivering an instructional program that reflects the educational needs of the individual students, a full-time special class can exert a very positive force on a youngster's development. It depends a great deal on the teacher, the resources that are made available to her, the extent of congruence between each child's educational needs and how well they can be provided for within the setting, and the degree to which there is enough flexibility within the entire system to allow a child to be reassigned out of or into the full-time special class program whenever necessary.

Level V—Special Stations or Special Schools This level of the plan presented in Figure 4-1 conceptualizes the notion that fewer children than at any other level will need highly specialized services over long periods of time. There will be some children, however, and provision must be made for them.

A number of possibilities exists within the broad category of special stations and special schools. A child might be placed in a special program within a psychiatric treatment center, but he could still live at home. Another youngster might go to a rehabilitation center within the community in preparation for work in a sheltered workshop program later on. And still a third child might have such extreme multiple disorders that the best possible setting for him would be a special school in which a complete program of education and therapy is provided. In Pennsylvania, for example, some parents in certain communities have chosen not to commit their moderately or severely retarded children to public residential centers but have elected to keep them at home. Since schools have responsibility for providing an educational program for all children, wherever their location or whatever their level of retardation, some school districts have collaborated with neighboring units to provide broad services in, for example, a residence that is sufficiently centralized for all.

Usually children who can profit most from special stations or special school programs have relatively severe and varied problems. The kind of attention they need usually requires advice and management from a team of professional experts who represent various fields of study. You can see that this form of programming is expensive.

Level VI—Homebound Most school systems are legally bound to provide instruction for all children, including those who are so infirm that they must stay home. Certain teachers, then, visit the home of each child—whatever his disorder—and provide appropriate instruction. In many school systems a homebound teacher could be responsible for several elementary as well as for a number of older children during the same school year. This situation is often a very difficult one for the teacher because of the tremendous differences in the types of lessons she must prepare. As a means of bringing the homebound child closer to the actual classroom, schools have often provided a two-way telephone connection between the child's bed and the class. Although expensive, this type of provision for the seriously infirm child has been successful.

For states in which the law requires that school systems provide for all children, whatever their level of mental retardation, the need for homebound instruction has increased. Many profoundly retarded children are unable to attend school. The alternative most frequently selected for educating these youngsters is a homebound program. (As a side issue at this point, consider the tremendous change in teacher-training programs that this fairly new educational responsibility has precipitated. Most teacher-training institutions have in the past focused their efforts on preparing teachers to work with mildly retarded children; very little effort has been directed toward training educators to work with the severely affected youngsters.)

Level VII—"In-Patient" Programs Residential centers, institutions, hospitals, and halfway houses are all examples of settings which Deno has described as in-patient programs. Children who are assigned to any of these programs usually receive whatever instruction is available within their domicile. In many states the educational services provided come under the aegis of a division or department other than education, such as welfare, health, or rehabilitation. This situation is changing rapidly as a result of several court suits that were initiated by parent groups who felt that state departments of education should be responsible for providing instruction for all children, irrespective of their level of disability or their location. This has resulted in planned programs of intervention being developed for and provided to youngsters who are profoundly retarded and who have lived for long periods of their lives on the back wards of residential institutions.

deciding on assignment

Usually either the special education supervisor or an administrator makes the final decision regarding the assignment of children to an educational setting. These decisions are typically made on the basis of recommendations by school psychologists, remedial specialists, former teachers, local school administrators, or guidance counselors, and they very often may be involved in the final process of deciding where the child's needs can best be served. Less often parents or children themselves request some form of special education.

In past years, the IQ score was the primary basis on which a decision was made to place a youngster in a special class, institution, or regular classroom. The injudiciousness of using this measure as the sole criterion for placement has been discussed in preceding chapters and will not be elaborated upon here. What approach, then, is professionally sound and has promise for being more "on-target" with respect to delivering the best possible instructional program to every child?

Although implementation will differ among school systems, the questions that must be considered before placement decisions are finalized remain largely the same. First of all, there is no possible way one can make an intelligent decision about placement until two kinds of inventories have been completed, namely:

1 The school system must have collected reliable, valid, and relevant data on each mentally retarded child. From these data individual instructional needs must have been generated, including precise statements about objectives, a delineation of priorities among these targets, preferred instructional methodologies for each youngster, and a specification of which instructional materials or devices will predictably aid each child in achieving the objectives. This, then, provides an individual and collective survey of the educational needs represented among the children within a school, district, system, or within whatever administrative unit you have concern.

2 In addition, the school system must survey and analyze the placement settings that currently exist within the administrative unit and the major characteristics of each individual who is responsible for participating in the special education program. Concerning the existing placement situations, it is necessary to inventory many items—the kinds of each type of programming configuration (special class, resource room, special school, sheltered workshop, etc.) and the location of each within the administrative unit, the possible ways in which students can flow from one level to the next without losing continuity, community resources and problems, transportation issues, and the degree to which administrators and staff within each school are willing to accept and assist the special education program within their individual locale.

It is equally important for the administrator to carefully evaluate the characteristics of each professional on the staff in terms of their particular strengths. That is, one must continuously ask what each teacher can do best within each setting. Mrs. Blanche may be more skillful than others in dealing with severe language and reading problems within a resource room at the elementary school level. Another teacher may be particularly successful with a full-time special class setting because of the instructional advantages a setting of this sort provides in program sequencing and continuity. Someone else may be especially accomplished in working with severely retarded children who have significant multi-handicaps.

Every administrator who is responsible for special education should comprehensively take stock of his educational resources (both teachers and other assets) with respect to instructional needs (kinds and numbers of educational problems that require special attention). With these data the problem becomes one of matching each youngster's instructional requirements to a teacher who can best respond to that child's problems at that time. Obviously this is administratively idealistic, and as one adds criteria, conditions, or restrictions, the matching of the two dimensions becomes more difficult. The process is not an easy one, and, along with the question of whether a particular teacher and placement are best for a certain child, in arriving at a final decision one must consider problems such as:

1 If the youngster is placed in a specific situation are there any potential indigenous problems that might deleteriously affect his rate of learning and level of performance, such as a predisposition by the teacher that the child will fail or not be accepted by other youngsters, previous failure experiences within the same setting, a cosmetic disorder that could serve to alienate the child from others within the program, or a wide discrepancy between the child's age and that of other children in the class?

2 Are the logistics of transportation unmanageable?

3 Will the child be expected to endure any unreasonable adversity in order for the optimum program of instruction to be provided?

4 Are the instructional resources for the teacher at the various locations proper for the child's educational requirements?

5 To what extent are the parents in sympathy with the potential placement setting?

6 Are the exit criteria from the anticipated setting well established so that everyone will know when the prominent targets, which are part of the reason for the child's being placed in the setting, have been achieved?

7 Is the proper and necessary teacher supervision available at the setting?

8 Do the social dynamics among students in the setting seem conducive to fostering development in the child?

COORDINATION AMONG PLACEMENT OPTIONS

The need for clear, explicit organization of each placement setting at all levels of instruction within the total special education program is an absolute necessity and will in large measure dictate the quality of skills attained by the children. If the coordination among units is poor and haphazard, the student's performance will be further impaired. An outstanding teacher at any one level of the program will exert only minimal long-term influence on children if the total program lacks integration and proper articulation among all segments. This suggests that school personnel need to develop units of instruction and lines of responsibility for each aspect of the total program—from preschool through the postschool level. To place junior or senior high school children who have been socially promoted within a regular class program in a special education program without their having had previous opportunities to proceed through a sequenced instructional program will usually be unsuccessful. Even under the most desirable conditions, this type of school program will typically not assist the mentally retarded to meet and solve the problems of becoming independent within society on a conceptual level. This whole *modus operandi* is incompatible with the basic theme and philosophy of effective development and delivery of appropriate programs of instruction for the mentally retarded within the public schools. This goal will be met only after coordination and collaboration have occurred among all levels of the school program. The diagrams and discussion that follow will serve as a point of departure in our consideration of how such coordination might be enlisted and maintained.

In the preceding chapter the proposition was advanced that it is potentially more productive to view a curriculum from the viewpoint of the skills or competencies youngsters need to acquire rather than in terms of subjects, per se. Further, it was proposed that task analyses of major skill areas be made, that the skills emerging from these analyses be ordered from simple to more complex according to their degrees of dependence on each other, and that this sequenced array of targets become the essence of the curriculum for mentally retarded children. It was emphasized earlier that this approach is parsimonious, it provides the basis for diagnosing where, within the sequence of competencies, the child is having problems, and it allows every teacher to know precisely his or her instructional responsibilities and those of every other teacher in the program.

The delineation of competencies to be acquired in various fundamental areas by the children at each of the landmark periods in their total instructional program is the beginning stage in establishing a coordinated effort among the different components of a special education program. Figure 5-2 shows the usual relative emphasis given to the different skill areas during various periods in many special education programs for children with mild to moderate degrees of retardation. Let me elaborate on the segments of this diagram. But first, it is important to realize that it is hypothetical and in actual practice will vary according to the prognosis for individual children, the program that a school system can best deliver, the child's age and rate of skill development, and the types of placement settings that are available.

In this figure the notion is advanced that *each* of the five time periods (preschool, elementary, junior high, senior high, and postschool) has associated with it a unique set of skills or competencies in pertinent subject areas that the program personnel desire children at each of these respective levels to acquire. This means that the instructional program at each stage will be focused toward increasing the probability that children at the various stages will develop those skills. This figure probably most realistically depicts the emphasis given in special class programs. At the preschool and beginning elementary years, instruction is aimed at helping children acquire the whole range of skills usually labeled as "readiness." By the time the youngster has reached the middle elementary school years, it is suggested that emphasis be given to competencies involved in reading, language arts, arithmetic, and other tool subjects.

During the junior high school years the program continues to stress

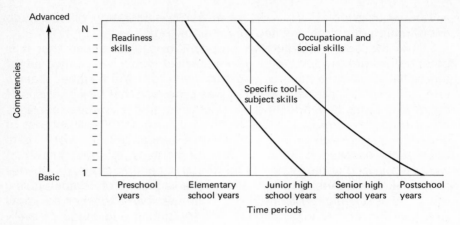

Figure 5-2
Relative curricular emphases within special class settings.

the development of specific tool-subject skills, and as the child proceeds through this period more attention is focused on the application of those skills involving occupational, social, and personal problems that he might expect to encounter in adulthood. The emphasis during the senior high school years is focused on arranging the adolescent's environment in a way that will maximize the possibility of his acquiring skills for daily living. A certain amount of attention is given to tool-subject skills in those instances in which youngsters either have not been exposed to certain developmental sequences in the past or might have acquired a serious learning disorder that special education personnel view as being so important for occupational and social self-sufficiency that remedial programming is needed.

Much as a sculptor begins by outlining the broad dimensions of a piece of art before making fine adjustments, so the proposition has been advanced that certain broad competencies should be focused upon during major instructional periods in a child's program. Figure 5-3 defines the same model as before, but in more detail, by breaking down the major time periods into smaller chunks. Within each proposed level, special education personnel would decide the specific group of competency areas to be focused upon. In this way, everyone would know what was to go on before, during, and after their individual periods of responsibility. Presumably, then, a child who is presently receiving instruction at Level B will have previously performed in an acceptable manner in those skills that are part of the program of instruction at Level

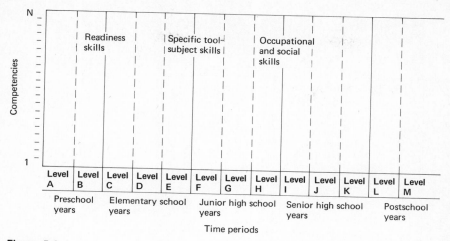

Figure 5-3
Relative curricular emphases within special class settings.

A. Moreover, before a child "graduated" to Level C we would assume that he had achieved the exit criteria required for those competencies in the Level B program. Continuity, therefore, is assured among the program units so that a child does not miss important stages in his educational experience. If a child or group of children lags in certain skill areas, one can ascertain at what point the program is faulty.

Up to this point the discussion and diagrams have centered on issues that pertain most obviously to special classes for the mentally retarded. How do the other placement settings that were discussed earlier relate to the concepts that have just been described? Let me try to suggest a possibility through a simplified and abridged version of the earlier figures.

Figure 5-4 shows how flexibility might be initiated among various units within the school program. For purposes of discussion only, the regular class and resource room possibilities have been identified with roman numeral I, special classes with a II, and special schools or stations and institution programs with a III. The notion suggested by the model is a simple one. The two-way arrows between the placement settings at I and the various levels at II indicate that a youngster can move among all these settings according to the location within which his educational program can best be served. If a student is able to move rapidly through a series of competencies within a level he should most certainly be given the opportunity to move into a setting in which the

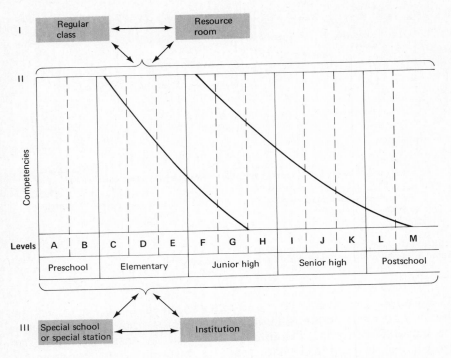

Figure 5-4
A schematic for possible coordination among regular and special education program units.

subsequent array of skills can be developed. At any time this may mean that placement in a regular class or resource room is recommended. Moreover, the preferred setting may differ according to the subject areas involved. This same perspective has pertinence to the interaction that should occur between units at II and III. Whenever the entrance or exit criteria are met by a child, movement to the next most-preferred setting should be promptly initiated.

You can see how important it is to have free lines of communication among teachers of the various instructional units. In addition, the various levels of administrators within the school system must maintain constant involvement and surveillance.

In-Service Training The procedures that have been suggested to coordinate efforts among all aspects of the school program may seem complicated and overly idealistic. There is no question but that someone must assume responsibility for coordinating the entire program.

Usually this becomes the duty of a special education supervisor, director, or coordinator. Urban and suburban school districts have traditionally had a position of this type within the central administration. In rural areas a special education director has not been customary; however, there is a definite movement toward a unification among districts in scattered areas into what is often called intermediate units, or cooperatives among districts. The districts within an intermediate unit together support a director and other staff personnel so that a coordinated program of educational services can be provided to all handicapped children within the unit.

Two factors will help to enhance the effectiveness of the total special education program—including those components that pertain most specifically to children with retarded mental development. First, open channels of communication must be guaranteed among all components of the network at every level. As soon as little factions of opinion or segmented practices develop which are outside the perimeter of the overall thrust of the program, all types of problems will ensue. Numerous opportunities must be provided for all teachers, supervisors, administrators, and parents to discuss any issues that pertain to the program. This can be done through reports, newsletters, open correspondence, and, above all, through frequent face-to-face visits.

The second factor that can have a definite positive influence on the program and its personnel is intelligently planned and executed in-service training programs. The rapid advancement of research and training with the mentally retarded has not made it possible for teachers to keep up with innovations and trends in the field. The time devoted to the day-to-day planning and activities within the special education program does not leave the teacher with much time for attending professional meetings, reading journals, or registering for extension courses. To remedy this situation, school systems must provide special education teachers with a chance to become familiar with new practices and procedures that may be of value to them. In-service training programs and workshops provide an excellent opportunity for new ideas to be discussed and tested. Teachers will benefit most from those in-service programs that are devoted to a translation and interpretation of results from those studies in psychology and education that have direct implications for education of the mentally retarded. To implement this procedure, school systems might give some thought to including educational psychologists on their staffs. These specialists would have the responsibility for interpreting research for teachers and translating findings into practical classroom application. Academicians have not traditionally provided this necessary service. The lag that exists between evidence and practice in programs for the retarded makes all the more imperative the need for including a professional such as an educational psychologist on every school staff.

In-service training programs should reflect a pragmatic view of education. Meetings that are of value to teachers in special education settings are usually those that: (1) focus on how best to deal with practical problems in the classroom; (2) reflect a consistent general philosophy that allows teachers to generalize the content of the workshop or institute beyond the immediate setting, situation, or example; (3) are on an extended and coordinated basis rather than a "one-shot" presentation; (4) contain ample illustrations and examples; (5) are not totally lecture-oriented but include demonstrations; (6) have been well planned and for which teachers are paid either financially or through college credit; and (7) include various types of integrated presentations by district teachers and personnel as well as college professors.

Itinerant Specialists Finally, the need for itinerant specialists, especially in rural communities where many teachers often lack formal training and experience in how to provide a good educational program for the mentally retarded, is particularly acute. Large urban centers have such specialists readily available and, in addition, often have consultants in specific subject areas such as reading, arithmetic, counseling, and technical and vocational education. Rural communities are usually not so fortunate. Mobile units offer the most reasonable approach for providing such services to teachers in these communities. This technique has proved successful in several sections of the country in which special diagnostic and remedial services are needed by children, such as the mentally retarded, who have unique learning problems.

Each mobile unit would have a schedule for traveling to various sections of a county or a state. All equipment and personnel required for offering these services would travel with the unit and provide comprehensive diagnostic and remedial consulting services to the appropriate school personnel. The coordination of this effort should emanate from the state or county department of public instruction and have the cooperation and collaboration of other state and county agencies. Plenty of time must be provided at each stop to answer questions of teachers, administrators, and parents concerning the children who have been examined by members of the unit. Systematic records should be kept by the unit secretary and specific recommendations reported back to principals of the schools visited. Periodic reevaluation of each child should be required in order for the system to operate effectively.

COORDINATION WITHIN CLASSROOM UNITS
Because retarded children tend to progress slowly and to advance in smaller increments than their intellectually normal peers, teachers in turn tend to be less diligent in organizing program sequences during the various time periods—of a year, a month, a week, or a day—as well as within each specific instructional encounter. Although it may not seem worthy of top priority attention, unless the sequence of instructional steps is given careful attention, one can expect the entire program (and especially the teacher's behavior) to become inefficient and ineffective. This situation, of course, results in the children not achieving appropriate goals, and, therefore, being maintained in special education classes without having an opportunity to be moved into one of the other possible placement options. To a very definite and obvious degree, the results from tests of children who are in special education programs depend more on what the teacher does within her classroom than on any other single factor. This is as true for regular as it is for special education teachers. Let us, then, consider some ways in which a teacher can organize her program to make it more efficient and to increase student performance in a desired direction.

Organizing the Day   One of the first issues with which a teacher of the mentally retarded must deal is how best to map out the daily activities. Every teacher wants to be "a hit" with students, and this is certainly a laudable ambition. However, one of the problems that many teachers experience is a gradual "running down" of the children's interest and performance as the day's activities progress. David Premack has suggested a very logical procedure that teachers might adopt to maintain student interest and motivation. He suggests that the major activities during the day be arranged so that the things that a child or a group of children enjoy doing most are always preceded by activities that are less desirable. Moreover, for a child to participate in the high-preference activity he must have demonstrated a preset level of accomplishment in the previous low-priority task. If a youngster enjoys art but dislikes spelling, see to it that he does whatever spelling work you believe to be proper and fair before he has the privilege of going on to art. Beginning the day with "The Good Morning Club" or "Show and Tell" may not be sequentially appropriate until the children individually, or even collectively, have met a prespecified level of performance in a less-preferred area. Make certain, however, that you do not define success in the same terms for each child. One child who has problems in attending to reading stimuli, for example, may have license to share in "Show and Tell" if he attends to a given stimulus for a given time. Another youngster, at a more advanced level, may be required to

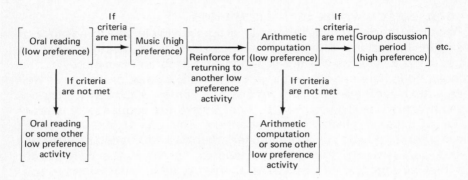

Figure 5-5
The Premack concept illustrated.

read a passage with fewer errors than he did on the previous day in order to have the same opportunity as the first child.

The Premack principle is nothing more than arranging the day or week so that low-preference tasks precede high-preference tasks such as are described in the hypothetical case that appears in Figure 5-5.

In an earlier section the suggestion was advanced that a great deal of progress toward the establishment of an effective special education program could be made by describing the skills embodied in each major content area, listing them in a general way by competency areas according to the major time periods or levels in the total program. A teacher at any one level, then, knows her responsibility and instructional focus as well as those of every other teacher in the program. It is the responsibility of each to provide an instructional environment in her room so that skill area targets are achieved quickly and with stability. These skill areas direct the thrust of the program for each teacher and are the basis on which units of instruction are developed and presented.

The concept of specifying and sequencing objectives and targets, so that everyone in the program knows his mission, has applicability to directing the teacher's behavior within the classroom. In the preceding chapter mention was made of the value of using series of objectives such as those developed by the Instructional Objectives Exchange. But how can all this be implemented on a daily basis and still have the teacher maintain the desire to truly individualize instruction? Let me describe how one teacher successfully did just that.

Mrs. Sara Forsberg, at The Pennsylvania State University Demonstration School, is responsible for a class of children who are adjudged to

Examples of Abbreviated Checksheets in Three Subject Areas*

Specific arithmetic skills

	Term 1		Term 2		Term 3	
	Date	Rate	Date	Rate	Date	Rate
1. Counts to 100						
2. Names numbers 1–10						
3. Writes numbers 1–10						
4. Says (recognizes) number groups 1–100						
5. Adds simple combinations up to 10						
6. Adds simple combinations over 10						
7. Simple column addition						
8. Adds 2 digit numbers—no carrying						
9. Adds 2–5 digit numbers—no carrying						
10. Adds 2 digit numbers with carrying						

Specific reading skills

	Term 1		Term 2		Term 3	
	Date	Rate	Date	Rate	Date	Rate
1. Says letter names						
2. Writes alphabet						
3. Says consonant sounds (list all and check each)						
4. Says blends (list all and check each)						
5. Says short vowels (list all and check each)						
6. Says long vowels (list all and check each)						
7. Reads phonically true words from reading program						
8. Reads sight words (Dolch Basic Sight Vocabulary)						

Specific spelling skills

	Term 1		Term 2		Term 3	
	Date	Rate	Date	Rate	Date	Rate
1. Identify (circle) beginning and ending letters in words						
2. Spell (identifying when heard and writing when heard) b, h, m, t (beginning and final position)						
3. Spell sh, ch, th, wh						
4. Spell words with blends at end						
5. Discriminate among 5 short vowel sounds (a, e, i, o, u)						
6. Change words to plural by adding s						
7. Spell two-syllable words						
8. Spell words with ay						

Figure 5-6
Examples of abbreviated checksheets in three subject areas.

be mentally retarded. In coordination with teachers of children at other levels in the program Mrs. Forsberg decided upon a group of targets to which instructional attention is directed. To aid in maintaining proper focus and in staying current on each child's progress in every subject area, she designed checksheets of the prominent skills involved in major subject areas. Each youngster has a checklist in his cumulative folder for all of the relevant areas, and Mrs. Forsberg records the date and rate of performances of each child in a given skill area. Figure 5-6 illustrates abbreviated versions of checklists in three subject areas.

For a child to receive a check in a skill area, the teacher maintains another kind of performance record on a planned (daily, if at all possible) basis. The procedure is as follows:

1 Every day each child in Mrs. Forsberg's class is given a folder in which the teacher has specified what is to be worked on during a given period. For example, in arithmetic the folder for a certain child might contain a series of two-digit addition problems that she has decided are compatible with the youngster's arithmetic targets at that time. The spelling, writing, and reading folders also contain individual activities and directions according to the instructional needs of each student.
2 The children are then expected to begin the work in their folders, and Mrs. Forsberg supervises, instructs, and reinforces appropriate on-target behavior.
3 After a certain time, or as each assignment is completed, Mrs. Forsberg quickly records on a piece of graph paper attached to each child's folder the progress he has made. She tabulates performance along a variety of possible dimensions. The number of problems done, words spelled correctly, or pages read might be used as the dimension of concern.

One could also record percent of errors per number completed—or rate of completion could be used as an indicator of progress. Figure 5-7 is an example of how one can quickly and simply record performance data.

In this instance Mrs. Forsberg decided to move to the next arithmetic skill in the sequence after Herbert had demonstrated a leveling-off of performance in his current skill area for seven successive days. At that time she simply recorded the date and rate next to item 8 on the checksheet of arithmetic skills (Figure 5-6) for which she has instructional responsibility.

In this quick and accurate way Mrs. Forsberg is able to maintain a consistent and up-to-date record of how each child is progressing in

Name: Herbert Acalculia
Target: Two digit addition without carrying

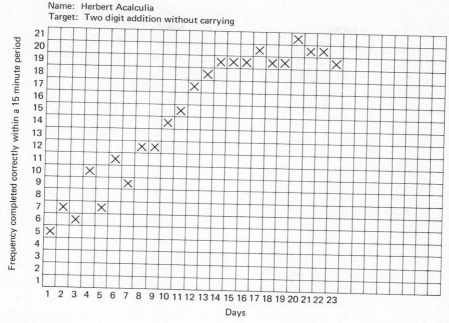

Figure 5-7
Example of charting daily performance data.

those areas for which she has a duty. The data are precise, they can be easily observed, and they communicate a lot of meaning to other teachers, to parents, and to administrators concerning each child's progress. Moreover, this kind of information helps the teacher by demonstrating how well the instructional program is going. If children are leveling off at too low a level, in her opinion, or are making a large number of errors, or demonstrate a poor rate of skill acquisition, the instructional procedures being used need to be reevaluated. In short, there is a "teaching disability" present in the classroom and not a "learning disability." And finally, this procedure is a truly individualized program in which each youngster works on his most appropriate goal with activities that are most pertinent to him and with a record system that avoids unnecessary labeling or suggestions of performance inadequacies that are caused by unverified etiologies. Here it is what he does or does not do and how he goes about dealing with the stimuli on which the teacher focuses attention that are of importance.

Grouping One of the most time-honored means for individualizing instruction has been to separate a class into smaller units which within themselves are relatively homogeneous in one or more characteristics. Level of achievement has been the criterion most often used for selecting groups. The children's performance is related to that of their fellow students in any of a number of possible subject areas. Because of the wide variation that typically exists within and between children, stability of the class groups between subject-matter areas rarely occurs. For example, a child might be in the top group in arithmetic but in a much lower group in reading. Other criteria are used only infrequently in determining groups; however, when used, chronological age and interest level are typically chosen.

From the perspective of clinical teaching, using achievement level as the sole criterion for grouping children is insufficient. It was suggested earlier that two or more children achieving at the same level and having the same chronological age and "intellectual ability" could be experiencing difficulty in a certain area, such as reading, for completely different reasons. To illustrate, one child could be underachieving in reading because of visualization difficulties; another child at the same level could be underachieving because of auditory difficulties. If the criterion of achievement alone is used for grouping these children, they would probably be placed in the same reading group. A more complete evaluation would lead to the conclusion that the most appropriate teaching strategy for these students should in no way be similar. In fact, the evidence suggests that one child should have a phonics emphasis and the other a look-and-say–oriented program.

Any scheme for grouping should consider the methods or techniques that children use to learn. Each of us tends to have our preferred strategy. The intellectually normal are usually equally adept in using various modes for learning, irrespective of the particular technique preferred by the teacher. Mentally retarded children are more inclined to prefer nonverbal strategies and the visual channel for learning instead of a more verbal or auditory approach. As children develop these preferences and styles, the teacher should know of the patterns and group students accordingly. Placing an auditorially oriented child in a group in which the reading program is visually oriented will result in a reduction in the level of performance of the child as well as in increased confusion for the entire group. In grouping, therefore, each child's achievement profile and the manner of presentation that will work best for him should be considered. Using this combination approach in grouping will realistically individualize instruction on those dimensions most crucial to efficient learning. Imprecise criteria for grouping, such as gross levels of achievement, could be more damaging than no grouping at all, should a child be placed with other students who are taught and learn best with an approach that is incompatible with his own style.

Instructional groups in classes for the mentally retarded should usually not include more than two or three children. Also, teaching will be less efficient when more than three groups are used in a subject area. Some heterogeneity will certainly exist within groups; however, this is preferable to the logical alternative of increasing the number of groups. The teacher must recognize that grouping should be very flexible in terms of the length of time each one is to be maintained. A group should be used only until its intended purpose is satisfied. Indeed, its makeup may change quite frequently, depending on the degree to which instruction results in the remediation of weaknesses of the individual group members. A clear rationale should be developed for forming an instructional group; as these reasons are satisfied the groups should be dissolved or altered accordingly.

There is an obvious instructional advantage in grouping children, but this advantage will be lost if the criteria used for determining the group's constituents are viewed as unimportant or are vague. Grouping is employed so that children with similar problems can be exposed to the most appropriate subject-specific method possible based on their unique characteristics and not solely on a broad-based achievement score.

Using Psychological Reports   The observation, evaluation, and analysis of a retarded child's behaviors by a school psychologist who is oriented toward and experienced in dealing with the instructional problems of children can be a real asset to the teacher. Such a person, skilled in identifying educationally relevant attributes and weaknesses in retarded youngsters, can be of immeasurable aid to teachers in helping to specify proper individual targets, preferred methodologies, materials compatible with goals and methods, procedures of maintaining data on individual children, and in helping to decide on placement options and in validating the observations of teachers concerning especially troublesome instructional problems. Whether this type of service can be provided depends on (1) the training and experience of the school psychologist and his awareness of important diagnostic clues, (2) the ability of the school psychologist to translate diagnostic findings into practical educational considerations, (3) the time available to the psychologist for administering the necessary evaluative procedures appropriate to each situation, and (4) the opportunity the psychologist has to consistently reevaluate each child or to train teachers to do so.

For many reasons, this optimum situation is more the exception than the rule; school systems are often unable to afford or to locate competent psychologists who are skilled educational diagnosticians. The most frequent alternative is for the schools to hire someone with limited experience to test large groups of children in order to satisfy state or local regulations concerning the placement of retarded children in special classes. All that is legally required in many locations is that the children be individually tested and, if found to meet the stated criteria, placed in a special classroom. Fortunately, the tide is changing, and school psychologists are suggesting placement options other than special classes, according to where within the placement possibilities in a given school system a child's instructional needs can best be served.

What position should a teacher take concerning information that appears in a child's folder, including reports by the school psychologist, psychometrician, or diagnostician? The problem is to identify and properly use the data that have educational meaning to the teacher. Data, that is, that can clearly characterize the child's performance characteristics and lead to an appropriate instructional program. Which data within a protocol are relevant and which should be ignored have and will continue to be an area for spirited debate among educators and psychologists. Guidelines for teachers on this issue will differ; however, the following are presented as reflecting the general beliefs and philosophy of this text concerning how best to provide retarded children and appropriate educational experience.

1 Focus your attention on achievement or performance data that have been collected with instruments or procedures that were originally designed for that purpose. Whenever achievement scores are reported, look for other evidence in the folder to confirm those data. Do not accept at face value a single score and assume that it reflects the true status of a child or of his performance.
2 Refrain from prejudging a child on the basis of an IQ score, an etiological classification, a symptom that has not been observed or adequately evaluated, and interpretations that stem from unverifiable sources that have not or cannot be directly observed.
3 Treat every statement about a child as a hypothesis that requires validation by you or by a competent examiner.
4 Pay special attention to data that have been collected continuously over a relatively long period and which have been focused on very specific subject-area goals or objectives. Look for information about rate of achievement along with performance-level data.

5 Be cautious not to make too much of information, observations, or assessments on a child when his performance has been compared with that of a population of which he is not a representative.

6 Look for precise, specific statements about educational priorities needed by the youngster. A good psychological report should cut through the usual maze of irrelevant words and focus on those targets, methods, and materials that are proper for the child. Vague statements about where a child should be placed without describing what kind of program he needs are worthless to teachers.

7 Be aware of the possible multiple interpretations that could result from use of the vague words that are so often used in reports to describe children. Another examiner or teacher may give an entirely different interpretation of the child's alleged problem than did the author of the psychological report.

8 Compare observations that have been expressed by different observers—especially when they have focused on the same dimension of the child's behavior.

9 Consider as important any information in a child's records that tells the teacher alternative procedures to try in case the primary suggestions appear not to work. A particularly helpful psychological report will include information about what kind of performance the teacher can look for in the youngster as an indication that the suggested procedures are indeed working. These types of performance criteria are extremely helpful as general guides for determining when to shift to an alternate goal, method, or material.

10 A report on a child that is helpful and practical is one that is as brief as possible, has few technical words (with understandable definitions for those terms that must be used), describes the basis on which interpretations and recommendations are offered, provides a map of the general direction in which the child's program of instruction might best proceed, and is more heavily oriented toward recommended management procedures than toward areas such as complex and lengthy testing information or presumed etiology.

Maintaining Records   To establish continuity between classes, and to allow for day-to-day and week-by-week checks on each child's progress, special education personnel must develop standard procedures for maintaining records. Earlier in this chapter the suggestion was made that records have particular meaning when teachers chart performance on a daily basis (see Figure 5-7) and then summarize each child's achievement in performance areas on a subject-area checksheet as each individual goal is achieved at an acceptable level. Obviously, this system requires that you clearly specify the essential components of a subject area.

Systematizing procedures for record keeping helps teachers to know where emphasis should be placed in teaching each child. Moreover, it gives a clear indication of the scope and sequence of instruction in each classroom and in the total special program. As children move through various phases of the program, consistent and periodic checks should be made to determine their progress. This is of particular value because of the integration it effects between levels. Further, it is of diagnostic value because it provides a basis for supplementing and revising the program structure according to those data collected on the special education students.

Although many teachers are tempted to collect a great deal of historical information and anecdotal description on a child, this orientation is often unnecessary if the individual skill analyses and charting of performance are initiated on a consistent and comprehensive basis. Second, and of less relative significance, teachers simply do not have time to maintain copious notes on individual children so as to obtain a representative sample of the child's usual behavior. Since our attention is usually drawn to negative behaviors of a youngster, anecdotal records typically contain lengthy descriptions of a child's wrongdoings and less about more positive behaviors. This unintentional bias may leave the uninformed reader with the impression that the youngster spends most of his time on off-target activities. The simple solution to this problem is to emphasize objective information gained through informal procedures within the classroom, and to supplement these data with periodic formal evaluations of performance.

Grading Procedures Procedures for grading the mentally retarded have been and still are of general concern to parents, children, teachers, and administrators. The major problem is whether the child should be graded in the same manner as other youngsters in the public schools. The retarded students and their parents are usually inclined to favor a grading system similar to that used in the regular classrooms. On the students' part, this position is taken because of their frequent association with normal children. Other possible reasons for parents' holding this belief are their greater familiarity with standard grading procedures, their wish to make comparisons with other children in the same school program, and their frequent feeling that perhaps an error in placement has been made by the schools.

Using the typical grading system is attractive to administrators because it reduces for them the possibility of being placed in a position of recommending that the mentally retarded children receive the same type of diploma as other students. Teachers of the retarded often find themselves caught between the intense opinion of the parents, children, and school administration on one hand and, on the other, the knowledge of the relative meaninglessness of grading the retarded students in the same way as the normal. Further complicating the picture is the decision that special education teachers must make as to whether a child should be graded in terms of progress made or in comparison with other class members. The research is unclear on these matters, and, therefore, the schools must base their decision about grading on a logical and commonsense basis.

In deciding on a grading procedure for special education students the key question to be answered is, "What information will be most beneficial to the youngster's parents and how can I best convey this to them?" Among the factors that must be considered in making a decision on this matter are: (1) the age of the child and his level of performance; (2) the types of placement situations he has experienced during the previous grading period; (3) the level of education, sophistication, and experience of the parents; (4) the extent to which they need to have or can deal with a detailed picture of their child's performance; and (5) the easiest manner available for delivering maximum information to parents about their child's achievement and his teacher's goals, but at a minimum cost of teacher time and effort.

Usually, using traditional grading procedures with mentally retarded children results in confusing the child's parents. They do not understand the basis on which the grades were given and the criteria against which their youngster was evaluated. They are uncertain about the real meaning of the grades because of the lack of specificity characteristic of the procedure. For many mentally retarded children, then, the typical approach to grading and reporting to parents is imprecise and confusing.

Because of this confusion, and in an effort to communicate clearly with parents, writing letters about the child's performance and progress is often the most effective way to make an evaluation meaningful. The content of these letters should summarize the teacher's observations as recorded on the daily or weekly checklists. This method allows teachers to point out specifically those areas in which each child is weak and strong. Moreover, it gives some indication of the direction the educational program will take in subsequent periods.

Do not overlook the educational level of the parents and/or the amount of information you believe they can handle. Always be sure that your letter says something positive about the child's *progress* as well as mentioning the tasks on which he needs further attention. Map out in some detail your major targets for the youngster during the next reporting period and tell how you propose to aid him in achieving them. It is also important to most parents to know specifically how they can become an active part in the management program which you, as the child's teacher, have decided upon. All these areas should be discussed in the letter. For some parents it should be detailed and in depth, for others it is necessary to proceed with caution and in much smaller steps.

The teacher will want to meet with the parents frequently to get their observations of their child's progress. This information will aid in the formulation of the classroom program. The youngsters should also be informed of their own progress in school. The older children can be interviewed by the teacher, and, in some cases, the parents might be present.

Using Other Available Services Because of the many associated problems characteristic of the mentally retarded, the teacher will need to call on specialists from other fields for evaluation and consultation. The schools will not be able to provide the comprehensive array of special services required, and, therefore, arrangements should be made to use private and community services whenever necessary.

Many of the mentally retarded require medical and paramedical services. The incidence of other types of handicaps is high among this group. Since some of their problems may be of a medical nature, the teacher should consult with each child's physician to be aware of and know how to handle all possible contingencies, unless the parents have discussed the problems in enough detail. Children from deprived settings often need to be referred to clinics, since their parents are usually not able to handle their medical needs.

Speech, social work, psychiatric, family counseling, and community mental health services may be needed by the retarded. As specialists on their educational problems, teachers should insist that all necessary ancillary services be provided for the retarded and their families. The school administration should be kept informed of the needs of each child; the teacher is responsible for making recommendations to the administration whenever appropriate. If the recommendations are not considered promptly, it may be up to the teacher to see to it that the needed services are provided for those in particular need.

Classroom Experimentation Advancement of knowledge within a profession is based in a large measure on the insights and observations of those directly involved in the work. For example, in repairing certain types of birth deformities, such as a cleft palate, plastic surgeons have contributed to an increase in scientific awareness of possible repair techniques that affect both the functional and cosmetic areas. Although most surgeons are aware of these technical advances, variations still exist in the final excellence of repairs. Many professionals believe that technical knowledge must be combined with artistic sensitivity to effect an optimum performance in any area in which human change is involved. This analogy holds true in teaching the mentally retarded. Libraries are filled with reports of studies outlining the learning characteristics of these children. Each study has some bearing on teaching and learning; however, effective learning can occur only after the material has been translated into classroom activity. The point is that a new technique is not necessarily accepted just because its value has been shown.

By virtue of having to deal with the practical problems of instructing mentally retarded children, the teacher is in an excellent position to test—through informal experimentation—any techniques or procedures that seem to have potential merit. Many of the best leads for tightly controlled investigations come from the experiences of classroom teachers. The special educator's laboratory is the classroom, and, although the academicians have an important contribution to make in research, the teacher's awareness of classroom practicalities is of great value. Schools should encourage special education teachers to conduct small pilot studies. For example, teachers could be of great service to the field by experimenting with and evaluating new techniques and media. Then, as they become more familiar with the capabilities of their children and the scope of the material to be covered, they can feel more free to develop and evaluate innovative practices.

6

PERCEPTUAL-MOTOR PERFORMANCE

Irrespective of the area of performance, if a child is to learn how to behave in an appropriate manner following the presentation of a stimulus, then the mechanism that is responsible for information gathering must operate effectively. Obviously, this is not the only factor that dictates how well a youngster performs in skill areas. For example, it was pointed out in an earlier chapter that appropriate reinforcement is a powerful influence in building a child's repertoire of responses. This chapter will focus on problems of performance that are most frequently characterized as "perceptual-motor." In spite of very active programs of research, theorizing, and writing in this field, there still remain vast areas of inconclusiveness, speculation, and uncertainty surrounding perceptual-motor development, the types of skills that are properly subsumed under this rubric, procedures for evaluating these postulated areas of competence, and the actual importance that perceptual-motor development has in the child's subsequent cognitive development. The relative newcomer to the field of special education may not immediately become aware of these areas of debate because of the enormous number of instructional devices that are available to teachers for remediating alleged disorders of this type. Unfortunately, most of these materials and devices have not been empirically validated, nor, in most cases, have they been associated with a systematic theory of development.

Because many of the traditional notions about the broad area of perceptual-motor development have not been adequately tested for scientific validity, we must be cautious not to automatically accept the propositions that frequently appear in the literature. The major reason for this uncertainty about the entire array of dimensions related to perceptual-motor areas is that so many of the factors are hypothetical and/or internal and cannot be readily observed. Body image, perceptual confusion, perceptual disintegration, associational problems, and perceptual matching are central concepts to many theories of perceptual-motor performance; however, each of these hypothesized entities defies direct observation. At this time, therefore, we are dealing with assumptions, postulates, and hypotheses about the presence of these phenomena, the interrelationship that is adjudged to exist among the various components, the impact that each dimension has on further development and appropriate assessment procedures. Do not be frightened away from study in this field because of this rather strong cautionary note. Just be prudent and carefully evaluate all different points of view, and continue to look for careful documentation from those who are ardent purveyors of perceptual-motor training programs.

presumed sequence of perceptual-motor development

Most authorities agree that the process by which perceptual-motor skills develop is complex. As a rule you can count on the number of theories that have been advanced to explain a phenomenon to be directly related to its complexity—i.e., the more complex the phenomenon, the more points of view there are. This is certainly true with perceptual-motor performance. It is very difficult to precisely identify the components of this process since they are not discrete. In fact, in many ways they build on each other in an interdependent way. In a very general sense, however, most authorities agree that there are four major components of the process: input, association or integration, output, and feedback. More elegant theories attempt to make much finer distinctions. Let us consider a series of propositions concerning these components from one theoretical stance, a point of view that is basically internal and hypothetical.

The receptive element of the perceptual process consists of the extraction of information from the environment by the sense organs and the translation of these perceptions into a message system appropriate for the cortex. A certain level of arousal is necessary for the perceptions to be received. The brainstem reticular formation has the function of awakening the higher centers so that information can be processed. If the organism is lethargic or is damaged to the point that arousal is not possible, information will not be received or processed. Similarly, if the organism is too highly aroused and the extreme activating effect of the brainstem reticular formation is not inhibited by those sections of the cortex responsible for this function, behavior, according to this point of view, will be hyperactive, resulting in inattentiveness, and inappropriate perceptions will be received. Therefore, either too low or too high a level of arousal will impede the accurate reception of information from the environment.

The receptive component of the perceptual process normally develops in early infancy and operates at a meaningful level before a commensurate degree of skill is manifested in areas of association and expression. The meaning of commands and admonitions is usually understood first; the integration of concepts occurs more slowly and must often be intentionally taught. As the organism gains skill in and satisfaction from the reception of stimuli, incidental learning begins to play a greater role in learning. With mentally retarded children, who often have difficulty extracting relevant stimuli from their environment or who are exposed to a restricted range of stimuli, learning cannot be left to chance and must be more intentional than incidental.

Perceptions must be received before association and integration can occur; there must be something to program into the repertoire. The integrity of the receptive components of the perceptual process is fundamental to the development of associational networks. Moreover, to inhibit the development of random patterns of association, stable and relevant stimuli must be presented in the early stages of learning. If a child receives different perceptions each time the same event is experienced, integration among the perceptions will not be facilitated and associational bonds, in a Hebbian sense, will be unstable.

Early learning should be structured so that new information is directly associated with existing, stable associational networks. It is usually necessary to call the attention of the mentally retarded to relationships between new and old learning so that bonds between perceptions can be more easily and accurately formed. There is some advantage in the organism being exposed to stimuli from all the sense modalities, as this results in associations that develop more quickly and allows for the increased probability of appropriate responses given to various stimuli. Such intersensory association suggests the need to combine auditory, visual, and tactile procedures into activities involving new learning.

The development of association skills follows closely the establishment of and growth in receptive perceptual capabilities. Infants quickly learn that the bottle means food and that this, in turn, results in comfort. Visual, auditory, and intra-individual stimuli associate rapidly; and in homes in which a routine has been established, the infant develops stable associational networks quickly. These networks provide anchoring points to which subsequent verbal and nonverbal learning can be related and subsumed. For example, if a child associates milk in a glass with the quenching of thirst and general comfort, at an early age the parents can introduce the vocal expression "milk." This allows the child to relate the appropriate label to the proper, well-established associational pattern. The introduction of additional perceptions to an established network can be done by using this same strategy.

The expression, or output, phase of the perceptual process, according to this point of view, occurs after the organism perceives that some type of response is appropriate or necessary in a situation. The organism must scan the repertoire for those responses that are correct for each situation and then assess each possible alternative for the most appropriate answer at that time. A response is made after the repertoire has been surveyed. Individuals vary substantially in their ability to perform this operation.

A response can be made by word, gesture, or both, in combination. Meaningfulness expressed vocally does not typically occur until a child reaches approximately eighteen to twenty-four months of age. Gestures and other nonverbal expressions are the primary means of communication before that time. A great deal of earlier development must occur before a child reaches the stage of vocal expression of ideas.

Initial responses by the child are motoric. Patterns of output are developed, systematized, and elaborated upon according to the perceptions the child receives from the environment. These motor patterns gradually become strengthened and generalized to more elaborate responses. For example, sitting leads to many types of locomotion, such as crawling, walking, running, skipping, and jumping.

It is critical that the perceptual process contain an effective system for monitoring the appropriateness of the output in order to be in harmony with the problem and with other information received from the environment. Apparently, some aspects of the output are internally fed back to the receptive components of the system. This monitoring results in any necessary modifications within the system and leads to greater discrimination, selectivity, and differentiation in the reception of subsequent stimuli. Other adjustments are often effected in the associational process as well as in subsequent output.

An important goal of special education is to help the mentally retarded to develop an internal monitoring system. These children often have difficulty in using their output to adjust the various components of this hypothesized perceptual process. When this is so, their attention should be called to the degree of consonance between their responses and the problem at the beginning stages of instruction. At first the teacher may need to act as the child's monitor, until sensitivity to and skill in using feedback are developed. Gallagher (1960) suggests tutors for those children who exhibit monitoring problems so that proper remediation can be given to this specific area of disability.

Children with specific or general difficulty in one or more of the components of the perceptual process presumably exhibit a reduction in effective learning. The causes of these difficulties might be traced to (1) the erroneous or random reception of stimuli including the misunderstanding of a problem or situation, (2) the introduction of irrelevant perceptions into associational networks, (3) the obliteration of existing networks because information has been programmed that is antagonistic to established associational chains, (4) too little or too much arousal in the higher centers, (5) an ineffective mechanism for surveying the cognitive structure to locate appropriate responses related to a situation, (6) improper response patterns, and/or (7) an inadequate mechanism for monitoring output and providing internal feedback.

Learning will not occur effectively if children have difficulty in receiving information, perceiving differences between figure and ground, making associations properly, making spatial-to-temporal translations, accurately perceiving objects in space, developing coordination between eye and hand, and sequencing. A major key proposition on which many of the previous and subsequent postulates are based is that *all these skills are prerequisite to adequate perceptual-motor development and are basically dependent on the effectiveness of control an individual has over the movement of his own body.* Information is not received nor are responses transmitted in a vacuum. An individual perceives accurately only after having developed some reference against which comparisons and checks can be made. Consistent and efficient motor patterns permit an individual to explore his environment and systematize his relation to it. An individual, therefore, compares aspects of the environment to himself and only after much experience is he able to receive and translate environmental stimuli without constant reference to his own body. This is a basic assumption on which most perceptual-motor training programs are based; however, it remains to be demonstrated on a solid empirical basis that certain groups of problems in school achievement are *caused* by previous difficulties in referring aspects of the environment to one's own body.[1]

---

[1]Studies by Maloney, Ball, and Edgar (1970), and by Edgar, Ball, McIntyre, and Shotwell (1969) have been directed toward testing propositions that are related to the effects of perceptual-motor training programs.

To illustrate the essence of this theoretical stance, assume that an individual is asked to compare the size of two objects and to indicate which is the larger. A young child who has not developed skill in perceptual orientation will find it necessary to compare each of the objects with his own body in order to judge which object is the larger. If, however, the youngster has completed knowledge of his own body in relation to the outside world and is able to project this information, he will no longer find it necessary to constantly check his perceptual experiences by referring back to himself. In short, for children with unstable perceptual organization, discriminations and comparisons between objects must be checked with themselves and their own position in space. As control of the body is gained and the individual begins to understand his relationship with external objects, more rapid comparisons can be made without establishing the constant time-consuming reorientations. If a person has not learned about his own body and its spatial position, an inadequate perception of outside objects may result.

Kephart (1963, 1965, 1971) has suggested that children develop understanding of themselves and, thus, a reference against which perceptions can be compared at an early age through the development of skill in motor-activity patterns. He, along with many other theoreticians, has suggested that four basic motor patterns—(1) balance and maintenance of posture, (2) locomotion, (3) contact, and (4) contact with a moving object with propulsion—constitute important central areas in which competence must be developed for effective interaction with and evaluation of the environment. Accordingly, if an individual has difficulty with any of these patterns, he will not develop a stable reference point for comparing external perceptions. This situation can lead to errors in any or all the components of perception (reception, association, and expression) and can subsequently result in learning difficulties.

Table 6-1 summarizes this postulated hierarchy of perceptual-motor development.

An example may help to explain this sequence. Suppose we have two pieces of pipe, one of which is large enough for a young child to crawl through and the other of which is too small. The objective is that the child eventually reach the point at which a correct judgment will be made concerning which of the two is larger. Prerequisite to the task is that the child be able to perceive sensations and transmit this information to the already awakened cortex. The child must also be able to move about and engage in enough motor movements to allow for the manipulation and exploration of the objects in space.

Table 6-1

HYPOTHESIZED HIERARCHY FOR PERCEPTUAL-MOTOR DEVELOP-
MENT

LEVEL 1 Integrity of the peripheral sensory mechanisms including vision, hearing, speech, and tactile senses.

LEVEL 2 *Development of basic* *Additional and more precise*
motor patterns. *motor patterns.*
  a balance **a** gross motor movements
  b locomotion **b** fine motor movements
  c contact
  d receipt and
  propulsion

LEVEL 3 *Development of a concept of one's own body in space.*
  At this stage the individual makes use of the body as a reference point for experimentation with the environment. Responses are formulated solely in terms of the position of the body in relation to the perceptions being received. For example, laterality is the internal appreciation of left and right with which all objects in space are compared. In short, at this stage of development of the child, the object is not perceived in itself as having a left or right since all comparisons are made in terms of one's own body and its position in space.

LEVEL 4 *Matching perceptions with established motor patterns.*
  As perceptual stability progresses and the organism gains experience, perceptions are compared with information the repertoire has programmed from previous motor learning. As these perceptual matches occur between the sensory experience and the motor experience, the object being perceived begins to have meaning in terms of general and unique characteristics. Eventually, the organism no longer has to depend on a perceptual-motor match when characteristics of objects are accurately perceived, and reference to one's own body is unnecessary.

LEVEL 5 *Accurate perception leads to efficient and effective learning.*
  As soon as the organism has reached the level of development at which perceptual stability is established and a dependable system for processing perceptual data created, effort can be devoted to increasing associational networks, further elaborating on the capabilities to establish external sources for reference, establishing a consistent means for evaluating alternative responses to problems emanating from the perceptual experiences, and responding in a precise and appropriate manner.

Assuming that the systems necessary for these functions are intact, the child will respond initially by indicating that one of the pipes is larger than the other totally on the basis of a comparison of each with himself. Pipe A may be large enough to crawl through, whereas pipe B may be too small. The child responds purely on the basis of comparison with his own body. Gradually, after having experienced this type of event on several occasions, the child will be able to begin using one of the pipes as the reference point against which other objects are compared. No longer will it be necessary to make a perceptual-motor match between himself and objects in space. Logically, then, this skill will result in more rapid, functional, and efficacious learning.

PERCEPTUAL-MOTOR DEVELOPMENT OF THE MENTALLY RETARDED

Because there are so many other influential factors to be considered, it is difficult to characterize the perceptual-motor development of children with retarded mental development. Level of skill development, the extent and types of multiple disorders, previous training experiences, hearing and visual characteristics, muscular development and the degree to which opportunities are available for a child to play, are but a few of many factors that will influence a youngster's perceptual-motor characteristics and development. To further complicate the picture, scientists disagree among themselves on what factors embody the broad area of perceptual-motor development. Spivack (1963), for example, in reviewing the literature on perceptual processes, elected not to include studies in which subjects were required to engage in some type of visual-motor performance. He felt that one cannot accurately study perception without being aware of nonperceptual components involved in response. Malpass (1963), Stein (1964), and Kral (1972), in their review of motor skills among the mentally retarded, noted that researchers tended to exercise very little control over the input side in their investigations of motor proficiency. Others have reported on research in which both input and output have been controlled and measured (Lipman, 1963).

Spivack (1963) and Benton (1964) surveyed the contemporary research studies describing the perceptual-input characteristics of the retarded. To summarize conclusions from the studies they review in depth, it was found that retarded children tend to have difficulties in (1) auditory and visual discrimination, (2) right-left discrimination, (3) locating the site of stimulation applied to various parts of the body, (4) color discrimination, and (5) general identification of complex stimuli. Because of methodological difficulties, including the use of brain-injured and non-brain-injured subjects in the same sample, the findings from investigations designed to assess perceptual-input characteristics of the retarded are ambiguous and often confusing. Spivack has presented an excellent summary of these possible methodological difficulties.

The results of research dealing with motor skills of the retarded have been summarized and interpreted by Malpass (1963), Denny (1964), and Kral (1972). In the broadest sense, there seems to be agreement that this population of youngsters is deficient to varying degrees in performance of tasks that are of a motoric character, such as strength, body flexibility, precision, balance, finger dexterity, and some forms of hand manipulation. The retarded appear to be significantly behind the national norms on most tests of gross motor proficiency, although their motor development seems to follow a pattern similar to that of normal children, and they are unusually poor in physical fitness (Stein, 1964).

The evidence suggests that the mentally retarded are responsive to training programs that focus on motor education (Maloney, Ball, and Edgar, 1970; Chasey and Wyrick, 1971; Solomon and Prangle, 1966; Oliver, 1958; Denny, 1964). Data from these studies document that when retarded children are provided with a program aimed at developing simple motor skills and given opportunities to practice, they often become capable of performing at a level commensurate with their chronological age (CA). It is important, however, that the perceptual-motor program be sequentially structured so that tasks build on and emanate from previously developed skills. Moreover, it should be pointed out that as the motor tasks increase in difficulty, the influence of intelligence becomes more apparent.

In a number of these studies a positive relationship was found between improvement in physical proficiency and increases in intelligence-test scores or on other measures of adaptive behavior. The exact character of this relationship is not clear; thus, one must be cautious not to prematurely infer a cause and effect relationship. Research in this area has been particularly vigorous in the past decade, and much of it is being directed toward establishing the extent to which there is a linear influence of perceptual-motor training on cognitive factors.

Studies of perceptual-motor performance and development in which input and output are relatively controlled and measured have typically required subjects to perform on tasks such as card sorting, rotary pursuit, block turning, mirror drawing, maze learning, or formboard work. Lipman (1963) has reviewed and interpreted the major research in these areas. In general, the data seem to suggest the following:

1 The retarded often exhibit initial performance difficulties that can frequently be overcome with practice if the task is not too complex.
2 A relationship seems to exist between the complexity of the task and intelligence.

3 In certain perceptual-motor tasks, the subject's CA appears to determine the upper limit of capability, whereas on other tasks the mental age (MA) determines the upper limit.

4 Establishing goals and providing verbal praise bring an elevation of a child's performance level.

5 The data have not clearly indicated the relationship between MA and competence on the various perceptual-motor tasks typically used in these experiments.

assessment of perceptual-motor competence

A number of formal evaluative devices have been developed to assess perceptual-motor capabilities. Most of them are standardized—that is, they have data from a standardization group against which a subject's responses can be compared. Some of the tests are broad-spectrum and attempt to assess a large number of perceptual-motor factors. Others are of much narrower focus; they are specialty tests that zero in on one aspect of the spectrum of skills in relatively greater depth. Many of the tests require the services of a trained psychometrician for both administration and interpretation. Table 6-2 lists several of the prominent formal tests used to assess various perceptual-motor factors.

Whereas most of the formal instruments require administration by a qualified examiner, there are several scales (principally those involving motor performance) that do not. Irrespective of the test, the examiner should always be sure that he has the proper background and training required. In most instances the manual of instructions will outline these requirements.

In addition to the above instruments, perceptual-motor development has often been evaluated by using tasks that involve rotary pursuit, mirror drawing, coding, maze tracing, card sorting, assembling objects, formboards, pegboard apparatus, ball and slot, and other similar activities. These procedures are used when the researcher wants to compare one group with another and is not primarily interested in evaluating an individual's performance in terms of a comparative normative group.

Teachers who provide various forms of special education services to children often suspect certain children of having some level of difficulty in perceptual-motor areas, but at the same time they either are untrained to administer the available formal tests or do not readily have

Table 6-2

EXAMPLES OF INSTRUMENTS DESIGNED TO EVALUATE VARIOUS
FACTORS RELATED TO PERCEPTUAL-MOTOR DEVELOPMENT

NAME OF TEST	AGE RANGE (IN YEARS)	FACTORS ASSESSED	PUBLISHER*
Marianne Frostig Developmental Test of Visual Perception	3–8	Eye-hand coordination, figure-ground discrimination, form constancy, position in space, spatial relations	CPP
Perceptual Forms Test	5–8	General visual-motor performance	WHLRF
Children's Embedded Figures Test	5–9	Dimensions of a field-ground nature	CPP
Bender-Gestalt Test	4 and above	Perceptual-motor skills in addition to personality factors	GS
Pre-Tests of Vision, Hearing, and Motor Coordination	12 to adult	Visual-motor and auditory-gestural association and coordination	CTB
Lincoln-Oseretsky Motor Development Scale (revision of Oseretsky Tests of Motor Proficiency)	6–14	Gross motor skills, speed, coordination, dexterity, rhythm, balance, jumping, manual ability (strength and power minimized)	AGS
AAHPER Youth Fitness Test	5–16	Various dimensions of physical fitness	AAHPER
Southern California Perceptual-Motor Tests	4–8	Balance, right-left discrimination, imitation of postures, crossing midline, and bilateral motor coordination	WPS

*The list of publishers and their addresses appears on page 353.

access to the services of a psychologist. Of course, it is important to identify the type of problem and gain some estimate of the magnitude of the youngster's performance difficulty so that the remedial program can have a more definite focus. To this end, then, a teacher should use more informal assessment procedures to screen for and characterize, in a preliminary sense, these possible perceptual-motor problems. These techniques, which are usually not standardized, can be used by the classroom teacher or by physical education specialists. There typically is no specified time limit for their administration, and, in fact, the tasks can be given in part, in total, or in any combination. This flexibility is bought at a price; intra-individual comparisons can be easily made, but interindividual comparisons are more imprecise when informal procedures are employed. They do, however, provide an excellent means for checking on a child's progress in those important foundation areas that may be directly related to future performance in more complex academic activities.

One technique for informally assessing perceptual-motor development is the Purdue Perceptual-Motor Survey which was developed by Kephart (1966, 1971). The scale is designed for children aged six to nine and surveys many auditory and visual perceptual-motor abilities. Tasks in the scale are easy to administer and aspects of the child's performance to which the examiner should pay particular attention are mentioned in the literature describing the procedures. Emphasis is placed on the response aspect of the process. Table 6-3 summarizes the tasks included in the Purdue Perceptual-Motor Survey and the dimensions each evaluates.

Eventually this scale will be standardized, and teachers will have a basis against which they can compare the achievement of their youngsters.

Another procedure you can use to informally check on a child's achievement, and to maintain records on progress in skill areas, is to begin a card file of evaluative activities that can be conducted within a classroom but without disrupting the rhythm and sequence of the usual program format. Each of the cards, which could be stored in a file and classified according to the area(s) of functioning it evaluates, should contain three bits of information. First, there should be a definite statement about the perceptual-motor factor that is being evaluated, and, if at all possible, a statement of the behavioral objective associated with that factor. Second, it is obviously important that a clear description of the activity be presented. And third, the card should contain the response you expect the child to give as an indication that he is able to adequately perform the task. Figure 6-1 shows a sample assessment card.

This figure illustrates only one activity you could use within a whole range that children might accomplish using the balance beam. For

Table 6-3

DIMENSIONS EVALUATED BY THE PURDUE PERCEPTUAL-MOTOR
SURVEY

NAME OF ACTIVITY	PRIMARY FUNCTIONS OBSERVED
1 Walking board	**a** Balance **b** Postural flexibility **c** Laterality
2 Jumping, skipping, and hopping	**a** Symmetrical behavior and body control **b** Laterality **c** Body image **d** Rhythm
3 Identifying body parts (auditory stimulus–motor response)	**a** Body image **b** Understanding significance of what is heard **c** Proper translation of an auditory stimulus to a gestural response
4 Imitation of movements	**a** Laterality **b** Body control **c** Directionality
5 Obstacle course	**a** Body image in terms of its position in space **b** Body control
6 Angels in the snow (visual stimulus–motor response with frequent auditory-vocal associations)	**a** Body image **b** Laterality **c** Directionality **d** Body control
7 Steppingstones (visual-motor)	**a** Laterality **b** Body control **c** Eye-foot coordination **d** Directionality
8 Chalkboard work	**a** Laterality **b** Directionality **c** Motor movement **d** Visual memory
9 Ocular pursuits (lateral, vertical, diagonal, rotary, monocular)	**a** Ocular control **b** Laterality
10 Visual achievement forms (copying various forms presented by the teacher)	**a** Form perception **b** Figure-ground relationships
11 Kraus-Weber Tests	**a** Gross motor coordination **b** General postural adjustment **c** Muscular fitness

The above is a summary of the material presented in Roach and Kephart, *The Purdue Perceptual-Motor Survey*, Charles E. Merrill Books, Inc., Columbus, Ohio, 1966.

Target Area: Balance (using balance beam)

Target Objective: The child will be able to maintain control of his center of gravity while walking forward on a balance beam

Activity: After verbal instruction and demonstration, the child will walk a balance beam (12 feet long and 2 1/2 inches wide) with his arms outstretched from his shoulders.

Response Pattern Expected:

1. arms outstretched throughout
2. heel–toe position throughout
3. feet touch during each step
4. eyes on target beyond beam
5. body erect

Figure 6-1
Example of an assessment card in the area of balance.

example, other cards in the "balance" category that you could use might include

1 Walking with arms at side
2 Stepping over an object placed on the beam
3 Walking with eyes closed
4 Walking forward on a longer board
5 Walking, squatting, and walking
6 Walking forward using longer strides
7 Touching toes while on the beam
8 Grabbing ankles while on the beam
9 Bouncing ball on the floor while on the beam
10 Throwing ball on the floor while on the beam
11 Walking backward on the beam
12 Walking sideways on the beam

By asking a child to perform in each of these areas on several occasions, the teacher will be able to gain a fairly clear impression of the current limits of his balancing ability. By maintaining a daily or weekly tally of whether he accomplished the individual activities to criteria, as well as where during the performance he had difficulty, a teacher can quickly determine not only a child's status but assess how well the program of management (with a perceptual-motor focus in this case) is working for the child.

When you use informal procedures such as an assessment card, remember to

1 Decide first on the behavior you want to check
2 Make sure you select an assessment activity that you believe most directly evaluates that behavior
3 Evaluate the child in that area on several occasions
4 Use a number of activities to evaluate the child's performance in the same area
5 Make certain that you keep a continuing record of the child's performance (which should indicate how often he has done the activity, where within the activity he has trouble, and the rate with which he has progressed toward accomplishing the task)

teaching for the development of perceptual-motor skills

This section is devoted to a specification of several broad instructional procedures that you might use to assist mentally retarded children to become more skilled in various perceptual-motor behaviors. Although the suggestions are organized according to reception, association, and expression categories, I am sure that you recognize that attention given to any one of these areas will strengthen the others. In many ways, then, grouping according to these three dimensions is arbitrary but useful for discussion.

TRAINING OF RECEPTIVE ABILITY
It is reminiscent of Montessori to devote a section to a consideration of the need to train retarded children to be alert and attentive to relevant stimuli. But if this area is not considered, there will always be a high probability of erroneous information becoming a part of the retarded child's response repertoire, and such a situation could lead to difficulties throughout the hypothesized perceptual process and could perhaps precipitate subsequent learning problems.

In a modern translation of Montessori (1965), suggestions have been made for helping children to develop receptive capabilities. The instruments and materials used are graded and are manipulated solely by the child. The perceptual input of children is refined through repeated exercises. Table 6-4 shows some sample activities recommended by

Montessori for training various types of perceptual sensitivity. Unfortunately, it is not possible to give unqualified endorsement to these suggestions because consistent empirical documentation of their efficacy has not appeared in the professional literature. This situation is not atypical in special education and should not deter the teacher from experimenting with procedures such as these in the classroom.

Many of the types of activities suggested by Itard, Seguin, and Montessori are appropriate for training receptive skills of the mentally retarded. By becoming familiar with materials and techniques suggested in the programs of these early educators, the teacher can easily elaborate on the basic principles inherent in the activities they suggest.

The following activities and pedagogical considerations illustrate the direction a teacher's instructional behavior might take to help the mentally retarded develop keener receptive capabilities. Each of these suggestions can be adapted according to the ability level and age of the children as well as to the local situation.

1 Before you spend a great deal of instructional time and energy stimulating children to develop various perceptual-motor skills of a receptive character, make sure that you have reasonably fair assurance that the youngsters are able to hear and see adequately. If a child continuously makes errors in response to the most basic visual or auditory stimuli, or tends to misperceive, have him see an eye or ear specialist immediately.

2 In presenting a stimulus (whether it be a verbal command, visual presentation, or combination) it is important to maximize the possibility of the child attending to it and acting on it instead of on peripheral events. In certain instances, and with some children, the teacher may have to:

a Reduce stimuli that are tangential to the relevant event or activity.

b Make sure that the stimuli that precede the presentation of a visual or auditory display are consistent from one time to the next. (This seems to set the stage for the activity so that the children learn to be alert to a stimulus they have previously experienced. For example, do the reading lesson at the same time each day and within the same section of the classroom.)

c Increase the stimulus value of the activity to which you desire to direct the children's attention.

d Be certain to consistently reinforce those youngsters who attend to the relevant display or stimulus.

e Do not fade out cues that attend an activity until you are sure that you will be able to hold the youngsters' attention throughout the activity.

Table 6-4

ILLUSTRATIONS OF PERCEPTUAL TRAINING SUGGESTED BY MONTESSORI

SENSORY CHANNEL AFFECTED	ILLUSTRATION OF AN APPROPRIATE ACTIVITY
TACTILE SENSE	The children touch materials with various types of surfaces, starting with those requiring discriminations between two highly different surfaces (sandpaper and silk) and gradually reducing the degree of difference between the surface characteristics.
THERMIC SENSE	The children feel the outside of two metal bowls each of which contains water of a different temperature. Slowly the difference between the bowls is reduced, requiring a finer discrimination by the children.
BARIC SENSE (SENSE OF WEIGHT)	The children are required to estimate the difference in weight among small blocks each of which is of the same size, texture, and degree of smoothness; however, the blocks are made of different types of wood and thus are of different weights.
STEROGNOSTIC SENSE (RECOGNITION OF OBJECTS THROUGH THE SIMULTANEOUS HELP OF THE TACTILE AND MUSCULAR SENSES)	The children are presented with a large pile of cubes and bricks each group of which has different composition characteristics. The task is to make two piles by placing the bricks on one side and the cubes on the other, while blindfolded.
TASTE	The tongues of the children are touched with various solutions which have different characteristics such as salty, sweet, sour, bitter, acid, or neutral.
OLFACTORY SENSE (SMELL)	The children learn to recognize various odors, first by associating the smell with the appropriate label. Later they are asked to discriminate among various odors while blindfolded.
VISUAL SENSE (A VARIETY OF DIMENSIONS RELATED TO VISUAL PERCEPTION IS ASSESSED SUCH AS SIZE, THICKNESS, COLOR, SHAPE, LENGTH, CONTOUR, ETC.)	Various objects of graded size, dimensions, and color are used with the children manipulating the objects according to a variety of possible criteria, such as the longest, the larger, red-colored objects, or placing them in the appropriate geometric inserts in a formboard.

Table 6-4 *(Continued)*

HEARING SENSE (THE PRIMARY CONCERN IN THIS CATEGORY IS IN THE DISCRIMINATION OF SOUNDS, AUDITORY ACUITY, PITCH, VOLUME, AND VARIOUS MODULATIONS OF THE VOICE)	In discriminating among sounds, the children are asked to strike a bell in one of a double series of thirteen bells and then to locate the same sounding bell in the second series. At a very early stage, the children are taught about silence by being asked to sit in absolute and complete silence for periods of time. Later, very small noises are introduced such as the tick of a clock or the buzz of a fly or bee. Comparisons are frequently made between noise and sound. Eventually, musical education is incorporated into this aspect of the program.

3 Auditory receptive skills can be developed by engaging the children in activities such as the following:
   a Have the children listen to various types of sounds they have heard during a class walk. Ask them to identify the source of each sound and to give it an appropriate label.
   b Ask the children to distinguish between various characteristics of sounds, such as between loud and soft, high and low, pleasant and obnoxious, and happy and sad. A tape recorder often helps to standardize the sounds and gives the children an opportunity to check their responses. The tape recorder also provides an opportunity for the retarded to make their own happy, sad, loud, soft, low, or high sounds, which will help receptive abilities and also help to develop basic expressive skills.
   c Have the children follow auditory commands by using a gestural or motor response.
   d Have the children listen to nursery stories, rhymes, and songs, and pick out details and other information or generalizations. At first they can be asked to listen for certain sounds or words on the records and eventually they can be required to repeat the sounds or words. This activity will help to develop association and response skills.
   e Ask questions of the children to make them more aware of the world around them.
   f Give the children opportunities to play with musical instruments and rhythm-band equipment. Work on the perception of rhythm through musical games.
   g Have quiet periods during which the children are to listen for various sounds.

4 Visual receptive skills can be developed by giving the children experiences such as the following:

a Have the children identify common objects by name, telling both their proper use and to whom each object belongs. Emphasis should be placed on tasks involving visual reception wherein the stimuli are obvious or intentionally presented, not on stimuli that must be perceived incidentally.

b Have the children examine objects and toys and report on their color, shape, size, texture, and the materials used in their construction. By comparing these objects in some way, visual discrimination skills will also be enhanced.

c Let the children stand in front of a mirror each day and comment on what they see.

d Have the children interpret pictures in terms of the objects seen—colors, sizes, motion—or by noticing details.

e Give the children opportunities to copy, cut, paste, and draw.

5 Tactile receptive skills can be developed by:

a Showing the children different scraps of cloth and allowing them to handle these scraps and learn the names of each. Place several scraps in a bag. Have each child feel the material and select the roughest, smoothest, largest, smallest, or most wrinkled. See if they can give the name of the scrap chosen. It would be best to introduce this activity by using objects that are grossly dissimilar.

b Have the children identify shapes and sizes of objects while blindfolded.

6 The olfactory sense can be trained in a way similar to that used by Montessori. Odors can be sniffed as the children are walking on a tour or field trip. Even in the classroom, bottles with distinctive odors provide an excellent medium for playing unusual games.

TRAINING IN PERCEPTUAL-MOTOR ASSOCIATION

The term "perceptual-motor association" is confusing in many respects and is subject to errors of interpretation and judgment among even the most erudite scholars. Just as it is virtually impossible to observe directly whether or not a person is receiving stimuli (using criteria other than the person's overt response), so is it almost impossible to know with sureness whether a child is properly integrating and associating stimuli that are allegedly being received with material in his repertoire so that a proper response can occur. With some degree of apparent exasperation, people refer to "the black-box phenomenon" when they consider cognitive functioning and integration like perceptual-motor association or integration.

When a child is able to see similarities and differences among several events that are either close together or far apart in time and space, he is engaging in an important association behavior that will be valuable to him when more complex reading and arithmetic problems are presented. Clearly, neurological activity is taking place, and equally clearly teachers should not spend time attempting to explain superiority or deficiencies in a child's association skills from the point of view of an internal-cognitive perspective. Focus your attention on how you can best arrange the environment to increase the likelihood that each child will begin to see relationships among things in his environment according to time and space, cause and effect, similarities and differences, and systems of classification and categorization. Here are some suggestions for you to think about if your youngsters have problems in seeing associations:

1 As in the previous section on reception, it is essential that the stimuli you wish to have associated be stable, prominent, unambiguous, simple, and consistent from one time to the next. Fade out only one stimulus at a time, very gradually, and then only after a child has been consistently accurate in demonstrating that he can relate events, objects, or other phenomena.
2 Be careful to use only two items to establish a relationship at first. Eventually, you can add items or make the activity more complex by introducing variations of time, space, quantity, or quality.
3 Consider the advantages of your acting as a model for proper responses to an activity involving the making of associations. In this way a child learns what you expect, how you went about doing the task, and what an acceptable response looks like. Of course, you must reinforce every instance in which a proper response is given.
4 Make sure that the child knows on which dimension you desire him to make an association. At least during the early stages of instruction, be clear about what you want him to do. One way of making your desires obvious is to emphasize the variables on which you want associations to take place and to deemphasize those that are unimportant, irrelevant, or potentially confusing. For example, if you want a child to classify a set of blocks according to color, make sure that they are all the same size and shape. This will avoid confusion and misunderstanding.

The following are illustrations of the types of activities that will promote perceptual-motor association:

1 Children learn to hear likenesses and differences among auditory stimuli by noticing sounds and words that are alike and by playing games in which they make up silly words. The tape recorder or record player can help in these activities.

2 Rhythmical moving to music helps children to establish relationships between input and response.

3 Have the children follow directions, play "Simon Says," sing songs, or make up stories in response to a situation or picture.

4 Cut construction paper of different colors into squares, triangles, circles, and oblongs; paste small strips of felt to the back of each and have the children group them according to color, size, or shape. The children can play a game by grouping objects in various ways after having received vocal directions.

5 Initiate and practice the development of sequence using such techniques as sentence completion. For example, "After we arrive at school on the bus we . . ."; "Before lunch we must . . ."; or "Before we go home from school we . . ." This can be done by using both auditory and visual stimuli.

TRAINING IN RESPONDING

One of the major propositions advanced in this chapter has been that sensory-motor development is related to a child's subsequent performance level in other areas. The exact character of this relationship is unknown; however, it is clear that attention during a child's early school years must be directed toward increasing skill in gross and fine motor movements including balance, posture, eye-hand coordination, locomotion, and similar skills. Kephart (1971) and Cratty (1970) have suggested practical procedures that teachers can use to help children develop these skills, a sampling of which is given here.

1 In developing gross motor skills, games should be planned in which the children walk, run, slide, gallop, skip, hop, run over uneven areas, dance freely and spontaneously, practice other methods of movement (cat, elephant, duck, crab, measuring worm), balance and walk along board or brick fences, crawl through equipment. Action songs or other types of rhythm music should be encouraged in all activities with particular attention given to the children making use of both sides of their bodies. Initially, the teacher should encourage the children's participation through imitation of her, since spontaneity on the part of many retarded youngsters may be lacking.

2 Fine-muscle movement and coordination between the eyes and hands can be developed by having the children draw on a blackboard or large piece of paper, by doing pegboard work, cutting and pasting, working on puzzles and lotto games, manipulating toys, handling and sorting small objects, throwing balls, climbing ropes, hanging from playground equipment by their hands, copying patterns, coloring, tracing, working with buttons and zippers, and engaging in rhythm activities. In their use of paper or the blackboard, it is wise to encourage a left-to-right progression whenever appropriate. When demonstrating, for example, the teacher should move in a left-to-right direction.

3 In many of these activities, vocal expression before, during, or immediately after the motor response is natural and desirable. Every attempt should be made to relate vocal expression to the appropriate motor response.

4 After the child has established a stable spatial world, some effort should be directed to emphasizing spatial-to-temporal translation. Adequately performing complex activities, such as batting a ball, kicking a can, drawing a triangle, and reading, requires that the child translate an object in space into an appropriate temporal sequence. For example, in batting a ball, the child must do certain things before swinging the bat. He has to throw the ball in the air, estimate how rapidly it will fall in relation to his own body, and judge the speed at which he should swing the bat. Unless the temporal translation of these spatial entities is accurate, an error of some type will occur. As soon as gross and fine-motor skills develop, attention should be directed toward working on spatial-temporal translations.

selected readings

Benton, A. L.: "Psychological Evaluation and Differential Diagnosis," in H. A. Stevens and R. Heber (eds.), *Mental Retardation: A Review of Research*, The University of Chicago Press, Chicago, 1964, pp. 16–56.

Chasey, W. C. and W. Wyrick: "Effects of a Physical Developmental Program on Psychomotor Ability of Retarded Children," *American Journal of Mental Deficiency*, 75:566–570, 1971.

Cratty, B. J.: *Perceptual and Motor Development of Inputs and Children*, The Macmillan Company, New York, 1970.

Denny, M. R.: "Learning and Performance," in H. A. Stevens and R. Heber (eds.), *Mental Retardation: A Review of Research*, The University of Chicago Press, Chicago, 1964, pp. 128–132.

Edgar, C. L., T. S. Ball, R. R. McIntyre, and A. M. Shotwell: "Effects of Sensory-Motor Training on Adaptive Behavior," *American Journal of Mental Deficiency*, 73:713–720, 1969.

Forgus, R. H.: *Perception*, McGraw-Hill Book Company, New York, 1966.

Gallagher, J. J.: *The Tutoring of Brain Injured Mentally Retarded Children*, Charles C Thomas, Publisher, Springfield, Ill., 1960.

Hunt, J. McV.: *Intelligence and Experience*, The Ronald Press Company, New York, 1961.

Kephart, N. C.: "Perceptual-Motor Concepts of Learning Disabilities," *Exceptional Children*, 31:201–206, 1965.

————: "Perceptual-Motor Correlates of Education," in S. A. Kirk and W. Becker (eds.), *Conference on Children with Minimal Brain Impairments*, The University of Illinois Press, Urbana, 1963, pp. 13–25.

————: *The Slow Learner in the Classroom*, 2d ed., Charles E. Merrill Books, Inc., Columbus, Ohio, 1971.

Kral, P. A.: "Motor Characteristics and Development of Retarded Children: Success Experience," *Education and Training of the Mentally Retarded*, 7:14–21, 1972.

Lipman, R. S.: "Learning: Verbal, Perceptual-Motor and Classical Conditioning," in Norman R. Ellis (ed.), *Handbook of Mental Deficiency*, McGraw-Hill Book Company, New York, 1963, pp. 391–423.

Maloney, M. P., T. S. Ball, and C. L. Edgar: "Analysis of the Generalizability of Sensory-Motor Training," *American Journal of Mental Deficiency*, 74:458–469, 1970.

Malpass, L. F.: "Motor Skills in Mental Deficiency," in Norman R. Ellis (ed.), *Handbook of Mental Deficiency*, McGraw-Hill Book Company, New York, 1963, pp. 602–631.

Montessori, M.: *The Montessori Method*, translated by A. E. George, Robert Bently, Inc., Cambridge, Mass., 1965.

Oliver, J. N.: "The Effect of Physical Conditioning Exercises and Activities on Mental Characteristics of Educationally Subnormal Boys," *British Journal of Educational Psychology*, 28:155–164, 1958.

Radler, D. H. and N. C. Kephart: *Success through Play*, Harper & Brothers, New York, 1960.

Roach, E. G. and N. C. Kephart: *The Purdue Perceptual-Motor Survey*, Charles E. Merrill Books, Inc., Columbus, Ohio, 1966.

Solomon, A. H. and R. Prangle: "The Effects of a Structured Physical Education Program on Physical, Intellectual, and Self-Concept Development of Educable Retarded Boys," *IMRID Behavioral Science Monograph*, no. 4, George Peabody College for Teachers, Nashville, Tenn., 1966.

Spivack, G.: "Perceptual Processes," in Norman R. Ellis (ed.), *Handbook of Mental Deficiency*, McGraw-Hill Book Company, New York, 1963, pp. 480–511.

Stein, J. V.: "Motor Function and Physical Fitness of the Mentally Retarded: A Critical Review," *Rehabilitation Literature*, 24:230–242, 1964.

7

DEVELOPING COMMUNICATION SKILLS

If mentally retarded children are to function adequately in society, they must be able to make themselves understood by their contemporaries. To do so requires that they be able to receive and interpret the significance of incoming stimuli and express themselves in an appropriate and understandable fashion. Speech, language, and written expression are three major components of communication. The teacher of mentally retarded children must emphasize the skills in each of these areas. Blending into society is typically no major problem for the retarded child until he is forced to communicate with others; if he is unable to do so adequately, he is immediately identified and labeled as a defective person. If, on the other hand, he is able to benefit from systematic training in communicating with others, potential problems in other areas will be minimized.

This chapter discusses some of the major facets of communication as they apply to the mentally retarded and suggests procedures that teachers can use to help them to develop capabilities in speech, language, and written expression.

some basic requisites for speech development

Speech is the manner in which sounds are made, whereas language is the expression of concepts. A poor speaker is one whose audience pays more attention to how he talks than to what he is saying. Retarded children typically have more difficulty developing adequate speech patterns than do intellectually normal children. The reason is directly related to the extent to which certain basic requirements for effective speech development characterize the individual child.

ADEQUATE PHYSICAL STRUCTURES

Speech depends in large measure on how well the mechanisms responsible for this behavior are able to function. The whole process involves an exceedingly complicated operation of many organic entities none of which has exclusive responsibility for speech and all of which serve other vital functions. For example, the tongue and teeth are essential to effective speech, yet they serve other important functions, such as mastication. Any number of malformations of these organic components could result in poor speech development. Difficulty in respiration, vocal-cord nodules, a short soft palate, lip abnormalities, central-nervous-system disturbances, or muscular difficulties are a few of the vast number of physical problems that may impede the development of speech.

The basis for speech disturbances can be environmental, organic, or a combination of the two. Typically the teacher is not trained to deal with organically based defects. These severe difficulties require the expertise of a trained speech therapist; however, the classroom teacher must continue to provide an environment wherein functional difficulties do not become added to the existing organic-based problem.

INTELLECTUAL CAPABILITIES

Learning to speak is an intellectual function based on adequate employment of the cortex, or higher neural centers. It is a complex process requiring a certain minimum level of intellectual ability as well as the rapid and unconscious manipulation of the various articulators. Thus, it is not astonishing to find that retarded children are slower in speech development, speak at a slower pace, and, finally, attain a lower level of success in speech than do the intellectually normal.

It would be difficult to identify the minimum level of intellectual ability below which speech will not develop. Likewise, it would be hazardous to suggest that speech will develop adequately in children who are above a certain intelligence level. In a general sense, the retarded have more difficulty with speech as well as with the peripheral mechanisms associated with communication.

AUDITORY DISCRIMINATION ABILITIES

Comparing and contrasting correct and incorrect sounds in isolation and in connected speech is a basic requisite for the development of speech. Children who have difficulty differentiating among sounds will subsequently have difficulty reproducing more complex components of speech. There are several possible reasons for a child having a disability in auditory discrimination. Poor hearing involving some general or specific difficulty with his ears or central nervous system, resulting in a reduction of auditory acuity, will impede discrimination capabilities. The literature reveals that retarded children tend to have substantial hearing disturbances (Birch and Matthews, 1951; Kodman, 1958; Lloyd and Moore, 1972). Although much of this research has been done with moderately and severely mentally retarded subjects, there is still enough evidence to justify concluding that retarded individuals have a higher number of and more serious hearing problems than the nonretarded population.

Inattentiveness on the part of the retarded could account for difficulty in auditory discrimination. This problem may be the direct result of too many peripheral stimuli, confusion or lack of clarity in the stimulus presented, or previous lack of success in related tasks.

Auditory discrimination is essential for ear training. To develop adequate speech and reap the benefits of any subsequent speech therapy, children must be able to isolate sounds that occur in various positions within words. For speech therapy to be effective the child must be able to hear differences between his productions and those of others. Speech development and the remediation of speech difficulties are based, in large measure, on these auditory discrimination capabilities.

Several studies have reported results in which training programs to assist the retarded in effectively utilizing their hearing have increased the auditory capabilities of children (Goda and Rigrodsky, 1962; Schlanger, 1962; Glovsky and Rigrodsky, 1963). It is indeed promising that capabilities of this nature can be learned—the implication being that activities to train auditory discrimination skills should be a major part of the classroom program in most special education settings.

ADEQUATE FEEDBACK AND MONITORING SYSTEMS

The character of our vocal and motor output is in part influenced by how well we continuously monitor our own speech and motor behavior and adjust our subsequent productions accordingly. You have heard people spontaneously correct themselves when an utterance was inappropriate in terms of the content, the pronunciation, or the quality of the speech. To make these kinds of self-adjustments a person has to be alert to his own output and evaluate it in terms of what he personally considers an appropriate response. Difficulties in self-monitoring of responses and feeding these data back for adjustments in output constitutes one group in a host of possible reasons for a youngster having difficulty performing satisfactorily in communication areas.

From one perspective, feedback can be viewed as a conditioned reflex that is automatic and self-regulating. This physiological process regulates the manipulation of the articulators so that the individual does not consciously think about their rapid movement and repositioning as his words are expressed. As the articulators move, signals are sent to the appropriate nerve centers for subsequent and sequential innervation and deactivation of muscle groups. Although these processes are of academic interest, educators do not need to be concerned about nor understand their complex interaction in order to develop management programs to train for better use of feedback.

Other aspects of feedback and monitoring are learned and should be of interest to individuals working with speech-defective children. If they have not learned to make use of their vocal output, modifications that are subsequently required for speech productions will be less well effected. Even with an intact speech mechanism, mentally retarded children frequently do not listen to themselves; that is, they do not make use of their own vocalizations to improve speech and language. Unless direct intervention by a speech therapist or teacher is introduced, the child will continue to practice his own errors. When this occurs on a continuous basis, poor patterns of speech become established. This situation, in turn, leads to a hard-core remedial problem which, if severe enough, is frequently beyond the training and experience of the special education teacher.

ADEQUATE MODELS

Speech is a learned activity that takes place through example and activity. An important factor in speech development is that a child have some reference against which he can compare his performance. This has some relationship to the development of auditory discrimination skills, the use of monitoring and feedback competencies, and the kinds of experiences the youngster has available. There is no doubt but that each child's pattern of speech and language is heavily influenced by his parents and siblings. Children who live in homes where members of the family have faulty patterns of speech and/or language will imitate these patterns. The family speech and language can become so sloppy and imprecise that members of the family may be the only ones who can understand each other. In a real sense, these families develop their own system of communication much of which is foreign and incomprehensible to outsiders. When the children reach school they can have serious problems of adjustment and certainly present difficult remedial situations.

Even within families that offer satisfactory levels of stimulation to children, parents often err by (1) not insisting on continuously acceptable speech productions from children, (2) not continuously rewarding good speech, (3) allowing sloppy productions or ignoring the child when he tries to speak well, (4) emphasizing how not to say things instead of modeling proper speech, or (5) placing undue pressure on a child to continuously perform under contrived circumstances or before strangers. All these issues are especially significant with the mentally retarded child who usually needs an environment that is maximally facilitating for speech and language development.

stages of speech development

To a substantial extent, speech and language develop simultaneously. As a child proceeds through the various stages of sound emission and gains skill in manipulating the articulators, he is at the same time gaining an understanding of the meaning of words and expressions. In considering the speech development of children, two major factors are worthy of emphasis: (1) speech and language do not develop in isolation from each other although a child can be disabled in one but not necessarily in the other, and (2) the stages of speech development are not mutually exclusive, discrete entities, but overlap substantially. Indeed, a child can easily be operating in more than one stage at the same time.

There is some inconsistency in the literature regarding appropriate labels for stages of speech development. Table 7-1 summarizes the major stages of speech development and the characteristic behaviors associated with each. The student interested in a more complete and detailed description of each stage is referred to the excellent discussion by Van Riper (1965). In addition, Fokes (1971) has developed a comprehensive scale of language acquisition which provides excellent landmarks in this area.

speech characteristics
of the mentally retarded

The historical and contemporary literature on the speech characteristics of the mentally retarded is difficult to characterize because (1) so many studies have used subjects from unique populations (e.g., severely retarded institutionalized residents), thus restricting the generalizability of findings; and (2) there have been fewer comprehensive

Table 7-1
SUMMARY OF THE STAGES OF SPEECH DEVELOPMENT

STAGES AND BEHAVIORAL CHARACTERISTICS

REFLEXIVE SOUNDS

The first sounds the child makes are related to either crying or comfort. Wide variation exists among infants during the first few months in terms of the type and extent of these vocalizations. Both crying and cooing allow the child to manipulate his articulators and form sounds, although more sounds relevant to speech emanate from cooing than from crying. Subsequent development of speech will depend to a great extent on how effectively the infant uses his tongue during sucking and swallowing.

BABBLING AND VOCAL PLAY

This stage usually begins around the end of the second month and is typified by the child emitting a variety of sounds, primarily front vowels with a few consonant productions. Most frequently the child babbles during periods of relaxation and when alone. Interruptions will often stifle the child's continuation of babbling. Toward the half-year mark, the child begins to interact more completely with his environment and develops a type of social vocalization. At this point he will make sounds at objects, repeat syllables, and begin making combinations of consonant-vowel blends such as "da-da" or "ma-ma." Eventually, the child develops a variety of capabilities including variation in volume, inflection, and tone. The repertoire of sounds increases, and the child uses his own feedback for repetition as well as exhibiting a tendency toward imitating sounds from other sources. During the latter half of the first year, the child develops skill in using the back vowels and elaborating on his consonant production.

FIRST WORDS

Emerging from the myriad of sounds are the child's first words. When stimulated and appropriately responded to, he develops an understanding of the significance of the first few words over which he has control. "Ma-ma" or "da-da" take on meaning, elicit a pleasurable response from the two observers to whom the words become attached, and thus provide a system of rewards to the child. Repetition of these sounds only brings more satisfying experiences. By judicious use of stimulation, the parent can foster a firmer establishment of these vocalizations and their meanings. It should be emphasized, however, that comprehension of the meaning of words is often a slow process and does not necessarily occur in close temporal contiguity with the first words. Comprehension of the meaning of words can be aided if the parents use gestures, so long as the child does not substitute this type of behavior for vocalizations. By the end of eighteen months, the child has typically developed a repertoire of ten to fifteen meaningful words, usually choosing from those which most effectively manipulate his parents.

JARGON

Midway through the child's second year, he will devote much time to vocal productions which are characterized by the term *word salad*. Distributed throughout these vocalizations are a few intelligible words with interesting patterns of inflection. Indeed, this seems like double talk. This period of speech development is often perplexing to parents because it contrasts sharply with the few intelligible words the child is able to use.

ECHOLALIA

Emerging from the stage of jargon is a second period of vocal play which is of greater breadth and sophistication than the earlier stage. At this point, the child plays with and repeats words, syllables, and combinations of words and phrases. The children parrot themselves and their parents. Fortunately for the parents, it typically lasts for a short time.

Table 7-1 *(Continued)*

MORE ELABORATE SPEECH DEVELOPMENT

The two-year-old child is able to communicate meaningfully in two- and three-word sentences. His articulation is typically not good, and variation occurs from normal rhythm, voice, and volume. By the time the child reaches ages three and four, speech and vocabulary have progressed at a dramatic rate. The child's skill in syntactical understanding is growing at this point, and he usually is not hesitant to attempt an explanation of almost anything. Articulation capabilities continue to develop because of maturity of the child's own feedback and discrimination abilities as well as his propinquity to appropriate models. Progress continues in articulation development, although the child typically does not master all sounds until about the age of eight, assuming a relatively normal environmental situation prevails.

---

studies in speech than in other areas of functioning. The problems of interpretation are compounded by the great inconsistency that prevails among speech studies in distinguishing between speech and language, the variability in the criteria that are used in identifying and classifying speech productions, and the techniques that are employed for assessing speech.

These difficulties notwithstanding, there is consistent evidence that the retarded have more defects in speech than the intellectually normal (Goertzen, 1957; Matthews, 1957; Spradlin, 1963; Kirk, 1964), although the literature reports a wide range in the percentage of speech problems among the retarded. In fact, percentages range from 5 to 100 depending upon the degree of retardation, the type of speech examination used, the speech factors studied, the age of the subjects, the criteria used, and whether the subjects were institutionalized or living at home. In considering the prevalence of speech defects among the retarded, one must be attentive to the divergency among these factors.

Most of the investigators that have studied speech problems of the retarded have used standard testing procedures for screening as well as for making more comprehensive diagnostic determinations. Many retarded children in schools and in institutions never receive a speech analysis because of both the high incidence of speech defects among this population and the restricted number of trained speech therapists available for conducting such examinations. Siegel (1962) studied the advisability of using inexperienced articulation examiners to screen the speech problems among retarded children. His report is particularly promising because it suggests that articulation screening can be effectively conducted by inexperienced examiners following a very brief training period. This is a key study because it suggests the wisdom of administrators considering using subprofessionals in the first-line evaluation of speech problems in retarded subjects who are in public schools or in institutions.

Some effort has been devoted to studying the types of speech problems most characteristic of the retarded. There are difficulties, again, in generalizing. The evidence seems to be clear in two areas: (1) The mentally retarded acquire speech much more slowly than do the intellectually normal, and (2) the greatest percentage of errors in speech among the retarded appears to be in articulation, with voice problems constituting the second area of greatest difficulty. The latter finding differs in no way from the data on the intellectually normal.

The types of articulation errors made by the retarded have also been investigated. Karlin and Strazzula (1952) and Bangs (1942) report that the kinds of articulation errors made by the retarded are similar to those characteristic of a normal population, although Bangs suggests that the retarded make more errors of omission in the final position.

Schlanger and Gottsleben (1957) and Blanchard (1964) present clear evidence that the mongoloid population is typically very defective in speech. The later study presents evidence that suggests a close relationship between etiology and speech difficulties among the retarded. Michel and Carney (1964) indicate that mongoloid children do not seem to have abnormal pitch characteristics as had been reported in previous studies.

A number of attempts have been made to analyze the influence of hospitalization and institutionalization on the development of the mentally retarded. McGunigle (1967) studied a large group of mentally retarded children in an institution and found that length of stay did not make a difference between good and poor speakers. Poor speakers, however, were admitted earlier than were good speakers. The important implication of this study is that speech does not seem to decay because of a lengthy period of institutionalization.

The influence of speech therapy with the retarded has received relatively little attention and, thus, does not allow for the formulation of clear generalizations. Those studies that have been reported suffer from methodological weaknesses that raise questions concerning their validity. Clinically, there is reason to believe that higher-level retarded children can benefit from speech correction. Similarly, the younger retarded child who comes from an environment in which good speech models are consistently available typically shows a more favorable prognosis than does the older institutionalized retardate. There is consensus in the literature that speech therapy with the retarded will prove beneficial in some measure irrespective of the degree of defect or the individual's intellectual capability.

Most speech therapists concur in the belief that significant and lasting changes in speech productions occur most reliably after therapy by a trained, experienced correctionist who is able to provide systematic intervention over a relatively long period of time. These beliefs are most strongly held when the therapy program involves mentally retarded youngsters. There is a general feeling in the literature that short-term therapy, whether by a trained or untrained correctionist, will probably be disappointing when retarded subjects are used. Many of the studies that have reported on the value of speech therapy with this group have been cross sectional. One notable exception to this is the work of Wilson (1966). This significant study casts doubt on the value of speech therapy as presently used in the programs for educable retarded children in the public schools. Usually, two half-hour weekly sessions are devoted to individual or small-group speech therapy. Other investigations, using institutionalized youngsters, have supported this general conclusion (Rigrodsky and Steer, 1961).

To summarize this brief review, the literature reveals that:

1 Speech problems are related to mental age (MA), with more communication defects among the moderately or severely retarded than among the mildly retarded.
2 Articulation disorders, followed by problems of voice, constitute the greatest percentage of speech defects. The frequency of stuttering among the mentally retarded is the same as in normal populations.
3 The influence of speech therapy has not been adequately assessed, although the evidence suggests the greater benefits of special corrective procedures with educable-level children than with the trainable and severely retarded.

assessment of speech difficulties

In the earlier section on the assessment of perceptual-motor functioning, your attention was drawn to the importance of being aware of the assumptions underlying the evaluation of human performance. Securing reliable samples of typical behavior, focusing on data collection within a natural environment, selecting instruments that were designed to measure the behavior on which you wish to focus attention, being sure that the examiner is competent, and comparing each child's performance against data drawn from a population from which he is a representative—all reflect some of the prominent concerns one should have in observing a child's performance and/or in using data for designing a program of management. These same issues have pertinence to speech and language evaluation, and it does not matter whether we are talking about formal or informal procedures.

FORMAL PROCEDURES

An adequate assessment of a child's speech capabilities should involve periods of observation in a variety of settings in which verbal communication is required. These observations should be made by a trained speech clinician who is skilled in identifying patterns of specific weakness. Standardized testing procedures and other instruments should be used to supplement data gathered through observation. The observation period should never be sacrificed in favor of using a standardized test on a single occasion.

Van Riper (1965) has presented a dossier of examinations and forms for recording relevant speech information. This material suggests procedures for examining children in voice production, articulation defects, stuttering, and the general collection of information. Techniques are given for task-analyzing speech processes. Although this information is of interest and is instructive to teachers of the mentally retarded, caution should be exercised in the use of these materials by one who has not had proper training and appropriate clinical supervision.

Tests such as the following provide data that support observations by the trained speech correctionist.

1 Templin-Darley Tests of Articulation (UI)
2 The Arizona Articulation Proficiency Scale (WPS)
3 Goldman-Fristoe Test of Articulation (AGS)
4 The Riley Articulation and Language Test (WPS)
5 Deep Test of Articulation (SH)
6 A Screening Deep Test of Articulation (SH)

INFORMAL PROCEDURES

Many teachers do not have adequate speech services available for the children in their special education classes. Among the reasons for this unfortunate situation are (1) the lack of enough trained speech correctionists, (2) the unusually heavy caseload of therapists, and (3) the difficulty in working with the retarded, who often show disappointing results even after extensive therapy. These problems necessitate that teachers become aware of the advantages of using informal procedures to assess and analyze speech defects in the retarded. In addition, teachers need to learn about guiding principles that they can use to assist in the development of speech among the mentally retarded.

As has been emphasized earlier, teachers must realize the limitations of their training and experience as the task of analyzing a child's speech difficulties is approached. Since the retarded tend to exhibit more difficulty with articulation than with other speech problems, focus is naturally on this area.

Perhaps the most practical and informative procedure the teacher can use to analyze the children's speech difficulties is to systematically record the types of errors made during a period in which the children are responding to a set stimulus designed to elicit a certain response. Errors of articulation can be tabulated in various ways. It is important to know the specific types of consonant and vowel misarticulations that each child makes, and whether these errors occur in the initial, medial, and/or final positions in words. Moreover, a record should be kept of the types of errors characteristic of each phonemic sound and position, such as substitutions, omissions, and distortions in any of the three positions. The tabulation procedures described previously can be adapted for use in recording speech behavior. From these records, the exact nature of a child's articulation weaknesses soon becomes obvious. Table 7-2 presents stimulus words that can be used by the teacher to test consonant and vowel difficulties, either as a single word, in a picture, or in a sentence. These will help to systematize the collection of data and should be included in each child's folder.

It is important not only to check on and tabulate a child's articulation errors in isolation but also to evaluate his performance during connected speech. Articulation errors may not necessarily occur with isolated sounds but may be present only when words are used in some type of relationship. These errors may be the result of slow and sluggish articulators that do not move and reposition quickly enough for the production of a new sound. The teacher should have the child repeat sentences or phrases and should listen for atypical sounds during casual conversations. Pictures can also be used as a stimulus for eliciting vocal productions. From all these procedures the objective of the teacher should be to classify the types of articulation errors the child makes and to note any specific environmental circumstances within which the errors most often occur.

If it is suspected that a child misarticulates because of environmental, rather than organic, factors, a visit to the home would help to discern the kinds of models available for speech. If the child is associated with faulty models, it may be necessary to consider offering speech services to other members of the family. The teacher is in the most advantageous position to ascertain these potential problems.

As is true in other areas of speech assessment, a comprehensive

Table 7-2 ARTICULATION TEST WORDS

CONSONANTS				CONSONANT BLENDS	
	Initial	*Medial*	*Final*		
[r]	rake, rabbit	carrot	door	[dr] [pt]	dripped
[l]	lamp	telephone	ball	[kr] [dl]	cradle
[s]	saw	glasses	house	[sm] [ʃt]	smashed
[z]	zipper	scissors	nose	[tw] [lv]	twelve
[k]	cat	cookies	book	[θr]	three
[g]	gun	wagon	flag	[br] [ðð]	brother
[w]	window	sandwich		[ldʒɚ]	soldier
[θ]	thumb	birthday cake	mouth	[gr] [vz]	groves
[ð]	that	feather	smooth	[rtʃ]	church
[j]	yellow	onion		[sn] [fl]	snuffle
[f]	fork	elephant	knife		
[v]	vase	shovel	stove		
[ŋ]		monkey	swing		
[ʃ]	shoe	dishes	fish		
[ʒ]		measure	garage		
[ʍ]	wheel				
[tʃ]	chair	matches	watch		
[dʒ]	jelly	soldier	orange		
[t]	table	letter	boat		
[d]	dog	ladder	bed		
[p]	pencil	apple	cup		
[b]	bus	baby	tub		
[m]	mouse	hammer	drum		
[n]	nose	banana	train		
[h]	hat				

VOWELS		DIPHTHONGS	
[i]	tree	[aʊ]	cow
[ɪ]	pig	[aɪ]	pie
[ɛ]	bell	[ɔɪ]	boy
[e] [eɪ]	cake		
[æ]	hat		
[ʌ]	gun		
[ɑ]	car		
[o] [oʊ]	comb		
[ɔ]	ball		
[ʊ]	book		
[u]	shoe		

SOURCE: *Handbook of Speech Pathology.* Edited by Lee Edward Travis. Copyright © 1957 by Appleton-Century-Crofts, Inc. Reprinted by permission of Appleton-Century-Crofts, division of Meredith Publishing Company.

examination of voice disorders requires the services of a trained speech clinician. Teachers should, however, be alert to difficulties children have in discriminating among various pitches, producing and duplicating a given pitch, inflecting appropriately, carrying a tune, and the spontaneous change of inflections and pitch. Intensity difficulties can be assessed by asking the child to engage in activities requiring changes in volume. The range might extend from whispering to calling hogs and vary according to pitch. Moreover, some attention must be given to changes in the voice patterns of children, especially in terms of hoarse voices, huskiness, gutteral qualities, nasal or denasal productions, breathiness, and other differential abnormal speech patterns of voice related to consonants and vowels.

Data that the teacher gathers on these speech patterns will be of benefit only to the degree that a systematic approach is used in their collection. The important point to remember is not that the *isolated* and *infrequently* poor production be focused upon but that patterns of *consistent* speech weakness be identified. To this end, observation should be made in a variety of speech situations with a standard form for recording information. In this way, patterns of strength and weakness will become self-evident. Again, it must be recognized that deep and penetrating speech evaluation is typically outside the training and experience of the special education teacher. Nevertheless, the exigencies of the special education situation often make it necessary that the teacher do some preliminary screening of speech problems among the retarded.

procedures for correcting speech difficulties

It is most important that the people who have responsibility for the training and rearing of each mentally retarded child make a coordinated effort in dealing with speech disorders. It is counterproductive, indeed, for the speech correctionist to be working in one direction, the teachers in another, and the child's parents in yet another. As with other types of behaviors, the fundamental principles of instructional methodology that were discussed in Chapter 3 are totally relevant to the efficient and effective correction of speech difficulties. Recalling for the moment principles of behavior management that are of special prominence and that can be used by all who are concerned about correcting speech problems of mentally retarded children, one would certainly want to incorporate the following principles into a child's program:

1 Reinforce desired speech
2 Ignore unwanted deviations
3 Shape up desired productions through successive approximations
4 Provide appropriate models of good speech
5 Provide cues to set the occasion for proper responses and gradually fade out antecedent events as the child's responses approximate the target behavior
6 Use a continuous schedule of reinforcement, followed by a variable-ratio format as responses become stable.

THE SPEECH CORRECTIONIST
The major techniques that a speech correctionist uses in dealing with complex speech disorders are beyond the scope and focus of this book; however, these procedures have been reviewed and discussed by Van Riper (1965), Lillywhite and Bradley (1969), Neisworth and Smith (1973), and Sloan and MacAulay (1968). Remediating hard-core speech disorders requires substantial clinical training and is typically the responsibility of a speech therapist or correctionist.

Ideally, the speech correctionist should provide the direction for the remediation of the retarded child's speech defects and should guide the teacher in deciding on the activities and tasks most suitable for resolving each child's problems. In addition, the correctionist should make the teacher aware of the general attitude she should assume in reacting to a speech problem in order to foster good speech as well as good mental health. For example, because of lack of specific training, questions such as the following often perplex the teacher of the mentally retarded.

1 How much attention should I call to the child's speech problem? For example, should I stop the child during recitation for a second attempt at articulating a difficult sound?
2 How much peer pressure should I allow? Will it help a child to speak better?
3 How can I make the other children understand speech defects and accept an individual with this type of disability?
4 What proportion of group and individual work should be given to speech? How can I provide individual work without losing the rest of the class?
5 How can I work with the families to provide more adequate speech models for the children?

The correctionist should clearly serve as a consultant to both the teachers of the mentally retarded and to their parents. Answers to

specific and general questions should be given, materials and suggested procedures provided, the child's speech development frequently
reassessed, and small-group or independent work provided for the
most severely disabled. Unfortunately, this ideal situation is more the
exception than the rule, with the result that teachers of the retarded are
being provided with only minimal services for their children, the most
frequent of which is some type of speech-screening assessment.
Because of this situation, much of the responsibility for dealing with
speech problems has fallen on the teacher's shoulders. What can the
teacher do to improve the speech of the retarded?

TECHNIQUES TEACHERS MIGHT
USE TO IMPROVE SPEECH IN STUDENTS
To promote good speech and alleviate potential difficulties, the teacher
will need to demonstrate and establish an understanding of speech
problems among the children. The rapport the teacher develops with
the students will serve as a model for how the children should react
toward one another. If the teacher unknowingly or unnecessarily
rebukes, embarrasses, or reprimands a child for speaking poorly or for
not trying to articulate properly, one could expect to see other children
exhibit the same type of reaction. The teacher, then, must establish the
class tone so that the children feel free to experiment with speech and
to spontaneously try to develop greater skill in being understood. If the
teacher chooses not to work on the development of this type of
atmosphere, the results from even specific units designed to develop
speech will be minimal at best. In a sense, then, the teacher should
model appropriate attitudes and behavior toward people with disabilities, such as the speech handicapped.

The teacher should also consciously, skillfully, and continuously
model proper speech for the students. In a way, the teacher should
present a standard against which students can compare their own
utterances. By being a good model, standards of acceptability in speech
are established. A certain behavioral set for speaking must be emphasized; children should realize through example that speaking can be
enjoyable. Presenting material in an informal fashion, in a relaxed
environment that allows for periods during which speech productions
are emphasized, illustrates the kind of situation that will encourage
communication among students and with adults. In trying to be a good
speech model, teachers often fall into the trap of overarticulating. This
hyperprecision is not normal, will call undue attention to defective
speech, and should be avoided.

Certain implications logically follow from these generalizations. It
would seem wise for teachers not to handle speech errors at the time

Table 7-3
SPEECH ACTIVITIES APPROPRIATE FOR THE CLASSROOM

PRIMARY AREAS OF SPEECH ACQUISITION AND TECHNIQUES FOR FOSTERING THEIR EARLY DEVELOPMENT

EXERCISE OF THE ARTICULATORS

A   Blowing, sucking, licking, and chewing exercises help the retarded to develop coordination of important articulators. The child can be asked to imitate various movements with the tongue, such as curling, clicking, moving from side to side, and rotating.

B   Drooling can be controlled, swallowing saliva encouraged, and the tongue strengthened by having children chew gum or taffy, suck through straws, or lick peanut butter from the roofs of their mouths with their lips closed.

C   As the children do mouth and tongue exercises, a mirror should be available so that they can appreciate the results of their activities. Moreover, using a mirror will provide the students with immediate knowledge of the results of their efforts, establish a more stable pattern for subsequent behavior by reinforcement through the visual modality, and provide immediate reward.

AUDITORY TRAINING AND IMITATION

A   Have the children identify sounds while blindfolded. Direct their attention to sounds around them, and ask them to identify the unique characteristics of each. Turn the task around and have the children make sounds of various animals or other things in their environment.

B   Encourage the understanding of differences between loud and soft, high and low, happy and sad, or noisy and clear sounds.

C   Begin exercises with gross sounds such as are produced by a bell, wood blocks, piano, or drums. Gradually bring the sounds closer together in terms of their characteristics, and require finer discriminations by the child. Eventually, speech sounds in isolation and in words should be introduced.

D   Pictures and objects can be used as stimuli for a variety of speech activities. Pictures or objects beginning with various sounds, such as the *b* sound, can be selected. Games can be played with the pictures and objects. For instance, have the children find hidden objects that begin with the *b* sound or paste pictures that begin with the *b* sound on a large piece of paper.

E   The tape recorder, or special records presenting auditory discrimination tasks, can be used by the teacher.

F   Having children imitate sounds and words will help them to establish standards for good speech. This can be done through music and rhythm activities. Follow-the-leader games are also beneficial if vocalization is included along with the nonverbal activities.

G   Reciting funny poems, nursery rhymes, and singing songs will help to develop imitation skills.

Table 7-3 *(Continued)*

CORRECTING A DEFECTIVE SOUND

A Assuming that the child has the physiological capability to make sounds correctly, the teacher should first work on discriminating between sounds so the child is able to identify both the correct and the incorrect one. The child's ability to discriminate between correct and incorrect can be checked by having the teacher say words in which either sound is used. The child is then asked to indicate when the correct sound is given.

B The correct sound should first be produced in isolation and gradually employed in and practiced with words. Practice should be given in the use of correct sounds in various positions in words, phrases, and sentences.

C A tape recorder is extremely valuable and will help an individual assess his own productions to determine if new sounds are being correctly used in conversation.

D Speech activities should be done as much as possible within the context of the classroom activities.

TEACHING NEW SOUNDS AND STABILIZING THEIR USE

A Assuming that the physiological mechanisms for speech are intact, the children can be asked to listen to a sound and try to imitate what they hear. This activity can be reinforced through games. For example, children find it interesting to blow a tissue in an attempt to make plosive sounds.

B After the sound has been articulated successfully in isolation, then repeated, and reinforced, it should be used in a variety of nonsense words, in the beginning, middle, and final positions.

C Gradually the sounds should be used in several words that are familiar to the child. His repertoire should not be expanded until the sound has been correctly and continuously used. Additional words incorporating the new sound should be introduced at this point.

D Eventually a group of key words that incorporate the new sound is given to the child, who learns to use these and other words in sentences. Reinforcement should always be provided for correct usage, and the task should be varied after the sound has become stabilized.

E With retarded children this entire process will take a good bit of time and often they regress to an earlier level of carelessness in speaking. The teacher should maintain stability in stimuli, be reasonable and consistent in her expectations, be cautious not to progress too rapidly, and certainly continue to reinforce proper speech performance—on a continual basis, at first. Determination of success is based on how accurately the child can consistently use the new sound in a variety of situations involving spontaneous communication. Whenever possible, all sensory channels should be used to stimulate the acquisition of proper speech utterances.

they occur. To stop a lesson destroys the natural rhythm and sequence of the material being presented, and it also alerts children to their own weaknesses, or to those of others, at a time when particular attention to remedial procedures cannot be given. This strategy could also result in embarrassment to the child.

Since many retarded children need individual or small-group instruction, certain times each day should be given exclusively to communication activities. This should come after the teacher has a general overview of the nature of the problems within the class. A variety of activities can be included as part of this period. A tape recorder, record player, and telephone can help provide the means for listening, stimulating speech, and working on specific speech problems.

Although seemingly too obvious to mention, time should be set aside for children to talk and discuss. Teachers often feel that it is desirable to establish and maintain control of the class through constant verbalization. When this occurs, the children have little opportunity to talk and find themselves in a situation in which listening constitutes the central activity in communication. Although the verbal stimulation by the teacher may be desirable for youngsters, giving children a chance to respond is equally important.

Table 7-3 lists several types of specific activities in which teachers can engage their students to improve both speech and language.

language: the primary means for communicating ideas

Language is the ability to express ideas and concepts. Most often it is viewed as ability in the vocal expression of ideas wherein the evaluation of one's performance is not based on how well sounds are made but on how effectively ideas are expressed. Ideas can also be expressed using nonverbal communication. This is an important component of language for the retarded since it is the area in which they usually exhibit their greatest strength.

Since the middle 1950s, research on language with the mentally retarded has escalated at an astonishing rate. This has been precipitated by (1) the prevailing view of many educators that language capabilities are directly related to performance levels of the mentally retarded in other areas, (2) the development of linguistic models to which new instruments and experimentation can be directly related and validated, and (3) encouraging reports from investigations that have directed attention to studying remedial procedures in language with the mentally retarded.

Language studies, and the implications emanating from this line of research, have resulted in a greater emphasis on a learning-disabilities approach in the education of the mentally retarded. This, in turn, has stimulated among professionals expressions of dissatisfaction with traditional disability categories. This movement is consistent with the theme considered in this book: that emphasizing a clinical approach in teaching the retarded will result in the teacher, psychologist, and parents focusing on relevant educational behaviors and considering procedures for dealing with these dimensions rather than consistently classifying children by using systems that have absolutely no instructional pertinence.

The range of needs that were discussed as vital for speech development are equally essential for language development. Discrimination skills, the availability of appropriate stimuli, the presence of adequate models, and the establishment and maintenance of an adequate feedback and monitoring system contribute to language development. Speech and language do not develop in isolation but are the result of dynamic interaction between an individual and his environment. Prerequisite to the development of language is the degree to which the mentally retarded are able to attend to stimuli and listen effectively. Suggestions for maintaining attention in these children have been detailed in previous sections.

Language is an omnibus term that encompasses several major dimensions not mutually exclusive or discrete, but highly interrelated. Deemphasizing the notion that language can be assessed only in terms of the length and/or complexity of a verbal production, Myklebust (1956) has suggested reception, association, and expression as its three major components. These factors are similar to components of the assumed perceptual-motor process. Although much of the research dealing with the language characteristics of the retarded has not been intentionally directed toward studying the three processes of language, contemporary experiments have employed theoretical positions or models that allow experimenters to focus on one or more of these processes.

language characteristics
of the mentally retarded

Dimensions of language development and ability have been comprehensively reviewed and interpreted in other publications (Goertzen, 1957; Harrison, 1958; Smith, 1962; Peins, 1962; Spradlin, 1963; McCarthy, 1964; Schiefelbusch, Copeland, and Smith, 1967; Jordan, 1972).

Although the major presentation by each of these reviews deals with language, there is some difference of opinion among writers in their delineation and definition of language and communication factors. For example, some authors include speech development in their review, whereas others do not consider this area germane. The reader should be aware of these differences in the literature.

RECEPTIVE LANGUAGE
This component of language involves two processes: (1) the receipt of auditory, visual, and haptic stimuli by the peripheral organs and (2) the ability of the organism to gain understanding from these sensory experiences.

Individuals with problems of hearing or sight will misperceive sensory data and, consequently, have difficulty in the subsequent stage involving the meaningful interpretation of sensory images. Studies have suggested that the difficulty that the mentally retarded frequently exhibit in making optimum use of the auditory channel is because of the high incidence of hearing difficulties, auditory discrimination problems, memory disturbances, and environmentally induced inhibiting factors. Relative strengths or weaknesses in the visual channel in these areas are less prominent in the literature.

The research that has compared language capabilities of retarded children at various intellectual levels and mental ages has strongly suggested that they seem to have less *relative* difficulty in understanding and interpreting auditory and visual stimuli at meaningful than at nonmeaningful levels. It should be recognized that this relative strength is in comparison to their performance level in other areas of language, for the total language age of the retarded is typically lower than their mental age. The literature is consistent in suggesting that nonorganically involved retarded children are stronger in visual than in auditory reception and interpretation of stimuli. Children exhibiting the "Strauss Syndrome" show the opposite profile. That is, they are relatively stronger in auditory than in visual reception.

ASSOCIATING MEANINGFUL MATERIAL
"Association" refers to the internal manipulation of symbols of language. The ability to deal with incoming symbolic information and to appropriately associate this cognitive material with the existing repertoire is an important component of general language performance and is apparently related to MA. McCarthy (1964) characterizes this skill as "thinking in words."

The results of research dealing with the language association skills of the retarded parallel the findings of investigations concerned with receptive capabilities. Although not outstanding in general language performance, the culturally disadvantaged retarded child tends to be relatively poorer in auditory-vocal than in visual-motor association. Again, the opposite profile is seen for "Strauss Syndrome" children. Relative to their MA, retarded children score less well than one would predict in both areas of association.

EXPRESSIVE LANGUAGE

The effective translation of ideas into vocal or motor expression involves a complex constellation of capabilities among which are (1) surveying the myriad possible responses to find those that are most appropriate for the situation, (2) the proper sequencing of the components of expression, (3) the choice of an effective mode for communication (vocal and/or gestural), and (4) the effective monitoring of earlier responses, using this feedback system to alter subsequent patterns of expression. Expressive components of language involve complex operations many of which have not been identified or adequately characterized and must still be viewed as postulates.

Investigations of the vocal and gestural expressive abilities of retarded children using the Illinois Test of Psycholinguistic Abilities indicate that mildly retarded children tend to do better in the vocal expression of ideas than in gestural expression. As intelligence decreases toward the moderate level of mental retardation, this pattern reverses, with the gestural modality showing greater strength. It should be recognized that other variables apparently influence the expressive skills of the retarded. For example, living in an institution or residential facility seems to be associated with a reduction in vocal expression, whereas this pattern is not true for children in public schools who often exhibit greater skills in vocal than in motor expression.

To place these results in their proper perspective, it should be noted that in many of the studies the performance of the retarded children is compared with mental-age norms, that differences among the areas of language are relative differences, and that the indication that the retarded are stronger in vocal expression should in no sense be interpreted as meaning that their vocal expressive skills are necessarily consistent with normal children of the same CA or intellectual capability.

AUTOMATIC-SEQUENTIAL ASPECTS OF LANGUAGE

Certain aspects of language do not have meaning in the sense of embracing a concept, although these skills are necessary to effectively communicate ideas. These automatic and imitative rote-learned aspects involve the development of skill in the use of grammar, visual memory, and auditory memory. Intellectually normal children seem to learn these skills incidentally. The evidence suggests that the automatic-sequential factors constitute one of the areas of greatest difficulty for the retarded. It is ironic, indeed, that they seem to have less difficulty with the meaningful than with the imitative and rote-learned factors. The literature has been inconsistent in demonstrating greater disability in either auditory or visual memory.

assessing language difficulties

As with other areas of functioning, language performance can be evaluated using both formal and informal procedures of observation and assessment. Both should be used on a consistent basis, with special attention to systematically and continuously recording precise language behaviors of the child on an informal basis. The procedures are identical to those that have been reviewed in previous sections of this book.

FORMAL PROCEDURES
The development of formal, standardized techniques for assessing factors of language has escalated rapidly since the middle 1950s. Particular attention has been given to relating measurement and instrumentation to accepted theoretical models and constructs. The positions of Skinner (1957) and Osgood (1957) have contributed immeasurably to the construction of formal-language measures.

Several of these instruments, the dimensions of language evaluated by each, and the age range of the standardization subjects are summarized in Table 7-4. The administration of these instruments and the interpretation of a child's responses must be done by a trained and experienced speech clinician or educational diagnostician.

INFORMAL TECHNIQUES
If a language program is to be effective, the teacher should have some idea of the types of language difficulties peculiar to each child. In most settings, formal-language assessment can be given only periodically. To check frequently on the progress of each child, a systematic sample of the language performance of the children will need to be taken. From these diagnostic efforts, modification can be made on a day-to-day and week-to-week basis. If children are having difficulties in the various areas of language, it is appropriate that each child's performance be

Table 7-4

EXAMPLES OF FORMAL LANGUAGE TESTS

NAME OF TEST	AGE RANGE OF NORMATIVE SAMPLE	DIMENSIONS ASSESSED	PUBLISHER
Illinois Test of Psycholinguistic Abilities (Revised)	2–0 to 10–0	**a** Auditory reception **b** Visual reception **c** Auditory association **d** Visual association **e** Verbal expression **f** Manual expression **g** Grammatic closure **h** Visual sequential memory **i** Auditory sequential memory **j** Visual closure **k** Auditory closure (optional) **l** Sound blending (optional)	UIP
Peabody Picture Vocabulary Test	2–5 to 18–0	Auditory word comprehension and association with an appropriate visual stimulus	AGS
Screening Tests for Identifying Children with Specific Language Disability (Revised)	6–0 to 10–0	**a** Visual copying far point **b** Visual copying near point **c** Visual perception memory **d** Visual discrimination **e** Visual perception— memory in association with kinesthetic memory **f** Auditory recall **g** Auditory perception of beginning and ending sounds **h** Auditory associations	EPS

compared with the other children in the class. For example, that most children in a class can remember the words of a song indicates that this is a reasonable, broad, performance criterion against which the achievement of others in the class can be compared. If a child or small group of children is unable to measure up to this level, it would be indicative of a possible disability in understanding what they are hearing, in discriminating among the various words of the song, or in remembering an auditory sequence. When specific difficulties are identified, teachers can provide remedial experiences, which are often similar to those tasks used to diagnose the difficulty. Effort has been made to provide teachers with a compendium of informal diagnostic and remedial tasks related to factors of language; the most notable among these has been the work reported by Wiseman (1965).

Table 7-5 illustrates the types of activities teachers can use to check on those areas of language in which the retarded may show significant weaknesses. These assessment activities can be used for groups as well as for individual children.

procedures for developing language skills

The broad guidelines used to encourage the retarded to develop skills in language are no different from those used to support their performance in other areas. It is of concern that the children be exposed to an environment conducive to free expression in order to stimulate oral communication. Moreover, an accepting attitude of each child's level should be clearly demonstrated by the teacher. These suggestions are consistent with the need to minimize external evaluation. If the mentally retarded are to be stimulated to give spontaneous productions, they must be secure in their realization that there will be no criticism, and the classroom teacher should provide the model for establishing this atmosphere of acceptance. If the teacher is prone to constant critical evaluation, the children will mimic this behavior.

The environment must be arranged so that the youngsters are placed in situations in which verbal communication is necessary and natural. Any child whose communication is satisfactorily accomplished by pointing or gesturing does not need to engage in vocal communication. This behavior is often observed in young children whose parents or siblings immediately respond to an unintelligible sound and gesture. This same phenomenon occurs with the retarded when the teacher or someone else speaks for a student. In such instances, there is no need for the child to talk. It is important, therefore, that this type of communication not be rewarded, and that children be placed in situations in which verbal language is required. At the same time, each attempt at

Table 7-5

INFORMAL LANGUAGE ASSESSMENT ACTIVITIES

LANGUAGE AREA AND APPROPRIATE DIAGNOSTIC ACTIVITY

UNDERSTANDING WHAT IS HEARD

A Ask the child to follow your verbal commands such as, "Place your hand on the top of your head." "Hold your right hand in the air and wave to the people sitting on both sides of you." "Go to the table at the rear of the room, take a piece of paper out of the tray, return to your desk, and crumple the paper into a ball."

B Have the child respond to the directions sung on records such as "Ball and the Jack."

C Ask the child various questions such as, "Do books walk?" "Does chalk write?" "Do elephants eat?" Have him respond by standing up or raising a hand if the answer is "yes" and do nothing if the answer is "no."

D Play records containing various sounds and have the child identify who or what makes each sound. Ask the child to listen for certain components in stories or nursery rhymes, or have him tell the story again in order to determine if he understands what is being said.

E Present the child with a series of unambiguous pictures which appear on a single piece of paper, say the appropriate word or words describing one of the pictures, and have the child point to the correct picture.

UNDERSTANDING WHAT IS SEEN

A Show the child a picture of an animal, e.g., a cow, and give him the appropriate label for the animal; then, present the child with a series of pictures and ask him to point to all the cows. It is possible to vary this exercise by using different objects and pictures. For instance, the selection by the child can be according to those objects that are moving, things that are red, pictures that show children, or things that are round.

B Have the child inspect a picture containing an object with a certain shape or characteristic which is a hidden part of the total scene. Show a picture of the object and see how many he can locate in the total picture. The backs of cereal boxes frequently contain these types of pictures.

C Present the child with a group of chips which are of various geometric shapes or which have pictures printed on each. Have the child locate and make piles of all of the squares, triangles, or pictures of donkeys. The same exercise can be done with letters of the alphabet.

D Show a silent film, filmstrip, or series of cards which tell a story. Ask questions concerning the general story sense as well as specific details, such as what people were wearing on their heads, how many cars were in the picture, if children appeared in the sequence, and so on.

E Have the children interpret pictures by looking for details in a story, sensing implied facts, and seeing cause and effect.

F Present a series of pictures; then, have them sequence the pictures according to a story and tell about the story sequence.

Table 7-5 *(Continued)*

G Show a silent film or filmstrip and ask the students to tell about the story. Dramatization by role playing will help to determine any difficulties they might have in decoding visual stimuli.

ASSOCIATING AUDITORY STIMULI

A Play a group of recorded sounds and ask the children to identify all those sounds made by birds or animals. A variation of this is to name an object for the children, following this with a series of sounds. Ask the students to indicate which sound is made by a train. The task is made complicated by reducing the dissimilarity among the sounds or by providing more than one sound made by a train.

B Ask the children to vocally list all the things they can think of that can carry other things, that have ears or hair, or that can be built from bricks.

C Present a series of objects, and ask the students to tell in which ways the objects are similar. A graded series of these tasks can be developed which range from obvious similarities to more abstruse likenesses. Initially, it may be necessary to present a visual picture of each object as the appropriate word is said.

D Present an incomplete story or show part of a short film, and have the children tell what they think will happen, how the story will end, and why.

E Present vocal absurdities such as, "What would happen if we were born with three fingers and no thumb?" or "What would happen if we suddenly could walk only on our hands?" This will help check on how well the child is able to see cause and effect situations.

F. Have the child complete sentences such as, "I opened the window and _____ ___."

G Ask them to interpret or tell you the general sense of a story which they have been told. Determine if the child can discern cause and effect by asking him "What would happen if . . . ?" types of questions.

H Give the students an opportunity to supply an ending to a story.

ASSOCIATING STIMULI PRESENTED VISUALLY

A Present the child with cards containing pictures of absurd situations, such as a child trying to brush his teeth with a hair brush or comb. Ask them to tell you why the picture is silly, or have them point to the funny part of each picture.

B Have the children look through old magazines or catalogs and cut out all the things they can find which are green, have wheels, or have buttons. Present them with a group of pictures or objects and have the students group the objects according to some criterion, such as those things that are used for work, contain at least two colors, could hold water, or grow in the ground. Gradually ask for grouping on multiple criteria, such as those objects that are round, green, and can be eaten.

C Using one of the commercial story puzzles, ask the children to arrange the pieces of the puzzle so that the story is told. At first, they should be shown the entire sequence and later be allowed to reassemble the components of the story.

Table 7-5 *(Continued)*

D Show a picture and ask the children to verbally or gesturally indicate what would happen if "such and such" had occurred. For example, a picture of cars stopped at an intersection for a red light could be used and the children asked to tell or show the possible consequences of a car going through the red light.

E Prepare a sheet with pictures of objects which have characteristic sounds. From tape, present the children with a sound and have them relate the sound to one of the pictures.

F Present a picture of an object followed by a second series of pictures showing a group of objects. One of the group should be the same as the initial picture, or a variation thereof, shown from a different perspective. Ask the child to choose the one which is the same as the first picture.

REMEMBERING WHAT IS HEARD

A Ask the child to repeat digits of varying lengths forward and/or backward.

B Present words or sentences of different lengths and complexity, and ask that they be repeated in the way that they were originally presented.

C Observe how well the children remember rhymes and songs.

D Read a story to the group and have each child recall specific and general aspects of the story.

E Sing or play records using music that allows for adding on, such as "Old MacDonald Had a Farm." See how well children remember the paired relationships within the song. For example, the cow goes "moo" and not "quack-quack."

F See if the students can follow a series of directions which increase in length and complexity. For example, say, "Charlie, I would like for you to get up from your chair, take this piece of paper to the trash can, go to the blackboard, draw a circle, place the open book on the table, and return to your desk."

REMEMBERING WHAT IS SEEN

A Show a group of objects which initially are quite dissimilar in their characteristics. Have the students close their eyes while one of the objects is removed, and after they have opened their eyes, have them recall what is missing. This task can be increased in complexity by increasing the number of objects presented, exhibiting objects with similar characteristics, removing more than one object, or by requiring that a child replace the objects in the same initial sequence.

B Present a series of cards with paired-associate types of tasks, mix the cards up, and ask a child to reconstruct the pairs. For example, you might have a series of colored chips with the name of each color printed on separate cards. The child learns to associate the blue chip with the card containing the printed word "blue." Several of these types of pairs can be presented with the child requested to match the appropriate word with the correct color after the objects have been mixed up.

C Show a picture and have the students remember all the objects they saw.

Table 7-5 *(Continued)*

D Remembering and reconstructing a pictorial sequence such as in a comic strip will help to assess visual memory and the visual interpretation of stimuli.

VOCAL EXPRESSION OF IDEAS

A Observe how well children do during the "show-and-tell" period or in their description of an object, event, or process.

B Have the children respond to questions which emphasize verbal fluency wherein any response a child gives is correct, such as, "How many ways can a toothpick be used?" "What would happen if everyone lived in a house made of glass?"

C Show a picture and have the children tell about the picture, what went on before the picture was taken, and what happened afterward.

D Have a child tell how to do something such as catch a fish, teach a dog to fetch a stick, or cut the lawn.

E Show a simple object and ask for a description of the object.

F Observe the extent of each child's vocabulary, the length and complexity of sentences used, and how correctly words are used.

MOTOR EXPRESSION OF IDEAS

A Have the children dramatize an event which has been seen or heard, such as threading a needle, sewing on a patch, cooking dinner, driving a car, or riding a horse.

B Have them listen to a record containing a short story or song and draw a picture on the blackboard or on a large piece of paper describing what was heard.

C Observe how effectively children communicate ideas in finger plays.

D Ask the group to draw objects having certain characteristics, such as things that have three corners, objects that carry other things, or illustrations of things that can be eaten.

E Ask the children to show how many ways musical instruments can be played.

F Observe the use of gestures in describing a happening or object during show-and-tell.

G Creative dramatics and role playing will provide excellent situations for assessing ability in motor expression.

H Present an object or show a picture. Ask the children to show what people usually do with the object.

oral expression should be rewarded. Specific periods should be set aside for language arts, and the children should become involved in the vocal communication of ideas.

Activities appropriate for an informal assessment of language reception, association, memory, and expression were presented earlier.

These suggestions are equally appropriate for teaching language skills in a developmental sense and for remediating in specific problem areas. The activities suggested can be used as presented or elaborated upon and extended to include more complex tasks. Other suggestions which the teacher should consider in formulating a language program include the following:

1 Auditory and visual discrimination and memory should be emphasized through a systematic training program.

2 Frequent formal and informal discussion periods should be scheduled to encourage the retarded to express themselves freely and to listen attentively to others. Critical evaluation should not be part of this activity.

3 As language skills develop, the teacher should be more direct in helping students to organize their thoughts and expressions so that they are logical, parsimonious, and appropriate.

4 Activities planned for the children should emanate from real situations that the teacher believes to be significant. For example, allowing teen-age children to use the telephone will provide an excellent and realistic situation from which language skills can develop.

5 In all language activities, the early association of the various senses should be encouraged. Stimuli can be presented using both the auditory and visual modalities. It is also desirable that vocal expressions be encouraged at the same time that nonverbal productions are given, and vice versa.

6 Liberal use should be made of musical activities, including recordings of songs and stories, tapes of children's voices, rhythm-band activities, add-on or sing-along songs, and recordings requiring activities by the children. These high-interest materials offer a relaxed environment and at the same time provide stimulation for encouraging communication by shy children.

7 Show-and-tell periods often become a daily ritual and, if handled intelligently, provide an excellent stimulus for encouraging language. Even older retarded children find it interesting to bring something to show their classmates, and they are frequently eager to instruct other students in procedures for correctly operating a machine or performing some process, such as rowing a boat.

8 Games and activities in which any response given by a child is correct offer excellent stimulants for encouraging verbal and nonverbal fluency. Questions such as the following can be used: "How many ways can you think of to use a screwdriver?" "What would happen if everyone had springs in his shoes?" In nonverbal areas, the children can be asked to draw as many different things as possible on a sheet of paper containing 30 one-inch squares.

9 Choral reading, reciting, and singing encourage participation from those students who have not developed minimal skills in expression.

10 Creative dramatics and role playing are good techniques for encouraging the development of nonverbal language skills.

a word about severe speech and language disorders

Although the main focus in this chapter has been on diagnosing and dealing with mild or moderate speech and language disorders, there is in nearly every school a small group of youngsters who evidence more extreme problems in verbal communication. Some of these children may not make a sound other than some vague and undefined vowel productions. Others may have seriously impoverished language competencies, perhaps even to the point of not having many verbal labels for common objects. On the other hand, such children are frequently highly skilled in nonverbal communication. It is almost as if their gesturing constitutes another language within a home or classroom, and with enough persistence the youngsters are usually able to make themselves understood and get what they desire.

On the premise that such children can be taught to speak, the special education professional often has the responsibility (sometimes by default) of deciding on and initiating a program of instruction. Most of the guidelines that were presented in Chapter 4, especially those that pertain to the reinforcement of desired behavior, are vital components of any program designed to stimulate speech and language. Suppose we assume that a child, Jonathan (aged three), has some vague vowel sounds, no consonant sounds, reasonably good receptive language skills, and many gestures. A teacher, or parent, might structure a program of instruction for Jonathan that is oriented along the following guidelines:

1 The most important initial step to take is to decide to ignore gestures. If you attend to his nonverbal signals and obey his gestured demands, you can expect to see this behavior increase and the problems in getting him to use verbal modes for communication will become even more difficult to overcome.

2 A worthy initial target for the child might be to seek to increase any form of verbal utterance by simple reinforcement, by modeling on the part of the teacher or therapist, and by prompting. Initially, the teacher might decide to increase the frequency of the child's existing vowel sounds by continuously rewarding them. Eventually, however, the child should be prompted, and subsequently reinforced, for variations and elaborations on these basic sounds.

3 After the initial vowel sounds have become established, the speech targets should change to include consonant sounds, taken one at a time. The *mmm* sound and the *p* sound are recommended, in that order.

4 Gradually, and often over a long period of time, the child's repertoire of speech sounds can be shaped up and the youngster taught to make consonant-vowel combinations. The procedure used at each level of difficulty is basically the same: (a) model the sound for the child, (b) prompt and cue him on how and when to use it, (c) reward movement toward the goal on which you are working, and (d) give him a great deal of practice in making sounds.

5 As the child develops more complex sounds and eventually is able to say words, it is natural to begin relating objects to words, such as in labeling activities. This is the beginning of the process of developing and establishing a more complex pattern of language usage.

developing skills
in written communication

Handwriting, spelling, and the written expression of ideas will be focused upon in this section. The procedures used by the teacher in providing instruction in these areas are basically similar to those used by the regular classroom teacher. In the regular class, many of the skills involved are learned incidentally; however, special class instruction in these fundamental subject areas must be conducted intentionally and sequenced. Entrance into adult life requires that the retarded acquire a certain level of skill in each area.

HANDWRITING

As is true with intellectually normal children, instructing the retarded in handwriting requires that they have a certain minimal level of muscular coordination. Children must be able to grasp a pencil or piece of chalk and maintain a certain posture while it is manipulated. Procedures for aiding the retarded to develop basic motor skills were suggested in Chapter 6.

Children should initially be given experiences which allow for the practice of basic writing movements. The configuration of circles and straight and slanted lines can be developed by encouraging freedom of movement in art and drawing. At first, it is unwise to force the students to do small motor tasks with a pencil or pen until they have first practiced the strokes on a blackboard or a large piece of paper with a soft pencil, felt pen, chalk, or crayon. Gradually, as they develop control, the children are taught to combine these circles and other strokes, formerly used for drawing, into the formation of letters and words.

After these basic skills develop, the retarded can be engaged in activities requiring the use of small motor skills. Tracing letters on paper by following appropriately placed arrows will help them develop a systematic procedure for properly constructing letters. Full attention should be given to the development of a clear image of the letter and an appropriate sequence for making the strokes. Paper with horizontal lines is recommended for this stage.

A word of caution should be given at this point. Care should be exercised so that the children focus on the total configuration of the letter rather than the line segments being traced. The mode of presentation and the activities at this stage of development should be varied so as not to encourage emphasis which is tangential to the main objective of the tracing activity. Moreover, long periods of close work should be avoided and special attention should be given so that the children do not need to constantly refocus from near point to far point and vice versa.

Combining letters into words requires a close relationship between activities of reading, spelling, and oral expression. To construct words, the child needs to be able to sequence and space letters appropriately as well as correctly read and spell the word. Many teachers believe that whole words with real meaning should be introduced into the handwriting program at a very early stage. This strategy will increase the possibility of maintaining the child's interest in writing activities.

There is no empirical documentation to suggest that the handwriting program for the retarded should stress manuscript or cursive writing. It seems logically reasonable that less confusion would result in using manuscript writing because of the close relationship this has to material from books and the typewritten reproductions teachers frequently prepare. There is a clear advantage in relating all these activities and skills. Professional opinions vary on which writing style is preferred. Strauss and Lehtinen (1947), for example, suggest the use of cursive writing early in the children's career because it facilitates the children's seeing words in their totality.

Accuracy and not speed should always be stressed. Retarded children should not be placed in competitive situations in writing. The able teacher should focus on intra-individual evaluations by demonstrating variations within each child's performance. Comparing students with each other will foster poor habits and reduce the legibility and accuracy of the retarded child's performance. Principles of learning presented earlier should be viewed by the teacher as basic and necessary to handwriting instruction.

Most educable mentally retarded will eventually be able to make the transition from manuscript to cursive writing. The appropriate time for this event will vary according to each child's manipulative capabilities, their success in other areas such as reading and spelling, and their level of development in manuscript writing. With normal children, cursive writing is typically introduced in the late second or early third grade. Anderson (1964) has suggested the need to proceed from the simple to the complex by introducing lowercase letters in the following sequence: *l, e, i, t, u, n, m, h, k, w, o, b, v, x, y, j, f, s, p, r, c, a, d, g, q, z.* Capital letters can be taught as the need arises, such as when a name is written.

SPELLING

It is reasonable to expect that most mildly mentally retarded children will advance in spelling to about the fifth-grade level. As in any subject area involving the use of complex skills, expectations for spelling achievement will vary according to any unique weaknesses an individual child exhibits. For example, children with visualization difficulties may have substantial problems in spelling. In like manner, children with auditory discrimination problems could have spelling weaknesses because they may be unable to hear the sounds peculiar to spelling words. For those who seem to have unusual difficulty in spelling, an informal assessment of each child's performance in the fundamental skills should be conducted. Some of these fundamental areas are (1) auditory and visual reception, (2) auditory and visual memory, (3) auditory and visual discrimination, (4) association of auditory and visual stimuli, (5) motor expression, and (6) vocal expression. Techniques for evaluating children in each of these areas have been presented in an earlier section of this chapter.

Teaching considerations which are paramount for effective instruction in spelling include the following:

1 There is a need to establish and maintain a close relationship between instruction in reading, writing, and spelling. Procedures appropriate for teaching reading to the retarded will help to strengthen their spelling performances.

2 In teaching spelling to the retarded, all sense modalities should be used in concert. Children should trace or write a word, say the word, and observe its configuration when written by someone else. Using all the sense modalities will help to develop firm patterns of association. In this regard, the suggestion of Kirk and Johnson (1951) for using the Fernald system seems wise.

3 Because English has such a confusing phonemic structure, teaching spelling through the use of rules will be less effective and more confusing to the retarded. As is true in no other area, rote instruction in spelling rather than emphasizing conceptual development and understanding is necessary. For a small number of the higher-level educable retarded, however, introducing a few basic spelling rules may help to elevate their general spelling performance.

4 Words which have utility for the children should be selected for the spelling program. Material which is to be learned should be appropriate and of potential use to retarded children.

5 The retarded should not be given a chance to practice their errors. Immediate knowledge of results with appropriate rewards for a correct response will control this possibility. Teachers must be sure that an effective and accurate monitoring device for feedback is available. This could take the form of a programmed device, a teacher's aid, or some type of team or buddy system. In this way, children can be given the necessary feedback required for reinforcing success and obliterating patterns of error in spelling.

6 If the child knows how to write, instruction in spelling will probably make more immediate impact. By knowing how to write letters, the child will provide his own reinforcement and encourage greater intermodality facilitation. However, knowing how to write is not absolutely necessary if the child can discriminate among letters. Children can be given a group of letters each of which is printed on a separate card in a procedure similar to that used in a chart story. Each child can be asked to spell out a word using his own group of letters and to compare his performance with the teacher's model. By moving their fingers over the letters placed in sequence, they will develop skill in seeing the sequence of letters in words and strengthen their writing performance.

7 The teacher should keep a log of words the children use and those each child has particular trouble with in reading, spelling, and writing. If an individual seems to be particularly bothered by a certain group of words which have a common characteristic, the teacher may find it helpful to teach the child the rule or principle appropriate for those situations. Clinical teaching, then, requires the maintenance of a careful record of specific weaknesses in spelling.

8 Spelling is often a boring and tiresome activity. Attempts should be made to provide interesting activities during the spelling period. Retarded children who can spell at a third- or fourth-grade level enjoy participating in spelling bees as long as the rewards and penalties are not too high. When too much pressure is exerted, their performance will decline.

WRITTEN EXPRESSION

With the exception of the research by Cartwright (1968) and Sedlak and Cartwright (1972) little attention has been given to investigating written language abilities of mildly retarded children. Their research showed that the retarded are significantly weaker than the intellectually normal in composition length, sentence length, type-token ratio (number of different words divided by the composition length), grammatical correctness, and spelling correctness. Apparently the degree of disability that the retarded exhibit in written expression is directly related to their level of performance in oral expression. Written language, then, is an extension of oral language.

Too much direct emphasis on grammatical structure and other technical aspects of writing should not constitute a large segment of the retarded child's program. Spending too much time and effort on developing these skills will result in shortchanging other more important areas. Moreover, the vast majority of educable children will not be able to develop substantial skill in the appropriate use of written syntax. There are, however, certain procedures teachers can take to upgrade the retarded child's performance in written expression. Among these are the following:

1 As in the case of oral communication, mentally retarded children will profit in their acquisition of skill in written expression by being exposed to a good model. Since most parents of children living in disadvantaged communities do not provide this type of model, it will be necessary for the teacher to expose the retarded to a wide spectrum of examples of written and oral expression.
2 Emphasis should be placed on interrelating oral and written communication. Vocal expression should be translated into written communication, and vice versa.
3 Any writing done by the child should be of a practical nature and viewed as significant by the retarded youngster. It will often be necessary to devote time to changing the attitudes of the children before they can be asked to participate in written exercises.
4 Attention should be given to making use of the retarded child's

relative strengths in nonverbal areas to facilitate development in written production. Dramatizations of some type of process, such as catching a fish, can be described in written discourse. This activity will make clear their need to develop more skill in written expression.

5 The teacher can help the child in written communication by encouraging the appropriate sequencing of ideas. Exercises to strengthen the presentation of written material in a logical fashion should be incorporated in all areas of the instructional program, particularly in those portions involving oral communication. The retarded should learn what ideas should logically come before or after a thought, expression, or activity.

selected readings

Anderson, P. S.: *Language Skills in Elementary Education*, The Macmillan Company, New York, 1964, p. 108.

Bangs, J. E.: "A Clinical Analysis of the Articulatory Defects of the Feebleminded," *Journal of Speech Disorders*, 7:343–356, 1942.

Bateman, B. D. and J. Wetherell: "Psycholinguistic Aspects of Mental Retardation," *Mental Retardation*, 3:8–13, 1965.

Birch, J. W. and J. Matthews: "The Hearing of Mental Defectives: Its Measurement and Characteristics," *American Journal of Mental Deficiency*, 55:384–393, 1951.

Blanchard, I.: "Speech Patterns and Etiology in Mental Retardation," *American Journal of Mental Deficiency*, 68:612–616, 1964.

Cartwright, G. P.: "Written Language Abilities of Educable Mentally Retarded and Normal Children," *American Journal of Mental Deficiency*, 72:499–505, 1968.

Fokes, J.: "Developmental Scale of Language Acquisition," in W. B. Stephens (ed.), *Training the Developmentally Young*, The John Day Company, Inc., New York, 1971, pp. 102–132.

Glovsky, L. and S. Rigrodsky: "A Classroom Program for Auditorially Handicapped Mentally Deficient Children," *Training School Bulletin*, 60:56–59, 1963.

Goda, S. and S. Rigrodsky: "Auditory Training Procedures of Certain Mentally Retarded Children," *Training School Bulletin*, 59:81–86, 1962.

Goertzen, S. M.: "Speech and the Mentally Retarded Child," *American Journal of Mental Deficiency*, 62:244–253, 1957.

Harrison, S.: "A Review of Research in Speech and Language Development of the Mentally Retarded Child," *American Journal of Mental Deficiency*, 63:236–240, 1958.

Jordan, T. E.: *The Mentally Retarded* (3d ed.), Charles E. Merrill Company, Columbus, Ohio, 1972.

Karlin, I. W. and M. Strazzula: "Speech and Language Problems of Mentally Deficient Children," *Journal of Speech and Hearing Disorders*, 17:286–294, 1952.

Kirk, S. A.: "Research in Education," in H. A. Stevens and R. Heber (eds.), *Mental Retardation: A Review of Research*, The University of Chicago Press, Chicago, 1964, pp. 57–99.

———— and G. O. Johnson: *Educating the Retarded Child*, Houghton Mifflin Company, Boston, 1951.

Kodman, F.: "The Incidence of Hearing Loss in Mentally Retarded Children," *American Journal of Mental Deficiency*, 62:675–678, 1958.

Lillywhite, H. S. and D. P. Bradley: *Communication Problems in Mental Retardation: Diagnosis and Management*, Harper & Row, Publishers, Incorporated, New York, 1969.

Lloyd, L. L. and E. J. Moore: "Audiology," in J. Wortis (ed.), *Mental Retardation: An Annual Review*, Grune & Stratton, Inc., New York, 1972, vol. IV, pp. 141–163.

McCarthy, J. J.: "Research on the Linguistic Problems of the Mentally Retarded," *Mental Retardation Abstracts*, U.S. Department of Health, Education, and Welfare, 1964, vol. 1, pp. 3–27.

McGunigle, D.: "Speech Performance of Mental Retardates as Related to Selected Aspects of Hospitalization," *American Journal of Mental Deficiency*, 71:558–560, 1967.

Matthews, J.: "Speech of the Mentally Retarded," in L. E. Travis (ed.), *Handbook of Speech Pathology*, Appleton-Century-Crofts, Inc., New York, 1957, pp. 531–551.

Michel, J. F. and R. J. Carney: "Pitch Characteristics of Mongoloid Boys," *Journal of Speech and Hearing Disorders*, 29:212–215, 1964.

Myklebust, H. R.: "Language Disorders in Children," *Exceptional Children*, 22:163–166, 1956.

Neisworth, J. T. and R. M. Smith: *Modifying Retarded Behavior*, Houghton Mifflin Company, Boston, 1973.

Osgood, C. E.: *Contemporary Approaches to Cognition: A Behavioral Analysis*, Harvard University Press, Cambridge, Mass., 1957.

Peins, M.: "Mental Retardation: A Selected Bibliography on Speech, Hearing and Language Problems," *Asha*, 4:38–40, 1962.

Rigrodsky, S. and M. D. Steer: "Mocorer's Theory Applied to Speech Habilitation and the Mentally Retarded," *Journal of Speech and Hearing Disorders*, 26:237–243, 1961.

Schiefelbusch, R. L., R. H. Copeland, and J. O. Smith: *Language and Mental Retardation: Empirical and Conceptual Considerations*, Holt, Rinehart and Winston, Inc., New York, 1967.

Schlanger, B. B.: "Effects of Listening Training on Auditory Thresholds of Mentally Retarded Children," *Asha*, 4:273–275, 1962.

———— and R. H. Gottsleben: "Analysis of Speech Defects Among the Institutionalized Mentally Retarded," *Journal of Speech and Hearing Disorders*, 22:98–103, 1957.

Sedlak, R. A. and G. P. Cartwright: "Written Language Abilities of EMR and Nonretarded Children with the Same Mental Ages," *American Journal of Mental Deficiency*, 77:95–99, 1972.

Siegel, G. M.: "Experienced and Inexperienced Articulation Examiners," *Journal of Speech and Hearing Disorders,* 27:28–35, 1962.

Skinner, B. F.: *Verbal Behavior*, Appleton-Century-Crofts, Inc., New York, 1957.

Sloan, H. N. and B. D. MacAulay: *Operant Procedures in Remedial Speech and Language Training*, Houghton Mifflin Company, Boston, 1968.

Smith, J. O.: "Speech and Language of the Retarded," *Training School Bulletin*, vol. 58, 1962.

Spradlin, J. E.: "Language and Communication of Mental Defectives," in Norman R. Ellis (ed.), *Handbook of Mental Deficiency*, McGraw-Hill Book Company, New York, 1963, pp. 512–555.

Strauss, A. A. and L. E. Lehtinen: *Psychopathology and Education of the Brain-Injured Child*, Grune & Stratton, Inc., New York, 1947, pp. 184–190.

Travis, L. E. (ed.): *Handbook of Speech Pathology*, Appleton-Century-Crofts, Inc., New York, 1957, pp. 286–287.

Van Riper, C.: *Speech Correction: Principles and Methods*, 4th ed., Prentice-Hall, Inc., Englewood Cliffs, N.J., 1965, pp. 74–101, 467–502.

Wilson, F. B.: "Efficacy of Speech Therapy with Educable Mentally Retarded Children," *Journal of Speech and Hearing Research*, 9:423–433, 1966.

Wiseman, D. E.: "A Classroom Procedure for Identifying and Remediating Language Problems," *Mental Retardation*, 3:20–24, 1965.

8

DEVELOPING READING SKILLS

The reading process is exceedingly complicated. An individual must master a series of complex skills to effectively perform and receive the maximum advantage from reading. Adequate reception, discrimination among sounds and symbols, association among various components involved in reading, remembering a visual and auditory sequence, understanding material, applying facts and concepts to earlier learned material, and the effective expression of ideas comprise some of the major factors involved in reading. The complexities involved in adequate mastery of these skills provide a reasonable explanation why mentally retarded children often have such great difficulty learning to read. The added ambition of helping them to develop a conceptual instead of rote competency only increases the magnitude of the problem.

Perhaps in no other area does the teacher need to place greater emphasis on skill development than in reading. There are several noteworthy reasons for emphasizing reading. First, the basic skills constitute the most significant common denominator for adequate achievement in other important areas. Without an elementary ability to read, mentally retarded children could be adversely affected in arithmetic, social and personal development, communication, and vocational performance. Satisfactory achievement in each of these areas presupposes a certain minimum level of reading skill. Although the influence of reading disability may not be severe enough to make an impact in the early school years, when the child reaches junior or senior high school age his inability to read will become obvious to him and to others and will cause increasing problems of various types.

Second, reading must be emphasized to provide the retarded with a means for acquiring general information. Enhancement of the child's response repertoire is a primary objective of the reading program. Reading provides a breadth of general information that can be assimilated into the repertoire with a minimum of outside direction if the youngsters have developed the basic skills of word attack and continue to expand their reading vocabulary. This additional information, acquired through independent reading, allows for the generation of alternative solutions to problems.

Third, reading depends on the use of a consistent style or method for systematically analyzing each reading situation. The transfer, generalization, and elaboration of such a style should characterize the manner in which the child solves problems in other areas of life. This thesis is that reading demands a consistent approach and that use by the child of a consistent approach in reading situations will lead him to employ a similar strategy in other areas, thereby reducing impulsive and random responses to problems.

Fourth, reading provides opportunities for pleasurable out-of-school activities. Further, ability to perform independently in these activities might well be expected to lead to a more positive self-concept. The side advantage of other children in a family, with possible disorders, seeing value in developing reading skills through independent reading is worthy of note.

Finally, skill in reading decreases the possibility of the child experiencing physical harm and provides an insulation against severe social and emotional difficulties. The adverse influence of these environmental difficulties alone amply justifies emphasis being placed on the reading program.

basic reading objectives

The basic objectives of the reading program for the mentally retarded differ little from those that are viewed as appropriate for intellectually normal children. Obviously, the teacher will want to help every child develop as high a level of sophistication in reading as he is able. The following specific objectives should be emphasized in the program for mentally retarded youngsters:

1 Development of a basic sight vocabulary with elaboration on the existing speaking and listening vocabulary.
2 Development of a consistent method for word attack which is appropriate for each child and is based on his idiosyncratic strengths and weaknesses.

3 Development of skill in and a desire to read independently for information, pleasure, and personal satisfaction.
4 Development of an adequate level of reading competence to allow for effective social and vocational participation in society.

The first two objectives are consistent with the earlier expressed need to focus on the development of skill in the fundamental processes of reading. By using the children's existing speaking and listening capabilities to develop a sight vocabulary, the teacher can capitalize on the intrinsic motivation of the activities and experiences with which the children have had success. The approach that the teacher uses to help in word attack depends basically on where the child shows strength. There is often a wide discrepancy between the skill with which a child deals with auditory and visual stimuli. Ideally, therefore, a formal, but at the very least an informal, assessment of every child should precede a decision as to whether a visual, auditory, or combined approach should be emphasized. Consistency in the approach should be maintained throughout the process.

The latter two reading objectives emphasize the areas to which a child's developing skill should be applied. A utilitarian theme should be stressed early in the program. This is not to imply, however, that pleasureful reading is to be minimized; indeed, for the mentally retarded, this type of reading is both useful and of immediate, tangible value.

evaluating reading skills

By this time you know that a major tenet of this book is that evaluation of a child's performance, in whatever area you are focusing upon, is necessary in order to intelligently decide on appropriate targets, instructional procedures, and materials. This assessment or diagnosis should be as detailed as necessary but it should by all means deal with behaviors that (1) can be reliably and directly observed, (2) pertain to the subject area in a very specific way, and (3) will lead to definite and describable management procedures, whether they be developmental or remedial.

One subject of substantial dispute among behavioral scientists is the place that intelligence test scores should have in a reading diagnosis. You have already read about the controversy over the use of intelligence test scores in Chapter 2; that discussion will not be repeated here. With respect to establishing a reading diagnosis, it has been a tradition in most sections of the country to routinely administer an intelligence test to children who are suspected of being mentally retarded and/or to youngsters who have what appear to be significant reading problems. In numerous instances the child's mental age has been calculated and interpreted as the major indicator of capacity or potential for learning to read. The child's reading achievement is then assessed, and a comparison is made between his adjudged potential and his present level of performance. If a discrepancy of approximately nine months or more exists between the two scores, the child is usually viewed as requiring special attention.

There are some advantages in administering an intelligence test to children who are having difficulties in learning (although it is of dubious value to do so on a routine basis); however, attempting to determine a child's capacity to read runs a definite risk of being counterproductive and of actually hindering the establishment of an objectively based program. In certain cases it might help to document an informal observation (such as when a child is believed to have greater nonverbal strengths than verbal) by using an intelligence test that assesses various categories of skills. The use of tests that tap a variety of skills, a youngster's performance among which you desire to make intercomparisons, is to be encouraged when the performance characteristics of the child can lead directly to the establishment of a preferred program or of its validation. But to administer an intelligence test to ascertain an IQ score or MA equivalent has questionable value.

The proposal that was made in Chapter 3 concerning a diagnostic sequence is directly applicable in areas of reading. One can decide if a child is deficient in reading by using a broad-range achievement test to profile his performance. If the child shows depressed achievement scores in reading, or in any of the skill areas contained therein, a more detailed probe should be initiated into his areas of weakness and an analysis should be made of the environment within which the problems occur. So, the technique of inquiry into characteristics of the child's performance problems remains the same among subject areas—the difference lies in the measuring tools that one uses and the peculiarities of the subject matter under study. For example, the content and targets in reading are obviously different from those in arithmetic, spelling, or motor development.

This section will suggest some formal and informal procedures for diagnosing certain prominent types of reading problems in children with retarded intellectual development. Do not misunderstand; there is no unique syndrome of reading disorders that is peculiar to the mentally retarded. The types of problems they exhibit are no different from anyone else's, although they do tend to have more in number and complexity than nonretarded children. The remainder of this section is arranged in an arbitrary way. The tests that are listed are but a sample of those that are available, and if you are interested in investigating reading tests more thoroughly you will find it helpful to refer to Roswell and Natchez (1964), Strang (1969), Bond and Tinker (1957), or Kaluger and Kolson (1969).

1. ASSESSING READINESS LEVELS

If a child has previously been unsuccessful in reading, if he is young and has not been exposed to a formal reading program, or if he is completely disinterested in participating in activities that involve reading, you might suspect that he has not experienced success in certain skill areas that are prerequisite to being able to read. In any of these instances, as well as in others you could think of, you should not delay in attempting to catalog the readiness skills in which the child is performing satisfactorily and those in which he is weak. As has been mentioned, it is vital to place mentally retarded children in instructional situations in which they will succeed because of the reinforcing character of success. If we push a youngster into a reading program without his having developed skills that are assumed to precede that program, there is little doubt but that he will fail, become frustrated, and learn to dislike reading. This happens, and it certainly is not the child's fault. The teacher is responsible for determining the proper character of each child's instructional environment.

There is no exhaustive list of reading readiness skills to which one can refer, nor is there a readiness test available to assess the entire array of presumed areas of competence. Among the areas of major concern in reading readiness are skills such as discriminating among sounds and visual displays, remembering an auditory or visual sequence, listening for details, following directions, recognizing letters, using context for cues to comprehension, eye-hand coordination, seeing relationships, and interpreting pictures. You could think of activities or tests to use in assessing performance in each of these skill areas. It is much more difficult to deal with readiness areas such as those involving emotional, social, or personal development. Although there are numerous personality inventories to assess the emotional readiness of a child to read, I suggest that you give evaluation priority to readiness skills that are more easily and objectively assessed (such as those just mentioned). These skills have more direct pertinence to reading. You can see that I am presenting a biased position, and I do not deny that emotions play a major role in being able to read. However, if success can be increased by providing a child with an effective program designed to deal with specific skills that have a direct relation to reading (e.g., seeing relationships between a letter and its name), the alleged emotional problems will have a high probability of becoming less pronounced and influential. You see, identify, and properly attack the skill weakness, assure the child's success in those areas, and watch the increase in his interest in reading activities when previously he could have been classified as "emotionally blocked"!

Formal Procedures Table 8-1 lists several of the standardized readiness tests that have relevance to the broad area of reading. None of these devices assesses the full spectrum of readiness skills, but each samples skills within that spectrum. Whichever you decide to use, make certain that you first select the precise skill areas you want to evaluate before selecting the instrument. Always attempt to directly observe a child's performance in a skill and eschew making interpretations about performance when there are no data or when inordinate assumptions are required.

Informal Procedures Teachers often do not have standardized tests available to assess a child's readiness for formal instruction in reading. Since it is important to be able to begin instruction at a proper point on the sequence of skills in reading, teachers may need to depend initially on their own, somewhat informal, assessment of each child's needs. Of course, we want to avoid unnecessary delays, random testing of procedures, and false starts in all aspects of the school program—and this is especially true in reading. To that end, you should try to systematize the informal procedures you intend to use in assessing readiness factors and, indeed, in all other areas of reading. One major way of doing this is to develop a card file of skills, activities, and criteria that can be unobtrusively inserted into the ongoing program to evaluate a youngster's performance. This same suggestion was advanced in the earlier chapter on perceptual-motor development. Table 8-2 illustrates some of the major areas of reading readiness and suggests activities that can serve as the *modus operandi* for your observation of achievement in each area.

2. ASSESSING THE GENERAL INSTRUCTIONAL LEVEL FOR READING

The rationale that has been presented for being concerned about establishing a child's performance level and characteristics in other subject areas, as well as in the immediately preceding section on reading readiness, is entirely appropriate here. Make use of those formal instruments you feel competent to administer and continue to check on the children's scores on these devices by using informal procedures.

Table 8-1

EXAMPLES OF STANDARDIZED READING READINESS TESTS

NAME OF TEST	FACTORS ASSESSED	PUBLISHER
Gates-MacGinitie Reading Tests (Readiness Skills)	a. Auditory blending b. Auditory discrimination c. Following directions d. Letter recognition e. Listening comprehension f. Visual discrimination g. Visual-motor coordination h. Word recognition	TCP
Lee-Clark Reading Readiness Test	a. Letter symbols b. Concepts c. Word symbols	MGH
Murphy-Durrell Reading Readiness Analysis	a. Learning rate b. Letter names c. Phonemes test d. Total	HBJ
School Readiness Survey	a. Color naming b. Discrimination of form c. General information d. Listening vocabulary e. Number concepts f. Speaking vocabulary g. Symbol matching h. Total	CPP
Harrison-Stroud Reading Readiness Profiles	a. Giving names of letters b. Auditory discrimination c. Visual discrimination d. Using auditory and context clues e. Using symbols f. Using context	HMC

Formal Procedures   Survey tests that are part of a general achievement battery can be used to assess the level at which a child is able to read. These tests sample a variety of reading skills including oral and silent reading, vocabulary, word knowledge, and comprehension. They can usually be administered by the teacher either to individual children or to groups of youngsters. Table 8-3 lists reading achievement tests that reflect current developments in this area.

Table 8-2

INFORMAL TECHNIQUES FOR ASSESSING READING READINESS SKILLS

READINESS FACTORS AND ASSESSMENT PROCEDURES

AUDITORY DISCRIMINATION

A   Present the children with sounds which are consistent in intensity but which vary in pitch. Ask them to tell which sound is higher and which is lower. Have them try to reproduce the sound. Gradually, bring the sounds closer together in pitch so that discriminations become more difficult. Hold pitch constant, vary intensity, and ask them to choose the louder or softer sound. Eventually, vary both intensity and pitch.

B   Read a story or poem with similar sounds. Ask the children to listen to the beginning sound of each word and to tell which is used, for example, "Carl cast copper coins into the creek."

C   Ask the children to recite a poem or to sing a song which they have learned earlier. Pay particular attention to whether the children exhibit a consistent pattern of difficulties in discrimination.

D   Tape record a series of sets containing two sounds, some of which vary substantially and others of which are alike. Using a numbered piece of paper, have the children listen to each sound and place a mark next to the number of each set which sounds alike. Gradually, develop a taped inventory of sets of words, musical selections, and sounds which differ on more than one dimension. This can be used as an assessment device as well as a procedure for training auditory discrimination.

VISUAL DISCRIMINATION

A   Observe the children grouping three-dimensional objects which differ in only one way, e.g., in shape, size, or color. Gradually, introduce variation on more than one dimension, such as by asking the children to choose the largest green box from a variety of other objects which differ in size and color.

B   By using jigsaw puzzles, check on visual-discrimination skills. This same technique can be used to assess the degree of spatial orientation children exhibit in placing a puzzle piece in the appropriate spot.

C   Ask the children to locate and cross out all the *b*'s in a short passage. Later the children can be asked to cross out words containing the letters *p* and *b*.

ATTENTION

The informal assessment of attention is similar in nature to the formal procedure suggested earlier. Observation of the child's general behavior and ability to attend to a task until completed will provide an indication of attention span.

AUDITORY MEMORY

(See Table 7-5, page 193.)

VISUAL MEMORY

(See Table 7-5, page 193.)

Table 8-2 *(Continued)*

PERCEPTUAL-MOTOR DEVELOPMENT

(See Table 6-4, page 160.)

UNDERSTANDING THE SIGNIFICANCE
OF WHAT IS SEEN

(See Table 7-5, page 191.)

UNDERSTANDING THE SIGNIFICANCE
OF WHAT IS HEARD

(See Table 7-5, page 191.)

VOCAL EXPRESSION

(See Table 7-5, page 194.)

GESTURAL EXPRESSION

(See Table 7-5, page 194.)

ASSOCIATION

(See Table 7-5, page 192.)

The evaluation of reading achievement infrequently during the school year can be done using one of the tests mentioned above. The advantage of using a well-standardized, systematically organized series of tasks based on a normative group against which the child can be compared should be recognized. Achievement tests do not typically require a highly trained examiner and can be administered satisfactorily by teachers who are familiar with the testing and scoring procedures.

There are times during the year, however, when the administration of formal tests is not possible or feasible. Nonetheless, the teacher may be interested in estimating the progress the children are making in reading. A similar need exists when a new child is enrolled in a class midway through the year. The teacher must decide at which level to start the student in reading. These situations suggest the need for an informal inventory of a child's performance level in reading.

Johnson and Kress (1965) have outlined a variety of techniques teachers can use to informally survey achievement in important areas of reading. They include techniques for surveying skills in listening, word attack, word recognition, oral reading, silent reading, and levels of readiness. Betts (1963) has also suggested techniques for administering informal inventories.

Table 8-3
READING ACHIEVEMENT SURVEY TESTS

NAME OF TEST	DIMENSION EVALUATED	GRADE LEVEL	PUBLISHER
California Reading Tests	Vocabulary Reference skills Following directions Interpretation of materials Comprehension Total	1–14	CTB
Gates-MacGinitie Reading Tests	Accuracy Comprehension Phrases Speed Vocabulary Words	1–6	TCP
Iowa Silent Reading Tests	Rate Comprehension Directed reading Word meaning Sentence meaning Location of information Total	4–14	HBW
Metropolitan Achievement Tests	Word knowledge Word discrimination Reading	2–9	HBW
SRA Achievement Series: Reading	Comprehension Language perception Verbal pictorial association Vocabulary Total	1–9	SRA
Stanford Achievement Test: Reading	Word meaning Paragraph meaning Vocabulary	4–9	HBW
Wide Range Achievement Test	Reading	K-college	GA

It is often helpful to inspect test scores from the years preceding the enrollment of students in your class to determine whether a unique pattern of strengths and weaknesses, particularly in reading, is obvious. For example, a child may have continuously shown strengths in word attack but weakness in sentence and paragraph meaning. These data

provide information concerning his general level of reading performance, and suggest the need to provide special and extensive remediation in one or more areas. Additionally, previous records will give vital
information in judging where further assessment should be directed.

An inventory involves asking the child to silently and orally read
selections from a graded set of basal tests. The child's general level of
word knowledge is first sampled by requiring the reading of a selection
of words which appear at the end of the test initially chosen for the
informal assessment. If no outstanding difficulty with the words is
exhibited, the child's vocabulary skills are assessed using the text at the
next higher level. If the child manifests some hesitation, he should be
asked to read several paragraphs aloud to the teacher and answer
questions about the content. During this reading, the examiner should
observe difficulties related to word attack, hesitations, pronunciations,
omissions, and lack of comprehension. The same procedure is used in
silent reading, after which the child is asked to read the passage aloud.
Approximately 80 percent of the teacher's questions should be answered correctly. The youngster should be able to read comfortably
without manifesting confusion and unnatural and inconsistent patterns
of recognition and word attack. If the book seems too easy or too hard,
the teacher should make the necessary adjustment until the proper level
of text is identified which allows for comfortable reading with some
degree of challenge.

Teachers can simplify the process by selecting vocabulary samples
and paragraphs from each of the basal series, typing the material on
cards, drafting questions for the paragraphs, and administering the
series to students throughout the year. Having several forms of this
material available will allow the teacher to frequently check on the
progress of each child without becoming overly concerned about the
children memorizing the evaluation selections or becoming test wise.

3. DIAGNOSIS OF SPECIFIC READING DIFFICULTIES
The evaluation procedures reviewed in the previous discussion were
concerned primarily with assessing the level at which a child operates
or his state of reading development in terms of a reference group. This
primarily involves an inter-individual assessment. Children have difficulty in learning to read for any number of reasons. For example, two
children may be underachieving at the same level, one having difficulty
because a consistent means of word attack has not been developed, the
other having a serious reversal problem. The problems are different,
although when compared with other children, both read at the same
level. Such inter-individual assessment will not typically lead to the

Table 8-4

DIAGNOSTIC READING TESTS AND THEIR CHARACTERISTICS

NAME OF TEST	CHARACTERISTICS	PUBLISHER
Gray Oral Reading Tests	This individual oral diagnostic test has four forms and consists of thirteen passages arranged according to level of difficulty from preprimer to adult. The passages are not only useful in assessing general level of reading but also provide an objective measure of growth in oral reading. In addition, they offer the opportunity to evaluate specific problems in oral reading, such as in vowel and consonant sounds, reversals, omissions, substitutions, additions, and specific position difficulties.	BMC
Spache Diagnostic Reading Scales	This scale, which requires individual administration, consists of three parts: three graded word lists, twenty-two graded paragraphs from preprimer through grade eight, and six phonics tests. Information is yielded in terms of a child's adequacy in silent reading, sight vocabulary, system for word attack and analysis, oral reading, phonics performance, and listening comprehension.	CTB
Gates-McKillop Reading Diagnostic Tests	Both forms of this test require a high level of skill in administration and interpretation by the examiner. A series of graded paragraphs to be read orally, tests for perception and word attack, and an oral vocabulary test all provide specific information concerning errors in oral reading and word attack. A total of twenty-eight scores provides a measure of difficulty in areas such as omissions, additions, repetitions, mispronunciations, position, recognition of usual forms, oral reading, syllabication, spelling, and sound blending. This is a revision of the Gates Reading Diagnostic Tests.	TCP
Doren Diagnostic Reading Tests of Word Recognition Skills	This group silent-reading diagnostic test can be administered to an entire class and offers a class profile which will assist in planning instruction and in grouping.	AGS

Table 8-4 *(Continued)*

McCullough Word Analysis Tests	This group of individually administered instruments yields ten scores from a battery which consists of 7 thirty-item tests, five of which assess phonetic-analysis skills, with two for diagnosing structural-analysis skills. This instrument is appropriate for children who are achieving above the fourth-grade level.	GC

development of a specific prescription for remediating reading difficulties. A more penetrating intra-individual assessment is required to determine which symptoms of poor reading are present, the manner in which the child approaches the reading task, the strengths and weaknesses of the child in terms of auditory and visual use of stimuli, and the degree to which other manifestations of disability are present in reading skills, such as in poor auditory fusion, sound blending, closure, visualization, and laterality. It is for these specific reasons that children often have problems in reading and require study extending beyond comparisons solely among children.

A number of formal procedures have been developed to diagnose specific reading difficulties of children. These diagnostic batteries vary according to individual and group administration. A basic requirement in using these instruments is that the test administrator be familiar with procedures of administration, scoring, and interpreting. The implication is that any teacher choosing to use these tests should have had specific training and experience in diagnosing and correcting reading problems. In most instances, the services of reading specialists should be requested by the teacher to help in the diagnosis and to suggest corrective procedures. Increasingly, though, special education teachers are being trained to do this type of diagnostic work. Table 8-4 summarizes the major characteristics of a sample of these tests.

The continuous appraisal of progress and specific weaknesses in the reading performance of children is necessary. The use of tests mentioned in the above table is often not possible; therefore, teachers should know of informal procedures available to them for obtaining this information. In some instances, with the older mentally retarded children principally, friendly discussions or astute questioning by the teacher will reveal possible sources of difficulty. The teacher can often estimate the eagerness of the child to read independently or his personal attitudes concerning developing skills in reading. These may be restricting or interfering to some degree with his progress.

More objective information can be obtained, and systematically recorded, when the teacher frequently appraises the nature of the oral reading errors made. The teacher should listen to the child read and attempt to detect errors of omission and substitution, repetitions, reversals, additions, and intonation problems. Strang (1964) has provided a systematic checklist for recording errors in oral reading.

A child's progress in silent reading can be checked by having the teacher ask questions related to the details and main ideas contained in a passage, inferences from information given by the passage or teacher, contradictory statements of fact or content, mood or characterization of the characters, and various possible reasons for the points of view expressed in the passage. This will reveal the extent to which the youngster has developed mature reading habits. Moreover, asking key questions will help to determine if the child is able to gain understanding from independent reading. Possible areas of difficulty can be checked by asking the student to reread portions of the passage orally.

Analyzing errors on workbook pages and in other types of work requiring independent reading provides an excellent procedure for assessing comprehension and work-study skills. The teacher can constantly assess specific areas of particular difficulty in this fashion. These exercises should have meaning, be related to the specific objectives of the lessons, and be evaluated by the teacher on a consistent basis. Children should not be led to assume that their seatwork is unimportant; the teacher can minimize this potential problem by carefully checking seatwork during and after the period devoted to this activity.

Comprehension and speed of reading can be evaluated by timing the children as they silently read a passage of known difficulty. Asking questions either before or after the reading will emphasize the need to read for comprehension of ideas. The teacher must be selective in the choice of a passage so that it is not too difficult for any one child. To do otherwise will sacrifice success for higher rates of reading speed.

Informal tests of auditory and visual discrimination and memory should be employed when it appears that a child is particularly weak in any of these areas. These tests are no different from those suggested in previous sections. Eye-voice span of the child can be checked by sliding a card over a page being read and asking for all the words seen prior to being covered by the card.

Finally, it is important that a systematic procedure be employed for reporting and summarizing information gathered by both formal and informal reading evaluations. Bond and Tinker (1957), Cleland (1954), and Strang (1964) have suggested various techniques and checklists for recording such information. Special attention should be given to providing subsequent teachers with complete data on children from these evaluations.

procedures for reading instruction

There is no approach to teaching reading to mentally retarded children that is especially unique to this group of children. The range of peculiarities in reading characteristics of these youngsters is as wide as among normal or bright children. It happens, however, that the magnitude of the reading problems that retarded children have and the frequency with which they occur in contrast to other children is significantly higher. There is always a number of mentally retarded students who will be able to proceed through a normal developmental program of reading (such as in a basal series, Distar, or Sullivan approach) without experiencing problems that require particular diagnostic or remedial attention. Many others, though, will become disabled and the teacher must be prepared to analyze the child's achievement, evaluate his program of reading instruction, and determine where to begin making adjustments in instructional practices to facilitate progress in those areas adjudged to have special priority.

This section will discuss a number of procedures that, to varying degrees, are appropriate in aiding the mentally retarded to acquire reading skills. None of the techniques will be presented in complete detail, because all can be found in standard reading textbooks. The important notion for you to grasp is the need to be systematic and enthusiastic in whichever method you choose for a certain child. The term "systematic" means being consistent, but it also means intelligently applying the principles, concepts, and guidelines discussed in Chapter 3.

Many systems have been designed to help children learn the fundamentals of reading. Each of these programs approaches reading from theoretical perspectives that differ. It is always necessary to make sure that you are aware of the bases, propositions, and assumptions on which an individual reading program has been developed before you select the one that you intend to use. The criteria suggested earlier for evaluating instructional materials will help you to systematize your evaluation of a reading system.

Since the term "reading system" might be somewhat confusing, let me briefly describe the direction certain publishers have taken in their development of reading programs. Since the middle 1960s professionals in the field of reading have undertaken to develop integrated packages of programs, each of which contains all that is necessary to deliver an instructional program in reading both developmentally and remedially. Further, each component of a system is usually consistent in terms of the theoretical basis on which the program is founded. The kinds of components vary among systems, but they usually contain teacher manuals, sheets for classroom activities, evaluative devices, storybooks, records or tapes, and even homework activities. The Distar Reading Program, the Sullivan Program, and the Scott-Foresman Reading Series are three examples of systems that have internally integrated components. In a sense, and to varying degrees, they provide for the teacher what might be broadly viewed as "a total reading environment." Not only is the behavior of the children directed but the systems provide specific focus for the teacher's behavior. It is certainly important for you to know that the research documenting the efficacy of these systems is not complete, nor absolute, in the findings with either normal or retarded children. At the same time, more research has been directed toward evaluating these comprehensive programs than has gone into studying the less well-integrated reading programs, such as the traditional basal reading series.

The kind of program one uses in teaching reading to mentally retarded children, especially during the period when fundamentals are being acquired, will not be very effective if it is legislated by someone other than the persons who are going to deliver the instruction. The program of instruction should not only be one in which the teacher believes but it is of utmost importance that the goals and procedures be congruent with each student's educational characteristics. This is an all-pervasive principle that is no respecter of subject or content area.

Since the three reading systems mentioned earlier (Distar, Sullivan, and Scott-Foresman) are relatively complete programs, a teacher of the mentally retarded may find it helpful to consider adopting one of these approaches in its entirety. The Distar Reading Program is a highly structured series and has more empirical documentation to support its use with mentally retarded children than the other programs have, but the Distar Program requires that the teacher be trained by a specialist and work for a while under supervision. The principles on which the Distar approach are based are completely compatible with those that are emphasized in this book.

For a number of reasons, some teachers are either unable or choose not to consider using a comprehensive reading system such as has just been suggested. They may prefer to teach in a less prestructured way and to develop their own procedures and materials according to the peculiarities of their children. There is nothing wrong with this position so long as the teacher's program is appropriate for each child, consistently applied, and continuously evaluated. The remainder of this chapter is directed to teachers who elect to organize their own program and who could profit from some suggestions on focus, sequence, and procedures for arranging the instructional environment.

READINESS INSTRUCTION
Many areas of readiness that were listed and discussed in preceding chapters have direct relevance to the reading program. Factors of perceptual-motor development and communication (speech and language) are fundamental readiness skills. In addition, there is evidence that a vital prerequisite is that the youngster have made the transition from dependence on the use of concrete objects as reference points to a pictorial representation of the object. Ability to deal with and understand the significance of this latter symbolic representation is at a higher conceptual level than its three-dimensional counterpart. It is usually of utmost importance that the reading readiness instruction be very well organized and precisely described so that incidental learning is not depended on in place of intentional instruction. Auditory and visual discrimination of various stimuli are considered important readiness areas. To illustrate a procedure you might use in constructing a program of instruction in the different readiness areas, a sequence of objectives and teaching procedures is presented below in the visual discrimination of letters, and a possible sequence in the major dimensions of auditory discrimination is also presented. These procedures can easily be adapted to other skill areas.

I Visual Discrimination
  A Rationale
    Research has suggested that certain perceptual-motor skills are prerequisite to the development of the visual discrimination (Zaporozhets, 1965; Meier and McGee, 1958; Walk, 1958) and that success in discriminating flat shapes is preceded by the ability to discriminate among three-dimensional shapes wherein the individual can engage in motor manipulation of the objects (Hicks and Hunton, 1964; Walk, Gibson, Pick, and Tight, 1959). These and other studies by Russian psychologists (Pick, 1963) clearly show that the more manipulative experience a child has in the early stages of development, the more skilled he will become in complex perceptual activities, such as those involved in discrimination. Indeed, there is reason to believe that early sensory-

motor experiences will facilitate skill development in areas involving sense modalities in addition to the visual. Pick (1963) has interpreted Soviet research as indicating that auditory discrimination will be facilitated by involvement in activities requiring motor mediation. Support of Piaget's position by these results is noteworthy.

Distinguishing among letters, and eventually between words, is important in the reading-readiness program. In order for children to develop this visual skill, the teacher must appropriately sequence activities so that skills learned earlier can be employed in subsequent activities. Moreover, a multisensory approach with particular emphasis on visual-motor experiences is indicated.

The work of Gibson (1963) is especially relevant to instruction in letter discrimination. She has identified four critical features of letters, viz., breaks and closes (*o* versus *c*), curves and corners (*u* versus *v*), rotations (*M* versus *W*), and reversals (*d* versus *b*). Her investigations have suggested that children must learn to discriminate differences in the unique characteristics within and between each of these pairs before being able to discriminate satisfactorily among letters per se. The following is an illustration of the sequence for teaching visual discrimination of letters which is suggested from this research.

B Sequence for Teaching Letter Discrimination[1]

  1 Level I

    At this level, activities should be designed to enable the child to distinguish the elementary features of shapes of letters, such as in breaks and closes, corners and curves, and lines and curves. They should be planned so that the manipulation of three-dimensional forms occurs in the early stages of instruction. The appropriate labeling of each form is also necessary. The two central components of this level are:

    a Manipulating letters according to the unique features of each

      (1) Behavioral Objective: The child can put all the three-dimensional objects (listed under materials) through the holes in the box (listed under materials) in any trial-and-error fashion.

      (2) Materials: Each child should have a set of three-dimensional objects of the following shapes: *C* (break), *O* (closed), *I* (line), *u* (curve), *v* (corner), and *U*, *V*, *h*, *b* (letters

[1]Appreciation is expressed to Mrs. Dina A. Deno for her substantial contribution to this section on visual discrimination.

which contain only one or two of these features). These shapes should be approximately 3 by 3 by 3 inches and red. Each child should also have a light blue cardboard box that has holes outlined in black which correspond in size and shape to the set of objects.

(3) **Procedure:** The children are told that they are going to work with certain letters and that they will learn to tell them apart. At first they should only learn to operate the *C, O, I, u,* and the *v,* because these are the elementary distinguishing features of letters. When the child can put all these forms through the holes, he can begin working with the remaining letters in the set. The teacher demonstrates putting the objects through the holes and makes clear that it is permissible to try different holes if the object does not fit in the first one.

b Visual discrimination of the distinguishing features of letters

(1) **Behavioral Objective:** When told to put an object through a specific hole (the teacher points), the child can pick up the correct object and put it through the hole without previously trying an incorrect object.

(2) **Materials:** The same as in the above lesson.

(3) **Procedure:** The procedure is the same as in the above lesson except that the teacher instructs the child to look from the hole to the object before picking the object up and trying it. The teacher works with the child until his glance automatically shifts from the hole to the object before he tries it. Studies have demonstrated the effectiveness of instructing the child to shift his glance in this way. After the child can perform this shift of glance, he is told to try to pick the correct one the first time.

2 Level 2

By the time the child has reached the second level, he should have developed stable associational patterns related to certain unique characteristics of letters and be ready to increase his present discrimination capabilities related to shape to include percepts of size and orientation. Discrimination in both these areas must be mastered. Two aspects of orientation are included at this level, rotation and reversal. Terms such as *smaller, larger, top, bottom, right,* and *left* should be presented and learned for subsequent communication to be effective. Tasks should proceed from sensory-motor experiences to purely visual. Up to this point, the materials used in the activities have been three-dimensional.

a Manipulation of identical objects which vary in size
   (1) **Behavioral Objective:** The child can put all the elements of a specific set (described under materials) inside one another in any trial-and-error fashion.
   (2) **Materials:** Each child must have sets of the following red, identically shaped elements which differ only in size: five bowls, five cardboard boxes, and five Chinese dolls all of which fit into one another.
   (3) **Procedure:** The children should be told that they are going to learn to put some objects inside other objects (they are not expected necessarily to know the meaning of "inside"). At first they should only work with the smallest and largest element of each set. The teacher should demonstrate and then have the child put one object into the other using trial and error. The teacher should name the objects as being smaller or larger and use these terms as the demonstration proceeds. The child, however, is not required to use them at this point. When the child can perform the task using two elements of each set, he can begin working with an additional element from each set until all the elements can be used with facility.
b Acquiring the concepts of smaller and larger
   (1) **Behavioral Objective:** After the child has put any two elements of a set (as used in lesson 3) together, he can point to the smaller one and to the larger one upon request.
   (2) **Materials:** The same as used in lesson 3.
   (3) **Procedure:** Only two elements of any one set will be used at a time. The concept of "smaller" will be introduced first, since that seems to be easier to learn. The child is asked to put two objects together while the teacher simultaneously points to the smaller object. The child should repeat the same procedure with each set, labeling the smaller object along with the teacher. When the child can label independent of help, he should continue to use other elements in the set and place a red sticker on the smallest object. The same procedure is used for the presentation of the concept "larger."
c Visual discrimination between sizes
   (1) **Behavioral Objective:** (1) The child can put all the elements within the sets (those used in lesson 3) together

without trying one incorrect object. (2) The child is able to point out the larger and smaller object of any two combinations of elements within a particular set.

(2) Materials: The same as used in lesson 3.

(3) Procedure: The procedure is the same as lesson 4 except that the child should be given specific instructions to shift his glance between the two objects to be used. He should also be required to vocalize the words "smaller" and "larger," until he can vocalize the correct word before the object is manipulated. When this point is reached, the child should be asked to always label objects before manipulating them.

d Acquiring an understanding of positional terms—*right, left, top,* and *bottom*

(1) Behavioral Objective: When asked to do so, the child can point to the left side, right side, top, and bottom of any paper placed on his desk.

(2) Materials: A marching record and the following items for each child: a piece of red material 12 inches long, a desk, and a stand-up calendar.

(3) Procedure: The first day the teacher introduces the concepts of "top" and "bottom" by showing the children where each position is relative to their own desks. A marching record should be played and the children asked to march around the room, touching the top and bottom of desks on a command. They should continue marching and extend their action of touching to any object near them. After they can do this, have them touch the top of a calendar which has been placed on each desk in an upright position. Next, have the students place their calendars in a flat position, keeping their hands on the top and continuing to refer to it as the top. After these concepts have been acquired, the children should be introduced to the concepts of "right" and "left" by attaching a piece of red material to each right arm and continuing to use the same types of activities.

e Tracing reversed and rotated figures

(1) Behavioral Objective: After tracing two flat cutout figures, the child can correctly verbalize their likenesses and differences with respect to position.

(2) Materials: The following materials should be provided to each child: a yellow feltboard, two sets of orange card-board figures with felt glued to the bottom side. These figures are as follows: (1) *V, U, C;* (2) *M, T, P.*

(3) **Procedure:** This program assumes that the child knows the meaning of "alike" and "different." It is the teacher's responsibility to be sure that the child knows these terms before proceeding. The teacher demonstrates tracing the figures from a set which has been placed on the feltboard. The child is assisted in tracing the figure. At the same time, the teacher should verbally emphasize the directions of the lines (such as from top to bottom) and position of the features (such as a corner on the right side). This proce-dure should be repeated with an identical figure with emphasis placed on the sameness of the directions. One of the figures should be rotated and the child helped to trace while the teacher emphasizes the differences in direction. The figure should subsequently be placed back in the original position. The child should trace and match shapes to identical positions until overlearning has oc-curred. After the performance is completed successfully on set 1, the child should continue the process with the more complex set 2. The child can then repeat the ex-ercises working with reversed figures.

f Visually discriminating between rotated and reversed figures

(1) **Behavioral Objective:** The child can name any pair of cutout figures (those used in lesson g) as alike or different without handling them.

(2) **Materials:** The same as used in lesson g.

(3) **Procedure:** The procedure is the same as in lesson g, only the teacher should have the child shift his glance from one figure to the other and try to judge them before tracing.

3 Level 3

At this level, the tasks are designed to give the child experi-ences which will help to develop visual discrimination among complex written letters. These skills build on the previously developed competencies in discrimination among two-dimensional letters. This association with earlier learned mate-rial is fostered by giving the child tasks requiring the construc-tion of letters from basic component parts. Three-dimensional lines and parts of circles of various sizes are used in the construction or modeling of letters. The child learns to match the concrete objects to the figures in terms of shape, size, and orientation. Initially, matching should be done along one dimension (e.g., shape) followed by various combinations of the above three components. At all times, the child should be asked to vocalize the characteristics of the elements being considered, such as "line" or "a smaller circle." Practice in constructing every letter should be given until the child can successfully discriminate among them.

a Concrete reconstruction

    (1) Behavioral Objectives: The child can construct every printed letter of the alphabet by matching three-dimensional cutouts of elements of letters to a graphic representation of each letter.

    (2) Materials: A set of papers containing upper- and lowercase 3- by 3-inch letters of the alphabet, with one letter per page, and a set of cardboard cutouts of elements of these letters, such as:

    (3) Procedure: The teacher demonstrates and gives the child practice in matching first in terms of form, next size, and next orientation. He then matches along two of the former dimensions and finishes with matching along all three dimensions.

b Visual discrimination between graphic letters

    (1) Behavioral Objectives: When presented with any two upper- or lowercase letters, the child can verbally indicate whether they are alike or different.

    (2) Materials: The same as those used in lesson 9, only one side of the paper must be folded under so that the letters can be presented in close proximity to one another.

    (3) Procedure: The child should continue with the preceding lesson modeling two letters successively and judging them as alike or different. The child is encouraged to make the discrimination decision as soon as possible, even before he is done modeling until discrimination can be made prior to modeling.

II Auditory Discrimination

  A Rationale

    The research is not as comprehensive in this area as in visual discrimination; this is particularly true for investigations which have employed mentally retarded children as subjects. The research related to the auditory perception and acuity problems of the retarded, reviewed briefly in Chapter 6, has relevance to this section. Auditory discrimination is more than just the fact that a sound is audible to a listener; indeed, auditory discrimination requires that individual sounds and their components be accurately recognized.

Auditory experiences can be distinguished from each other in terms of intensity (loudness), pitch (frequency), and timbre (quality of tone). The ability to discriminate among sounds does not happen all at once. Wepman (1960), for example, has suggested that higher-level discrimination capabilities do not fully mature until a child reaches the age of eight. With the mentally retarded, optimum development in this area may not occur until the early teenage years. Poor environmental backgrounds and/or organic difficulties of a peripheral or central nature often mean that a child never reaches full maturity in auditory discrimination. Combinations of slow speech, language development, and problems of inattentiveness only further compound the situation.

As in other areas involving skills which are learned, when the child gets older, the difficulty in teaching the auditory discrimination increases because of the ineffective and inefficient habits already established. A planned program of early intervention should be initiated to encourage the development of auditory discrimination skills. This will require that a sequential program be used which requires the child to begin making discriminations among sounds which are very difficult but which gradually require finer and finer distinctions to be made. For skill development in reading readiness, a sequential program of auditory discrimination might consist of the following six levels: (1) sound discrimination, (2) rhyming, (3) initial-consonant discrimination, (4) final-consonant discrimination, (5) initial-blend discrimination, and (6) final-blend discrimination. The following suggests objectives and activities that are appropriate for fostering the development of auditory discrimination skills with the retarded.

B Sequence for Teaching Auditory Discrimination[2]
  1 Sound Discrimination
    a Purpose: to be able to differentiate between loud and soft

---

[2]Additional exercises and activities to develop auditory discrimination can be located in Betts (1946); Queen Anne's County Teachers Manual, 1954–1955; Russell and Russell (1959); Smith, 1963.

sounds (volume), long and short sounds (duration), high and low sounds (pitch), sounds of different instruments and voices (timbre), and to follow directions

b Activities:

(1) Volume: Children can raise hands if sound is loud and leave hands down if sound is soft.

   (a) Tap on desk loudly and softly.

   (b) Clap two erasers or two pieces of wood together loudly and softly.

   (c) Ring a bell or beat on a drum loudly and softly.

   (d) Walk across room and then tiptoe across room.

   (e) Slam door and then open it gently.

   (f) Talk and whisper; talk and shout.

   (g) Drop a book and a pencil.

   (h) Listen to a clock and a watch ticking.

   (i) Use boxes filled with different objects and shake them.

(2) Duration: Children can raise hands if sound is long and leave hands down if sound is short. Almost any instrument can be used for this and the procedure would follow the same lines as that for differentiating between long and short sounds.

(3) Pitch: The same procedure can be followed as for volume and duration activities. The teacher can make use of the piano, a pitch pipe, or a whistle.

Responses to these activities can be varied by having children walk to sounds that are long, loud, or low; or tiptoe to sounds that are short, soft, or high. The students can clap their hands or stand up and sit down according to the earlier established criteria.

(4) Timbre

   (a) Play "Who Is It?" or "Who Said it?" by blindfolding one child and having another pupil make a comment with the blindfolded child trying to identify the speaker.

   (b) Hit a triangle and a drum. Ask the children to name each instrument as you strike it. Any combination of instruments may be used.

   (c) Have children listen to and differentiate among sounds that are inside the room or outside the room or sounds that are near and far away.

   (d) After an animal noise is made, have the children identify the animal or pretend that they are animals.

Throughout all these activities, begin with gross discrimination. After the children master these, require them to make finer discriminations.

(5) Using music as children become more proficient in sound discrimination

    (a) Children can be asked to identify simple tunes or songs.

    (b) Have the children skip, hop, jump, etc., to suitable music. Afterwards, have them stop when the music stops.

    (c) Beat on a drum a certain number of times, and have child clap back the identical number of beats. As a child is correct, he then becomes the next drummer. Instruments should be varied in this activity.

(6) Following directions

    (a) Have them respond to simple individual directions such as, "Come here."

    (b) Present group commands to the class such as, "Stand up."

    (c) Require the children to do errands when asked.

    (d) Play games requiring commands such as "Simon Says" or "Bring me the _____ (e.g., book)."

2 Rhymes

  a **Purpose:** to develop ability to hear rhymes, acquire a sense of rhythm, rhyme words, complete rhymes, compose rhymes, and pick out those words that rhyme in a group of words

  b **Activities:**

    (1) Read nursery rhymes and other rhymes to children.

    (2) Engage them in choral speaking of nursery rhymes and other simple poems.

    (3) Read simple rhymes to the children, and have them fill in the last word, e.g., "We have fun when we _____."

    (4) When reading rhymes, have children clap hands on the rhyming words.

    (5) Have them think of pairs of rhyming words, such as "cat" and "hat."

    (6) Say a short rhyme leaving off the final rhyming word. Give the children two words from which to choose, and have them select the correct word.

    (7) Read a short rhyme leaving out the rhyming word. Show the children a picture which finishes the rhyme, and have them supply the missing word. Later, use two or more pictures.

(8) Have them compose their own short rhymes.

(9) Give the children three words, one of which does not rhyme with the others. Have them pick out the nonrhyming word.

3 Initial Consonants

  a Purpose: to develop ability to note the beginning sound of words, become aware that many words begin with the same sound, and develop recognition of like and unlike beginning consonants

  b Activities:

    (1) Read short sentences that have a great deal of alliteration. Simple songs also can be used. Have the children pick out the words that are alike in their beginning sound.

    (2) After taking a trip, ask the children to think of all the things they saw. Point out the similarities in the beginnings of the words they choose to use.

    (3) In taking the class roll, point out that many of the children's names begin with the same sound, e.g., Jim, Joe, Judy.

    (4) Have them collect pictures of words that begin alike.

    (5) Present two words to the children, and vary the likenesses and differences in the beginning sounds. Have them tell if the words begin with the same sound.

    (6) Present three words to them, of which two are alike. Have the pupils pick out the two that begin with the same sound.

    (7) Encourage descriptive word activity. Say, "I have a book." Ask the students to think of adjectives, beginning like book, that could be used with the word, e.g., beautiful, big.

    (8) Show the children two pictures, and ask them if the pictures begin with the same sounds.

    (9) Have the children draw a picture, such as a ball, and ask them to think of other words beginning with the same sound.

Consonants should be learned in the following order (from easiest to the most difficult): b, p, m, w, h, d, t, n, g, k, ng, y, f, v, th (as in *then*), sh, zh, l, s, z, r, th (as in *thin*), wh, ch, and j (Wepman, 1960).

4 Final Consonants

5 Initial Blends

6 Final Blends

The purposes for the activities related to these three levels of auditory discrimination are the same as for the initial consonants. Here, of course, final consonants, initial blends, and final blends are substituted for the initial consonant sounds.

Vowel discrimination should be introduced as the need arises within the program. The activities employed should be similar to those for the initial consonants. Generally long vowels are taught first, followed by instruction in short vowels.

Within each level, considerable time should be spent on each activity. No new level should be introduced until the previous level has been well mastered.

DEVELOPING A SIGHT VOCABULARY AND WORD ATTACK SKILLS

It is really not right to separate reading comprehension skills from those skills that are subsumed under this paragraph heading, for certainly they are complementary throughout reading instruction, whatever the focus of the moment. It is most desirable that the acquiring of reading skills not become totally mechanistic because of the danger of a youngster becoming a "word caller" for whom reading has little or no meaning.

The effective recognition of words in print hinges to a large degree on how well developed the mentally retarded child is in vital areas of readiness. Assuming that these readiness skills have reached a satisfactory level, the teacher is faced next with the need to assist the child in developing a sight vocabulary. Several considerations are paramount in selecting sight vocabulary words. Sampling words from the child's previous experiences or from areas of current interest will help to stimulate his desire to learn to read. Selecting words will be simplified if the teacher is aware of the mentally retarded child's speaking and listening vocabulary.

Of central importance is that the children be successful in their early experiences in reading. As is true in all areas involving initial learning, the retarded become discouraged if their early efforts meet with failure. The teacher, then, must wisely select words of high stimulus value to the children and with which they will be successful, thus allowing for ample positive reinforcement.

Establishing a consistent and effective method for attacking words is equally important. Mentally retarded children should be instructed in a word-analyzing procedure on which they can depend and which they can use with facility. Instruction in this procedure must be consistent within and among classrooms. Intellectually normal children are able to learn incidental relationships that exist between visual and auditory approaches to learning; mentally retarded children often have difficulty transferring from one approach to another.

Developing a sight vocabulary and a skill in word attack are interdependent. Although word-attack skills may at first be underdeveloped while the sight vocabulary is more extensive, as a systematic approach in word analysis develops, the child will usually be able to simultaneously extend his sight vocabulary. There is, then, a relationship between a child's skill in word attack and the comprehensiveness of his sight vocabulary. Controlling the possibility of failure is important and calls for attention to be given to all possible avenues to success for the child. Various approaches should be analyzed to determine which have the greatest potential for helping each child to develop reading skills according to what the diagnostic data suggest. Among the approaches you might want to consider are the following:

1 Using a printer primer series is one approach for introducing reading. In a series of this type, certain basic words are used along with pictures. The children learn the words in association with the illustrations, gradually building a more extensive repertoire of sight words. Although these materials are usually carefully prepared, there are some disadvantages in using them with the retarded. One major problem is that the retarded often place too great a reliance on relating the words with the associated pictures. Dependence on specific page cues will then result in rote recall of a particular selection and make it more difficult for them to develop fine discriminations among the shapes of words and letters.

2 A spelling or alphabet approach is another technique for introducing reading. Emphasis is placed on the analysis of single letters before the child is exposed to letter combinations and words. The sight vocabulary is gradually established by using drill on isolated words before exposure to a passage or story. The primary disadvantage in using this approach with the retarded is the danger of their becoming inclined toward "word calling." In reading instruction with these children, there is need to emphasize the meaning of words in a variety of contexts. To teach the analysis of words, or their basic components, without focusing on meaning and comprehension from the beginning of a child's reading program will restrict progress, convey a biased and narrow perspective of reasons for learning how to read, and hinder fluency.

3 Too much emphasis on phonetic elements is equally stifling during the initial stages of teaching the retarded child to read. In addition to all the disadvantages of the spelling method, early reliance on the phonics approach often causes confusion between the names of the letters and what they should say at different times when they appear in various combinations. This potential for confusion cannot be allowed during the early stages of reading. It is important that words be learned in context, that the child enjoy the process, that experiences be successful for each child, that use be made of the child's existing repertoire and background, and that the initial focus be global rather than narrowly emphasizing elements or basic parts of words.

4 The experience approach to reading minimizes many of the disadvantages in the techniques mentioned above for introducing reading to the retarded. Using the cooperative story and experience chart at the outset enables the retarded to gain a clear picture of the reason for reading. Reading should become a basic part of communication. The children should be helped to see that it is possible to communicate not only vocally but also in reading and writing. The children's experiences should be used as a stimulus for wanting to learn to read and as a means for encouraging the development of a more flexible use of all the components of communication. There is no lock-step characteristic of the experience approach as there frequently is with the primer series wherein stories and pictures are often inappropriate for various groups of children. Moreover, the experience approach allows for complete integration with other subject areas in ways not easily possible with other procedures for reading instruction with the mentally retarded.

stages in teaching reading using an experience approach

The teacher of the mentally retarded can present material in a progressively differentiated manner by using the experience approach. Three levels, or stages, of instruction characterize this technique. The mass stage is exemplified by the child reacting to the whole story, the differentiation stage is characterized by emphasis on learning details, and the integration stage is typified by the child being able to read without awareness of details. These three levels constitute the core of the approach and will be treated separately.

First in the sequence is the need for the children to understand that reading is an extension of speaking. Emphasis should not be placed on details at this point. The children should be encouraged to see that reading results in meaning and that it is possible to record what has been spoken and then later, by reading, to gain understanding from what has been said.

When the teacher elects to use the experience approach or cooperative story at the mass level, the children should be asked to help record a past, present, or future experience. The incident can be direct or vicarious, but ideally it should be reported by a group or by an individual. A short passage, no longer than three or four lines, should be interesting to the children and should contain words from their own speaking vocabulary. The sentence structure should be the same for each sentence, and the words the children use most frequently should be repeated. The teacher should write each sentence on the blackboard or a large piece of tagboard as the story unfolds. Stories such as the following illustrate the type that might be written.

We went for a walk.
We saw a bird.
We saw a dog.   or
The dog barked.

Snow is falling.
It is on the ground.
We can ride our sleds.
It will be fun.

After the story has been written, the teacher should repeat each sentence and follow along with a pointer. As the children remember the sentences, they should be asked to read with the teacher. The entire class should eventually be able to read in concert as well as individually. Emphasis should be placed on the notion that the entire story tells about something interesting that has or will take place. The idea of conveying a message should be stressed and no particular attention paid to any of the story components. Moreover, the configuration of the entire story should be emphasized and left-to-right progression clearly reinforced throughout all stages of reading instruction.

After the children understand that reading makes sense and that it conveys a message, they should be ready for instruction in the differentiation stage of reading. This second stage has several levels, each of which contains some characteristics of the massed stage of instruction. At this level, the children should be encouraged to see that the story components make sense in isolation.

The first step in this process is for the children to understand that each line says something different from the other lines, has a unique meaning, and looks different from the others. After they learn to differentiate among the sentences, the children should be asked questions which test their ability to discriminate, such as by the teacher saying, "Show me the sentence that tells us what the dog did." "Which line tells what we saw first on our walk?" "Which sentence tells us what we can do when snow is on the ground?" The chart can be cut into sentence strips and the children asked to replace them in order. The same general strategy can be used for sentences that can be employed for phrases.

After the child has developed ability to distinguish among words, several procedures can be initiated. An individual flash card for each word can be constructed so that each child can see how the printed word follows a unique configuration. The following illustrates this procedure:

In a certain sense, this involves temporary movement back to the massed stage. A variety of drills and activities can be used to facilitate the learning and reassembling of the words in the proper sentence sequence. As examples, the child can be asked to locate any word that he knows on the chart, the teacher could pick a word by giving the child a position cue, a child could be asked to identify all the words that look alike, or the teacher could give an auditory cue and ask the child to identify the appropriate word, phrase, or sentence. The children should not be required to reconstruct more than one sentence at a time until the concept has been overlearned.

At this point the process of word analysis can begin. You will have to determine which children seem to be inclined toward a phonics approach, which toward a more visualized approach, which toward a kinesthetic method, and which seem to have no particular preference. Use informal evaluative procedures to determine this and then group the youngsters according to their apparent learning styles or instructional needs. As children attack words and acquire progressively higher levels of skill, you can begin to fade out prominent configuration cues. When the children no longer need extra cues they will be ready for instruction at the integration stage. Plenty of drill is needed to help them reassemble sentences and place individual components in their proper order. As skill in these activities develop, the children should be able to assemble complete stories. It should be noted that differentiation and integration are not mutually exclusive but share certain areas of skill development. For example, during each of these stages some effort should be given to developing a consistent means for word attack (whether it be auditory or visual), a left-to-right progression, skill in proper sequencing for clarity in the comprehension of ideas, and a more extensive sight vocabulary.

The experience approach can be as effective with older retarded children as with the younger if the following points are considered:

1 Each story should be simple, clearly express several main ideas, and reflect the vocabulary and interests of the children.
2 The story should be a cooperative venture, although the teacher

should exert some control over the vocabulary according to the children's reading capabilities. To illustrate, in choosing a story with beginning readers, it would be important to emphasize initial consonant sounds and short vowels so that procedures for word attack can be systematically introduced.

3 Care should be given to reduce the tendency of the retarded to depend primarily on memorization and the use of context clues. This can be controlled by using new words in a variety of ways on several experience stories.

4 Each student should be asked to develop his own book of experience stories to which reference can be made. These will be of diagnostic value to the teacher from the perspective of reading, spelling, sequencing ideas, and in comprehension.

5 Instruction during the early stages should adhere to the basic learning principles which were reviewed earlier. In no case should the child be forced to discriminate or integrate before showing some competence at the massed level of instruction. The children should understand that meaning can be gained through reading before being required to analyze the components of the reading process.

6 Integration with other subject areas should characterize all instruction involving reading.

7 Continued development of auditory and visual discrimination, moving from left to right in reading, sequencing for meaning, and elaboration of the child's vocabulary should be considered an important part of the child's early reading activities whatever their chronological age.

Systematically attacking words constitutes a vital component of reading instruction for the retarded. The teacher should be concerned about minimizing random behavior and guessing. In no other area will such behavior be manifested as extensively as when a child has not developed skill in the analysis of words.

There is no best single approach for instructing the retarded in word attack. Books on beginning reading emphasize different procedures. Because of their unique characteristics, certain children will learn to read best when an auditory approach is employed, whereas other children will acquire reading-analysis skills more effectively when emphasis is placed on a visualization procedure. Research in reading with the retarded has been more of an ex post facto type with only minimum systematic effort devoted to studying the reading process with retarded subjects. Suggestions in this area, therefore, are extrapolations from the literature on remedial-reading subjects. The debates concerning which is better for retarded readers—a sight-word or a decoding approach for word attack—have been especially prominent in the literature since the middle 1960s. You might be interested in learning about the various positions that have been taken on this issue by consulting Chall (1967), Brown (1967), Cohen (1969), Cawley and Pappanikou (1967), Sheperd (1967), Delacato (1963), Robbins (1967), Kershner (1968), Pope and Haklay (1970), and Cegelka and Cegelka (1970).

The teacher of the retarded may find greatest success in using an eclectic approach, one that combines the phonics, visualization, context, and kinesthetic methods in different ways but according to each child's performance patterns. This procedure would seem to have greatest merit because of the frequent difficulties the retarded have in visual-perception development, auditory memory and discrimination, remembering and applying rules or principles, and a host of other skills. The wide spectrum of difficulties in these necessary skill areas forces the teacher to employ components from many methods, placing particular emphasis on those procedural techniques appropriate to each child's pattern of strengths and weaknesses. For example, children who show weakness in using the visual but not the auditory channel would probably learn best by emphasizing a phonics approach with a gradual introduction of the appropriately associated visual components. Differential emphasis, therefore, is needed according to any significant characteristic of each child.

Comprehensive coverage has been given to the procedures for teaching word-attack skills according to the various points of view. The procedures described by Kirk (1940) have also been reiterated in more recent volumes (Anderson, 1965; Otto and McMenemy, 1966; Spache, 1964). Their treatment of the principal characteristics of each word-attack method differs little from that of the early proponents of these different methods. The reader who is unfamiliar with these techniques will find coherent discussions of each method in these sources. Although it is important that the teacher have a firm grasp of these procedures, the need for parsimony here will not allow for the reiteration of the basic tenets of each technique. Instead, the generalizations and principal teaching considerations listed below illustrate the relationship that would be allowed to exist among these methods in teaching reading to the retarded.

1 Two important advantages for using a combination of several word-attack methods are:
a The teacher can quickly see which method should be emphasized by observing how effectively each child performs with different means of

presentation. This procedure, then, has diagnostic value and will readily show which method or combination of methods should work best with each child.

b There is more opportunity for association of stimuli received from different sources. This will have a direct influence on the level of initial learning, recall, association, and general skill development.

2 In word attack, the attention of the children should not be continuously directed toward learning rules. Such an approach would prove disappointing because of the retarded child's weakness for applying and generalizing rules to various situations. In addition, there are many problems inherent in the frequent exceptions to rules, such as those exemplified in the unique phonetic structure of the English language.

3 Primary use should be made of words learned in the cooperative stories and experience charts. In this beginning stage of reading, the children should be made aware of the entire spectrum of auditory and visual clues related to words and their combinations. Attention should be given to the use of context clues, the configuration of letters and words, and the sounds of words, letters, and letter combinations. Each child should be encouraged to engage in kinesthetic experiences during this early stage of reading development by systematically tracing and writing words contained in the stories. Full use should be made of each sense modality.

4 New words should be said, traced, and written when they are introduced. Early in the process the teacher should write the new word on a card and make it available to the child for tracing and for reference as he learns to write the word, thus allowing for quick comparison of his performance with that of the model. The use of some type of translucent material for the child to write on, which, after he has written a word, can be placed on top of a model response, will allow for an immediate check on errors of omission and commission. This provides immediate knowledge of results and proper reinforcement of success.

5 When using a predominately visualization approach, whole words should first be presented. When too much emphasis is placed on details, children often have trouble with comprehension. When using a phonics approach for word attack, try backward chaining with children who have trouble with sound blending. For example, in trying to blend the sounds "g-r-an-d," a child might be instructed to begin by making the "d" sound, then the "*an*" (then put it with the "d" making "and"), then the "r" (then put it with the "and" making "rand"), and finally the "g" (then put it with "rand" to make "grand"). You will find this an excellent way to teach sound blending, and it also will help a child who exhibits some articulation problems.

6 Similarities between old and new words in sound, appearance, and meaning should be explicitly pointed out. The closeness between this concept and the desirability of employing minimal change in learning new words is worthy of note. For example, after the child has learned c-a-n, by changing only the initial consonant he can form r-a-n or t-a-n, and thus a basis for new instruction from previously successful experiences will be provided.

7 Attention should be directed to identifying and responding to all areas of significance in which the retarded children are particularly weak. For example, blending small units or words, discriminating among *b*, *d*, *g*, and *p*, and reversing letters in words are areas of frequent weakness with the mentally retarded.

8 Children should move naturally and as rapidly as possible from total use of the cooperative story and experience chart to books of high interest and low vocabulary. This is a gradual weaning process and one that should not take place before word-analysis skills have been developed from the first formal reading activities associated with the experience chart.

**DEVELOPING SKILLS
IN READING COMPREHENSION**

Reading is essentially useless exercise if the reader does not understand the meaning of the words he calls. Comprehension cannot occur unless the individual has the necessary skills to expand his sight vocabulary and attack words in a systematic manner. It is reasonable, therefore, that the teacher of the retarded devote attention to assisting the youngsters in developing reading comprehension skills.

The importance of stressing accuracy instead of speed in all aspects of reading cannot be overemphasized. It is natural for children to want to rush ahead in reading after having achieved some competence in basic skills. The competition engendered by such achievements is quickly kindled between students in terms of the number of pages each is able to read or the speed with which a child is able to complete an assignment passage. Every attempt should be made to reduce this tendency and to encourage accurate reading. Pronounced focus on speed will result in the development of sloppy and inadequate word-analysis skills which, in turn, will reduce comprehension. Gradually, as these basic skills develop, the children will be able to gain speed in reading without sacrificing their understanding of what appears on the printed page.

In teaching for comprehension, the teacher needs to give attention to the vital role of the feedback and monitoring systems. As children read selections of various lengths, gaining meaning will depend on their remembering what has been visually and/or auditorially read. If words are being called and the child is not alert to the meaning contained in each passage, comprehension will be reduced. A central aim of the reading program is for each child to eventually move from overattending to the process of attacking words to focusing on their meaning and content. Often it will be necessary for the teacher to act as a monitor during the reading process by stopping the child at the end of a sentence and questioning him concerning the meaning of what was just read. In more difficult cases, it will help for the teacher to read short passages in concert with the child so that feedback and memory are emphasized more dramatically. Gradually, the child will develop a "style" which is characterized by greater attention being given to thoughts contained in passages.

For the mentally retarded, reading comprehension should center on instruction which will allow the children to (1) understand thoughts contained in sentences, (2) comprehend the meaning contained in paragraphs, and (3) grasp the meaning and implications of entire selections. For some children, these objectives are reasonable; for other children, intellectual limitations will decrease the possibility of their satisfactorily achieving these three aims. Otto and McMenemy (1966) have suggested certain informal diagnostic techniques for assessing comprehension skills in each of these areas and have outlined procedures for remediating weaknesses in these types of comprehension.

For meaningful reading comprehension to be encouraged the teacher should

1 Provide reading material of high interest that is compatible with the social interests of the children
2 Rewrite stories and other reading materials that are interesting to the students but too difficult
3 Continually integrate reading lessons with other school subject areas
4 Consistently reinforce students for attending to content in reading passages and especially reward those who are able to discuss progressively complex issues that pertain to the material being read (such as cause and effect relationships; what happened before or after the story; implications of the conclusions of the story for their own lives; and increasingly complex understanding of the material being read)
5 Make sure that the questions asked students are of the type that give the children an opportunity to not only talk about the material they have read but to express themselves spontaneously and thoroughly

selected readings

Anderson, P. S.: *Language Skills in Elementary Education*, The Macmillan Company, New York, 1965.

Betts, E. A.: *Foundations of Reading Instruction*, American Book Company, New York, 1946.

Bond, G. L. and M. A. Tinker: *Reading Difficulties, Their Diagnosis and Correction*, Appleton-Century-Crofts, Inc., New York, 1957.

Brown, V. L.: "Reading Instruction," *Exceptional Children*, 34:197–199, 1967.

Cawley, J. F. and A. J. Pappanikou: "The Educable Mentally Retarded," in N. G. Haring and R. L. Schiefelbusch (eds.), *Methods in Special Education*, McGraw-Hill Book Company, New York, 1967.

Cegelka, P. A. and W. J. Cegelka: "A Review of Research: Reading and the Educable Mentally Handicapped," *Exceptional Children*, 37:187–200, 1970.

Chall, J. S.: *Learning to Read: The Great Debate*, McGraw-Hill Book Company, New York, 1967.

Cohen, S. A.: *Teach Them All to Read*, Random House, Inc., New York, 1969.

Delacato, C. H.: *The Diagnosis and Treatment of Speech and Reading Problems*, Charles C Thomas, Publisher, Springfield, Ill., 1963.

Gibson, E. J.: "Perceptual Development," in H. W. Stevenson (ed.), *Child Psychology*, Yearbook of the National Society for the Study of Education, Part I, The University of Chicago Press, Chicago, 1963, pp. 144–195.

Hicks, L. and V. Hunton: "The Relative Dominance of Form and Orientation in Discrimination Learning by Monkeys and Children," *Psychonomic Science*, 1:411–412, 1964.

Kaluger, G. and C. J. Kolson: *Reading and Learning Disabilities*, Charles E. Merrill, Columbus, Ohio, 1969.

Kershner, J. R.: "Doman-Delacato's Theory of Neurological Organization Applied with Retarded Children," *Exceptional Children*, 34:441–450, 1968.

Kirk, S. A.: *Teaching Reading to Slow-Learning Children*, Houghton Mifflin Company, Boston, 1940.

Meier, G. W. and R. K. McGee: "Re-evaluation of the Effect of Early Perceptual Experience on Discrimination Performed During Adulthood," *Journal of Comparative and Physiological Psychology*, 51:785–878, 1958.

Otto, W. and R. A. McMenemy: *Corrective and Remedial Teaching*, Houghton Mifflin Company, Boston, 1966, pp. 181–186.

Pick, H. L.: "Some Soviet Research on Learning and Perception in Children," *Monographs of the Society for Research in Child Development*, vol. 28, 1963, pp. 185–190.

Pope, L. and A. Haklay: "Reading Durability," in J. Wortis (ed.), *Mental Retardation: An Annual Review*, Grune & Stratton, Inc., New York, 1970, vol. II, pp. 132–149.

Queen Anne's County Teachers Manual: *First Steps in Word Recognition*, Queen Anne's County, Maryland, pp. 1954–1955.

Robbins, M. P.: "Test of the Doman-Delacato Rationale with Retarded Readers," *Journal of the American Medical Association*, 202:389–393, 1967.

Roswell, F. and G. Natchez: *Reading Disability: Diagnosis and Treatment*, Basic Books, New York, 1964.

Russell, D. H. and E. F. Russell: *Listening Aids Through the Grades*, Teachers College Press, Columbia University, New York, 1959.

Sheperd, G.: "Selected Factors in the Reading Ability of Educable Mentally Retarded Boys," *American Journal of Mental Deficiency*, 71:563–570, 1967.

Smith, Nila Banton: *Reading Instruction for Today's Children*, Prentice-Hall, Inc., Englewood Cliffs, N. J., 1963.

Spache, G. D.: *Reading in the Elementary School*, Allyn and Bacon, Inc., Boston, 1964.

Strang, R.: *Diagnostic Teaching of Reading*, McGraw-Hill Book Company, New York, 1964, pp. 62–63, 199.

Walk, R. D.: "Visual and Visual-Motor Experience: A Replication," *Journal of Comparative and Physiological Psychology*, 51:785–787, 1958.

———, E. J. Gibson, H. C. Pick, and T. J. Tight: "The Effectiveness of Prolonged Exposure to Cutouts vs. Painted Patterns for Facilitation of Discrimination," *Journal of Comparative and Physiological Psychology*, 52:519–521, 1959.

Wepman, Joseph: "Auditory Discrimination, Speech and Reading," *Elementary School Journal*, vol. 60, 1960.

Zaporozhets, A. V.: "The Development of Perception in the Preschool Child," *Monographs of the Society for Research in Child Development*, vol. 30, 1965, pp. 82–101.

9

DEVELOPING ARITHMETIC SKILLS

Among studies conducted in subject areas, perhaps the least attention has been directed toward investigating factors of arithmetic performance among the mentally retarded. Cruickshank (1946, 1948a, 1948b) reports that, compared with the intellectually normal of the same mental age, the retarded (1) are reasonably alike in areas of computation, although they are more careless and exhibit a greater incidence of "primitive habits" such as making marks and counting on their fingers, (2) have greater difficulty in understanding and identifying which process should be used in solving a problem, even when it is presented verbally, (3) lack the skill to separate irrelevant facts from significant dimensions of a problem, and (4) have greater difficulty with the reading and language peculiar to arithmetic. The literature agrees that the retarded tend to achieve at a level consistent with their mental age in arithmetic computation but are often significantly below that level in arithmetic reasoning (Dunn, 1954; Bensberg, 1953) and in problem solving (Cawley and Goodman, 1968; Cawley, 1972).

Studies seeking to identify a relationship between etiology and arithmetic achievement have been contradictory and inconclusive (Strauss and Werner, 1938; Fouracre, 1958; Capobianco, 1954). Teaching methodology has been studied by only a few investigators (Burns, 1961; Costello, 1941). These investigations suggest the value of emphasizing an experience approach in teaching arithmetic to the retarded.

Although lacking in empirical documentation on mentally retarded subjects, several authors have suggested the potential value in applying the work of Piaget to the arithmetic problems of the retarded (Clarke and Clarke, 1965; Woodward, 1961, 1962a, 1962b, Cawley and Vitello,

1972). Their position is that traditional teaching strategies do not allow the retarded to develop an understanding of number concepts, which, in turn, relate directly to reasoning ability. Teaching computational skills solely through "devices" is to be eschewed according to this school of thought, since it results in a level of skill similar to "word calling" in reading. Bereiter and Engelmann (1966) have assumed a closely allied position by suggesting that arithmetic skills can be effectively taught to disadvantaged preschool children by focusing on the numerical concepts embodied in the language of arithmetic and by deemphasizing specific computational facts.

basic arithmetic objectives

There are few other areas where the implications of ignorance are more severe or longlasting than in the management of personal finances. A person who is unconcerned about or unable to manage his monetary affairs is a ready target for unscrupulous members of society whose primary goal is to make an easy dollar without concern for the difficulties they precipitate for others. A great many areas of personal and social interaction depend on an ability to apply to practical situations fundamental arithmetic skills and concepts. Since most mildly retarded children will become part of the social and occupational world, their success in this environment will depend on their performance level in these important areas. By the time they leave school, the retarded should be skilled enough to handle affairs that require a minimum level of arithmetic skill and understanding.

The basic objectives of the arithmetic program for the mentally retarded differ significantly from those for the intellectually normal in terms of breadth and depth of treatment. As was true in other subject areas, great variation will be observed between the children in ability and performance. The most dramatic differences occur between arithmetic computation and arithmetic reasoning. To delineate the specific emphasis of an arithmetic program for retarded children, the following objectives should be focused upon:

1 Development of an understanding of numbers and the processes involved in arithmetic computation
2 Seeing relationships among various computational processes and the manner in which they can be used for solving various types of problems
3 Development of a more structured and organized repertoire of

responses that comes about through having acquired an understanding of the logical structure of arithmetic
4 Development of more dependence on and comfort in using symbols or abstractions as points of reference instead of total dependence on concrete reference points
5 Movement toward greater dependence in using a consistent method for solving problems in place of random, impulsive behavior

The first two of these objectives focus on developing basic understanding and skills in computation and in using these skills to solve everyday arithmetic problems. The latter three objectives are broader and suggest the important potential role arithmetic instruction can play in helping the retarded to develop a general style for effectively dealing with issues and problems. This has pertinence for solving problems in nonarithmetic areas of life as well.

evaluating arithmetic skills

Adequately diagnosing a youngster's arithmetic difficulties involves observation, testing, and assessment procedures similar to those used in the other developmental areas. One would want to assess achievement in arithmetic vis-à-vis other primary content areas, to attempt to identify the character of specific arithmetic weaknesses, to determine if there are faulty procedures of solution that the youngster needs to have remediated, to identify any peculiarities in his instructional environment that need to be altered, and then to proceed to formulate a specific program of educational management. You recall, of course, that the instructional program you must specify as a result of the data collected during the diagnostic phase should always include performance objectives, instructional procedures, and a description of materials that are compatible with the targets and methods.

1. ASSESSING READINESS SKILLS
The concept of readiness has emerged as being vital to subsequent success in reading. In arithmetic, readiness is of equal importance, although this area usually receives less attention in most special education arithmetic programs.

Readiness for arithmetic can be viewed from two perspectives. First, adequate arithmetic achievement is fundamentally dependent on the student's ability to discriminate among and remember auditory and visual stimuli, attend to a task, accurately perceive spatial orientation and translate these phenomena into temporal sequences, associate stimuli, and express himself. For rote counting alone, a very elementary arithmetic skill, students must listen carefully, perceive accurately, discriminate among sounds, remember the components and their appropriate sequence, and vocally or gesturally express the numerical chain. This simple task requires a certain minimum level of achievement in each of these basic areas. As computational and reasoning problems increase in complexity, the fundamental readiness skills become increasingly significant techniques for assessing various readiness dimensions that have been reviewed in the previous chapter.

The second way for viewing readiness for arithmetic is in terms of how far into the logical arithmetic sequence the student has proceeded with satisfactory achievement. To illustrate, the student would not be able to satisfactorily perform a two-digit addition problem involving carrying before understanding concepts of grouping; addition is based on this fundamental understanding. From this perspective, then, readiness to do arithmetic requires the developmental and sequential ordering of arithmetic skills. The evaluation of each retarded child should be made in terms of the degree to which prerequisite skills are understood and accomplished before the child is allowed to move to the next level of instruction.

The importance of language development as a precursor to formal arithmetic instruction should be recognized. The students must understand the significance of what is being said and exhibit some facility for using the language of arithmetic. If any of the children show weaknesses in language, problems in computation and reasoning will be more frequent.

2. ESTABLISHING THE GENERAL INSTRUCTIONAL LEVEL IN ARITHMETIC

Formal Procedures   Most survey group-achievement tests contain a number of subtests that sample arithmetic achievement. These tests can usually be administered individually or in a group. It is most important that you assure yourself that you are properly trained and experienced in administering and interpreting any test before you proceed. Individual administration is always preferred over group because of the greater control one has over the student's behavior during individual sessions. Presumably, then, you could expect to obtain more representative samples of the child's performance in this setting. Table 9-1 lists several achievement tests that sample various arithmetic factors.

Informal Procedures   As in reading, a teacher may wish to evaluate arithmetic achievement infrequently during the school year by making

Table 9-1

SURVEY TESTS THAT ASSESS FACTORS OF ARITHMETIC
ACHIEVEMENT

NAME OF TEST	DIMENSIONS EVALUATED	GRADE LEVEL	PUBLISHER
California Arithmetic Tests	Fundamentals Reasoning	1–9	CTB
Metropolitan Achievement Tests	Computation Problem solving Concepts and skills	1–9	HBW
Stanford Achievement Tests	Computation Applications Concepts Total	2–9	HBW
Wide Range Achievement Test	Computation	K-College	GA
SRA Achievement Series	Concepts Reasoning Computation Total	1–9	SRA
Bobbs-Merrill Arithmetic Achievement Tests	Computation Concepts Problems Total	1–9	BMC

use of one of the formal standardized procedures. This strategy will allow for systematic comparisons over time. There is the added advantage of an achievement test typically not requiring a specially trained examiner for administration. It is inadvisable to use formal achievement survey techniques too frequently. Students become test wise, and, consequently, instruments lose their meaningfulness.

To circumvent this problem, the teacher will find it beneficial to frequently check on a child's progress using informal means of evaluation. Appraising the value of a different method of instruction, the instructional regrouping of students, and the placement of new children in an appropriate arithmetic group all require constant evaluation of achievement. The purpose of this assessment procedure must be understood before an informal arithmetic survey is constructed. If computational skills are to be studied, tasks should be presented so as to minimize the need for the child to do anything other than computation. He should not be penalized for errors of arithmetic reasoning at a time when you are dealing with assessing computation. If, on the other hand, the teacher is interested in sampling arithmetic reasoning skills, it would be wise to control any reading requirements needed to solve arithmetic reasoning problems. Being aware of this differentiation will provide a more accurate estimate of achievement, strengths, or weaknesses which require special attention.

The assessment of arithmetic achievement is closely associated with the identification of specific arithmetic difficulties. The latter typically involves a more intensive analysis, usually individual testing of some type. Informal group checks of achievement do not provide a situation which allows for the accurate observation of processes or habits a child might exhibit in attacking a specific arithmetic problem. Informal individual checks of achievement, however, will provide general indications of specific weaknesses, such as difficulties in carrying, borrowing, grouping, combinations, or counting problems.

In sampling computation and reasoning performance, tasks should be designed to include a variety of arithmetic processes and skills. Adequate samples of these various arithmetic skills should be included in an informal survey. To this end, specific items can be gathered from arithmetic workbooks or texts. The following illustrates a set of items which might be included in an informal computational survey designed to sample achievement in a number of areas.

Examples of items appropriate for an informal test of computational achievement

Addition

6	3	4	10	8	11
+ 2	+ 5	+ 0	+ 5	+ 3	+ 4

			11		
17	33	67	12	42	523
+ 5	+ 15	+ 71	+ 9	+ 9	+ 162

692
+ 349

Subtraction

6	3	4	17	98	47
− 4	− 3	− 0	− 3	− 4	− 32

10	14	27	7 − 5 = _____
− 3	− 6	− 24	

$17 - 12 =$ _____ $18 - 9 =$ _____ $\begin{array}{r} 462 \\ -\ 321 \\ \hline \end{array}$

$\begin{array}{r} 176 \\ -\ 36 \\ \hline \end{array}$ $\begin{array}{r} 253 \\ -\ 89 \\ \hline \end{array}$

Multiplication

$\begin{array}{r} 3 \\ \times\ 2 \\ \hline \end{array}$ $\begin{array}{r} 2 \\ \times\ 2 \\ \hline \end{array}$ $\begin{array}{r} 2 \\ \times\ 8 \\ \hline \end{array}$ $\begin{array}{r} 6 \\ \times\ 0 \\ \hline \end{array}$ $\begin{array}{r} 33 \\ \times\ 1 \\ \hline \end{array}$ $\begin{array}{r} 22 \\ \times\ 4 \\ \hline \end{array}$ $\begin{array}{r} 3 \\ \times\ 22 \\ \hline \end{array}$

$\begin{array}{r} 232 \\ \times\ 3 \\ \hline \end{array}$ $\begin{array}{r} 204 \\ \times\ 2 \\ \hline \end{array}$ $8 \times 6 =$ _____ $7 \times 7 =$ _____

$\begin{array}{r} 1403 \\ \times\ 2 \\ \hline \end{array}$ $\begin{array}{r} 105 \\ \times\ 3 \\ \hline \end{array}$ $\begin{array}{r} 2675 \\ \times\ 3 \\ \hline \end{array}$ $\begin{array}{r} 1760 \\ \times\ 5 \\ \hline \end{array}$ $\begin{array}{r} 22 \\ \times\ 33 \\ \hline \end{array}$ $\begin{array}{r} 17 \\ \times\ 12 \\ \hline \end{array}$

$\begin{array}{r} 46 \\ \times\ 32 \\ \hline \end{array}$ $\begin{array}{r} 60 \\ \times\ 16 \\ \hline \end{array}$ $\begin{array}{r} 328 \\ \times\ 21 \\ \hline \end{array}$ $\begin{array}{r} 6023 \\ \times\ 34 \\ \hline \end{array}$

Division

$3\overline{)3}$ $2\overline{)4}$ $3\overline{)963}$ $6\overline{)18}$ $5\overline{)155}$ $2\overline{)1864}$

$3\overline{)10}$ $4\overline{)1208}$ $7\overline{)56714}$ $7\overline{)1500}$ $22\overline{)484}$

$36\overline{)864}$ $15\overline{)3666}$

In this suggested informal schedule, a general sequence was followed wherein each subsequent task requires an additional skill not necessary for a correct response on any of the preceding items. This sequencing allows for a quick check on the approximate level of achievement each child exhibits in the various arithmetic processes. Moreover, if the teacher observes that a youngster consistently misses problems involving certain skills, a more intense follow-up assessment can be made by presenting additional tasks which require a further demonstration of skill in those areas of particular weakness. Without difficulty, a tally can be made of the types of errors each child manifests in the informal computational tests during the entire year. Data from these informal surveys can then be related to the performance of the retarded on standardized achievement tests which are usually administered at the beginning and end of each school year. The comparison of these data will help the teacher to get some indication of the validity of the informal techniques.

Reasoning skills, controlling for the possible influence of reading difficulties, can be informally assessed by having the teacher read to the children a problem which requires the use of one or more of the arithmetic processes. At the most elementary level, these problems should contain no irrelevant information and should be sequenced according to the computational level attained by each child. The computational requirements of the reasoning problems should move from problems demanding the application of very simple skills to those requiring greater sophistication in the application of arithmetic fundamentals.

Reasoning capabilities of retarded children can be further analyzed by introducing irrelevant information into the problem and determining the facility of a child for identifying those facts essential for a correct solution. Reading the word problem will further complicate this task for the retarded student. As the results of the word problems are analyzed, specific difficulties of computation should be separated from those problems related to reasoning and problem solving. This procedure is needed to check for process, or computational, difficulties which the child may exhibit. As errors in computation and reasoning are delineated, the arithmetic program should be adjusted according to each student's needs. In some instances, this may simply mean that a child is placed in another group. For other children, a totally different methodological attack or curriculum revision may be necessary.

In addition to using teacher-constructed achievement surveys, a review of the previous arithmetic work done by students will be revealing. This material will provide clues to the general achievement level and progress each child has made during the course of formal instruction in arithmetic. Further, each child's record should be compared with his present daily performance. Some attention must be given to daily activities and awareness shown of any errors the child makes or poor habits acquired during the course of instruction. A daily check of workbooks and seatwork will help to maintain control over these potential difficulties.

3. DIAGNOSIS OF SPECIFIC ARITHMETIC DEFICITS

A child may be achieving poorly in arithmetic for any of a variety of specific reasons, which if allowed to go unremediated will result in the accumulation of deficits which deleteriously influence other areas of arithmetic performance. For example, lack of understanding of the concept of zero could influence each of the fundamental computational processes in addition to reasoning. The potential influence of this type of problem could be even more widespread and possibly result in guessing, impulsivity, lack of cooperation, antisocial responses, or a general dislike for anything dealing with a particularly difficult subject or even the entire school program. The illustration is by no means overstated; lack of success will characteristically result in atypical behavior. It is significant, indeed, that difficulty in a very specific component of a process, if unremediated, has the potential for mushrooming into negative attitudes and poor behavior.

The point has been emphasized that the teacher must be alert to diagnostic clues and formulate the total program accordingly. Factors related to successful performance in arithmetic computation and reasoning will require evaluation in order to identify any specific disabilities. The process of identifying possible difficulties should be combined with the formal and informal assessment of arithmetic achievement, assuming that these instruments have been administered individually to the students. With arithmetic, as well as in reading, the teacher's interests should be focused on the *types of errors* made by each child and also on the *process* each student uses in solving problems.

Formal Procedures Less recent attention has been given to the construction of diagnostic instruments in arithmetic than in reading. In most instances one can use a standard achievement test and diagnose problems directly from it with accuracy and depth that is impossible to attain in a broad-range reading achievement test. However, since some effort has been given recently to techniques for teaching "modern math," and interest has been shown in applying the observations of Piaget to arithmetic instruction for the mentally retarded, academicians are reconsidering the traditional approaches for arithmetic assessment and instruction (Stephens, 1966).

The formal procedures available to check on specific arithmetic defects do not usually require the extensive formal instruction and experience for administration characteristic of most reading diagnostic tests. Teachers will find it helpful to have samples of these diagnostic tests available. It is not always necessary to administer the entire test each time it is given. The teacher may wish to select items from only certain areas of relevance. Table 9-2 summarizes a sample of the formal tests available to help diagnose arithmetic problems.

Informal Procedures The evaluation of a child's arithmetic performance in attempting to identify the kinds of problems he is experiencing and the possible reasons for such difficulty does not require the "ruffles anf flourishes" of psychometric sophistication to be successful and meaningful. Basically the procedures involve the commonsense approach of (1) stating the arithmetic behaviors in which you wish to observe the youngster perform, (2) providing the child with enough situations in which that behavior is required to secure an adequate sample, and (3) accurately and reliably recording his performance in the

Table 9-2

INSTRUMENTS FOR IDENTIFYING SPECIFIC ARITHMETIC
WEAKNESSES

NAME OF TEST	DIMENSIONS EVALUATED	GRADE LEVEL	PUBLISHER
Diagnostic Number Tests	Addition Subtraction Multiplication Division Weights and measures Fractions Decimals Percentages	2–5	ACER
Stanford Diagnostic Arithmetic Test	Number facts Computation Concepts	2.5–8.5	HBJ
Wisconsin Contemporary Test of Elementary Mathematics	Facts Concepts	3–6	PP
Stanford Modern Mathematics Concepts Test	Ten general categories of content	5.5–9.5	HBJ

areas of concern. Perhaps the major way in which this procedure differs
from the practices of evaluating level of achievement is that one usually
looks with a more powerful microscope at the molecules of performance when there is a suspected underlying disorder than when a routine
achievement test is given to survey many areas of performance. Actually, an astute observer can gain some appreciation of the nature of a
child's arithmetic problem by carefully studying the products of his
efforts over a period of time. A key to the whole issue of informal
observation of behavior is to systematize your efforts and to make the
recording of your observations as easy on yourself as possible.

Errors of computation can be identified and recorded at any time in
the arithmetic program and in a variety of situations. Use can be made
of workbooks, seatwork, and informal or formal tests to gather such
data. The types of errors made by the children and their habits used in
arriving at incorrect answers to problems should be surveyed. When a
certain type of mistake is revealed, the reliability of this observation and

the consistency of its occurrence should be studied by giving the child more problems of the same type. Computational errors in addition, subtraction, multiplication, and division are often the result of (1) the use of incorrect procedures or sloppy work habits, (2) problems in counting and in combinations, (3) difficulties in carrying, borrowing, and in the use of remainders, (4) guessing or the need to use crutches, or (5) an inability to understand what type of solution is needed from the language of arithmetic.

Perhaps the most reasonable approach to informally assessing computation is to develop a procedure much like that suggested for other content areas. First, develop a group of sets of arithmetic problems, all of which can be used to basically evaluate the same dimension. For example, you might have five or ten sets of addition problems, with each set containing ten problems that require the youngsters to add a one-digit number to a two-digit number, with no carrying and with a sum of less than thirty. When you suspect that a child is having trouble with some of the skills contained in that task, you simply provide him with a set of the problems within that category, have him solve the problems, and record the frequency of correct responses, error rate, or types of problems within the set in which errors were consistently made (e.g., numbers with zero in the addend). Use a frequency chart, such as that in Figure 4-6, to maintain your records, or use some criterion (say, 90 percent correct on five successive sets, each of which evaluates the same factors) and make movement to the next level in the arithmetic program contingent on his meeting that level of success. You can see how important it is, though, to specify the skills you wish to assess, outline the sequence of skills, and develop your file of evaluation sets before you begin to implement these procedures.

To survey errors in arithmetic reasoning requires that the teacher consider possible difficulties in (1) reading, (2) attention and listening, (3) understanding the nature of the problem, (4) extracting the significant elements from the problem and selecting an appropriate computational procedure, (5) translating the word problem into a proper medium for computation, (6) correctly computing the answer, and (7) using the computed answer in adequately responding to the problem. Arithmetic reasoning is a complex process that involves a variety of high-level intellectual skills. The more mechanical components of arithmetic computation are much easier for the retarded to master than are the more complex skills required for a child to reason through a problem that is presented either visually or vocally and then to decide which, if any, arithmetic processes are needed to solve the problem—and then to actually solve it. Care must be taken in the evaluation to differentiate between the factors involved in these two components of arithmetic. The suggestions given for dealing with assessment problems involved in computation will work equally well in this area of arithmetic application, reasoning, or problem solving. Set up a group of problems that are sequenced along lines of difficulty (e.g., judgments needed regarding the proper process to use, amount and nature of irrelevant information, language level used, or use of multiple operations). Have the students attempt a response to each, at their individually appropriate level, and then try to identify where within the process errors of judgment and/or application have been made.

procedures for arithmetic instruction

Experiments in arithmetic using retarded subjects have been descriptive in the past and not designed to provide evidence concerning the efficacy of various methods, materials, or curricula. Those studies which have been designed to shed light in these areas have been inadequate in terms of program duration, research questions asked, subjects used, and alternative control procedures employed. Hence, specific direction from research for instructing the retarded in arithmetic is relatively nonexistent. The singular exception to this sweeping generalization is the recent developmental work of Cawley (1972). He and his colleagues have constructed an instructional model that allows for the delivery of an individually appropriate arithmetic program to a child with certain prespecified performance characteristics. Several thousand lessons have been generated from the model and are being field tested with various types of children in different instructional settings.

Special educators are in agreement on several points concerning the teaching of arithmetic to the retarded. First, instruction must be practical and utilitarian with especial emphasis given to a social and vocational orientation. Second, the retarded must be instructed in a manner which will facilitate the development of a conceptual understanding of arithmetic processes instead of the rote manipulation and application of figures. Teachers of the retarded should ask questions such as the following about the arithmetic program:

1 Is the material under consideration potentially important to the retarded child's future success?

2 What procedures can be employed to teach the important components of the topic under consideration in the most efficacious and practical way?
3 What procedures can be used to foster a conceptual understanding of the material by the youngsters, and how can they be encouraged to generalize and apply these understandings?

Mathematicians view success in understanding arithmetic to be basically dependent on the establishment of a firm understanding of numerical concepts. This skill encompasses more than the simple recitation of numbers; indeed, many believe that arithmetic instruction designed to help children develop a conceptual understanding of numbers should not begin with tasks involving rote or rational counting. Their point is that practice of this type encourages number calling and limits the possibility of children developing an appreciation of the full meaning of numbers. Equally damaging is the tendency of many teachers to spend too much of a child's time in mechanically computing sums and differences of progressively larger figures without ever having an opportunity to apply the concepts and skills of computation to solving problems.

Various authors have suggested different approaches for teaching arithmetic to the retarded. Kirk and Johnson (1951) propose that emphasis be placed on counting, in the early stages of instruction. Bereiter and Engelmann (1966) stress a language approach for disadvantaged preschool youngsters, many of whom find their way into a special education class unless some type of early intervention is provided. Their work has resulted in the Distar Arithmetic Program, a system of instruction in arithmetic that has a language orientation and that carefully directs the teacher's behavior throughout the instructional sequences. As with the reading system, trained teachers of children with retarded intellectual development find the program to be successful with children in regular as well as special classes. Stern (1949) suggests a structured approach in teaching arithmetic, one in which children are engaged in various activities with blocks of different sizes. It is believed that youngsters will acquire the basic concepts and skills that underlie mathematics through manipulation of the blocks and experimentation under the guidance of the teacher. The Cuisenaire program is philosophically similar to the Stern Structured Arithmetic approach although the materials are not the same. Although school systems have selected these approaches in their programs for mentally retarded youngsters, there is still very little research reported on their efficacy.

Cawley (1972) has been involved in the development of an arithmetic program—initially for mentally retarded children, but later expanded to include other types of youngsters. Although the description here is an oversimplification of his entire system, the lessons in his program are designed so that each reflects the tenets of the four major units within his model: (1) learning set, (2) verbal information processing unit, (3) cognitive processing unit, and (4) interactive unit. The developers were concerned about incorporating into their lessons activities that touched on the various types of learnings (the learning set unit) such as discrimination, incidental and paired-associate learning, retention, meaningful learning, and others. In addition, they wanted to give attention to those tasks of a "cognitive nature" that are presumed to be mainly developmental (and allegedly more resistant to change as a result of premature intervention) and those competencies that are more amenable to direct intervention and less dependent on developmental timing (cognitive processing unit). The "verbal information processing unit" pertains mainly to problem-solving tasks. Arithmetic reasoning depends to some extent on the language structure and context within which the problem (whether in written or oral format) is formulated and presented. The designers of this arithmetic program have varied the language within the problem-solving lessons—some are straightforward and lead directly to a computational solution; others include distractions, interruptions to solving the problem, or indefinite quantifiers with which a student must deal before the computational requirements can be met.

The fourth dimension of the arithmetic program being developed by Cawley is the "interactive unit." On the horizontal dimension the unit is separated into two sections: (1) mode of teacher presentation (input), and (2) mode of student response (output). The columns in Figure 9-1 represent three possible ways in which a stimulus can be presented and responded to, viz., (1) by manipulating objects, (2) by using or acting on a visual stimulus, and/or (3) by speaking or writing. The figure generates nine possible combinations among the six cells. It is assumed that the "do-do" combination is easier than the "see-see" dyad, and that it in turn is more elementary than the "say-say" pair. However, all the combinations and their relative order of difficulty are yet to be researched.

These are a few of the prominent programs that are either available or are in the development stage and appear to be particularly promising for use with the mentally retarded. Most experts in arithmetic agree that if the mentally retarded are to develop a basic conceptual understanding of arithmetic so that they can properly apply the skills to social and

Figure 9-1

The Interactive Unit of Cawley's Arithmetic Program

	Do	See	Say
Input			
Output			

Examples of each of the nine possible combinations:

Mode combination		Teacher behavior illustrated	Student behavior illustrated
Input	Output		
Do	Do	The teacher has three toy cars and three balls. She says, "Watch me." She groups the three toy cars into a set and the three balls into another set. She says, "Now, you do what I did."	The child has the same kind and number of toy cars and balls. He is expected to group the objects into two sets similar to his teacher's groups.
Do	See	The teacher lays seven pieces of string on a table. All of the pieces are of the same color and texture, three are five inches shorter than the other four, all of which are the same size. She separates the three short ones from the four longer ones—making two sets.	The child is shown four pictures, only one of which contains two sets. The remaining three pictures contain more than two sets. The child is asked to point to the picture that is like the display which the teacher constructed.
Do	Say	The teacher combines three sets of blocks, each of which contains two blocks.	The child is asked to write the algorithm that describes what was done and to solve the problem.
See	Do	The teacher presents the following stimulus to the child: $8 - \square = 6$	With a group of blocks, the child is asked to solve the problem by stacking the number of blocks that belong in the box.
See	See	The teacher presents the following problem: $3 + 2 - 1 =$	The child is asked to point to the correct response among the following alternatives: 5 1 2 4 6 0
See	Say	The child is presented with the following stimulus and asked to tell what time it is: 	The child is expected to say, "Three o'clock."

| Mode combination | | Teacher behavior | Student behavior |
Input	Output	illustrated	illustrated
Say	Do	The teacher says to the class, "With your Cuisenaire Rods, prove that 6 + 2 is the same as 4 + 4 and that both are different from 5 + 4.	The children manipulate the rods so that they have a combination of rods for each of the three algorithms. They place the three groups side-by-side to prove the relationships which the teacher requested.
Say	See	The teacher presents the following problem in written form: "Bill has four dogs, Bertha has two cats, and Mark has a hamster. How many more animals does Bill have than Bertha and Mark together?"	The child points to one of the following alternatives: 7 1 3 5 2
Say	Say	The teacher says, "How many ways can you think of to make six?"	The child responds verbally with as many ways as he can generate.

Figure 9-1
The interactive unit of Cawley's arithmetic program.

occupational problems, great attention and care must be given to the character of early basic instruction in numbers. Because the under-standing of basic number concepts is so crucial to subsequent arith-metic performance, substantial emphasis should be placed on this area. After this basic conceptual foundation has developed and as the retarded youngster increases in age, a more utilitarian application of the principles and skills can be provided. Throughout the process of instruction, the principles of learning, reviewed earlier, should assume a central position in all pedagogical practices. Factors such as active participation, overlearning, reinforcement of success, fading out, shap-ing, and reducing aversive stimuli that could be inhibiting to achieve-ment in arithmetic should be considered. The remainder of this chapter will focus on instructional procedures you can use to aid mentally retarded students to develop the skills in computation and reasoning that are so important for independent living.

TEACHING NUMBER CONCEPTS
The most promising suggestions of Piaget (1952), with interpretation by others (Lovell, 1961; Churchill, 1961; Hood, 1962; Mannix, 1960), seem to have relevance to the problems of early arithmetic instruction for the

mentally retarded. Piaget indicates that numerical concepts do not develop from the use of symbols, mechanical procedures, or verbalization by the child or teacher. Instead, he suggests that the manipulation of objects and active participation during the stage of *concrete operations* provide the necessary and most desirable circumstances for the establishment of two important concepts which, in turn, form the foundation for understanding numbers. These two central concepts are *classification* and *seriation*, both of which will be described and illustrated along with several other key areas that are relevant to number concepts.

Classification   The grouping of objects according to some common property is basic to understanding other arithmetic processes. In order to be successful in classification activities, a retarded child must be able to perceive the unique characteristics of and differences between objects. Discrimination, then, is a sequential precursor to classification. Additionally, a certain level of language capability will enhance the development of skill in classifying.

Learning how to group according to a common characteristic must be acquired first in the process of developing the concept of number. This initial skill may take a long time for the retarded children to understand well at a conceptual level. Briefly, the steps of instruction are the following:

1 An object with obvious, but somewhat limited, characteristics could be shown to the class. The object should be named or labeled, discussed, and the children encouraged to attend to its outstanding characteristics. By using a simple object, such as a spoon or a ball, the number of possible characteristics is controlled allowing the class to quickly see what is wanted and decide on the most unique characteristics of the object.

2 The children might be presented with several small objects which have common characteristics. They should be asked to describe the one or two most outstanding features of each. For example, the spoon and ball each have a unique shape and are used in certain types of activities. Through the use of a variety of similar experiences, some with variations, the retarded will gradually develop skill in grouping objects into classes. Eventually they will begin to understand that most sets of objects can be subsumed under progressively large classification systems.

As many sense modalities as possible should be employed in helping the retarded children to form concepts of classification. To this end, opportunities to manipulate objects in gamelike situations should be provided. A stable understanding will not become established if the teacher hurries through this stage of instruction by too quickly requiring children to respond to seatwork which has been duplicated on paper. Exercises of this type should come only after each youngster has demonstrated some capacity for organizing objects by characteristics. This suggestion is consistent with the perspectives of Hebb and Piaget. It has especial relevance for the retarded.

3 Gradually the teacher should require that more abstract objects and pictures be classified. For example, Cuisenaire Rods are excellent materials to use at this level. These rods, which are of ten different colors, vary in length from 1 to 10 centimeters and are 1 centimeter in cross length. Rods of the same length have similar colors. The rods offer an excellent instructional medium for classifying and grouping. In addition, pictures of various objects requiring grouping can be presented; those shown the children initially should be meaningful and have limited and very obvious characteristics. The more difficult tasks requiring classification might involve more inclusive criteria, e.g., color, size, and shape, or use of objects which are abstract or without meaning.

Correspondence   Moving to the next prenumber stage, the understanding of correspondence requires that the retarded have previously attained an understanding of the concept of class. This concept will need to be reinforced frequently during the instruction. Relating a unit in one group or set to a unit in another group or set, regardless of the possible dissimilarity in the characteristics of the groups, requires that the children understand one-to-one correspondence. There are many subtleties involved in the notion of correspondence which may prove to be very difficult for the retarded unless the teacher is especially aware of potential areas for misunderstanding or misinterpretation.

Correspondence is vital for the subsequent teaching and learning of addition and subtraction. Instruction can be initiated at this stage by the teacher placing two sets of three-dimensional objects, each of which contains the same number of objects, in front of a retarded child. The child is asked to match an object from one set with an object from the other set, for example,

As in the earlier level of arithmetic, after the children have gained an understanding of the concept, the materials of instruction can gradually become more obtuse and remote in contrast to the first presentation which involved three-dimensional objects having meaning. For example, in asking a child to associate one object in a set with another object in a set, during the early stages of teaching one-to-one correspondence, the relationships of the units between the two sets should be logically realistic. The children might be asked to relate a piece of candy with a coin or a picture of a mustache with a picture of a man's face.

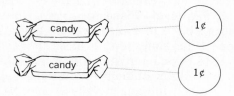

Practical activities for developing this notion of equivalence between sets might include playing a game of musical chairs, setting a table for the members of the class or for a family, or checking to see if enough cups or glasses of milk are available for the class members.

As they begin to see that any time two groups contain an equal number of units the sets are equivalent, the teacher can move to exercises which involve some type of variation, such as differences between elements of sets whose members vary in terms of size, shape, color, or purpose.

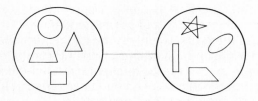

Exercises should evolve gradually from the manipulation of three-dimensional objects to responses by the children on paper. Those students who have a firm understanding of classification and equivalence should be able to relate members of sets on more than one criterion. For the children to perform well in this skill, the teacher should present material sequentially so that the retarded can proceed from working at a concrete manipulating level to a more abstract level of response.

The activities of one-to-one correspondence, which follow instruction in classification, should always include elements from sets having the same number of objects. The number of objects presented in teaching correspondence should include sets with no more than two members. This number should gradually increase, but never exceed nine. Movement to the higher numbers should be based on a criterion of success exhibited by a child during the course of instruction.

In activities of correspondence, children should first be asked to pair elements of sets whose members, although grossly different in certain unique characteristics, are equivalent in number. After this concept is understood, they should be asked to pair sets in which one set contains more members than the others. To illustrate:

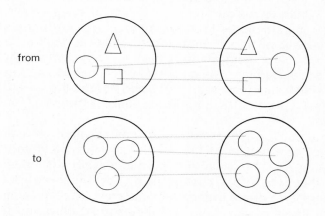

from

to

Here, as in the earlier stages of instruction in classification and correspondence, the objects presented for pairing should have an obvious relationship. In fact, the principles of obviousness and concreteness should always be followed whenever a new activity or experience is introduced to these children. In this case, one set might contain four units with pictures of birds; the other set might contain three units of pictures of birdhouses. The children are asked to associate a bird with the birdhouse and to mark the set containing more elements than the other set. As in the earlier exercises of this sort, using three-dimensional objects which the children can manipulate is recommended. Employing paper and pencil exercises should occur only after success with the concrete objects has been observed.

Conservation and Reversibility Two additional concepts should be taught at this point in the arithmetic program. The first is conservation, i.e., that the number of units within sets remains the same irrespective of any changes made in the arrangement of the units contained in each set. The second concept is reversibility, i.e., the idea that it is always possible to restore units to their original positions without changing their nature or relationship with other sets. The teacher will find the Cuisenaire Rods to be a valuable instructional device in teaching these concepts. By altering the position of groups of rods, the teacher can demonstrate that the number of rods and the characteristics of each remain the same irrespective of their location or position relative to other sets. The children will gradually realize that the space between members of a set and the relative position of each unit is totally irrelevant and in no way alters the number of elements or the relationship existing among groups. These concepts will be difficult for many retarded children to acquire without a great amount of practice and repetition. Children below the mental age of eight will find it most difficult to separate all the irrelevant perceptual components related to shifting element positions within groups. Most children at this age perceive that a set changes in number simply by virtue of the elements having been rearranged. The concepts of conservation or equivalence and reversibility are necessary for later instruction in addition and subtraction. Opportunities, therefore, should be provided for overlearning to occur.

To reinforce the earlier notions of conservation and reversibility, members of sets, which at this stage should be unequal, should be altered by moving the units into various positions in order to further reinforce the notion that change in number does not occur simply because elements are rearranged. As the children relate elements from one set to those of a second set, they should be asked to describe exactly what they see and what they are doing. This will help to encourage overlearning, provide immediate knowledge of results, facilitate feedback, and be of diagnostic value to the teacher. By observing and listening to the students, the teacher can identify specific areas or concepts which are not clearly understood.

By the time the child has reached this stage of arithmetic development, the language of arithmetic begins to become commonplace. The children will be able to react to situations involving the use of words such as "more than," "as much as," "less than," "large," and "small." Much of arithmetic language deals with qualitative differences such as the dichotomies between hard and soft, light and heavy, or large and small. The language of arithmetic, therefore, can be viewed as the result of perceptual outgrowth and develops basically because of the active interaction an individual has with the environment. To estimate qualitative dimensions accurately requires that an individual be able to compare an object with himself. The relationships existing among certain factors of the language of arithmetic, perceptual-motor development, communication, and reading are worth considering.

Ordering The ability to order sets into a series according to the number of members contained in each is another major concept the retarded must understand in order to grasp the idea of number. The notion of relations or seriation is as important as classification and one-to-one correspondence. Indeed, the number system is based on a blend of the operations of classification and ordering. The idea of five, for example, requires the child to classify in his mind five objects and to place five between four and six in the proper order. When able to deal with these operations in combination, the student will simultaneously see the cardinal and ordinal meanings of number; that is, the number five is both understood conceptually and correctly located between the fourth and sixth position.

Seriation must be taught to the retarded by using concrete objects. This is required for two reasons: (1) Research employing Piaget's concepts reports that seriation of objects can be accomplished by children by the age of seven or eight; whereas seriation of verbal abstractions rarely occurs at an appropriate level of competence before the age of eleven or twelve, and (2) mentally retarded youngsters are relatively stronger in nonverbal than in verbal areas of performance. The teacher, then, should make use of the retarded child's relative strengths in nonverbal areas to help develop the concept of ordering. At the same time, these children should be required to verbalize their observations during the process of ordering.

The Cuisenaire Rods are ideal for beginning instruction in seriation. By providing each child with three or four rods of different lengths and requiring the ordering of these rods according to size, seriation skills can be facilitated. Materials other than those produced commercially can be used for this activity. For example, the teacher could cut cardboard strips which vary in length from 1 to 10 inches. Each 1-inch interval can be identified and the children asked to tell the number of smaller strips of cardboard required to make one of the larger strips. Both ordination and cardination can be taught using this approach.

It is interesting that although a great amount of formal instruction in arithmetic has taken place up to this point, little has been said about numbers either by the child or the teacher. The classification and seriation exercises used with the retarded do not explicitly have the development of rote or rational counting as a primary objective. As the children work with various combinations and groups, however, they will begin to realize the concept of "twoness," "threeness," "fourness," and so on. Association with a specific numeral, however, should not be formally introduced prior to the presentation of seriation activities. It is particularly interesting and significant that understanding the concept of number does not depend on ability for rote and rational counting prior to classification and grouping instruction. In many respects this is the reverse position presently held by many teachers of the mentally retarded. Although rote counting and rational counting can be taught relatively quickly to the mentally retarded, this procedure does not allow for development of concept of number which, in turn, forms the basis for understanding and correctly applying concepts concerned with simple addition and subtraction.

Associating Numbers with Numerals After the children have demonstrated skill in ordering sets of objects in terms of their relationship to other sets, they are ready to focus their attention on the association of numerals with the number of elements contained in appropriate sets. By this time the notions of oneness, twoness, and threeness will have been introduced, and the children will know that sets containing a like number of elements exhibit a common property which differentiates them from other sets. The common property of sets having a similar number of elements can be associated with a certain name and symbol.

The following procedure might be employed in teaching the retarded to make this association. First, identify for the children a variety of three-dimensional sets each of which contains a different number of elements. Place the sets around the perimeter of a large table, allow the children to manipulate them and rearrange the position of the objects within an individual set in any way they wish. After they have had a chance to study the various sets, choose a set which contains one element; and explain that whenever we have a set with this many members, holding the set out so that all the children can see, we think of the number 1. At this point, the teacher should place a large cutout of the numeral 1 in the center of the table which contains the various sets of objects. After the relationship between the numeral 1 and the appropriate set has been established, the children should be asked to select from all the sets on the table those which can be described by the numeral 1. The children might be allowed to work in groups at first. The teacher must be careful to give clear directions and provide numerous examples concerning the association of sets with the number 1. Emphasis should be given to the common characteristic of all the sets which have been selected as being descriptive of oneness and described by the numeral 1.

This same type of exercise can be used for sequential presentations through number nine. Similar types of activities can be given which make use of paper and pencil tasks, but only after they have had plenty of opportunity to work with three-dimensional objects. As they are required to move beyond sets containing more than four members, it may become difficult for them to identify the correct sets at a glance without counting the elements of each set. At this point, rational counting should be encouraged. The advantage of emphasizing rational counting here is to make the point that "Whenever we need to know how many, we should count." The additional advantage of having children count the members of sets is the clear vocal feedback provided to them. This exercise will also be of diagnostic value to the teacher.

In teaching the relationship between a numerical symbol and the appropriate set, the teacher will find it helpful to proceed from one through nine in an ordinal fashion. Objects can be arranged to contain two elements, three elements, four elements, and five elements, as a means for reviewing and reinforcing earlier concepts prior to introducing the relationship between the numeral 6 and sets containing six members. Following this review, the teacher can introduce the numeral 6 by saying that by adding one member to the set which has five members we no longer can think of the set as five, but we must now think of it as six. Have the children count the elements of the set.

The concept of cardinal numbers from one through nine must be constantly reinforced. The child's ability to recognize the standard numerals and to associate the numeral with the correct number of elements is important. Exercises such as presenting them with the numeral 6 and asking them to draw six balls or make six X's will help to reinforce the idea and provide a means for evaluating the degree to which the concept becomes overlearned. Numerous variations from this activity are possible. For example, the teacher could reverse the procedure and supply the children with a certain number of circles of X's and ask the students to indicate how many objects were in each row by writing the appropriate numeral. Ordinal positioning should not be overlooked in these activities.

Teaching concepts related to number are basic for children to develop flexibility in understanding and correctly applying even the most elementary arithmetic process. Substantial attention should be given to these fundamental arithmetic matters in special classes for the retarded. The teacher should not be overly concerned if the children spend a great amount of time with these basic concepts. The advantage of establishing a firm understanding of the prenumber concepts will become visible as they move toward the more difficult aspects of the arithmetic program.

The special education teacher will find that many of the contemporary arithmetic workbooks and texts used with children from the kindergarten to second or third grade will help to design and sequence arithmetic activities for the retarded. Some selection of arithmetic exercises and activities will need to be made with the principal criterion being their potential value for the future social and occupational skills required of the retarded. Revision of workbook activities may be necessary. It should be emphasized that the child must spend time manipulating three-dimensional objects. For this reason, materials such as the Cuisenaire Rods are particularly useful for instruction in combinations, classifications, and seriation. Not only will these materials help in presenting concepts, but the children can work individually with these materials at their own desks.

TEACHING SIMPLE ADDITION
Although it is true that the teacher will view the operations of simple addition and subtraction as being closely related, they should be taught separately to the mentally retarded so that the retarded do not become confused in using and applying these processes. Eventually, they will begin to see that addition involves combining groups into a new, larger group.

The initial introduction of simple addition should emerge from the earlier study of classification and grouping. The children should move from a consideration of the characteristics of a group, to more than one group (involving the study of correspondence), to activities involving combining two separate groups into a new group. The first activities in addition should be very concrete and involve dramatization; for example, having two small groups of children join to form a single line. Subsequent activities might involve the use of inanimate three-dimensional objects. Verbal statements should be made which describe the process of combining groups. These will help the retarded pupils become familiar with the language of addition. For example, at this first stage a command, "Mary and John, go and join Herb for lunch," will gradually evolve into a more precise statement, "Two people and one person make a group of three."

When the teacher feels that the children understand conservation and reversibility, the instructional program should move into the use of pictorial materials. Although the appropriate numerical terms should be used to verbally describe the quantity in each set or group, the instruction should be broken into basic sequential steps. The printed numeral should not be used at this point for instruction in addition. The retarded should not be required to perform too many operations at once, particularly at this point, where the emphasis should be placed on understanding the process of combining, or adding, groups of things. The terms *and* and *make* can be used to describe the process of addition. The following illustrates the type of exercise appropriate at this level:

△△ and △ △△ make △△△△
two cents and three cents make five cents

Whenever the students want to know how many are in a group, they should be encouraged to count. It is quite proper for the youngsters to do rational counting at this point.

The next step in the process is to focus on developing association among the figures, appropriate verbal statements, and numerals. To illustrate:

△△ and △ △ make △△△

becomes   *2*   and   *3*   make   *5*

and later   *2*   +   *3*   =   *5*

At the same time, a transition should take place from the less precise verbal statement "Two tents and three tents make five tents" to "Two plus three equal five." The more generalized statement will be understood and used only after presenting many concrete examples of making combinations in a variety of situations. The children's achievement at this stage will be slow since they must adjust their thinking, principally in terms of seeing relationships between sets and among symbols involved in addition.

It should be realized that placing an algorithm in a horizontal position instead of in a vertical arrangement during the first stages of simple addition will help to reinforce the left-to-right progression necessary in reading. Moreover, this type of placement is more consistent with the earlier arithmetic activities involving the use of concrete objects and pictures. In order to aid the retarded child to know where to start in the process, an arrow could be drawn below each algorithm.

$$2 + 3 = 5$$
$$\longrightarrow$$

If the retarded child has developed an understanding of conservation, reversibility, and correspondence, it will be relatively easy for a transition to be made to a vertical arrangement of the algorithm. This conversion should be made before instruction is given in carrying and borrowing. In teaching simple addition, the teacher should concentrate on helping the children to use their newly developed skill for solving problems which have been presented verbally. This will help them to relate arithmetic computation skills to arithmetic reasoning situations early in the sequence of instruction and thus emphasize the utilitarian value of arithmetic. Exercises of this type can be given before the children develop a comparable level of achievement in reading.

The use of zero in simple addition is introduced after the children have had many opportunities to work with combining sets up to nine. Zero can best be introduced by indicating that it represents an empty set or group. There is nothing in the group to add to the other set, and, therefore, the total is the same as the number of members found in the nonempty group. The teacher will find it best to return to a more concrete stage of instruction by using people or three-dimensional inanimate objects to illustrate the point.

A variety of exercises should be used with the retarded in order that they firmly understand the addition process, know when it can be appropriately used, and become able to use the process in a flexible way.

TEACHING SIMPLE SUBTRACTION

The procedures used in teaching simple subtraction are basically similar to those employed in simple addition instruction. The concept of groups is used to begin teaching subtraction. Instruction should proceed from total use of concrete objects to abstract forms. Verbal statements will help to emphasize the process at all stages; the utilitarian theme should be stressed. The terms *take away* and *leaves* instead of *minus* and *equals* can be used when the children engage in subtraction activities initially.

Subtraction instruction can be started by illustration or through some type of dramatization. For example, start with a group of four children, and ask one child to leave the group. Ask the class how many children are left in the original group. Emphasize that the large group was separated in some way and two smaller groups formed. Even at this stage, the use of the language of subtraction should begin.

The same types of activities suggested for addition are applicable in teaching subtraction. Moreover, the same sequences can be followed. The children should manipulate objects first and gradually be introduced to more abstract stimuli including the use of the signs and symbols of subtraction. Making the transition from descriptive statements to the more precise language of subtraction must be done gradually. Placement of the algorithm in a horizontal position will provide a helpful reference point from the child's earlier experiences with addition. Eventually the students will become familiar with the vertical arrangement.

The use of zero in simple subtraction should emerge in the same relative sequence as it did in addition. Constant focus on the use of groups and the concept of an empty set will help the notion of zero to develop.

Certain students may eventually see that subtraction is the opposite of addition. *The important point is that the retarded understand when the process of addition is applicable and when subtraction is to be used.* If they are skilled in the computational aspects alone, and have no understanding of when to use the various processes, the objectives of the arithmetic program will not be met. For this reason, therefore, early experiences in addition and subtraction should be combined with activities which will help the students develop a firm understanding of number. If each of these skills develops in isolation without the other being considered, arithmetic instruction will be rendered relatively useless.

TEACHING CARRYING AND
BORROWING THROUGH PLACE VALUE
Understanding place value is necessary for the accurate execution of two- and three-place addition and subtraction, particularly when it involves carrying and borrowing. Place value should be introduced as part of instruction in simple addition and subtraction. As children

engage in arithmetic activities involving two- and three-place addition and subtraction without carrying and borrowing, the teacher should use the place-value box. This is a small plywood box with three equal-sized compartments into which sticks, such as tongue depressors, can be inserted. The compartments are appropriately labeled "Ones," "Tens," and "Hundreds."

As the children add and subtract, they can simultaneously add to or remove from the groups located in the various compartments. This introduction to the place-value box, using number combinations that do not exceed nine in any column, will help the students become familiar with using the device. Moreover, the concept and habit of correct column positioning will be developed; this is vital in the process of carrying and borrowing. Throughout the introductory stage, arithmetic activities should focus on experiences with manipulating objects (such as the place-value sticks), writing the appropriate algorithm, and using the child's computational skills to solve practical problems.

The next stage in the teaching of place value follows logically from the earlier instruction involving combinations and grouping. At this point, the retarded must understand that whenever the "Ones" compartment reaches ten, the group of objects is to be bundled together (with a rubber band to emphasize) and placed in the "Tens" compartment. The principle of "overcrowding" should lead to the realization that each bundled group now represents one group of ten. A great deal of practice should be given in making and taking apart bundles of ten so that the children realize that 1 ten is the same as 10 ones. The concepts of conservation and reversibility are inherently a part of place-value manipulation at this stage.

As the children make numbers and experiment with the use of the place-value box, the close association between this activity and the appropriate written and oral numerical symbols should be emphasized. As they manipulate the materials, the children should discuss, with the teacher or another student, what they are doing and the proper numeral which describes how many are contained in each compartment. To emphasize accuracy in this calculation operation, paper with vertical lines should be used to help impress on the children the need to execute accurately this important task.

Zero should be introduced during this early stage of experimenting. Some controversy exists as to whether zero should be explicitly called a "place holder." Since there is always the possibility that an additional rule or new concept will confuse the retarded child in beginning arithmetic, the concept of zero might best be introduced by pointing to an empty "Ones" compartment and asking the children, "How many ones are here?" A response by the children, such as "None," or "I don't see any," will lead to the teacher simply saying, "Correct. When we have none, we call that zero." This concept can be further reinforced by asking questions such as, "How many cats are with us today?" By continuing this line of questioning, with infrequent nonzero questions inserted, the retarded will soon gain a more realistic understanding of the concept of zero.

At the appropriate time the symbol zero should be introduced and the statement made that whenever there are none, the figure 0 is used. This point can be reinforced by having the children first write numbers which contain zeros when there are no sticks in any of the compartments in the place-value box; the same procedure can eventually be used in simple addition and subtraction with algorithms containing zeros. The teacher must not move too rapidly during this stage of instruction, nor should the logical sequences involving minimal change be ignored. Throughout this process, the retarded must be given plenty of practice in number building by relating numbers in the place-value box to written numerals.

By the time the children have developed reasonable levels of competence in the skills outlined above, they will be ready to begin learning the process of carrying in addition. Carrying can be introduced best by using the place-value box. In demonstrating, ask a child to place sixteen sticks (1 ten and 6 ones) in the appropriate compartments. The number should be recorded on the blackboard. Ask another child to add six more sticks. With twelve sticks in the "Ones" compartment, the previous experiences of the students in building should alert them to the "overcrowding" in the "Ones" compartment. The solution to group 10 ones and "carry" them to the "Tens" compartment should come from the students.

Throughout the process, the teacher should construct the algorithm as the students do the grouping and carrying. With the retarded, it is particularly advisable that the number of tens being carried to the next column be recorded at the top of the algorithm. The process for this sequence is shown on page 274.

Developed in this fashion, carrying is initially mechanical and greatly dependent on the use and manipulation of concrete materials and the concepts learned earlier. The retarded youngster will need to continue using these devices until practice has led to overlearning and the concept of carrying is understood by the child at an abstract level. This development may take a great amount of time, and, indeed, some

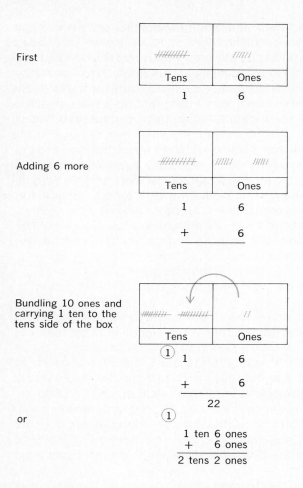

First

Adding 6 more

Bundling 10 ones and carrying 1 ten to the tens side of the box

or

1 ten 6 ones
+   6 ones
2 tens 2 ones

retarded youngsters may continue to need concrete crutches even into the high school program. If these devices are needed, the students should be allowed to use them by all means. As the children learn how to do simple carrying, the teacher should introduce addition which requires the carrying of two-digit numbers and, eventually, introduce instruction using the hundreds column.

The fundamental principles employed in borrowing are no different from those used in carrying; thus, these two operations should be taught in close contiguity. Most teachers will elect to use the decomposition method in connection with the place-value box. This process is the opposite of grouping in addition and involves breaking down a bundle of ten into ones and relocating them in the "Ones" compartment. For example, in the preliminary stages of instruction in borrowing, the students would break down 31 (or 3 tens and 1 one) into 2 tens and 11 ones. At first the children may argue that the "Ones" compartment should contain no more than 10 ones. The teacher must quickly indicate that this situation involves only a temporary grouping which is necessary in certain types of subtraction.

The retarded should make use of the place-value box with the algorithm during the subtraction process. As the minuend undergoes decomposition, appropriate changes should be made in the written numerals. The sequence is as follows:

First

Tens	Ones
2	1

Subtracting 5 requires breaking down 1 ten and relocating the 10 ones into the "ones" slot

Tens	Ones
2	1
−	5

This results in

Tens	Ones
11	11
2	1
−	5

Remove 5 from the "ones" compartment

Tens	Ones
~////////~	/////

1	11
2	1
—	5
1	6

or

2 tens 1 one
—   5 ones
1 ten 6 ones

Again, as in carrying, the use of the place-value box or a similar device should not be denied the retarded. They must be given plenty of practice in manipulating the objects and associating the changes in the grouping with the numerical alterations required in the algorithm. The students should understand that they can check on the accuracy of their subtraction by adding the subtrahend and difference to see if the sum equals the minuend. Their earlier developed understanding of conservation and reversibility again comes into focus as being an important basic concept to be emphasized in early arithmetic instruction.

Throughout the instruction in borrowing and carrying, the retarded should be given opportunities to employ their developing skills in a practical and realistic way. The early introduction of problems involving reasoning should constitute an important segment of the arithmetic period. A utilitarian theme must characterize the problems presented to the students.

MULTIPLICATION AND DIVISION

Retarded children who have developed a firm understanding of addition and subtraction and who can use each of these processes with flexibility in proper situations will be able to solve most problems involving arithmetic computation. For this reason, therefore, great emphasis should be placed on teaching these fundamental skills. Multiplication is a shortcut for addition and essentially a more efficient procedure for adding equal-sized groups to form a new group. Division is a shortcut for performing successive subtractions. Certain retarded children will be capable of learning the more elementary skills involved in each of these areas, frequently depending on crutches for successful achievement. Many other retarded youngsters will find multiplication and division too difficult. The teacher must make a decision as to whether further, more comprehensive instruction or tutoring in multiplication or division constitutes the most efficient use of time. The decision will differ for each child within a classroom and should be primarily based on the diagnostic clues each student exhibits. When the teacher judges that multiplication or division either confuses or has the potential for not being adequately understood by a youngster, greater emphasis should be placed on the further development of skills in addition and subtraction.

Those children who show some promise for being able to learn simple multiplication can be introduced to the process by first adding three numbers, e.g., $2 + 2 + 2 =$ ____. The next step is to introduce the notion that this algorithm can be viewed as 3 twos or, more technically, two times three. The children should realize that multiplication is a shortcut way to do addition and that a check can be made on the accuracy of their multiplication by repeated addition.

Multiplication will save time for the children, and, if they can develop an understanding of the computational procedures as well as accurately apply the process, eventually it should become part of the retarded students' arithmetic program. To be sure, they will need to commit some of the multiplication tables to memory or use a multiplication chart during the initial stages of instruction. A chart such as the following will often be helpful.

NUMBER TO BE MULTIPLIED

	1	2	3	4	5	6	7	8	9	10
	1	2	3	4	5	6	7	8	9	10
	2	4	6	8	10	12	14	16	18	20
	3	6	9	12	15	18	21	24	27	30
	4	8	12	16	20	24	28	32	36	40
X	5	10	15	20	25	30	35	40	45	50
(TIMES)	6	12	18	24	30	36	42	48	54	60
	7	14	21	28	35	42	49	56	63	70
	8	16	24	32	40	48	56	64	72	80
	9	18	27	36	45	54	63	72	81	90
	10	20	30	40	50	60	70	80	90	100

The use of a mnemonic device or a chart, such as the one illustrated above, is valuable to the retarded because it provides immediate knowledge of results, fosters an emphasis on accuracy, reinforces the correct response through the use of a variety of sense modalities, and gives the students opportunities for active participation. The teacher should not be hesitant to allow the retarded to use these devices.

Two-place multiplication is more difficult than simple multiplication and would be appropriate for only selected children in the special class. The combination of multiplication, addition, and the proper placement of numerals is often too difficult an operation for retarded children. Those students with the potential for satisfactorily performing this relatively complex task should be instructed in a fashion which prevents errors being practiced. Weaknesses in using the process must be identified quickly and properly remediated. Teaching two-place multiplication to the retarded is different from instruction with the intellectually normal. In the former case, the special class teacher must allow for the extended use of concrete devices and crutches, pace the instruction at a very slow rate, adhere to principles of learning, and not push the children beyond reasonable expectations.

Learning the process of division is a major stumbling block for many intellectually normal children, but it is especially difficult for the retarded. In reality, the retarded will find relatively few social or occupational opportunities for which knowledge of division is required. The teacher, therefore, should give some thought to the value of spending time teaching division to the retarded.

It would be wise to go back to the earlier stage of instruction in combinations to dramatize the meaning of division. Emphasis should be placed on the notion that division is the process of successively subtracting subgroups, each of which contains a certain restricted number of members, from a larger group of objects. For example, present a group of six blocks to the students and ask them to break down the group into subgroups, each of which contains two blocks. The question to be answered is, "How many groups of two are contained in six?"

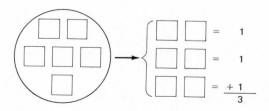

The problem can be written in another way using successive subtraction.

Problem: How many twos are in six?

$$
\begin{array}{r}
2 \div 6 \\
\quad(1 \\
-2 \\
\hline
4 \\
\quad(1 \\
-2 \\
\hline
2 \\
\quad(1 \\
-2 \\
\hline
0 \quad 3
\end{array}
$$

There are 3 twos in six.

Or

$$
\begin{array}{r}
3 \\
2 \div 6 \\
-6 \\
\hline
\end{array}
$$

In every division problem, the retarded should be taught to use the long-division approach which requires that the divisor and quotient be multiplied as a check of the dividend. Some children will be able to estimate the quotient when there is a one-figure divisor; most of the retarded will find it too difficult to learn the technique of estimating the quotient with a two-figure divisor.

As in other areas of arithmetic, the children should have plenty of practice using division by applying the process to practical problems. A great deal of manipulation of concrete objects which allows the child to return to the earlier stage of combinations should characterize early instruction in division. If a retarded child has not developed the basic concepts of reversibility and conservation, division, as well as other computational processes, will at best be done in a rote fashion. This situation will make the correct application of the appropriate arithmetic process to practical problems all the more difficult for the child. The assumption is that an understanding of the concept of number will reduce the incidence of random application of the appropriate process to a problem situation. Indeed, it could be suggested that reasoning skills will be substantially increased after a child has developed an understanding of these basic concepts.

FRACTIONS

Certain fundamental notions concerning fractions should be part of the retarded child's arithmetic program. The instruction, however, must have a decidedly practical flavor. A number of commercially developed visual aids are available to supplement the teaching of fractions. Charts such as the two below will help the retarded see relationships of fractional parts to a whole.

1							
$\frac{1}{2}$				$\frac{1}{2}$			
$\frac{1}{4}$		$\frac{1}{4}$		$\frac{1}{4}$		$\frac{1}{4}$	
$\frac{1}{8}$	$\frac{1}{8}$	$\frac{1}{8}$	$\frac{1}{8}$	$\frac{1}{8}$	$\frac{1}{8}$	$\frac{1}{8}$	$\frac{1}{8}$

The teacher should emphasize that (1) the bottom numeral of a fraction tells into how many pieces an object was equally divided, (2) the top numeral tells the number of pieces we have or are talking about, and (3) that the larger the bottom numeral, the smaller will be the pieces.

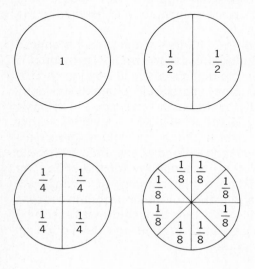

Instruction in fractions should be varied and related directly to areas in which the children will need to make use of this information or skill. They should understand what is meant by one-half loaf of bread, one-third cup of flour, or one-quarter spoon of medicine every half hour. Activities of this type, which require a basic understanding of fractions, should be stressed.

MEASUREMENT

The mentally retarded will need to understand and accurately use several types of measurement. Their depth of understanding will be totally dependent on each child's demonstrated ability and achievement along with some general prediction of future occupational expectations. Higher-level competence in specific areas of measurement which are required of certain occupations should be stressed during the work-study program. Instruction in basic skills in measurement, however, should begin much earlier in the school program.

Money   Beginning instruction with money must be concrete and allow children to manipulate the real thing. Fundamental operations of changing a coin into an equivalent sum using other coins, purchasing objects, making change, recording the amount of a purchase and calculating the amount of money to be returned, and understanding reasons for saving money should be introduced and practiced in a variety of ways throughout the instructional program. The more practical and real the situation, the greater assurance the retarded child will have in engaging in experiences with money.

Time   Its abstract nature and the minimum number of ways available for children to manipulate objects related to time often make teaching this concept to the retarded a long, arduous task. Empirical data describing a preferred strategy for teaching time are not available. Because of the more obvious switches between days of the week, the teacher can introduce time using days of the week instead of discussing relationships between minutes and hours. In the initial stages of teaching, no attempt should be made to use anything other than the names of each day. Gradually, dates, months, and years can be introduced. Activities should be provided to help the children remember the ordinal position of the days.

The relationship between hours and minutes can be introduced by the teacher adhering to a certain time schedule during each day. This schedule should become part of each child's activities. They will eventually begin to see relationships between the position of the hands on the clock and the activities typical of a particular time period in the day. Gradually, the children will show readiness for more systematic instruction in telling time. A variety of visual aids are available, or can be constructed by the teacher, to aid in this instruction. Each child can make his own model of a clock from tagboard for use at his desk.

Distance   The inch, foot, and yard are the concepts of distance on which emphasis should be placed in the special class program for the retarded. At a more advanced instructional level, the concept of mile can be introduced. Special attention should be given to techniques for making conversions from one dimension to another. The need for accuracy in measurement must be stressed, with practice in measuring and converting to another dimension included in all phases of the program. A variety of situations which occur during the day offer opportunities for the students to measure distance.

Weight   This subject can best be introduced by each student weighing himself and maintaining a weekly record. Attention should be focused primarily on the concepts of pound and ounce. The students should gain skill in converting ounces to pounds and vice versa. Activities of various types, which involve measuring the weight of flour, sand, sugar, wood, or any other commodity, using a kitchen scale, will allow for concrete experiences in this area of measurement. Experiences in the home economics and industrial arts classroom are particularly important in this regard.

Volume   The use of half-pint, pint, quart, half-gallon, and gallon containers will help develop an understanding of relationships among the various measures of volume. It will be conceptually helpful for the children to understand the significance of conservation of matter, i.e., when two containers of equal size are filled with fluid and the fluid in one vessel is poured into a smaller but taller container, the amount of fluid is altered in no way. Understanding this principle will help the retarded to conceptually see relationships among measurements of volume. The notion of conservation of matter in many ways is similar to conservation of number which was discussed earlier.

selected readings

Bensberg, G. J.: "The Relationship of Academic Achievement of Mental Defectives to Mental Age, Sex, Institutionalization, and Etiology," *American Journal of Mental Deficiency*, 58:327–330, 1953.

Bereiter, C. and S. Engelmann: *Teaching Disadvantaged Children in the Preschool*, Prentice-Hall, Inc., Englewood Cliffs, N.J., 1966.

Burns, P. C.: "Arithmetic Fundamentals for the Educable Mentally Retarded," *American Journal of Mental Deficiency*, 66:57–61, 1961.

Capobianco, R. J.: "Quantitative and Qualitative Analysis of Endogenous and Exogenous Boys on Arithmetic Achievement," in L. M. Dunn and R. J. Capobianco, "Studies of Reading and Arithmetic in Mentally Retarded Boys," *Monographs of the Society for Research in Child Development*, 1954, pp. 101–142.

Cawley, J. F.: "Teaching Arithmetic to Mentally Handicapped Children," in E. L. Meyen, G. A. Vergason, and R. J. Whelan (eds.), *Strategies for Teaching Exceptional Children*, Love Publishing Company, Denver, Colorado, 1972, pp. 250–263.

—— and J. Goodman: "Interrelationships Among Mental Abilities, Reading, Language Arts, and Arithmetic with the Mentally Handicapped," *The Arithmetic Teacher*, 15:631–636, 1968.

—— and S. J. Vitello: "Model for Arithmetic Programing for Handicapped Children," *Exceptional Children*, 39:101–110, 1972.

Churchill, E. M.: *Counting and Measuring*, University of Toronto Press, Toronto, 1961.

Clarke, A. M. and A. D. B. Clarke: *Mental Deficiency: The Changing Outlook*, The Free Press, New York, 1965.

Costello, H. M.: *The Responses of Mentally Retarded Children to Specialized Learning Experiences in Arithmetic*, unpublished doctoral dissertation, University of Pennsylvania, Philadelphia, 1941.

Cruickshank, W. M.: "Arithmetic Ability of Mentally Retarded Children: 1. Ability to Differentiate Extraneous Material from Needed Arithmetic Facts; II. Understanding Arithmetic Processes," *Journal of Education Research*, 42:161–170, 279–288, 1948b.

——: "Arithmetic Vocabulary of Mentally Retarded Boys," *Exceptional Children*, 13:65–69, 1946.

——: "Arithmetic Work Habits of Mentally Retarded Boys," *American Journal of Mental Deficiency*, 52:318–330, 1948a.

Dunn, L. M.: "A Comparison of the Reading Processes of Mentally Retarded Boys of the Same Mental Age," in L. M. Dunn and R. J. Capobianco, "Studies of Reading and Arithmetic in Mentally Retarded Boys," *Monographs of the Society for Research in Child Development*, vol. 1, 1954, pp. 7–99.

Fouracre, M. H.: "Learning Characteristics of Brain-Injured Children," *Exceptional Children*, 24:210–212, 1958.

Hood, H. B.: "An Experimental Study of Piaget's Theory of the Development of Number in Children," *British Journal of Psychology*, 53:273–286, 1962.

Kirk, S. A. and G. O. Johnson: *Educating the Retarded Child*, Houghton Mifflin Company, Boston, 1951.

Lovell, K.: *The Growth of Basic Mathematical and Scientific Concepts in Children*, University of London Press, Ltd., London, 1961.

Mannix, J. B.: "The Number Concepts of a Group of ESN Children," *British Journal of Education Psychology*, 30:180–181, 1960.

Piaget, J.: *The Child's Conception of Number*, Routledge and Kegan Paul, Ltd., London, 1952.

Stephens, W. B.: "Piaget and Inhelder—Application of Theory and Diagnostic Techniques to the Area of Mental Retardation," *Education and Training of the Mentally Retarded*, 1:75–86, 1966.

Stern, C.: *Children Discover Arithmetic*, Harper & Brothers, New York, 1949.

Strauss, A. A. and H. Werner: "Deficiency in the Finger Schema in Relation to Arithmetic Disability," *American Journal of Orthopsychiatry*, 8:719–725, 1938.

Woodward, M.: "The Application of Piaget's Theory of the Training of the Subnormal," *Journal of Mental Subnormality*, 8:17–25, 1962b.

————: "Concepts of Number in the Mentally Subnormal Studied by Piaget's Method," *Journal of Child Psychology and Psychiatry*, 2:249–259, 1961.

————: "Concepts of Space in the Mentally Subnormal Studied by Piaget's Method," *British Journal of Social and Clinical Psychology*, 1:25–37, 1962a.

10

DEVELOPING PERSONAL AND
SOCIAL SKILLS

Compared with the research effort related to learning, relatively less attention has been directed toward studying the social and emotional characteristics of the mentally retarded children or investigating the impact of programs specifically designed to develop desired social and personal skills. Nonetheless, it is the general opinion of the professional community and, indeed, of society itself that mentally retarded individuals should take their places as members of the community and contribute to its stability and enhancement. Without appropriate experiences leading to the achievement of this aim, the probability of the retarded being skilled enough to react appropriately to social demands will be minimal. It is necessary, therefore, that a great deal of attention be given to developing and directing the behavior of the child early and continuously during the course of the school program. It is equally essential that community members prepare themselves to accept the mentally retarded as contributors to an open society.

To be effective in social interchange, an individual must be sensitive to the requirements of his environment and responsive to appropriate ways of dealing with these social demands. Evidence suggests that the retarded are often unskilled in these requirements, particularly when placed in situations in which interaction is required with the intellectually normal. Goldstein (1964), in reviewing the literature, has noted the difficulty frequently characteristic of their adhering to social demands and the lack of tolerance of others in accepting their behavior. These observations are particularly relevant to the employment situation in which the mentally retarded commonly have more difficulty with the social and personal requirements of a position than with the occupational and manipulative demands (Goldstein, 1972). The need for special instructional programs to give more comprehensive and continuous attention to the social development of the mentally retarded has been clearly demonstrated.

Additional support for placing greater emphasis on the development of socialization skills in programs for the retarded comes from the research that has examined delinquency among this group. Although the evidence suggests that a marked relationship does not exist between intelligence and delinquency, there is reason to conclude that mental retardation is a complicating factor of particular significance when combined in some as yet unidentified mix with other environmental elements. Substantial effort has been given to studying reasons for criminal behavior among the retarded; included among the suggested causes are the difficulties they often have in telling right from wrong (Harrington, 1935), their problems in controlling their impulses (Gregg, 1948), their frequent lack of association with an appropriate school situation (Kvaraceus, 1944; Wallin, 1924), and their typical association with a deprived or impoverished environment (Poucher, 1952; Gregg, 1948). The retarded tend to commit more minor than major crimes, and, of those committed, the great majority seem to be the results of impulsive acts and not of planned aggression (Gregg). This finding underscores the possibility of a lack of social awareness on their part in those areas typically learned incidentally by intellectually normal children who are often also associated with a more stable family situation.

Along with these difficulties is the higher level of emotional and personal problems often observed in the retarded. For a variety of reasons, the retarded often view themselves as being generally inadequate (Heber, 1964). Certainly a frequent history of failure can be generalized and can reduce the child's eagerness to participate in activities in which success has not been experienced earlier. Developing friendships and a satisfying association with others are areas in which the mentally retarded often fail. The possibility of increased emotional disturbances among this group exists because of (1) their inflexibility in behavior and tendency to persevere on a goal even when it is out of reach, (2) their restricted range and background of experiences which delimit the possibility of an appropriate response and reduce insulation against personal degradation by others, and (3) their difficulty in interpreting personal and social situations and reacting in an acceptable fashion.

dimensions of personal, emotional, and social growth

PHYSICAL HEALTH AND PERSONAL ATTRACTIVENESS

Chapter 6 emphasized the relationships that exist between early perceptual-motor development and subsequent achievement in school-related activities. The need for the teacher to give attention to the early perceptual-motor development of the retarded and the desirability for providing the children with activities designed to increase skill in these areas were emphasized. An equally significant reason for an early emphasis on motor activities is to give children opportunities for consistent and vigorous exercise. This is particularly important for those youngsters from a depressed environment, which is frequently characterized by overcrowding and a lack of space in the surrounding neighborhood for sustained physical activity.

Rarick, Widdop, and Broadhead (1970) have documented the extent to which mildly mentally retarded boys and girls lag behind other children in certain important physical fitness categories. Using the AAHPER Youth Fitness Test (American Association for Health, Physical Education, and Recreation, 1958), they found that the mentally retarded children (aged eight to eighteen) performed less well than normal youngsters in flexed arm hang, sit-ups, shuttle run, standing broad jump, fifty-yard dash, softball throw, and 300-yard run-walk. Although there were some differences in the findings at various chronological ages, the generalization can safely be made from this and other studies (Campbell, 1971) that mentally retarded children are typically less fit than other youngsters—who, incidentally, may also be suffering from an increasingly sedentary life-style during early developmental periods.

For reasons of health, therefore, it is advisable that the teacher establish some time each day, twenty to forty minutes at the very least, for vigorous physical activity. This should extend beyond the typical recess and lunch periods of free play and have more organization and structure so that everyone can participate. Many of the children will need to be shown how to exert themselves actively. Often a collaborative effort between the special education teacher and the school's physical education department can provide a perceptual-motor and physical education program that satisfies health aims as well as the development of certain basic perceptual skills.

I urge that you and the physical education teacher decide on the kinds of skills you believe each child needs to develop along with those involved in establishing general physical fitness. Some children may need to develop better balance during walking or running, other youngsters may need to work on strength in the upper body, and a few may require particular attention to endurance. Decide on a small group of skills on which your program will focus, evaluate each child's level of activity/performance in a group of activities or games that tap the skills, record the child's level of achievement before your program begins and periodically thereafter, and be sure to make the entire experience pleasurable for everyone. Make sure that you continue to be systematic by (1) keeping records, (2) analyzing where each child's program should focus and specifying individual performance targets, and (3) using the principles or guidelines on managing behavior that were presented in Chapters 3 and 4. Campbell found that physical fitness could be increased, without an accompanying decrease in individual motivation, when retarded children were exposed to a fitness program that adhered to these principles. The teacher's behavior and the manner in which the child's instructional environment is arranged seem to be crucial if the youngster is to make progress—even in factors related to physical fitness.

The teacher of the retarded should attempt to exercise some control over the diet of the students. This is a particularly difficult expectation, for to have any lasting effect, control of nutrition must begin in each child's home. A parent education program is one approach for exerting influence in the home. Within the school program, the children should be instructed about reasons for eating carefully. Most teachers of educable retarded children who live in a depressed environment are aware of the need to devote time during the instructional program to considering proper nutrition. In the early stages of their education, the mentally retarded should develop some awareness of the reasons for eating certain kinds of food and the advantage in using various dietary supplements as frequently as possible. For example, being aware that a small amount of meat included in a large pot of beans will substantially increase the protein value of the food is an important fact of which few deprived families are aware. One can always hope that by presenting young children with a systematic program aimed at informing them about nutrition some of these ideas will be communicated to their parents. The older retarded children should come to realize the significance of appropriate nutrition. Many of these children will find themselves in situations in which they will be forced to decide on the kind of food to purchase for their families. The teacher can dramatize the impact of poor nutrition by using a variety of experiments with different types of plants which receive or are denied a certain type of nutritional supplement. In connection with the experience, films or slides can be shown to illustrate the relationship between the experiments with plants and problems resulting from nutritional deprivation among people.

A logical relationship exists between physical fitness, nutritional considerations, and the need for the children to learn more about bodily functions. The teacher should capitalize on the youngster's natural curiosity about his own body by systematically presenting units on the primary functions of the various bodily systems. A detailed explanation of the functioning of each system is beyond their capacity; however, the major bodily processes should be considered. The degree to which they understand these processes will be related to their motivation to care for themselves physically. For example, teaching the children about the process of elimination will help them conceptually understand the reasons for eating certain foods in moderation and keeping their bodies clean and make them aware of other types of difficulties that might result from not caring for themselves. In considering the respiratory system, a desired goal should be that they become aware of the disadvantages of smoking and of being near toxic vapors. Understanding the functions of the reproductive system, for example, provides a basis for an awareness of the physiological concerns of reproduction and the moral and social considerations as well.

Personal grooming and appropriate dress are other important areas for instructional concern. These are not only of social significance but have some direct relevance to physical health. Students should learn about the relationship between health, good grooming, and appropriate dress. For example, a clear difference can be shown between a person with clean hair and another with dirty hair. A strand of hair can be taken from each student and placed under a microscope. Differences in cleanliness between the strands will be quickly seen. This will be very revealing to most students and has the potential effect of altering the behavior of the child with dirty hair. Further, the level of motivation of the class may increase because this type of activity uses equipment often used by students in other classrooms.

It is much easier to work with older mentally retarded children in the areas of grooming and dress since peer pressure is often so firmly established. The teacher should use this situation by continually reminding the students of the danger of offending others by not maintaining good grooming. By the time the retarded have reached the secondary school special classes, they should have had experiences that will allow them to understand the health reasons for cleanliness and good dress. The importance of spending enough time in this area is obvious when one realizes that it is easier to detect a dirty and untidy person at a glance than it is to identify an academic problem.

EMOTIONAL GROWTH AND MENTAL HEALTH

Emotional development and interest in promoting good mental health among the retarded are other areas of concern to the special education teacher. Systematic attempts at studying personality factors among the educable retarded in the community have been predominately clinical and many are not based on empirical research. This situation is not unusual because of the great difficulty in adequately identifying and controlling the many influential, active variables that affect personality development. Heber has summarized the results of a number of investigations in which some control has been exercised. His findings indicate that (1) the retarded are poorly motivated after having once acquired a generalized expectancy of failure, (2) being located in a regular class is associated with more personality maladjustment than is placement in a special class, (3) educable individuals in the community show susceptibility for personal maladjustment, and (4) the retarded tend to have a more unrealistic picture of their own abilities.

We know that an individual's view of his own capabilities and his level of achievement are founded to a large degree on his history of success and failure within a given environment. If a child has not had an opportunity to succeed in school activities and has constantly failed, for example, a complex network of antagonisms toward those activities in which he has failed will develop with the result that the youngster will eventually exhibit a general dislike for anything associated with school, will begin to view himself as inadequate, and may even develop a dislike for or become hostile toward authority figures, such as teachers.

Factors that will help to foster good emotional development and mental health include

1 Helping the retarded to develop a positive, realistic view of themselves
2 Helping them to understand how to use healthy, adjustive mechanisms in situations that are personally troublesome
3 Providing experiences that will allow for the development and acceptance of reasonable goals and objectives
4 Helping them to develop the capabilities for controlling impulsive behavior

Figure 10-1 illustrates a hypothetical interrelationship that can occur

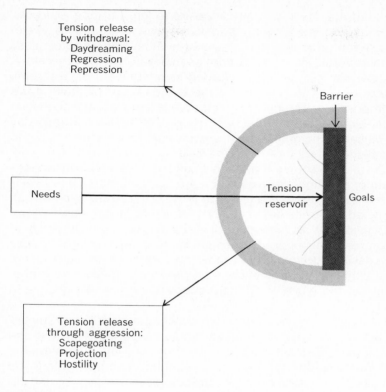

Figure 10-1
Examples of behavior resulting from tension produced by frustrated
needs. (From G. M. Blair, R. S. Jones, and R. H. Simpson, *Educational
Psychology*, The Macmillan Company, New York, 1962, p. 170. Used
with permission from the publishers.)

among these factors, shows the type of behavior that often results from
a person's not being able to satisfy his presumed individual needs, and
suggests possible procedures for dealing with some prominent difficulties which, in turn, have direct implications for one's mental health.

This figure indicates that behavior is goal-directed and is the result of
a desire to satisfy needs. These needs are the result of the normal
interaction that takes place between an individual and his environment.
They do not result from the person alone, nor from the environment
alone; their origin is a consequence of the environment-individual mix.
Certain goals are highly positive, and the need for achieving them is
high. Other goals are not as positive. For example, because of peer

pressure a child may have an intense desire to learn to ride a bicycle, whereas he may not view learning long division with the same degree of positiveness. Each of us is often frustrated in achieving goals because the necessary repertoire of skills has not been developed and, therefore, we do not have the requirements needed to circumvent or overcome obstacles that often arise and make the achievement of these goals difficult or impossible. The mentally retarded are constantly faced with this problem. Most frequently the obstacle of intellectual subnormality prohibits their satisfying goals which, unwittingly, they often consider to be highly realistic in terms of their abilities.

Figure 10-1 also assumes that each of us has a certain moment-by-moment level of tolerance for frustration and tension. When this level is reached or exceeded, there is a need for tension to be released through some type of adjustive or defensive behavior. The proposition, therefore, is advanced that an individual decides to use any of a variety of behaviors to protect his integrity because his original goal could not be satisfied. Behaviors that might broadly be classified as aggression, substitution, withdrawal, projection, suppression, and reaction formation are some of the types of adjustive mechanisms people choose to relieve this tension.

The components of the hypothetical behavioral network diagrammed in Figure 10-1 have important educational implications. Although the system is dynamic, constantly changing and undergoing alteration, the teacher will find it helpful to think about the factors of this system and their relationship to instructional methodology in classes for the retarded.

Needs and Goals The types of needs of the mentally retarded are basically no different from those of the intellectually normal. Attention, affection, activity, acceptance, and success are only some of the needs characteristic of all children. Among the strongest of these needs for the mentally retarded—and this is certainly not unique to them alone—is the desire to blend into the normal social matrix and not stand out as lacking basic skills. This wish is clear and obvious among high school children. Adolescent mildly retarded youngsters usually show extreme concern over the possibility of their making a social faux pas and, because of their apprehension, do all in their power to avoid situations in which a "social goof" might occur. At the same time, they have the same need as the normal to be accepted by their peers. These needs are strong, although the motivation for achieving them often becomes diminished after repeated failure.

Goals held by the mentally retarded for themselves are commonly unreasonable and usually more consistent with the types of objectives

characteristic of their intellectually normal peers of the same chronological age. It is not at all atypical for older mentally retarded youngsters
to consider themselves capable of eventually becoming lawyers, physicians, or teachers. When such unrealistic goals are held over an
extended period, even under optimum circumstances, the influence of a
program designed specifically to help them reconsider altering these
goals will have little impact and will most often meet with increased
perseverance and rigidity on their part. This is a common problem
among older children.

To illustrate this point, the author worked with a teenage boy whose
primary occupational desire was to become a concert drummer. This
lad, who was also legally blind, had held this ambition for a number of
years. The teacher of the class considered attempting to alter this
unrealistic goal held by the child as a worthwhile objective. A program
was designed to assist him in restructuring his occupational aims so
that they were more consistent with his capabilities. The reading period
was devoted to reading about occupations which were more consistent
with his potential; the occupational education period included activities
that would help him learn about possible positions for which he could
qualify, and the individual and group counseling sessions held with this
boy were designed to stimulate him to reconsider his occupational
objectives.

At the end of the school year, a summarization session was held. The
boy volunteered to have himself used as an illustration in the final class
on occupational education. The class decided to make three lists. The
first list contained all those skills that were needed by a concert
drummer; the second list contained all the problems which would make
it impossible for this boy to ever realize his occupational goal; and the
third list was made up of all the skills that he had which would assist him
in becoming a concert performer. As the lists developed, members of
the class spontaneously decided that their close friend should reconsider his occupational objectives. As this opinion was expressed
throughout the class, the boy listened intently to the suggestions of his
classmates. At the appropriate time, the teacher decided that the boy
seemed to be grasping the message and asked him to summarize his
feelings on the matter. With great delight, he acknowledged the
thoughtfulness of his fellow classmates in considering his problem and,
in the face of overwhelming data to the contrary, indicated that their
deliberations had provided the stimulation that he needed. He ended by
saying that he now was determined and would devote all his efforts to
become the best concert drummer in the country.

This situation, although humorous and somewhat unfortunate, is not atypical among retarded children. Their long-term goals are often extremely unreasonable, and they usually have no accurate perception of the short-term, intermediate goals on which an individual needs to focus in order to satisfy the more long-range objectives.

Barriers The mentally retarded face a variety of barriers that obstruct the achievement of their goals. Perhaps the most obvious barrier is their lack of experience with and skill in dealing with problems in their environment, along with their associated physical and health problems. These might be considered primary difficulties. There are, however, a constellation of secondary constraints that also impede the satisfaction of goals. These barriers, mostly social and psychological, result from the conflict between the child's aptitude to perform in a given area and society's expectations of his performance—that is, that it must be within reasonably normal limits. The mildly mentally retarded typically do not stand out in the community, and because they meet minimum demands of cultural acceptability, most people expect them to achieve and behave in a manner characteristic of the general population. Being in such an environment, where society expects him to achieve as others do, and is not aware of any intellectual or physical weakness, could cause any number of psychosocial difficulties. Factors such as self-derogation, reduced tolerance for frustration, antisocial behavior, regression to earlier and more satisfying stages of development, and overdependence on family members are often observed in people who are associated with such a situation. Each of these factors could be considered a barrier to the successful completion of goals.

To speak in a most unscientific and hypothetical way, the capacity of a child's "tension reservoir" is related to his emotional development and mental health. The amount of tension each of us is able to tolerate varies every day and is directly related to specific individual and constantly changing circumstances. At times one can be extremely tolerant of frustrating situations; at other times it is more difficult to deal effectively with the same tension-provoking situations. Retarded individuals seem to have a lower tolerance for frustration and tension. The reason for this can be related directly to their frequent history of failure in such a wide range of areas. When people are unsuccessful in a task, they have a tendency to avoid future experiences with it, and, in fact, many people feel so strongly about some specific lack of success that they are openly aggressive or hostile and wish never again to engage in that type of activity. Because the constraints are often so substantial with the mentally retarded, it is reasonable that they are often less tolerant of frustration and tension.

Behavior Resulting from Frustration When one is thwarted in achieving a goal, he can either make another frontal attack, attempting to penetrate or circumvent the barriers, or, after repeated failures, he can search for a reasonable substitute for the goals that he finds unattainable by direct means. Mentally retarded children should be encouraged to attempt goals that are reasonable. Tension can be released, however, by engaging in some type of adaptive behavior. Withdrawal and aggression of some variety constitute the two major types of adjustive mechanisms. It is often necessary for each of us to use mechanisms of this sort in certain situations. There is nothing inappropriate or unhealthy about them so long as they are not used more frequently than is goal-satisfying behavior.

Implications for Education   Some of the implications for teaching that emerge from this discussion of conditions presumed to be related to emotional development and mental health are the following:

1 The teacher should assess the types and extent of each child's specific desires, interests, or personal targets and identify those that seem to be in most urgent need of attention.

2 Some attempt should be given to surveying the long-term goals of each child, which in many instances will be unrealistic. The teacher should minimize long-term goal striving and emphasize a series of well-defined, short-term goals that are reasonable, and that, predictably, will allow each child to be successful. As the youngsters achieve each successive short-term goal, they will gain some ability to see the direction in which these goals lead.

3 Attempts should be made to minimize the influence of the barriers. Barriers created by physical problems and those related to lack of previous experiences can be only partly reduced, and any impact that the teacher can make in these areas will be minimal. Some attempt, however, can be made in the school program to reduce secondary barriers—that is, those resulting from differences between the aptitude for performance and the expectations of society. The child can be shielded from discouraging and disappointing situations until a tolerance and capability for handling dissonant situations has been developed. The child will begin to see himself as a more capable person, able to handle difficult situations in a more appropriate, systematic, and healthy way.

4 The teacher needs to be aware of the extent to which each child can tolerate frustration in various areas of performance. This frequent informal assessment of the level of frustration should be combined with some general prediction of how far to allow each child to go in potentially frustrating situations before the teacher decides to intervene. For example, if a child seems to be having some difficulty in using scissors to cut paper, some judgment has to be made by the teacher as to how far the child should be allowed to go. A major key to success here is how well the activity has been task analyzed, how appropriately reinforcement is being applied with each successive approximation to the goal, and what kind of reinforcement schedule is being used.

To reduce tension, an individual must either achieve his goal or engage in some type of socially accepted and situationally appropriate alternate behavior. The retarded must learn that aggressive behavior and hostility are inappropriate responses. Similarly, certain types of withdrawal behaviors, if used in the extreme and continuously, are not mentally healthy ways of reducing frustration and tension. The teacher, therefore, will need to provide the children with appropriate and helpful experiences and to reward socially appropriate behaviors that can be used in various situations. For example, when someone teases a child, he needs to be able to determine if striking out, cursing, worrying about what has been said, verbally attacking, or leaving the scene are appropriate reactions to the situation. For mental health reasons, and to support emotional development, the teacher cannot consider the major goal one of satisfying the child's immediate needs. Instead, the job is one of manipulating the social and physical environment in such a way that the child builds up a repertoire of behaviors that he can use with assurance to solve problems within a social and/or personal context.

SOCIAL AWARENESS AND BEHAVIOR
Many of the mildly mentally retarded children in the public schools come from lower socioeconomic levels in which standards of acceptance in social interaction are often at variance with the general mores and folkways of society. Lying, cheating, stealing, and vulgar language are often considered acceptable in impoverished environments. Children in these surroundings are frequent observers of various immoral and illegal acts by adults with whom they have direct association. It is not surprising, therefore, that the middle-class teacher of the retarded is often shocked at the pronouncements and demonstrations of behavior of these young, deprived, and retarded children. It is difficult for many teachers to understand and accept this type of behavior.

Without pursuing the philosophical arguments concerning whether the special class teacher has a responsibility for attempting to change the cultural patterns of the mildly retarded children from a deprived environment, most people would agree that some attempt should be made to help the children become aware of two interrelated facets of our social order: (1) the mores and folkways of our society, including the legal, moral, and social expectations of the citizenry, and (2) the reasons for and the need to become sensitive to the feelings of others. Each of these factors is an important interacting component of social awareness and should be given attention in all subject areas and at each level in the instructional program for the retarded.

Specific focus in the socialization program for the mentally retarded is suggested in the following areas. Procedures and practices for implementing their understanding by the children will be detailed later.

1 The students must develop an understanding of reasons for laws and rules in our society and the implications of breaking or violating these established standards.

2 The retarded child must develop an awareness of the need to be alert to the attitudes, feelings, and opinions of others and learn to respect these opinions as sources of possible additional information which could be of direct value to him personally. This type of awareness can be developed most easily by engaging the child in various activities within a very restricted social circumstance. For example, it would be inappropriate to expect the child to gain an understanding of these concepts by engaging in experiences with a large group of people before having had the opportunity to interact with smaller groups. We must first be interested in each child's understanding and respecting the feelings and attitudes of the one sitting next to him in the class, tentatively understanding the mores associated with effective social interaction with this person, and then finally generalizing this principle to others around him within a large social context. It is advisable, therefore, that the children be given initial experiences in a rather restricted milieu, gradually enlarging their sphere of contacts to include more complex associations among people.

3 Concepts associated with personal care and good grooming need to be stressed throughout the school program. The children should learn to care for their personal needs so that they are viewed as attractive and better accepted as compatriots and models of appropriate behavior by their fellow students.

4 The value in the children's showing mannerly behavior, honesty, and truthfulness needs to be stressed. One approach to encouraging this type of behavior is to place particular emphasis on the personal advantages of such behavior. Children at all ages are sensitive to what their peers think of them. By judiciously arranging the classroom environment, the teacher can place certain children in direct contact with other children who will often be able to serve as models and, in fact, idols for the one who is socially unsophisticated. Through propinquity and with appropriate rewards provided by the teacher to those modeling appropriate behavior, the more social child will continue appropriate behavior; the asocial child will begin to see the value in modeling his behavior after the child being reinforced.

Perhaps in no other area is the teacher more of a manipulator of the environment than in the area of social development. It is important that the teacher learn to accept the often repulsive social and personal characteristics of some mentally retarded children and begin to provide a sequential and systematic program aimed at shaping more desirable behavior. As a side benefit, by example there is always the possibility that the child will communicate some of these social skills to other members of his family. The first responsibility of the schools is to the children. Nevertheless, it is entirely proper to use each child's developing skills as a wedge into the family in an effort to begin the arduous process of altering family patterns of behavior.

methods for teaching social, personal, and emotional skills

Behavior is the result of a person interacting with his environment; this proposition has been stressed earlier. Continued behavior of the same type occurs because of the individual's expectation that the environment will in some way reinforce his behavior with an agent that is of value to him. In studying this complex process, psychologists have attempted to alter, manipulate, or control the environment in various ways in an effort to modify an individual's behavior. The term *behavior modification* has been used to describe this approach—the major principles of which have been discussed in Chapter 4. Since the procedures have such promising implications for altering the social, personal, and emotional behaviors of mentally retarded children, the prominent concepts in the behavioral approach will be re-emphasized in the next several paragraphs.

You remember the major premise we discussed before—behavior is changed by its consequences. What happens after a child, or anyone else, behaves in a certain way will affect the direction, intensity, and frequency of that behavior in the future. If you provide a child with something he wants after he has behaved in his certain way, that behavior will increase. If you withhold that same reinforcer, the behavior will eventually disappear. If you punish, the behavior will decrease immediately but will probably occur again soon.

The immediacy with which the reinforcer is applied and the degree to which you are consistent with the consequence are both important considerations. After a behavior has become established, it can be maintained by reinforcing every once in a while or on a gambling schedule—where the child never knows when he will receive the reinforcer and so he tries harder and longer in anticipation.

You must also be careful not to expect so much from a child at first that you end up by never reinforcing him because your goal for him has not been reached. Remember, reinforce successive approximations to the goal but never reward the child when he returns to a level of performance he had already attained.

Caution should be exercised so that undesirable behavior is not rewarded. This occurs frequently, particularly in cases involving discipline. Many children, whether intellectually retarded or not, seek attention by misbehaving. All too frequently teachers, as well as parents, reward misbehavior by calling attention to it. Children seeking attention are reinforced in this behavior, and, in fact, the behavior is strengthened by acknowledging its presence. In most instances, the preferred technique for handling a social or behavior problem is to ignore the person misbehaving. Certain reprehensible circumstances require that the teacher remove the child from the environment or administer some type of punishment. Punishment should always be administered in ways which have some significance to the child. Every attempt should be made to control the possibility that the child is being rewarded for misbehavior.

Procedures for helping retarded children understand and develop satisfactory social, personal, and emotional behavior are often characterized by the teacher telling or lecturing the children about how and why they are to behave in a certain fashion. Even with the best intentions in mind, this method of instruction will have only minimal impact for several reasons. First, lecturing assumes that the children have developed the language and conceptual skills needed to understand abstract notions. Moreover, lecturing is a poor strategy since opportunities are not provided for the children to look at themselves and evaluate their own performance. The importance of each child to be given opportunities to engage in activities which will demonstrate reasons for and against behaving in a certain fashion in various circumstances cannot be overstated.

Acceptable patterns of behavior will be most rapidly and effectively acquired by using the dual influence of models and differential reinforcement. Children will value and reflect the behavior of models whom they consider to be of high prestige. Moreover, they will react more favorably to the reinforcement provided by these "high-prestige" individuals than to those dispensed by a "low-prestige" person. In contrast to the less effective teaching strategy of lecturing, the teacher will find that the behavior of children can be dramatically changed and subsequently controlled when models are used in ways which allow for imitation by the youngsters. For example, if a high-prestige person begins to clean up the classroom, within a short time those students who value the model will begin to conform, and they, in turn, will serve as models for their other classmates. When this behavior is differentially rewarded by the model, the acquisition of the new behavior patterns is facilitated. There is, then, a clear teaching advantage in making use of imitation in concert with reward to modify general or specific behavioral patterns.

Developing procedures for presenting concepts related to social, personal, and emotional development is difficult because of the abstract nature of the material to be covered and the lack of effectiveness that the retarded have for operating at a level other than the concrete. It is also of significance that effective social, personal, and emotional development requires that the individual be flexible and have the ability to understand and apply principles in various situations. The important point here is that the teacher should not be satisfied with developing an automaton who can mechanically apply the correct solution to the appropriate problem. These situations demand an individual who understands principles, morals, and the variety of appropriate behaviors that are suitable for a particular situation at one specific moment. For example, if a child learns to withdraw whenever he encounters conflict with another individual, he will have difficulty satisfying certain requirements of employment when faced with a questioning foreman. If a retarded child is "programmed" to respond with, "Good morning," in a robotlike fashion any time greeted before noon, he may find himself in an embarrassing position when another type of response might be more appropriate. Such errors quickly alert others to weaknesses and are emphasized out of proportion and used by insensitive associates for their own amusement and advantage.

The types of activities in which the youngsters should be engaged should reflect the teacher's evaluation of individually appropriate social, personal, and/or emotional targets. There is room for individual goals as well as group goals within the instructional program. You can discern where the focus should be placed by simply observing how each child responds to various social situations. For example, one child may be particularly weak in interacting with authority figures and in accepting their directions; whereas the same child may interact very effectively with people his own age. Another child when facing a particularly difficult personal situation might respond by striking out at an individual; whereas the child sitting next to him may withdraw when facing the same situation. These patterns of variation between and within children under different circumstances will eventually become obvious to the teacher. The learning situation must be structured to allow the children to gain value in considering a range of possible responses, each of which could be dramatized in some fashion.

It is clear that the principles of educational management that were suggested earlier as being appropriate for directing student performance in academic areas are equally pertinent to social, personal, and emotional behavior development. Their application to social-personal situations is comprehensively illustrated in Neisworth and Smith (1973), O'Leary and O'Leary (1972), Dollar (1972), Thompson and Grabowski (1972), and Gardner (1971). In addition to these general procedures, sociodrama and classroom counseling have been used by teachers with success in dealing with specific social and personal problems that the mentally retarded often experience.

SOCIODRAMA
To produce appropriate social behavior, it would be desirable to set up actual social situations and systematically reward desired responses while ignoring undesired ones. Obviously, the teacher does not have the resources available to provide actual social situations in all the areas in which the retarded require training. It is possible, however, to duplicate these situations to some degree through the use of classroom sociodrama. This technique allows the teacher to call on the full array of reinforcement, shaping, and modeling procedures that characterize behavior-modification techniques. Because of the relative realism of this approach, sociodrama offers a particularly promising approach in classes for the mentally retarded; hence, the technique will be discussed in some detail.

Follow-up studies done with the retarded suggest that their most pronounced weaknesses lie in areas of social adjustment and not in how well they handle the mechanics of employment. They seem to have difficulty in all employee-employee, employee-employer relationships, but especially in relationships with authority figures. No systematic attempts have been made to pinpoint those areas of the school curriculum that are not reflecting the need for greater devotion to problems of social adjustment, although Goldstein's (1972) Social

Learning Curriculum provides a comprehensive taxonomy of social areas that warrant special attention by educators who are concerned over scope and sequence in this important area. It can legitimately be hypothesized that an obvious weakness of most secondary programs is that the retarded are not given opportunities to practice responding to situations similar to those in which they will eventually find themselves. Apparently, characteristics of real community situations are either totally foreign to the young retarded adult or else the youngsters are unable to transfer classroom experience and instruction into actual practice. Because of this apparent weakness in the typical school experience of the retarded, sociodrama has been suggested as a technique to facilitate the acquisition of social concepts and skills (Kirk and Johnson, 1951; Blackhurst, 1966).

Sociodrama, also called role playing, is the dramatization of some social situation with individuals assuming the roles of the characters involved in the situation. The process involves four steps: (1) identifying a specific problem; (2) delineating the roles to be played, describing the specific situation to be enacted, and selecting the participants to play various roles; (3) dramatizing the problem and alternative solutions; and (4) having a comprehensive discussion with a reenactment of other possible solutions if necessary.

Identifying the Problem In the beginning, when the students are becoming familiar with this technique, the dramatizations must involve relatively simple, specific problems. Since the procedure is new to the students, they should select a precise topic from their own experience that can be easily dramatized. Using this process of selection at the beginning encourages more spontaneity and causes less personal embarrassment. As the students gain experience with the technique, problems for dramatization evolve in a variety of ways. Perhaps a child had an experience at home that was particularly perplexing. Or other problems could arise out of group discussions, or from the teacher making certain suggestions, or out of the reading done by the students in other subject areas. In every case the teacher should have the specific goals for each session clearly formulated. The overall aim is to assist the youngsters in developing greater social awareness and better mental health as a result of being successful in the actual experience of solving problems in a familiar environment.

Delineating the Roles After a problem has been defined, the group should identify characteristics of the personalities to be involved in the plot. Clarification and simplification on this point should be encouraged by the teacher asking questions such as, ''What is this person like?'' or ''How could we describe this individual?'' Gradually the problem will come more clearly into focus for the students. The characters will be realistic and the nature of their roles will be clearly defined and understood. Students should then be selected or should volunteer to participate in the dramatization of the roles previously defined.

After selection, the students involved in the various roles should get together with the teacher to discuss their parts and plan the manner in which they intend to enact their role. At this point the teacher should impose any limits felt necessary. These limits are to help the students focus on the specific problem and not run too far afield. Encouraging the role players to maintain the intended direction can be aided by using only one scene or a single situation such as might occur in a living room, lunchroom, or during a coffee break at work. Choosing such a scene or situation will help to establish more circumscribed components for the dramatization during the early stages of role playing. At the same time, the teacher should discuss with the nonparticipants in the class how to observe and what they should look for in the dramatization. Before the role players begin, the players and observers will find it helpful to describe the setting in detail and elaborate on any specifics of the problem which they intend to emphasize.

The Dramatization   The sociodrama can begin most easily by one of the players asking a question or making a declarative statement to another player. Such a statement might express an opinion which has the potential for stimulating discussion more easily than if the statement is neutral. To get the dramatization moving initially, it may be necessary for the teacher to feed lines to the students or coach them when the enactment loses its value or tapers off. The behavior of the participants and their conversation should be allowed to flow freely from their own experiences, and the dialogue should not have been previously practiced nor memorized. Members presenting the characterizations should feel free to express their thoughts and feelings frankly during the enactments and in the discussions which follow. No pressure should be imposed on the members to respond in any certain manner. When such pressure is brought to bear, the value of sociodrama is reduced.

The major objective of this technique is to clarify issues concerning a certain problem and to help the students consider various types of behavior resulting from the dramatizations. Clearly, the role playing should not concentrate on "play acting"; instead, focus should be on the kinds of behavior exhibited by members playing the roles. The players should gradually begin to realize that problems can be appropriately handled in a variety of possible ways.

Postdramatization Discussion   After a situation has been dramatized, members of the group should discuss the enactment and consider all the ramifications of the solution presented. These should include a discussion of the interpersonal behavior accompanying the solution, the potential effectiveness of the solution, and the reactions of the observers. Criticisms by the class or the teacher should be directed at the role which was played and not at the acting qualities of the role players. The teacher should act as a friendly supervisor and one who reflects attitudes as the students discuss the earlier dramatization among themselves. All the players and observers should be given a chance to make suggestions of alternative ways to solve the problem. This discussion should be followed by another enactment which either redramatizes the former solution or develops an alternative explanation to the situation. Members of the group should switch roles in order to obtain a better understanding of the types of situations others were in, situations which might have been misunderstood by fellow participants and observers. The spontaneity encouraged by this procedure will help the students gain experience in meeting new problem situations and encourage behavioral flexibility.

Following the final enactment of a problem for the day, the teacher should summarize what has been learned from the dramatization and generalize the solution to other similar situations. The relevance of the various solutions for solving any problems the students might en- counter should be indicated. Any similarity among solutions should be focused upon in order to help the students develop an appropriate generalized style of behavior.

As the students develop skill in using this technique, more complex and sensitive topics can be considered. With the advantage of a comfortable and nonthreatening environment which has the support of the teacher, the retarded children will begin to show less hesitation in expressing their attitudes and feelings with freedom.

Each student should have the opportunity to assume a variety of roles. Here again, however, the teacher will need to consider each child's strengths and weaknesses and place those youngsters who need to develop skills in certain areas into roles which will allow them to experience solving problems in these less well-developed areas. Soci- odrama, therefore, is as much a diagnostic procedure as it is a technique for developing social and emotional maturity among the participants. Through careful observation, the teacher can reliably identify any unique response patterns of the children to certain situa- tions. This information will provide for subsequent manipulations of the child's environment in an informed fashion and according to each child's needs.

Dramatization of problems should eventually include individuals other than the students and classmates. As the youngsters engage in sociodrama, they tend to become familiar with the techniques used by their classmates. This sensitivity allows them to predict the responses of other players. Spontaneity is lost because of this awareness, and the value of the technique is reduced. To make situations realistic, other students and adults should be invited to participate in the dramatizations. The object is for the youngsters to gain experience by interacting with all segments of society. The teacher, therefore, must make a conscious effort to sequence the order of activities to be encountered by the students and select other people to cooperate in these activities from time to time. It is important, of course, that outside participants be fully aware of the goals and procedures of the dramatization. Eventually, the more experienced mentally retarded child might find himself alone in a dramatization with several intellectually normal or intellectually superior children or adults. The degree to which the child is able to handle everyday situations in a reasonably normal fashion is the appropriate criterion for evaluating the technique.

Since the mentally retarded will be expected to interact satisfactorily in the community setting, they must have breadth of social experiences with others. Cloistering them in a special class during their *entire* schooling experience will work to their disadvantage by not providing them with chances to experience the problems and appropriate behavior which emanates from social and emotional integration into society. Children at all levels should be allowed to move beyond the walls of the special class, into a more socially realistic setting, at least for a portion of the day. This can be effected by locating the children in small groups, or as a total class, with teachers whose subject areas do not particularly engender intense competition among students. Teachers of art, music, industrial arts, home economics, and physical education are in a position to substantially assist the mentally retarded in personal and social development.

The special education teacher has a responsibility to encourage other teachers to include retarded children in their programs as much as realistically possible. Sociodrama is a particularly useful approach for use in connection with activities in almost any subject area. A valuable interrelationship between other school areas and the special education program is possible when other teachers include mentally retarded children in their program. This united effort combines the best of both situations—the practical environment of the regular class and the unique tools and techniques characteristic of the special class. This is particularly true in the case of home economics and industrial arts classes. The unique physical facilities characteristic of these classes provide a realistic setting for the dramatization of problems that eventually will have direct relevance to the retarded child's social or occupational life. In these classrooms, numerous problems can be staged which are particularly unique to the home situation or the industrial situation. The teacher of these subject areas, in consultation with the special education teacher, has the best situation available to provide a program which will aid the retarded in synthesizing the many facts and concepts to which he has been exposed throughout his school years. This experience, which can be made very practical, will provide another means for evaluating each child's readiness to move toward occupational training or into a specific job situation.

The following list describes certain specific problems about which the mentally retarded often exhibit some confusion. Each of these problems offers a situation which is specific enough to be dramatized, yet each is broad enough to allow for generalization to other situations. The advantage of dramatizing these problems within the industrial arts or home economics laboratory is one of providing as realistic a setting as possible.

1 "My friend Charley says that I don't have to report to the foreman that I broke the bandsaw."
2 "If that fellow keeps talking behind my back, I'm going to meet him in the back alley."
3 "Bill said that we could take an extra fifteen minutes for lunch without anyone knowing that we were late."
4 "When I get tired on the night shift, I go into the bathroom, lock the door, and try to get a few winks of sleep."
5 "The best way to find out what you are supposed to do is ask old Bert; he's a good guy and doesn't mind being bothered."
6 "What shall I say tomorrow when I'm interviewed for the welding job?"
7 "He's making me do the dirty work because I'm an apprentice."
8 "Herb says that if I don't know how to run a machine not to worry about it because he'll teach me before the foreman finds out."
9 "The reason I'm slower doing my job on the production line is because I have more work to do than the others."
10 "If I get laid off, I'll get back at the boss either by breaking a machine or breaking the windows in his car."
11 "I wonder what would happen if I put a down payment on a new car this month instead of paying the rent?"
12 "If Charley is going to be cross with me when he leaves for work in the morning, I'll get back at him by not giving him a good supper."

13 "I think that I will ignore the baby today and maybe he won't cry so much."
14 "Should I tell the grocer that he made an error in counting my bill? It was in my favor."
15 "I don't know whether to go and get a job because the baby is only six months old."
16 "How can I tell my next door neighbor that I simply don't have time to come over each morning for coffee? I don't want to offend her."

Each of these problems is commonly experienced by mentally retarded adolescents and adults. By using sociodrama in the industrial arts or home economics classroom, the retarded will more realistically experience the variety of problems often characteristic of their situation. Using role playing in these settings provides an opportunity for the youngsters to use skills acquired in other classrooms for solving actual problems. Transfer of understandings from one subject-matter area to another, therefore, does not need to be assumed. Moreover, incidental learning does not need to be presumed. This results in the retarded developing a greater understanding of concepts of acceptable behavior that may have been unclear to them.

COUNSELING IN THE CLASSROOM
Offering counseling and guidance to children is typically considered to be totally within the domain of the professional counselor. Although people are generally aware of problems faced by the mentally retarded, most counselors find that they do not have enough time to work with these youngsters in as comprehensive a way as is needed. The guidance counselor in most school systems is often completely inundated with other responsibilities that involve all the populations of children in the school. The counseling and guidance needs of the mentally retarded typically are left up to the special education teacher, unless certain hard-core cases exceed the teacher's professional training and require highly professional advice.

In one sense it is reasonable that the special education teacher work with the retarded in responding to their counseling and guidance needs; the special education teachers in all likelihood know the children best. Moreover, most training programs designed to prepare teachers to work with these youngsters include units on counseling the retarded in their programs. Teachers must realize, however, that it is outside their professional responsibility and authority to provide anything other than informal counseling to the retarded. The teacher's knowledge of each child's weaknesses, needs, ambitions, attitudes, and general environment situation in no way suggests that the proper qualifications are held to offer diagnostic or other psychological assistance. In the following discussion, therefore, counseling and guidance should be viewed more as an informal discussion period than as a formal counseling session in the traditional sense. Those retarded children who are seriously disturbed should be referred for proper psychological or psychiatric assistance.

Informal counseling sessions with the mentally retarded will work best when they occur spontaneously and are not contrived. The sessions can be conducted with an entire class, small groups within the class, or with an individual. The topic for discussion should emanate from the students and may frequently occur during the course of instruction in some other area. If the teacher views the problem or topic as important, placing the scheduled lesson aside and moving logically into a more comprehensive discussion of the topic or issue which has been raised should certainly be done. To schedule a certain portion of each day or week for sessions of this type will usually be unproductive because of a lack of spontaneity and the consideration of problems out of context.

The types of issues discussed in these sessions are similar to those considered in the sociodrama section of this chapter. When all the basic facts of a situation are understood by the group, they should be given ample opportunity to discuss the facts, relate them to existing concepts, and consider possible appropriate alternative responses to the situation. Reactions to the expressions of others should be encouraged. Whenever possible, information and concepts used to solve previously discussed social or personal experiences should be directly related to the current problem or issue.

The teacher should realize that these sessions will be most beneficial when their structure and direction is flexible. This is particularly true when some authority figure is present. Since the major objective of the counseling sessions is to have the children gain a better perception of themselves, help resolve their own difficulties, and strengthen their weaknesses, the teacher does more harm than good by lecturing or giving an opinion at inappropriate times. The suggested role for the teacher in these sessions should be one of providing reflection about or clarification on points expressed by the students as well as subtly manipulating the discussion through the judicious use of leading questions. This manipulation of the conversation will help the youngsters to see relationships between points discussed and the problem. In addition, this strategy will help the children gain experience in generating alternative ways for reacting to problems. Only when asked directly should the teacher express an opinion; even in these situations alternative suggestions should be provided. The teacher, thus, should never be placed in a position of making a decision for a child concerning a specific social, personal, or emotional problem. Instead, the children should be instructed to generate a variety of solutions to problems and evaluate each alternative in terms of its relevance and personal appropriateness.

As was true with sociodrama, counseling sessions in the classroom require that certain ground rules be understood and accepted by all the participants. Regulations such as not interrupting someone else who is talking, not being critical of an opinion or point of view, being accepting of the behavior of others, and recognizing that there is often more than one correct answer to a problem illustrate basic ground rules necessary for a successful group discussion.

Because of the informal and spontaneous nature of these sessions, the teacher should be prepared and willing to abandon her prepared lesson when an issue seems important enough. Although this approach may seem most valuable with older mentally retarded children, a modified version of this technique will work effectively with primary- and intermediate-age retarded children. The types of problems discussed by the younger children should be narrowly described and involve concrete problems and illustrations. Further, the number of possible interactions within a group should be kept as small as possible for the young children. The author has observed upper-level primary and intermediate children participating in group discussions of this sort and considering with eagerness topics such as, "How should we act during our free time?," "What should I do when someone says that I am dumb or look funny?," and "Should I learn how to smoke like my friends?" Older retarded children at the upper intermediate and secondary levels will profit by considering topics such as, "What should I do when a boy makes advances toward me?," "How can I get my mother to allow me to wear cosmetics?," "Why can't I quit school and go get a job even though I don't know how to read?"

Counseling in the classroom is an effective method for helping the mentally retarded to develop social, personal, and emotional awareness and stability. The teacher must capitalize on the specific and immediate concerns of the children and allow them to initiate and engage in this type of discussion when beneficial. In no case should the teacher be considered the leader and dictate the direction of the discussion. It is true, however, that some manipulation, through the use of appropriate questions, must be done so that focus is maintained and the results of the discussion are profitable to the children. The solutions decided upon by the children can be reinforced by introducing them as topics for sociodrama at a later date. In this way the children can check on the validity of their deliberations. If viewed by them as constituting a suitable response to the issue or problem, the retarded will gain increased confidence and be eager to continue participating in the information discussion sessions. There is not only habilitative potential in these discussions, but the nature of the issues and problems raised by the children has diagnostic value because it allows the teacher to appraise any specific momentary concerns or interests of the children.

OTHER TEACHING CONSIDERATIONS

The following points have a direct bearing on the effectiveness of instruction in social, personal, and emotional development of the mentally retarded:

1 Liberal use should be made of films and other audio-visual aids. These aids allow a child to experience a variety of typical and atypical personal, social, and emotional situations on repeated occasions and, by stabilizing stimuli, allow each child to analyze and reanalyze faulty behavior. Moreover, use of audio equipment gives each child a chance to monitor his own responses and reflect on their appropriateness.

2 Throughout instruction in these areas, emphasis should be placed on appropriate behavior, with inappropriate behavior deemphasized or even ignored. The mentally retarded tend to remember best what *not* to do instead of what *to* do. Whenever appropriate, the teacher should use models, idols, and authority figures to emphasize important points or correct behavior.

3 Older mentally retarded children should see a clear association between vocational requirements and appropriate social and emotional behavior. Correct behavior for both should be reinforced when they are correctly applied to various situations.

4 Each child's experiences and activities should be based on what the teacher predicts will constitute the child's future social and occupational situation. The program, therefore, may differ substantially for each child.

5 Professional advice from school psychologists, guidance counselors, clergymen, local health officers, and other experts should be sought by the teacher whenever their advice is appropriate.

6 Opportunities to interact in practical situations with children and adults who are intellectually normal should be provided whenever possible or desirable.

7 For the more mature youngsters, some variety of self-government within the classroom will help to demonstrate the dimensions and advantages of government. This practical involvement will encourage students to participate in social and community affairs.

selected readings

American Association for Health, Physical Education, and Recreation: *AAHPER Youth Fitness Test Manual*, AAHPER, Washington, D.C., 1958.

Blackhurst, A. E.: "Sociodrama for the Adolescent Retarded," *Training School Bulletin*, 63(3):136–142, 1966.

Campbell, J. W.: *Evaluation of a Contingency Managed Physical Fitness Program for Mentally Retarded Boys*, unpublished doctoral dissertation, Pennsylvania State University, University Park, Pa., 1971.

Dollar, B.: *Humanizing Classroom Discipline: A Behavioral Approach*, Harper & Row, Publishers, Incorporated, New York, 1972.

Gardner, W. I.: *Behavior Modification in Mental Retardation: The Education and Rehabilitation of the Mentally Retarded Adolescent and Adult*, Aldine-Atherton, New York, 1971.

Goldstein, H.: "Construction of a Social Learning Curriculum," in E. L. Meyen, G. A. Vergason, and R. J. Whelan (eds.), *Strategies for Teaching Exceptional Children: Essays from Focus on Exceptional Children*, Love Publishing Company, Denver, 1972, pp. 94–114.

————: "Social and Occupational Adjustment," in H. A. Stevens and R. Heber (eds.), *Mental Retardation: A Review of Research*, The University of Chicago Press, Chicago, 1964, pp. 214–258.

Gregg, A. E.: "Criminal Behavior of Mentally Retarded Adults," *American Journal of Mental Deficiency*, 52:370–374, 1948.

Harrington, M.: "The Problem of the Defective Delinquent," *Mental Hygiene*, 19:429–438, 1935.

Heber, Rick: "Personality," in H. A. Stevens and R. Heber (eds.), *Mental Retardation: A Review of Research*, The University of Chicago Press, Chicago, 1964, pp. 143–174.

Kirk, S. A. and G. O. Johnson: *Educating the Retarded Child*, Houghton Mifflin Company, Boston, 1951, pp. 336–341.

Kvaraceus, W. C.: "Delinquency: A By-Product of the Schools?" *School and Society*, 59:350–351, 1944.

Neisworth, J. T. and R. M. Smith: *Modifying Retarded Behavior*, Houghton Mifflin Company, Boston, 1973.

O'Leary, K. D. and S. G. O'Leary: *Classroom Management: The Successful Use of Behavior Modification*, Pergamon Press, New York, 1972.

Poucher, G. E.: "The Role of a Juvenile Court Psychiatric Clinic in the Management of the Defective Delinquent," *American Journal of Mental Deficiency*, 56:275–282, 1952.

Rarick, G. L., J. H. Widdop, and G. D. Broadhead: "The Physical Fitness and Motor Performance of Educable Mentally Retarded Children," *Exceptional Children*, 36:509–519, 1970.

Thompson, T. and J. Grabowski: *Behavior Modification of the Mentally Retarded*, Oxford University Press, New York, 1972.

Wallin, J. E. W.: *The Education of Handicapped Children*, Houghton Mifflin Company, Boston, 1924.

11

PREPARATION FOR GAINFUL EMPLOYMENT

The complete assimilation of the mentally retarded into the community as active participants must be given serious consideration by the public schools. In fact, in an increasing number of states the public schools have been ordered to provide training that will lead to integration into the community for all mentally retarded youngsters, irrespective of their level of subnormality. The increased tendency for institutions to accept only the most severely retarded and to disallow placement for the less retarded, unless extenuating circumstances are present, dramatizes the urgency for such systematic training. It is not enough that the mentally retarded simply fade into the ranks of the unskilled and semiskilled workers; it is important that they become socially and occupationally prepared to function as contributors within the community setting and that the community become prepared to accept them in a spirit of warm colleagueship. Social and personal considerations were focused upon in the preceding chapter; the material discussed in this section will be devoted to those components of independent living related to occupational development.

The relative instability of the labor market due to increased production efficiency and the many demands imposed upon workers is substantial enough to restrict the occupational flexibility of even the intellectually normal. Now that specific training is required for even the most elementary task, employers are hesitant to employ those whose work careers are checkered or who show a restricted potential for maximum efficiency. The escalation in production and automation of most industries has reduced the wide spectrum of unskilled and semiskilled positions heretofore available to those less well endowed intellectually. The parallel increases in service occupations have been filled by individuals brighter than the mildly mentally retarded. Such persons demonstrate a greater ability to understand and deal with the semitechnical requirements of the service professions. These employment trends have resulted in fewer positions being available to the mentally retarded and a higher incidence of competitive failure and job skipping among these individuals.

pragmatic considerations for occupational education

The initial thrust for preparing mentally retarded youngsters for gainful employment should not occur suddenly, just as the youngster reaches the high school work-study program. Instead, throughout the child's class experiences the subtle flavor of occupational skill development required for mastery of appropriate work situations should permeate the program's activities. The child should be encouraged to first participate in parallel play with others and develop the fundamental skills required to learn the tool subjects. All of these experiences should be geared to the youngster's eventually becoming firmly situated in a rational occupational setting; throughout the program, the prime goal should be on successful job placement and community living. Whereas in the primary and intermediate grades the emphasis was on developing skills in subject matter areas, the work-study program during the late junior high and senior high years should make practical use of these academic skills in a more vocationally oriented program. Figure 11-1 illustrates the relative amount of emphasis that the tool subjects and the occupational skills should receive at various stages of the special education program.

Most of the classroom time during the primary years is devoted to helping the children gain skill in the basic tool subjects. Instructional emphasis should be on reading, arithmetic, perceptual-motor development, communication, and social and personal adjustment. At the same time, during these early school years, some attention should be given to those specific work skills which are vital for subsequent successful employment. To help the young to develop sensitivity and skill in this area, for example, the teacher should expect class members to assume a major responsibility for maintaining the classroom. Specific jobs should be assigned to the youngsters, and all the ramifications of conducting the jobs should be discussed during the instructional periods. Even during the early school years, the children must become aware of proper job behavior. It is at this time, therefore, that they

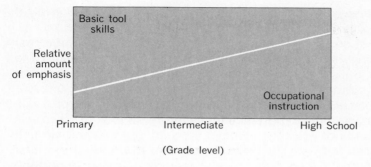

Figure 11-1
Relationship between emphasis in basic tool subjects and occupational instruction.

develop attitudes and concepts concerning proper care, completing a job, respect for others, satisfying responsibilities, and appropriate responses to authority figures. All this instruction should be aimed at the children acquiring foundation skills which can be further elaborated upon as the program unfolds.

During the intermediate grades, after certain elementary tool skills have been developed, relatively more attention should be devoted to occupational instruction than in the early primary grades. At this stage of instruction, the children should be exposed to a more realistic occupational environment characteristic of the industrial arts laboratory and the home economics classroom. In these classrooms the children have opportunities to make use of the tool skills which have constituted the core of the instruction in the special class program. Perhaps at no other time than during the intermediate grades is there so crucial a need for the teacher to blend components of the special education program into other aspects of the school program. At this very time, the children begin to "try their wings" and are at a propitious period for learning about the practical application of the tool skills. Children in intermediate classes often raise the question "Why do I have to learn this stuff?" Precisely at this point, the teacher must clearly demonstrate the practical application of and need for developing skills such as word attack, learning how to carry in addition and borrow in subtraction, communicating with adults, or being able to write legibly.

As the youngsters move through the school program and are placed in a work-study situation at the high school level, ostensibly they should be at a point at which the basic tool skills have developed to the eleven-

or twelve-year level. General achievement should be at the level of grades five or six.

The impact of an earlier assumption which is felt at this point is that the children have had a sequential instructional program designed to develop those tool subjects which are relevant to their predicted future occupational and social circumstances. If somewhere in the child's prior instruction too much time was devoted to the development of a skill which has relatively little importance to his future, or too little time was spent on concerns of greater urgency, the child and teacher will find themselves faced with a very difficult problem. It is during the high school program that the educable mentally retarded have an opportunity to use the previously developed skills in a practical way outside the cloistered environment of the special classroom. If they have not developed the skills required for reading, for example, the opportunity for becoming integrated into the community is substantially reduced. If, on the other hand, skills have been mastered at a level adequate enough for a satisfactory performance in the demands required of occupational and social situations, the child will have a more promising chance for complete integration into everyday society.

The high school program, therefore, is in sharp contrast to the emphasis given in the primary school special class. It must emphasize practical occupational considerations. Some time, however, should be devoted to remediating any specific weaknesses in the basic skill armamentarium of the children. At this point, directed attempts should be made to diagnose and remediate those weaknesses in the children's performance which might predictably impair effective interaction in the community.

Although personal and social development should have been emphasized throughout the school program, children in the secondary-level program need especially to learn appropriate techniques for interacting with others and procedures by which they can eliminate any obnoxious personal or social habits. Sociodrama has been suggested as a technique whereby the children can learn appropriate social and personal skills in practical situations. In the late junior high and early senior high school years, this tactic is most beneficial. As the older mentally retarded child gains experience, he should be placed in social situations which require interaction with members of the community other than classmates for extended periods of time. When experiences of this sort are provided early, an evaluation can be made of any major problems in the child's social and personal development. As specific difficulties are identified, proper remedial procedures can be provided.

In practical terms, it is much more difficult for the mentally retarded to develop satisfactory skills in the tool subjects and achieve healthy and adequate emotional and social adjustment than to perform the manipulative requirements of a position in a competent way. Not only do these academic areas demand greater conceptual skill for a satisfactory performance, but mentally retarded children simply are less responsive to instruction in areas of minimal development (such as in verbalization areas) and show greater responsiveness and eagerness to participate in those activities in which they have been more successful. As a group then, they are more responsive to nonverbal stimuli and usually enjoy becoming involved in manual and manipulative activities. From the perspective of clinical teaching, therefore, it makes sense for the teacher to use the child's relative strengths, typically in nonverbal areas, to strengthen the relative weaknesses in verbal and conceptualization skills. In the face of this consistent finding, it is puzzling, indeed, that teachers of the retarded tend to eschew the use of laboratory experiments (such as can be easily provided in industrial arts, home economics, and vocational education settings) as the major basis for teaching, applying, and extending the academic skills of retarded adolescents.

The high school work-study program should provide opportunities for them to develop skill in those specific manipulative tasks which may be required in various occupations. Whereas before they were engaged in more general nonverbal activity, during the high school years it is important that instruction in the manipulative activities become job specific. The child can no longer assume the casual, cavalier approach often characteristic of the early school years in finishing a task. The high school teacher must require that each individual learn to complete the requirements of a job in the shortest time and in the most effective way. If these types of skills and attitudes are not encouraged, the youngster will find himself in the tenuous position of producing less than a reasonable level of expectation. Although he may have all the personal and social expertise needed to effectively participate in a job, if the required level of manipulative skill is lacking, the young person will be a likely candidate for dismissal. Here you will find that the instructional procedures that characterize the behavior-modification approach can be used with great effectiveness (Gardner, 1971).

Society expects mentally retarded children to interact in an acceptable way within the community. This requirement will not be met if the youngsters are not given frequent opportunities to associate with others around them. To cloister the children in a special class for an entire school career may have certain academic advantages, but this placement strategy is bought at a price that will probably exceed any academic advantage. Children who are not integrated into other components of the school program will be viewed as defective by other members of society. A legitimate aim of special education programs should be to reduce any social stigma associated with atypical conditions. That is, the environment should be viewed as prosthetic whereby the possible personal and social consequences of the condition are reduced. The children, then, must learn how to deal with teasing and personal insults made by insensitive members of society. If these youngsters are not offered an opportunity to be exposed to problems of this type throughout their school career, but are secluded from the world in a special class or school, they will lack the necessary skills for facing these problems when they move more fully into the community. The newness of the situation will be so dramatic that the unthinking responses of aggressively striking out or withdrawing into safety will become predominant.

In high school, retarded children should be integrated into the industrial arts and home economics programs, physical education, art, music, and extracurricular activities. Competition between students in each of these areas does not have to be as intense as in the more academic areas. Further, by their very character, each of these areas mixes well with the main focus in the high school special class.

basis for a
successful work–study program

An effective work-study program requires the coordination among various in- and out-of-school agencies and the expertise of any number of specialists. Developing a close relationship with other agencies occurs at every level of the special education program; this combined effort, however, becomes more intense as the youngsters move closer toward complete integration into the community. The tools required for preparing them for gainful employment far exceed the available resources within most school communities. For example, many work experiences cannot be duplicated in the schools even under the most astutely contrived conditions. Moreover, the kind of information required by the adolescents prior to entering an occupation will often exceed the training and experience of the classroom teacher. A great deal of mutual understanding needs to be established between labor unions, employers, and school work-study coordinators concerning the relationship that should exist between these groups and the retarded employee. To illustrate a potential source of difficulty, it is reasonable to anticipate that a mentally retarded worker could qualify for promotion to a supervisory level simply because of having worked longer in the shop than other workers. Most labor unions would demand that this individual be promoted. A promotion of this sort probably would not be wise for all concerned. A clear understanding of the dimensions of the situation must be agreed upon by all groups involved with the program.

The coordinator of the work-study program for the mentally retarded should establish a close relationship with the local division of vocational rehabilitation. Vocational rehabilitation provides a variety of services and training opportunities for all types of handicapped people. Retarded adolescents, in most cases, qualify for these services. A variety of diagnostic, remedial, and occupational placement services are available from vocational rehabilitation. The extensiveness of the services typically exceeds the resources available from the public school's work-study program. The work-study coordinator should register each student with this agency as soon as he enrolls in the work-study program. It is the coordinator's responsibility to maintain liaison with vocational rehabilitation and to keep the assigned rehabilitation counselor informed of each student's progress in the work-study program, noting any change of status or special problems the student encounters during the course of the program.

In many respects, the success of a secondary program is based on the level of skills each student has mastered in the specific subject areas. The high school teacher must spend a large amount of time on the application of the basic skills; therefore, only minimal time will be available for extensive subject matter instruction. The retarded child in a high school program should have developed academic skills at a level which will allow the teacher to emphasize their social and vocational use.

In a great number of school systems, retarded high school students have not developed satisfactory understanding and skill in academic areas. This unfortunate situation is frequently the result of the youngsters having been socially promoted prior to being placed in a special education program. Social promotion, frequently the result of administrative expediency, only pacifies the child, his parents, and the schools temporarily. When the youngsters are later placed in a special education program they will not be able to demonstrate the required degree of proficiency in all the percursive skills required for dealing with academic material. The result is that the child will be able to operate less efficiently and effectively in an occupational setting. Under these circumstances, the only recourse the high school teacher has is to initiate a large-scale "crash program" designed to program the students with certain kinds of responses for specific situations. The foolishness of this procedure was stressed in previous discussion. Logically, then, school systems must provide such children with a systematically designed special program from the early school years through post high school and in doing so, provide them with opportunities to sequentially develop their capabilities in a total fashion.

The need for the special program to be sequential, wherein skills are built on earlier skills, has been stressed throughout this book. The degree to which instruction has been ordered will be felt most directly in the work-study program. Criteria which one might use to judge the appropriateness of the sequence employed in previous instruction include (1) the number of remedial cases in reading, arithmetic, and language at the high school level, (2) the attitudes of the children toward engaging in activities related to academic skills, (3) the incidence of specific types of learning difficulties such as borrowing or carrying in arithmetic, and (4) the degree to which the children have developed an understanding of the employment of various processes to solve problems, such as in learning to pronounce unfamiliar words.

Clinical teaching in the high school work-study program for the retarded implies that an analysis has been made of the social and occupational components of a job and that the position has been matched with an individual whose background and areas of competence are congruent with the demands of the job.

The requirements and components of each job under consideration should be analyzed and related to the students in the work-study program. The major factors to be considered in this job analysis include

1 The specific type of job, level of competence required, and amount of previous experience necessary

2 The employment procedures, types of certificates needed, and degree of involvement required with labor unions

3 The extent to which the employee is required to interact with fellow workers and members of the public

4 The types of working conditions prevalent and the potential for being relocated or moved to a different shift

5 The specific types of requirements needed for job success, the amount of training provided by the employer, and the type of supervision given to the employee

6 The types of educational skills and background necessary to satisfactorily perform on the job including the amount of reading required, the type of arithmetic skills needed, the demands for handling money, and the level of communication skills required for satisfactory employment

Locating jobs for the students is an important component of occupational education. Equally significant is that placement be decided according to the degree of congruence between the job requirements and the characteristics of the job candidates. Locating jobs is only the first step of the process and must be followed by skillfully relating the right job situation with the most appropriate student.

The evidence suggests that the mentally retarded worker rarely remains established in his first or second position. In the first few years of employment, they show a history of movement among jobs, with little or no upward movement to positions requiring higher-level skills. The reasons for this movement seem to be directly related to their frequent inability to get along with others.

It is probably unreasonable to assume that most retarded children will remain in the original job in which they were located during the work-study program. The instructional component of the work-study program, therefore, must be of great enough breadth to allow each child to generalize understandings to other occupations easily. The individual must be prepared to perform satisfactorily in a variety of settings and not in a circumscribed, narrowly defined occupation. The coordinator should realize that movement to a more skilled position will not occur readily and that large-scale retraining of the retarded would and should not be possible. Instructional success will be accomplished when all the experiences allow the retarded to formulate a pattern of acceptable behaviors which are easily transferred to other occupations requiring similar levels of accomplishment.

The degree of student success in the work-study program is related to the degree to which they become actively involved in all aspects of the program. Showing and telling these high school youngsters how and when to act will be ineffective. They must be given a chance to try out their responses in a realistic setting.

teaching considerations

PRELIMINARY CLASSROOM EXPERIENCES

The high school program for the mentally retarded must vary enough to allow for training and placement according to each child's skills, interests, and promise for success. Some children may be unable to operate within a competitive situation because of temperament or lack of skill in certain crucial areas. Other retarded high school students will be successful in occupational training and placement. The former group may require a more sheltered and restricted environment, the latter group perhaps a more normal vocational situation which allows for interaction among other members of society.

Suitable placement and success on the job demands a certain level of academic skill as well as a commonsense understanding of practical matters. These practical matters which are related to vocational employment include (1) social awareness and a sensitivity by the child for the needs of others, (2) realization of the dimensions of good citizenship and reasons for adhering to the principles contained therein, (3) skill in the rudimentary manipulative requirements of a job, and (4) an understanding of the manner in which facts learned in subject areas are applicable to practical day-to-day problems. To some degree, overlap exists among these five areas in terms of the teaching units that might be developed within the work-study program. The common threads characterizing these principles include (1) factors related to personal problems and (2) factors specifically concerned with occupational placement and effective participation on the job.

Personal Factors Techniques for emphasizing good grooming, good health, and care of personal belongings and clothing were previously considered. These factors require special emphasis because of the potentially deleterious effects poor personal appearance will have on an employer and fellow employees. Lack of concern for one's personal appearance will result in the individual's being labeled as mentally retarded even before the opportunity is presented to demonstrate academic or occupational capabilities. Some attention in the work-study program must be given to the children developing sensitivity to these important factors.

During the first few years of the work-study program, time and effort should be devoted to considering factors of personal finance. The public school program offers the most logical place for controlling the tendency of the retarded children to engage in impulsive behavior. The risks of their handling personal finances in an unfortunate manner are high, unless some systematic attempt is made to encourage proper management of these affairs. One of the important dimensions in this regard is the need to give particular stress to wise budgeting of their salaries. The students should actively practice the process involved in saving in order that stable patterns of behavior be established. Lecturing or your demonstrating the process will not suffice.

Employment for the first time often results in the new employee being deluged by various dealers interested in selling their services and products. These offers range from providing management of personal finances to a lifetime guarantee for a picture each month of every child born into the family. Mentally retarded adolescents and adults are especially vulnerable to accepting these deals without considering all the implications. The factors involved in wise purchasing must be realized by the youngsters so that they do not find themselves in situations which are irreversible. To illustrate, even non-mentally retarded individuals have some difficulty justifying the amount of insurance coverage carried after being exposed to the magic of a loquacious and mesmerizing insurance salesman. Certain guidelines or criteria, therefore, should be presented to the retarded students very early in the work-study program concerning issues such as what constitutes a reasonable amount of health, accident, and life insurance coverage.

In almost every employment situation, a variety of elective and nonelective programs is available to the employees. If uninformed, the mentally retarded employee will have difficulty understanding the nature of and reasons for the many payroll deductions. The high school program, therefore, should include experiences which emphasize the employer and employee responsibilities concerning income tax, social security, pension plans, and health and accident coverage. A good deal of instruction and activity should go into those units which consider the employee's responsibilities concerning income tax. Instructional materials from the Federal government are available to illustrate and practice the procedures required for submitting annual returns. A "one shot" program in this area is not enough; these matters need continual repetition throughout the work-study program.

The many goods and services available in our society make it difficult for most people not to succumb to acquiring the symbols of status and comfort even at the expense of going into debt. The sharpened skills of salesmen, who are totally informed about the advantages of their product as well as the products of others, tend to reduce the resistance of prospective buyers. The combination of the retarded child's lack of perspective with his difficulty in perceiving the implications of present actions for the future, and the ease with which goods can be purchased on time and money borrowed beyond all rational suitability, makes for a particularly difficult situation. These factors denote areas to which the high school program must give comprehensive and systematic attention. If the retarded are to understand the problems of installment buying, borrowing, and lending money, the dangers of impulsivity must be dramatically pointed out. The technique of sociodrama and the evolutionary process of the work-study program, extending from total in-class participation to final placement on the job, will provide opportunities for the children to "box themselves in" within a somewhat restricted and safe environment under supervision. This period of practice provides a circumstance whereby the results of their behavior can be demonstrated and in which failure will not have too severe an effect on the students.

Occupational Placement Factors   Preliminary to actual job placement, the work-study students should have some experience finding jobs which are consistent with their own capabilities, interviewing for occupational placement, and in making application for a position. A great deal hinges on the first impression made on the personnel officer dealing with the youth's application. Considerations concerning pay, working conditions, advancement possibilities, fringe benefits, inservice training programs, and other important factors are often deliberated and conclusions reached when the initial application is made. By the time the retarded are ready for employment outside of the relatively restricted environment of the school, each youngster should understand the procedures employed in applying for employment. It is highly important that they develop an attitude of self-assurance in making such applications. This attitude cannot be completely achieved unless the students have experiences of this type outside of the confines of the special education program. The activities in which the children are engaged must not be perceived by them as contrived. At the same time, the students must be placed in situations in which success will be forthcoming in order that the desired attitude concerning abilities develop.

The potential difficulties inherent in the aspects of employment which precede the actual work experience must be considered during the work-study program. For example, the issue of solving transportation problems, getting to work on time, or the relationship the workers should establish with the union should be discussed with the students and considered by the entire class. Alternatives to purchasing an automobile should be clearly delineated. The retarded youngster just entering the occupational scene will feel pressures to minimize transportation problems by purchasing an automobile. They should have a complete understanding of the problems which will be encountered after making such a purchase.

Two components of employment which are relevant to all occupations and which require constant attention include (1) the need to maintain an appropriate standard of excellence in terms of the accuracy and quality of each child's performance and (2) the requirement that principles of safety be maintained on the job. It is the coordinator's responsibility to continually focus on each of these factors and to remind students of their importance by rewarding behavior which exemplifies these tenets. If sloppy or unsafe work is tolerated, the child's potential for subsequent employment is reduced. Because of poor work habits, rapport between the work-study program and potential employers could be seriously damaged.

Finally, each retarded student must be given opportunities to develop appropriate response patterns to the often antagonistic and disrespectful behavior of fellow employees. The retarded employee must learn how to handle these situations gingerly, but effectively. These potential workers, therefore, should have certain experiences prior to placement on a job which will help them understand the need to respect authority. They should realize that employers and others may often appear antagonistic and that this is not because of any personal vendetta but for reasons of maintaining the effective use of workers and maximizing production. As members of the production team, the retarded worker should understand his responsibility for constantly giving his best performance.

RELATIONSHIP BETWEEN WORK AND STUDY

Kolstoe and Frey (1965) have suggested a three-level sequence for the work-study program, each level of which allows the retarded child to gradually assume more responsibility and exercise greater independence within an occupational setting. These levels are defined as:

1 Prevocational: students able to participate in sheltered, supervised, and semi-competitive work environments for a portion of each school day, but who by nature of their handicap or age are not eligible for vocational adjustment placement
2 Vocational adjustment or work try-out: students who have demonstrated a sufficient degree of work and social and personal skills to become eligible for part-time competitive work placement in selected jobs in the community
3 Placement: students who are capable of performing work at a minimum competitive level and who have completed the general academic requirements for graduation from the work-study program.

This program, which is evolutionary, allows the retarded child to move from total in-class involvement to full-time placement in a position, with ample opportunities for counseling and guidance on a follow-up basis from one to three years after leaving the school program. Because of the variation in characteristics of the retarded, the work-study program must be flexible enough to allow students to move from one level to another and, perhaps, return to an earlier level on the basis of the demonstrated ability each child exhibits in solving problems. It is difficult, therefore, to structure a program rigidly so that certain experiences occur only during a school year and never again. Moreover, some of the retarded children in the work-study program will not be able to operate effectively within an unstructured occupational environment. The determination of the location of each child within the total spectrum of work-study activities and his graduation into full-time employment require careful assessment of every student's characteristics in relation to the demands of each specific occupational situation.

The following sequence is an elaboration and extension of the levels of the work-study program as suggested by Kolstoe and Frey.

In-Class Activities (Exclusively) During the first year of the work-study program, the children should be given a heavy concentration of prevocational information. Some of the specific content of this first stage of instruction was discussed in the preceding section. Emphasis should be placed on the personal and social demands of employment with substantial time devoted to such job prerequisites as interviewing for a position, filling out all the required forms of application, developing those manipulative skills required of unskilled and semiskilled workers, and making practical use of the academic skills developed during the primary and intermediate school years.

During this preliminary stage, the teacher should begin to formulate some general impression as to how well each child will be able to accept responsibility and handle the requirements of a job. Some broad estimate of suitable placement should be made at this point. This judgment should be based on each youngster's ability to use and apply skills in the academic subjects and how well he comprehends occupational information demanded for employment success. At the same time, an estimate should be made of each child's personal and social development and maturity.

A work situation which is as realistic as possible should be replicated in the special education classroom in order to make the activities, situations, and experiences very meaningful to the children. This can be done methodologically by using sociodrama. During this period, the younger students will find it informative to hear about the experiences of the older retarded pupils who have some familiarity with the demands of employment. These older youngsters, by introspecting a bit on the difficulties encountered in employment, can help to alert the younger, more naive child to some of the possible areas of difficulty. At this level of their development, the teacher could use peer pressure and student models to aid in the formation of proper attitudes. In certain instances, the more experienced students will be able to make a greater impact on the young retarded children by describing the need for learning the

skills and information required for a successful employment experience.

   *In-Class Activities with Supervised Work of a Short-Term Duration
within the School Building, Gradually Becoming More Extensive as
Experience Is Gained*   At this second level, the retarded child should be
encouraged to relate classwork to practical problems within an environment in which certain controls are maintained. This propinquity allows
for the close observation of each child and at the same time, provides a
certain sense of security during each child's first experience at work. By
working in the school building, the children find themselves in a familiar
environment in which the regulations for appropriate behavior are well
known. The adults with whom the children will be associated or
supervised during the period of work should know about the objectives
characteristic of this stage of the program and what constitutes reasonable expectations for the children. This relatively structured environment and work situation gives the work-study student a chance to try
out an actual job situation.

   It is important that the work experience at this level of instruction not
be so contrived as to detract from the program objectives. If the
students develop a feeling that their performance level is unimportant
and their best effort not required, work performance at subsequent
levels will be manifestly ineffective. Attitudes of the adult supervisors
must be such that the children realize that a serious, concentrated effort
is required of them during the work-study program. It should be made
clear to each student that subsequent opportunities and job positions
will be jeopardized if they view their responsibilities in too casual or
cavalier a fashion.

   In order to replicate the work situation as closely as possible, the
children involved at this program level might be given a series of
realistic incentives and rewards. Financial remuneration should be
provided for work done. These rewards should be given only after work
has been accomplished at a satisfactory level. Control should be
exercised over the quality of work by paying students only when the
work is well done. Here again, accuracy and not speed should be
emphasized. Although some components of external evaluation of a
student's work will be required for determining remuneration in this
situation, the final goal should be for the child to learn to evaluate his
own performance according to established criteria. As they move to
higher levels within the work-study program, the children should move
away from total dependence on others to dependence on themselves
for evaluating the quality of achievement. The older retarded child
should gain an appreciation for what constitutes acceptable and satis-

factory work and not what he can get by with when someone is not keeping tabs on his performance. Some reward system, then, must become an integral part of this aspect of the program, not only because it replicates to some degree the actual work situation, but also because it helps to reinforce appropriate behavior.

Activities at this level of the work-study program will allow the teacher and work supervisor to collect meaningful and realistic data which subsequently can be used to gain a more precise estimate of the occupational expectations and apparent needs of each child. At this level when the students are actually working, their pattern of strengths and weaknesses will become obvious. As this profile is manifested, the teacher should restructure the classroom segments of the program in line with the weaknesses of each child and the requirements of the occupations with which they are or will be associated.

In-Class Activities with Periodic Out-of-School Experiences in Combination with Extensive In-School Work   This level of the work-study program allows the retarded to be gradually introduced into a new and less familiar work situation. The more cloistered environment characterizing their former situation will slowly move to the background, and the children now should be encouraged to use their skills and experiences in another type of occupational situation. It is significant, at this level, that they should still return to familiar territory for reorientation. This stable environment places them in a situation wherein the appropriateness of their behavior and that of others can be more accurately predicted. Moreover, in- and out-of-school experiences in concert with certain class room activities provide them with an opportunity to test the reactions of themselves and others to situations arising during the out-of-school aspect of the program. When a youngster faces problems on the job, the in-school program component will provide him with a stable environment which allows the study of reasons for his behavior, or that of others, to certain situations.

The teacher should place each youngster in an out-of-school occupation which is closely related to his previous experience within the school building. The alternative placement opportunities should be studied so that some consistency is maintained between the in- and out-of-school experiences and job demands. For example, the youngsters might be employed in another school building as part of their out-of-school work.

The in-class activities characteristic of this stage of the program should focus on (1) helping the student maintain those previously developed skills and (2) rehabilitating or "beefing him up" in any areas in which certain deficiencies are exhibited. Continued emphasis should be given to using academic skills during the work experience period. A close relationship should be maintained between the child's academic skills and the occupational demands in order to strengthen this bond.

In-Class Activities with Half-Days Supervised Out of School   At this stage of the program, the retarded should gradually move into a work situation which requires greater skills in independent living and personal responsibility. Each student should devote half-days to a specific employment situation and return to the classroom at which time problems experienced on the job are considered and any needed remedial training is provided. At this stage, the retarded children must be exposed to a variety of occupational experiences and moved from one setting to another for at least one year's duration.

The responsibilities for supervision during this stage should be clearly delineated so that the employer and the work-study coordinator understand the limits of their responsibility. At no other time during the students' program will closer supervision and the complete analysis of strengths and weaknesses be as necessary and valuable. Likewise, an easy transition can be facilitated for the children from one relatively short-term work experience to another by the work-study coordinator identifying employment situations which are somewhat similar. A rational sequence should be identified which allows the students to move from one job to other jobs in a logical fashion without experiencing dramatic changes and alterations as they move. Factors requiring consideration in this sequencing include the job's manipulative expectations, level of intellectual ability required, type and number of possible social interactions to which the child will be exposed, academic qualifications required for success on each job, and the degree and types of responsibilities demanded of the retarded. The major point to be remembered is that the children move from one job to another in a fashion that requires some minimal change. As they move toward the final experiences at this stage of instruction, the characteristics and requirements of any final employment situations will no doubt differ substantially from expectations required during the students' early occupational activities.

The need for close coordination between the work-study supervisor and employers is obvious. One important dimension of this coordination must be a clear understanding and agreement by the employer of the objectives of the work-study program. Records should be maintained by the employer and work-study coordinator of each child's performance, areas of difficulty or potential difficulty, and indications of any additional experiences believed necessary to work in a satisfactory manner. The work-study coordinator should clearly identify for the employer any possible areas of difficulty for those students involved in a job. Likewise, the coordinator should continuously inform the employer about the student's activities and performance within the classroom environment.

As was true in the stage of instruction immediately preceding this, there is need for a systematic and intelligent reward system in all stages of the program. It must be recognized by all involved in the program, including the students, that they have been placed in the job situations for half-days not primarily for purposes of supporting themselves or for making money. This is to be viewed as part of a training program.

The pedagogical advantages in properly reinforcing desired behavior should be recognized even at this stage. The students should receive some type of financial remuneration for work properly accomplished during the period on the job. At the same time, accuracy of performance should be emphasized instead of speed, and control should be maintained over the quality of the students' work. To this end, the coordinator and the employer might find it wise to reimburse the students according to the quality of their performance instead of on the basis of piecework or by the hour. The efficacy of this procedure requires study. In the absence of empirical support, teachers should not be hesitant to test innovative approaches as long as they are consistent with the program objectives and purposes.

Total Out-of-School Work Experience, Carefully Supervised, Leading Eventually to Placement By the time the students have reached this stage of the work-study program, they should have systematically worked out any major weaknesses which might impede their success in occupational, social, and personal self-sufficiency. At this stage, it will no longer be necessary for the students to return to the classroom. They should have developed the basic skills required for total participation and integration into society.

The wide spectrum of experiences gained during the earlier stages of this work-study sequence will often result in students demonstrating an interest for being employed in a specific type of industry or employment situation. It should be recognized that some of the students may require transfer from one situation to another even during the course of their total out-of-school work experience. Along with the students, the work-study coordinator should analyze the various positions available and decide on the best situation. By using this approach, the retarded child will learn the practicalities of job analysis. This should aid the child to develop a keener awareness of his own abilities and weaknesses in relation to the expectations of various occupations.

It is the responsibility of the work-study coordinator to try to place each child in a permanent occupational situation. The division of vocational rehabilitation will be able to offer assistance during the stage of work placement. Full-time placement should not be attempted until the child reaches age eighteen or nineteen.

Follow-up   By the time a retarded child has been placed on a job, substantial investment has been made by the public schools and other cooperating agencies. This fact suggests the need for a careful evaluation and scrutiny of each child's performance after leaving school. A systematic follow-up of former students of the work-study program for one to three years after graduation should be undertaken to help those youngsters having difficulty as well as to introduce any needed modifications in the program sequence. Systematic assessments of job performance and integration into the community should be made. The retarded employee should be questioned and interviewed, the facts and attitudes of the employer studied in detail, and a remedial program immediately provided the employee if necessary. Ideally, then, the schools should be concerned about the total program effectiveness and provide any additional educational services required by the retarded employee. Adult education, then, constitutes a necessary part of the special education program for the retarded.

THE EVALUATION PROCESS

The need for consistent evaluation of the components of the work-study program has been stressed as central to the program's success. The coordinator must instruct employers of the students about techniques for evaluating those dimensions of significance encountered on the job. Moreover, evaluation is needed to identify potential employment situations and to determine the basic tasks and work components characteristic of each potential job situation.

Concerning the students, evaluation is necessary to identify significant weaknesses in those areas which require a certain level of achievement for successful employment; it is also necessary that each student's performance be measured against the specific goals at each stage of the work-study program. As the students satisfy the criteria at each level, they should proceed to the next stage of the program.

Evaluation of progress is conducted not only to adjust and modify a child's program, but also to provide students with feedback concerning their progress. It is important that focus not be placed on a child's weaknesses but that each student be rewarded for correct responses. Whenever one is made aware of his shortcomings, an opportunity to practice appropriate responses to the situation should be given. Likewise, it is important that the work-study coordinator inform employers of the desirability not to place undue emphasis on a child's weaknesses without demonstrating the correct and proper manner in which to perform. The situation requires some clinical sensitivity on the part of those working with the retarded. Errors should not be practiced. At the same time, the youngsters should not assume that their responses are satisfactory because they have not been alerted to their errors. Feedback from evaluations, therefore, needs to be provided to students.

Evaluation should effect some modification in the instructional program when patterns of weakness are exhibited consistently among children. It should be purposeful, the basic aim being to assess the degree to which the youngsters are able to satisfy the established program objectives. Suggestions for temporary or permanent revision of the work-study program will emanate from the data collected. The goals for each child will not necessarily be alike because of the variations which exist between the children.

A variety of techniques might be employed to check on the progress of students. If a child seems to be having difficulty in any of the academic areas, the employment of a selection of the evaluative techniques discussed in other sections of this book would be appropriate. If performance in social, personal, or occupational factors needs to be evaluated, the teacher may find checklists of various types helpful. These checklists, which do not necessarily require standardization, are primarily a means for determining certain general patterns of achievement. Kolstoe and Frey (1965), in the appendix of their book, have provided illustrations of several scales and checklists which work-study coordinators will find helpful in assessing the progress of students. Vocational rehabilitation has also developed evaluation forms of this nature.

The employers of work-study students should be required to cooperate in the evaluation process. Because of time limitations, they are frequently unable to schedule extensive conferences with either the employee or the work-study coordinator. The most parsimonious and practical means of gathering information from the employer about the work-study students is to provide him with a progress checksheet similar to those mentioned earlier.

Another factor requiring assessment is the attitudes of potential employers toward the retarded. Assessing the motives of the employer and his willingness to cooperate is a difficult problem. In most cases, the work-study coordinator will need to devote a great deal of time selling the school program to the various levels of management. The search for and identification of placement possibilities require an enormous public relations effort and may involve other members of the community and local agencies to help locate job possibilities for students. The coordinator must not only sell the philosophy of the work-study program, he must sell the student as well. Employers should come to view the entire program in a positive fashion.

ADDITIONAL CONCERNS
RELATED TO THE WORK-STUDY PROGRAM
The program requires the services of a coordinator whose primary responsibilities involve locating potential employment situations, supervising students in their out-of-school vocational placement, and integrating the practical problems experienced by the students on the job with the in-class activities. The primary responsibility of the classroom instructor should be for all of the in-class activities and a portion of the in-school work program. Both of the instructors should coordinate their efforts closely and be responsible for consistently and systematically assessing the students under their direction.

The classroom in which these youngsters might be located should not differ significantly from a regular classroom in terms of the kind of equipment available. It might be advantageous to the program if the classroom were located in close proximity to an industrial arts laboratory and home economics classroom. This setting would provide closer coordination between the special education instructor and other facets of the school program. This integration should occur in a realistic way and not be contrived.

The teacher can be of great personal assistance to the children and help maximize the possibility for their success at work by spending time helping the students be as attractive as possible. Much of the early instruction of the work-study program will deal with various practical ways for making themselves attractive to others. This means that attention should be given to grooming, cleanliness, personal relationships with others, the use of toilet articles, neat and appropriate dress, and other such factors. The judicious use of peer pressure may provide the stimulus for the younger mentally retarded youngsters understanding the value in attending to these personal and social considerations.

Active participation, reducing the newness of the various situations, and integrating past experiences with new problems and situations are important considerations for the success of the program. The sequence of activities provided during the entire course of the program should consider these vital principles.

selected readings

Beckman, A. S. : "Minimum Intelligence Levels for Several Occupations," *Personal Journal*, 9: 309–313, 1930.

Bobroff, A.: "Economic Adjustment of 121 Adults, Formerly Students in Classes for Mental Retardates," *American Journal of Mental Deficiency*, 60: 525–535, 1956.

———: "A Survey of Social and Civic Participation of Adults Formerly in Classes for Mentally Retarded," *American Journal of Mental Deficiency*, 61: 127–133, 1956.

Capobianco, R. J. and H. B. Jacoby: "The Fairfax Plan: A High School Program for Mildly Retarded Youth," *Mental Retardation*, 4: 15–20, 1966.

Clark, G. M.: "A State-Wide School-Work Program for the Mentally Retarded," *Mental Retardation*, 5: 7–10, 1967.

Collman, R. D. and D. Newlyn: "Employment Success of Educationally Subnormal Ex-Pupils in England," *American Journal of Mental Deficiency*, 60: 733–743, 1956.

——— and ———: "Employment Success of Mentally Dull and Intellectually Normal Ex-Pupils in England," *American Journal of Mental Deficiency*, 6l: 484–490, 1957.

Delp, H. A. and M. Lorenz: "Follow-Up of 84 Public School Special-Class Pupils with IQ's Below 50," *American Journal of Mental Deficiency*, 58: 175–182, 1953.

Deno, E., R. Henze, G. Krantz, K. Barklind: *Retarded Youth: Their School-Rehabilitation Needs*, Minneapolis Public Schools, Minneapolis, 1965.

DiMichael, S.: "Vocational Rehabilitation Works for the Mentally Retarded," *Personnel and Guidance Journal*, 31: 428–432, 1953.

Dinger, J. C.: "Post-School Adjustment of Former Educable Retarded Pupils," *Exceptional Children*, 27: 353–360, 1961.

Engel, A. M.: "Employment of the Mentally Retarded," *American Journal of Mental Deficiency*, 57: 243–267, 1952.

Eskridge, C. S. and D. L. Partridge: "Vocational Rehabilitation for Exceptional Children through Special Education," *Exceptional Children*, 29: 452–458, 1963.

Gardner, W. I.: *Behavior Modification in Mental Retardation: The Education and Rehabilitation of the Mentally Retarded Adolescent, and Adult*, Aldine-Atherton, New York, 1971.

Gill, R. C.: "Individualizing the Curriculum for Educable Mentally Retarded High School Students through Prevocational Evaluation,"

Education and Training of the Mentally Retarded, 3: 169–179, 1968.

Goldberg, I. I.: "Coordination of Retardates' Experiences from School to Occupational Center," *American Journal of Mental Deficiency*, 62: 823–825, 1958.

Gruenberg, E. M.: "Epidemiology," in H. A. Stevens and R. Heber (eds.), *Mental Retardation: A Review of Research*, The University of Chicago Press, Chicago, 1964, pp. 259–306.

Harvey, J.: *Special Class Curriculum and Environment and Vocational Rehabilitation of Mentally Retarded Young Adults*, University of Alabama, University, 1964.

Heber, R. F.: *Proceedings of a Conference on Special Problems in Vocational Rehabilitation of the Mentally Retarded*, Rehabilitation Service Series Number 63–62, Vocational Rehabilitation Administration, Washington, 1963.

Hitchcock, A. A.: "Vocational Training and Job Adjustment of the Mentally Deficient," *American Journal of Mental Deficiency*, 59: 100–106, 1954.

Kokaska, C.: "In-school Work Experience: A Tool for Community Adjustment," *Mental Retardation*, 2: 365–369, 1964.

Kolstoe, O. P.: "An Examination of Some Characteristics Which Discriminate between Employed and Not-Employed Mentally Retarded Males," *American Journal of Mental Deficiency*, 66: 472–482, 1961.

Kolstoe, O. P. and R. M. Frey: *A High School Work-Study Program for Mentally Subnormal Students*, Southern Illinois University Press, Carbondale, Ill., 1965, pp. 95–96.

McCartney, L. D.: "Providing Occupational Readiness for Young Mentally Deficient Children of the Non-Familial Type," *American Journal of Mental Deficiency*, 62: 625–633, 1958.

Michael-Smith, H.: "A Study of the Personal Characteristics Desirable for the Vocational Success of the Mentally Deficient," *American Journal of Mental Deficiency*, 55: 139–143, 1950.

Neuhaus, E. C.: "A Unique Pre-vocational Program for Educable Retardates," *Mental Retardation*, 3: 19–21, 1965.

————: "Training the Mentally Retarded for Competitive Employment," *Exceptional Children*, 33: 625–628, 1967.

Payne, J. S. and J. D. Chaffin: "Developing Employer Relations in a Work-Study Program for the Educable Mentally Retarded," *Education and Training of the Mentally Retarded*, 3: 127–133, 1968.

Peck, J. R.: "The Work-Study Program—A Critical Phase of Preparation," *Education and Training of the Mentally Retarded*, 1: 68–74, 1966.

Peterson, L. and L. L. Smith: "A Comparison of the Post-School Adjustment of Educable Mentally Retarded Adults with That of Adults of Normal Intelligence," *Exceptional Children*, 26: 404–408, 1960.

Peterson, R. O. and E. J. Jones: *Guide to Jobs for the Mentally Retarded*, American Institute for Research, Pittsburgh, 1964.

Porter, R. B. and T. C. Milazzo: "A Comparison of Mentally Retarded Adults Who Attended a Special Class with Those Who Attended Regular School Classes," *Exceptional Children*, 24: 410–412, 1958.

Shawn, B.: "Review of a Work-Experience Program," *Mental Retardation*, 2: 360–364, 1964.

Strickland, C. G.: "Job Training Placement for Retarded Youth," *Exceptional Children*, 31: 83–86, 1964.

—————— and V. M. Arrell: "Employment of the Mentally Retarded," *Exceptional Children*, 34: 21–24, 1967.

Switzer, M. E.: "The Coordination of Vocational Rehabilitation and Special Education Services for the Mentally Retarded," *Education and Training of the Mentally Retarded*, 1: 155–160, 1966.

Wolfensberger, W.: "Vocational Preparation and Occupation," in A. Baumeister (ed.), *Mental Retardation: Appraisal, Education and Rehabilitation*, Aldine Publishing Company, Chicago, 1967, pp. 232–273.

12

ADULT EDUCATION FOR THE MENTALLY RETARDED AND THEIR PARENTS

Educational programs for the adult mentally retarded and for parents of the retarded attending public schools have traditionally not been provided by the schools. Rehabilitation counselors have been most directly responsible for the adult retarded if they are registered, have been evaluated by the agency, are of the appropriate age, and reside in a community in which needed services are available. Unfortunately, in many instances, special education teachers and coordinators fail to establish a close working relationship with vocational rehabilitation. This results in the retarded adults not being provided with professional advice, counsel, and other needed services. Parents of retarded children who are attending public schools are usually not incorporated in any of the existing programs unless they elect to join a parents' group, such as the National Association for Retarded Children, or are fortunate enough for their child to be taught by a teacher who is aware of the need to work with the parents as well as with the children.

The position taken here is that the schools must include adult education programs for former students who are retarded as well as for parents of all retarded children who are enrolled in the special program. This suggestion may seem idealistic when one considers the many other educational needs, such as extending school programs downward to include younger children, particularly those from lower socioeconomic communities. By attending to the needs of parents of former students, a complete program can be developed which will have impact on the participants and their families in terms of enhancing their potential stations in life. Moreover, the data gathered from this type of program will help to evaluate the efficacy of the activities, experiences, objectives, and rationale of the total special education sequence provided retarded students. This longitudinal view of the special education program provides the type of evaluative procedure needed to develop comprehensive educational services for the mentally retarded. The most commonly existing program structure, which dismisses the retarded at age eighteen never to see them again, not only lacks comprehensiveness and necessary follow-up but provides no basis or opportunity for testing the value of the student's éarlier special education experiences. Special education, therefore, must combine forces with vocational rehabilitation in each of these two important areas of adult education.

dimensions of the postschool program

The objective of the immediate postschool program is one of helping former students with any particular difficulties they are encountering as members of the community. This aim, although broad in terms of the possible variety of problems the retarded individuals could experience, should deal with specific difficulties. In all aspects of this program, however, attempts should be made to have the retarded person generalize appropriate behavior related to a certain situation to all other areas of functioning in which such behavior would be equally appropriate. The degree to which the individual adjusts to his occupational situation and the extent of his satisfaction in personal and family development should constitute the two broad areas for emphasis in the adult education program for the mentally retarded. Before considering the specifics of each of these areas, the following points will help to focus more precisely on what might constitute the broad structure and intent of the postschool program.

1 When the students are placed on a job, they should understand that one condition of their employment is that they attend school one evening each week in order to meet with either the work-study coordinator or a counselor trained in special education for the retarded. The length of time each student must continue attending these sessions should be variable and based totally on the mutual evaluation by the employer and the school representative. Factors considered before a retarded person is dismissed from the weekly sessions should include (1) the degree of success in the basic occupational expectations; (2) attitudes and values held by the student; (3) any specific weaknesses of an academic nature which deleteriously influence his performance on the job; (4) family difficulties; and (5) any personal, emotional, or social problems

2 Each weekly session should be relatively unstructured in terms of content. This strategy will allow the instructor to capitalize on concerns and difficulties expressed by members of the group as well as by each individual's employer. Although unstructured, the sessions should be informative for the participants and viewed by them as being a valuable activity. Information dispensing, as well as formal and informal counseling and guidance, will constitute major segments of each session. As specific difficulties are identified, the instructor may wish to dramatize alternative ways of solving the problem by using role playing

3 Each session should contain a relatively small number of participants with some group stability being maintained so that the participants will interact freely with other group members. Small groups are mandatory since many of the students' problems may be personal or specific to them although, no doubt, of general interest and importance to other members of the group. With large groups, it would be impossible for the instructor to adequately respond to the problems as they are presented, and the promise for wide group interaction would be minimized

4 Although many of the problems and issues raised by the retarded employees and their employers may be real and legitimate, neither of these groups of people is trained to observe and assess the subtle factors which are frequently causative of difficulties. The instructor of the postschool program, although making use of information provided by others, should attempt to identify and focus on specific weaknesses exhibited by members of the class. This requires that the instructor be broadly trained and particularly sensitive to clues of diagnostic relevance

5 The entire post school program must become closely associated with the division of vocational rehabilitation and other community agencies in order to operate effectively. As specific weaknesses of an employee are identified by the instructor or employer, a decision should be made as to whether the program for rehabilitating the individual could be done most efficiently by the schools, vocational rehabilitation, or some other community agency such as mental health, crippled children's commission, or a legal advisory service. Although the schools have some responsibility for the post school program, they and others should realize that effective integration of the retarded adult into the community will come about only after coordination has been effected among all the community services

FOLLOW-UP OF OCCUPATIONAL ADJUSTMENT

Specific characteristics of the follow-up components of the work-study program were discussed in the preceding chapter. The information gathered by the work-study coordinator when the work situation of the retarded employee is visited and observations by the employer should be discussed with the evening instructor and by the students in one of the early group sessions. Follow-up of the work-study program should be done for two reasons: first, to assist the public schools in revising or reorienting their program and, second, to evaluate the performance of each retarded individual and to provide any needed rehabilitative services. The latter point is probably the most important and suggests that a close collaborative relationship should exist between the work-study coordinator, the employer, and the evening instructor.

Social development, manipulative skills, personal and emotional adequacy, employee-employer relationships, and even training in specific academic areas are subjects which should receive attention in the postschool program. As information is gathered concerning how well the retarded adult performs in these areas, some judgment can be made regarding the necessity for any additional training. By the establishment of a close relationship with vocational rehabilitation, it will often be possible to schedule a series of short- and long-term training programs or relocate a retarded adult in a more restricted or sheltered occupational situation. It may not be possible to accurately diagnose the degree to which an individual will be able to become assimilated into a job during the course of the regular school program. When the more structured environment is removed, the retarded adult, no longer under the aegis of the work-study coordinator, may demonstrate significant weaknesses in behavior and management.

The type of data collected on the prospective employee during the course of the work-study program should continue to be gathered, although perhaps less formally, during the most immediate post-school period. These data will provide some general indication of the degree of employee growth and stability of performance over time. Recording segments of behavior periodically, but consistently, throughout the duration of the in- and out-of-school program has the potential for being helpful to the individual being studied and is also important to the total program structure as other students move through the various program components. Further, staff attrition requires objective, consistent, and systematic reporting so that communication among professionals at all levels and during various periods of time can be unambiguous and as efficient as possible.

COUNSELING THE RETARDED ADULT

Irrespective of the type of educational situation with which the mentally retarded might have been previously associated, as adults they will probably blend into society. This in no way suggests that they will become community leaders or major contributors to the social order; instead, the aggressive and active participation of those members of the community who are more astute often camouflages any weaknesses which the retarded members might exhibit. To be sure, the schools should and in some states are mandated by the courts to provide the retarded with experiences and activities which will allow them to move into the community on an independent and self-sufficient basis. The evidence indicates that as a group they will be able to do this irrespective of the type or caliber of their educational program. There is an increased use of various types of community advocates on behalf of the mentally retarded to assure a smooth transition into community life from the school environment.

The more crucial issue is how effectively the retarded will be able to manage their own affairs as adults. As much as possible must be done to help the retarded not find themselves in situations which require that they constantly solve a host of minor problems which have been precipitated by their ineffectiveness as problem solvers or by becoming associated with unscrupulous persons. If these little difficulties continue to occur, the retarded adult will become more deeply in debt, experiencing a host of problems—solutions for which are often not easily obvious to them. Eventually they will find themselves resorting to illegal or unethical behavior in an attempt to resolve these difficulties. Even after exposure to an outstanding social class program, the impact and significance of problems of adulthood are typically not felt. Because of youth and inexperience during the school years, problems of independent living as adults are not realistic facts of life. A postschool program, therefore, should help the retarded adult to sharpen his skills in solving the variety of personal and family problems which most will face.

Financial problems are among the most difficult problems for the retarded adult and have the greatest potential for causing severe difficulties. During the work-study program, and also during the intermediate school grades, mentally retarded youth should have a complete exposure to a program of effective management of money. As students, however, they are not faced with the problems of feeding and clothing themselves, providing their own transportation to and from work, renting or purchasing a house, or judging when and under what circumstances a major item should be purchased. As adults, with money in their pockets, many will succumb to any number of a variety of pressures to spend their money foolishly. As students, most of the retarded will be able to repeat back to the teacher in a correct and appropriate manner all the advantages and disadvantages of installment buying. As adults, many of the retarded either will have forgotten or be unable to apply what they have previously learned about intelligently spending money. The weekly postschool sessions, then, should constantly consider problems related to the management of money. Although the retarded tend to marry partners with greater relative intellectual ability, it would be unwise to assume that clear thinking will always prevail when financial considerations are at stake.

Family planning should be another vital part of the postschool program. Most retarded adults are totally unaware of the many problems involved in marriage and in raising a family. Their impulsive nature will result in many of them marrying without considering all the ramifications of making such a decision. In addition, the postschool sessions should consider topics such as how to provide suitable housing, planning children and providing for their complete care, sharing responsibility between the husband and wife, and appropriate techniques for child rearing.

Mentally retarded children and adults should know of the large number of unscrupulous persons in our society who are interested in taking advantage of them and their families. The importance of the retarded realizing the seriousness of associating with people of this type cannot be overstated. The potential harm in dealing with such people should be made dramatic by using actual case material for instruction or by asking authority figures, such as the local police inspector, to visit with the students to discuss how to avoid these unprincipled people. The retarded should be aware of when they are being taken advantage of and what course of action to follow when they find themselves in this type of situation.

The postschool curriculum should also contain a program which centers around the worthy use of leisure time. They must be encouraged to make use of all their capabilities and engage in activities which foster good physical and mental health. Moreover, a stable, socially acceptable pattern of extracurricular behavior, which provides a means for relaxation and enjoyment, should be encouraged. Financial considerations related to these leisure time activities require explicit instructional attention. Examples of recreational activities which do not require heavy expenditure from the family budget should be described during the postschool program. The enjoyment of church groups or neighborhood activities should be emphasized.

The areas suggested as requiring special attention in the postschool program constitute only a sample of the types of concerns frequently manifested by the mentally retarded adult. It is impossible to predict all the potential areas of difficulty to be encountered by the retarded prior to the postschool years. Even if these factors could be identified, restrictions in time during the school program make it impossible for each to be considered in depth. Further, the unique situation of each mentally retarded person upon leaving the schools will result in problems which are specific to each individual and situation. To gain maximum advantage from a consistent and sequentially developed special program for the mentally retarded, small practical problems encountered on the job by each retarded person should be discussed before the difficulties become too large to handle, are generalized to other situations, or place the retarded in a relatively irreversible situation. The postschool program for the adult, in cooperation with programs offered by other agencies such as vocational rehabilitation, will offer the most ideal situation for them to learn how to appropriately solve practical problems faced every day.

Every aspect of the special education program for the retarded is important and, in concert with other aspects of the program, provides the desired scope and sequence for them to develop into adequate citizens. Some educators would suggest that the preschool and the immediate postschool years are particularly crucial in the instructional program for the retarded. During the preschool years, the children learn to develop skills in those foundation areas on which academic skills are later based. During the immediate postschool years they have a chance to use the many skills developed during the school program in practical surroundings. The school should check on each child's effectiveness to apply those things learned earlier in their special program. Moreover, the retarded adult should be provided with remedial services when certain weaknesses are manifested.

adult education for parents of the mentally retarded

Any comprehensive school program for the mentally retarded should include adult education for parents as any integral part of the total program structure. Although the children will spend most daylight contact hours in the public schools, the potentially deleterious influence that the uneducated or insensitive parent can have is often substantial enough to completely nullify the advantages of even the best special education program. In considering the structure of an adult education program for parents of the retarded, the schools are faced with the need to deal with two somewhat unique and different populations, each of which requires a separate educational emphasis. On one hand, certain retarded children located in the special education program have some type of presumed organic dysfunction. These children often represent families from better educated situations.

The second population represented in special education programs for the retarded are those children who, because of severe environmental deprivation, have not had the full spectrum of experiences which would allow them to develop at an intellectual level commensurate with their chronological ages. Parents of these deprived children require a different orientation in an adult education program than those parents whose children represent some type of organic etiology. The nature of the concerns represented by each of these groups and recommendations for program emphasis will be considered in this section.

PARENTS FROM NORMAL ENVIRONMENTS

Children who are retarded because of some type of presumed organic dysfunction which is not directly related to environmental deprivation typically present a perplexing problem to their parents. The situation is particularly difficult for those parents whose families are without a history of mental retardation. Because of some type of prenatal, perinatal, or postnatal difficulty, the child may have experienced minimal neurological damage which results in a certain degree of intellectual subnormality. Parents with this type of child are immediately placed in a new psychological situation wherein appropriate goals and paths by which these goals are reached are not well delineated. This situation results in wandering, vacillating, and trial-and-error behavior; parents in this situation often engage in clinic hopping. They are often unsure of the type of specialist whose advice they should seek, and their perplexity only increases when subsequent births produce intellectually normal siblings. Anxiety and tension surrounding the retarded child in this family are increased because of various intra- and extrafamily pressures brought to bear on the parents. Many individuals with whom they come in contact act as, and often are preceived as, experts. This results in the parents' becoming more tense about the situation and future of their child.

The special education teacher is often the first professional concerned with behavior from whom parents with this type of child receive specific advice. The general practitioners and pediatricians, although frequently having had experience with intellectually subnormal children from a medical perspective, most often will not be aware of what should constitute an appropriate educational program for this type of retarded child. The special education teacher, therefore, must be prepared to respond intelligently to the questions and concerns of the parents. One major educational thrust in this matter can be achieved by the schools including an adult educational program within the total structure of the special education program.

Throughout the adult education sessions parents of the retarded must understand the teacher's willingness to help with everyday problems. The teacher must not be perceived by the parents as an expert in areas other than education. When the problems raised by parents exceed the professional training of the teacher, a referral should be made to experts in the areas of concern. Professionals representing these disciplines should be invited periodically to visit the class during the adult education program. Early in the parent education sessions, the problem of etiology or cause will come up. Parents must have the opportunity to freely discuss all the possibilities. Intelligent leadership by the teacher will help them arrive at the realization that the child's future should receive primary focus. It will be personally satisfying and advantageous for the parents to spend time discussing the range of possible reasons for their child's being mentally retarded. Parents should be left with the belief that it is probably impossible for anyone to specify the cause of the condition and that any of a variety of difficulties could have resulted in the problem.

Each parent session should be informal. Parents should feel free to discuss any area of concern with other members of the group. The sessions should be such that the parents realize that the techniques used in handling their child are not being critically evaluated by others, including the group leader. Emphasis should be placed on the need for a coordinated effort between the home and the school. To this end, the school's objectives for each child should be clearly delineated, each parent informed of the present educational level and educational prognosis for his child, and the specific instructional procedures that are being employed with their child clearly described along with periodic reports on performance.

Parents of the organically retarded typically have an unclear picture of the capabilities and future of their children. Many feel that their child will outgrow the intellectual slowness presently exhibited and eventually move into the regular class program. Other parents look for miracle cures, special diets, or unique kinds of therapy for rehabilitating their child. It is important that the parents gain a clear picture of the present status of their child and gain a reasonable perspective of the future for their child. This will take a long time to effect for many parents, and indeed, some will never arrive at a reasonable understanding on this matter. Before any interaction can occur between the home and school, the teacher must devote time and effort in helping parents place their understanding and expectations for the child in proper perspective.

Early in the adult education program the translation of the school's program in terms of each child's situation should be thoroughly explained. Although this can be covered through planned lectures, it is recommended that the parents be allowed to observe demonstrations of various aspects of the school program. The atmosphere characteristic of a contrived demonstration should be avoided and a warm, realistic, and informal situation provided for parent observations. This technique provides parents with a more realistic picture of the dimensions of the school program and the strategies by which the aims are realized, and there is the added advantage of the parents' becoming more aware of the limitations of their own child's ability and level of achievement. The parents, thus, gain an appreciation of the special program and, at the same time, become aware of the techniques used by the teacher in handling each retarded child. Many of these same strategies are appropriate for use in the home.

Too much pressure on the mentally retarded to achieve is a common characteristic of the middle-class home. For reasons that may be related to lack of understanding or social pressures, parents, unknowingly, will often place their retarded youngster in an unreasonably stressful situation. For example, they may require the child to study or do homework beyond all reasonableness. This will result in the youngster's becoming overly anxious in relating to the parents and others in the family. Moreover, the child will probably develop an attitude of disgust toward everything related to school activities. This situation is precipitated by well-meaning parents. The special education teacher has the responsibility to clearly define the limits of what parents can reasonably expect of their child. If homework activities are recommended, parents must be given precise directions concerning the types of activities, the manner in which the activities are to be handled, and the amount of time the child is to devote to them. Characteristic of parents of all handicapped children is their desire to force the child into a position of being extended beyond the point of maximum effectiveness.

Middle-class parents of mentally retarded children are often hypersensitive to the social dimensions of the defect. For a variety of reasons, the parents will often be ambivalent toward their child. Attention during the parent counseling sessions must be given to all the emotional and social ramifications of the problem. This will involve the need for the sessions to be attended periodically by specialists such as a clinical psychologist, child psychiatrist, or psychiatric social worker.

If a mentally retarded child is to develop emotional stability and social assurance, and the parents to assume a health posture toward their child, the parents must attempt to understand their feelings toward the child before deliberating on other kinds of habilitative concerns. In addition to this, there is the need for all involved in the school program to assure parents that they are welcome to visit with any member of the professional team whenever the need arises in order to ask questions or express any concerns they might have. The school must communicate its willingness to assume leadership in the provision of an educational program which contains appropriate experiences leading to the retarded becoming successfully integrated into the community. In fact, the special educator should supply the means for coordinating efforts of various specialties. To illustrate this point, the special education personnel should take leadership by relating their program with that offered by vocational rehabilitation and by constantly keeping the parents informed as to what is happening and what they can look forward to as the child's program progresses.

PARENTS WHOSE CHILDREN
ARE ENVIRONMENTALLY DEPRIVED

An adult education program must also consider parents of those retarded children who have been reared in environmentally deprived areas. The type of focus for this program will differ in some important ways from the emphasis placed on the adult program for parents of organically involved mentally retarded children. Parents of deprived children may not be as eager to participate in the adult education programs as parents of organically involved children.

Working with families from lower socioeconomic situations presents a particularly difficult problem because their attitudes are inextricably associated with the poverty they have experienced and all that it entails. The initial thrust in any adult education program for these parents must be aimed at altering their attitudes toward their children as well as toward the total school program. These parents will not tolerate being preached to or badgered about the poor condition of their children and that they have incorrectly reared them. Each individual must realize the advantage of his participation in the adult education program and the benefits that could accue to him and to his children. Indeed, perhaps the most difficult problem is the initial one of getting parents to attend the adult sessions. It may be necessary for the schools to make special provisions for these parents by conducting the sessions according to the best time in their schedule. If the educational program for the deprived retarded is to be effective, the schools must make some substantial effort to systematically work with these parents.

The first order of business in this program must be to assist them in realizing the advantages of working closely with the schools. Their attitudes toward the school program will change only after they can clearly see the personal advantages in cooperating. This must not be treated in a cavalier fashion; the instructor must understand that firmly entrenched attitudes which have been established over years because of constant frustration and an inability to provide for themselves and their families can be altered, at best, only very slightly and over an extended period of time. One strategy for helping the parents develop a positive view of the school's objectives is to provide some type of immediate and tangible evidence of the advantages in cooperating. Initially, then, the instructor should survey needs of the parents in an attempt to identify their most difficult problems and, in a forthright manner, make every attempt to assist them in resolving these difficulties. Eventually, as the parents gain greater experience with and confidence in the adult education program, their perception of the school's program in relation to their own retarded child will be altered. Although there is a need for focusing the initial thrust of the adult education program on changing attitudes of parents toward the schools, it should be recognized that dramatic changes in attitudes will be difficult to effect in relatively short periods of time.

Many parents living in lower socioeconomic circumstances are not aware of the aims of the special education program for the mentally retarded. The most common view is that their child, because of his performance problems in a regular class situation or because of a substantial behavior problem, has been placed in a situation wherein greater controls can be exercised by the schools. At the same time, many parents will believe that this new classroom situation is not designed to help their child develop skills for independent living. In short, parents from a deprived environment are usually unclear about the advantages of their child being located in a special education situation and are often antagonistic toward this placement. Early in the adult program objectives and aims of the special class program should be clearly discussed. Further, if the parents are to understand the practicalities of the situation, the instructor will need to describe what the school expects of each child and the specific instructional sequence planned for the students as they proceed through the special program. Throughout this session, the schools should help parents understand the variety of difficulties the children and teachers encounter in the day-to-day classroom situation and ways in which the parents can provide support at home so that the program objectives are more easily achieved. The advantage of a close relationship between the parents, their treatment of the child, and the activities and experiences of the school program should be emphasized.

Because of inordinately large families and the difficulties in social behavior frequently characteristic of children from lower socioeconomic situations, the instructor will find that these parents are interested in topics related to child rearing and techniques for dealing with personal and social difficulties. Problems in these areas are usually difficult for parents to fully understand or deal with in a healthy and socially acceptable manner. Because of their propinquity to the deprived environment, parents do not have a reasonable perspective and, therefore, judge the behavior of their children and themselves from a social reference point which differs from the middle socioeconomic strata. When everyone around you misbehaves, it is easy to lose sight of another reference point. The school program, therefore, must help these parents to understand some of the major factors related to healthy child-rearing practices, and instructors must suggest the range of activities and experiences in which parents can engage their children in the home to foster normal and healthy physical, social, and emotional development. Special attention should be given to the reactions of parents to the behavior of their children. Demonstrations, small group discussions, role playing, and films and other visual aids will help to make an impact on the parents.

Many parents from slum areas or pockets of poverty will exhibit a desperate need for information and counseling concerning family planning and occupational security. In most cases they will have inordinately large families and find themselves unable to adequately support the home. In a great number of the homes, the mother will be head of the household and often the only source of income. Other adults, often found living in these homes, will be indigent or handicapped and unable to contribute in any beneficial and tangible way. Welfare may be the only source of financial support; consequently, they will be unable to handle the continuous array of difficulties which arise.

The school's role should be one of providing these parents with information concerning those community services which will assist in resolving these difficulties. The school, obviously, cannot solve each of the many specific problems presented during the course of the parent program. A more reasonable approach is to inform parents of services provided by various agencies and to act as a liaison between the parents and these agencies. In this respect, therefore, the schools should both dispense appropriate information to parents and help to coordinate the various services relevant to each parent's situation.

Recent research has demonstrated the deleterious influence of poor nutrition on general physical and intellectual development. Adult education for parents of retarded children living in a deprived environment must provide detailed information concerning the dietary needs of these children. Clearly, it is important that this area be explored with parents in terms that are realistic. To present them with suggestions for properly feeding their young without considering the financial difficulties of this group will only serve to undermine the entire adult education program. A variety of alternative means for satisfying the basic nutritional requirements should be given and examples of ways to solve nutritional deficiencies actually demonstrated for the parents.

selected readings

Albini, J. L. and S. Dinitz: "Psychotherapy with Disturbed and Defective Children: An Evaluation of Changes in Behavior and Attitudes," *American Journal of Mental Deficiency,* 69:560–567, 1965.

Auerbach, Aline B.: "Group Education for Parents of the Handicapped," *Children,* 8:135–140, 1961.

Barber, T. M.: "Better Parent Education Means More Effective Public Relations," *American Journal of Mental Deficiency,* 60:627–632, 1956.

Beck, Helen L.: "Counseling Parents of Retarded Children," *Children,* 6:225–230, 1959.

Begab, M. J.: "Factors in Counseling Parents of Retarded Children," *American Journal of Mental Deficiency,* 60:515–524, 1956.

Coleman, J. C.: "Group Therapy with Parents of Mentally Deficient Children," *American Journal of Mental Deficiency,* 57:700–704, 1953.

Cotzin, M.: "Group Psychotherapy with Mentally Defective Problem Boys," *American Journal of Mental Deficiency,* 53:268–283, 1948.

Dalton, J. and H. Epstein: "Counseling Parents of Mildly Retarded Children," *Social Casework,* 44:523–530, 1963.

French, A. C., M. Levbarg, and H. Michael-Smith: "Parent Counseling as a Means of Improving the Performance of a Mentally Retarded Boy: A Case Study Presentation," *American Journal of Mental Deficiency,* 58:13–20, 1952.

Goodman, L. and R. Rothman: "The Development of a Group Counseling Program in a Clinic for Retarded Children," *American Journal of Mental Deficiency,* 65:789–795, 1961.

Gordon, E. W. and M. Ullman: "Reaction of Parents to Problems of

Mental Retardation in Children," *American Journal of Mental Deficiency,* 61: 158–163, 1956.

Grebler, A. M.: "Parental Attitudes toward Mentally Retarded Children," *American Journal of Mental Deficiency,* 56:475–483, 1952.

Hale, C. B.: "Parent Need for Education and Help with Family Problems," *California Journal of Education Research,* 6:38–44, 1955.

Jensen, R. A.: "The Clinical Management of the Mentally Retarded Child and the Parents," *American Journal of Psychiatry,* 106:830–833, 1950.

Kanner, L.: "Parents' Feelings about Retarded Children," *American Journal of Mental Deficiency,* 57:375–383, 1953.

Kirk, S. A., M. B. Karnes, and W. O. Kirk: *You and Your Retarded Child,* The Macmillan Company, New York, 1955.

Leichman, N. S.: *Parent Attitudes in Rearing Mentally Retarded Children,* California State Department of Education, Sacramento, Calif., 1962.

McDonald, E. T.: *Understand Those Feelings,* Stanwix House, Inc., Pittsburgh, 1962.

Mahoney, S. C.: "Observations Concerning Counseling with Parents of Mentally Retarded Children," *American Journal of Mental Deficiency,* 63:81–86, 1958.

Morris, E. F.: "Casework Training Needs for Counseling Parents of the Retarded," *American Journal of Mental Deficiency,* 59:510–516, 1955.

Mullen, F. A.: "The Teacher Works with the Parent of the Exceptional Child," *Education,* 80:329–332, 1960.

Murray, M. A.: "Needs of Parents of Mentally Retarded Children," *American Journal of Mental Deficiency,* 63:1078, 1088, 1959.

Peck, J. R. and W. B. Stephens: "A Study of the Relationship between the Attitude and Behavior of Parents and That of Their Mentally Defective Child," *American Journal of Mental Deficiency,* 64:839–844, 1960.

Rankin, J. A.: "A Group Therapy Experiment with Mothers of Mentally Deficient Children," *American Journal of Mental Deficiency,* 62:49–55, 1957.

Rheingold, H. L.: "Interpreting Mental Retardation to Parents," *Journal of Consulting Psychology,* 9:142–148, 1945.

Roos, P.: "Psychological Counseling with Parents of Retarded Children," *Mental Retardation,* 1:345–350, 1963.

Rose, J. A.: "Factors in the Development of Mentally Handicapped Children, Counseling Parents of Children with Mental Handicaps," *Proceedings of the 1958 Woods School Conference,* May 2–3, 1958.

Rosen, L.: "Selected Aspects in the Development of the Mother's Understanding of Her Mentally Retarded Child," *American Journal of Mental Deficiency,* 59:522–528, 1955.

Ross, A. O.: *The Exceptional Child in the Family: Helping Parents of Exceptional Children,* Grune and Stratton, Inc., New York, 1964.

Sarason, S. B.: "Individual Psychotherapy with Mentally Defective Individuals," *American Journal of Mental Deficiency,* 56:803–805, 1952.

Scher, B.: "Help to Parents: An Integral Part of Service to the Retarded Child," *American Journal of Mental Deficiency,* 60: 169–175, 1955.

Sheimo, S. L.: "Problems in Helping Parents of Mentally Defective and Handicapped Children," *American Journal of Mental Deficiency,* 56:42–47, 1951.

Stacey, C. L. and M. F. DeMartino (eds.): *Counseling and Psychotherapy with the Mentally Retarded,* The Free Press of Glencoe, New York, 1957, pp. 615–851.

Sternlicht, M.: "Establishing an Initial Relationship in Group Psychotherapy with Delinquent Retarded Male Adolescents," *American Journal of Mental Deficiency,* 69:39–41, 1964.

Thorne, R. C.: "Counseling and Psychotherapy with Mental Defectives," *American Journal of Mental Deficiency,* 52:263–271, 1948.

Tizard, J. and J. C. Grad: *The Mentally Handicapped and Their Families,* Oxford University Press, Inc., New York, 1961.

Watson, E. H.: "Counseling Parents of Mentally Deficient Children," *Pediatrics,* 22:401–408, 1958.

Weingold, J. T.: "Parents Counseling Other Parents," *Children Limited,* 12:2, 1963.

——— and R. P. Hormuth: "Group Guidance of Mentally Retarded Children," *Journal of Clinical Psychology,* 9:118–124, 1953.

Wiest, G.: "Psychotherapy with the Mentally Retarded," *American Journal of Mental Deficiency,* 59:640–644, 1955.

Yepsen, L.: "Counseling the Mentally Retarded," *American Journal of Mental Deficiency,* 57:205–213, 1952.

Zwerling, I.: "The Initial Counseling of Parents with Mentally Retarded Children," *Journal of Pediatrics,* 44:469–479, 1954.

appendix

NAMES AND ADDRESSES OF PUBLISHERS OF TESTING MATERIALS

Abbreviation	*Name and Address*
ACER	Australian Council for Educational Research Box 210 Hawthorn Victoria, Australia 3122
AGS	American Guidance Service Publishers' Building Circle Pines, Minnesota 55014
BMS	The Bobbs-Merrill Company, Inc. 4330 East 62nd Street Indianapolis, Indiana 46206
CPP	Consulting Psychologists Press 577 College Avenue Palo Alto, California 94306
CTB	California Test Bureau Del Monte Research Park Monterey, California 93940
EPS	Educators Publishing Service 75 Moulton Street Cambridge, Massachusetts 02138
GA	Guidance Associates 1526 Gilpin Avenue Wilmington, Delaware

GC   Ginn and Company
2550 Hanover Street
Palo Alto, California   94304

GS   Grune & Stratton, Inc.
757 Third Avenue
New York, New York   10017

HBJ   Harcourt Brace Jovanovich
757 Third Avenue
New York, New York   10017

HMC   Houghton Mifflin Company
53 West 43rd Street
New York, New York   10036

HBW   Harcourt, Brace, & World, Inc.
757 Third Street
New York, New York   10017

MGH   CTB/McGraw-Hill
Del Monte Research Park
Monterey, California   93940

PP   Personnel Press, Inc.
20 Nassau Street
Princeton, New Jersey   08540

SH   Stanwix House, Inc.
3020 Chartiers Street
Pittsburgh, Pennsylvania   15204

SRA   Science Research Associates
259 East Erie Street
Chicago, Illinois   60611

TCP   Teachers College Press
Teachers College
525 West 120th Street
New York, New York   10027

UI   Bureau of Educational Research and Service
University of Iowa
Iowa City, Iowa   52240

UIP   The University of Illinois Press
Urbana, Illinois   61801

WHLRF   Winter Haven Lions Research Foundation
                P.O. Box 111
                Winter Haven, Florida   33880

WPS   Western Psychological Services
                12031 Wilshire Boulevard
                Los Angeles, California   90025

index